Rambles & Scrambles:
A Peakbagging Guide to the Desert Southwest

Second Edition

Courtney Purcell

First edition 2008. Second edition 2015

Front cover photo: Courtney Purcell slacking off while en route to Fleur de Lis Peak.
Front cover photo by Harlan W. Stockman
Back cover photo: Little DB below the summit of Escalante Butte.
Back cover photo by Courtney Purcell

All photos by Courtney Purcell unless otherwise credited.

Warning

Hiking, scrambling and climbing are outdoor activities where you may be seriously injured or die! **Read this warning before using this book.**

This book describes a wide variety of adventures, some of which involve considerable risk. Those who wish to pursue the outdoor objectives outlined in this guidebook should be fully cognizant of these risks and take appropriate steps to minimize them. Some of these steps include:

-**Consulting** with other information sources about current conditions and to verify the information in this book;

-**Applying** common sense in regard to current, past and likely future weather conditions, and condition of the environment, as well as your own capabilities to deal with emergencies and unforeseen events;

-**Carrying proper equipment**, such as a map and compass, plenty of water, cold-water and cold-weather protective clothing, and any technical equipment that may be needed.

The objectives outlined in this book are primarily intended for experienced hikers, scramblers, and often, climbers who will exercise informed judgment and caution. **Still, the dangers should not be minimalized.**

Pursue adventures that are appropriate to your physical conditioning, experience and skill set. Enjoy the easier routes and objectives first, and gradually work your way toward the harder ones.

-**Class 1 & 2** routes will be fun for most hikers;

-Class 2+ & 3 routes require greater fitness and more advanced skills, such as assessing natural hazards and taking care of oneself in remote and/or topographically complex locations. These routes carry considerably more risk than class 1 & 2 routes;

-**Class 3+ to Class 5** routes typically require steep, loose and exposed climbing (and downclimbing), sometimes of a sustained nature, potential ropework and specific skills in a challenging and sometimes technical environment. You must be proficient at rappelling and setting anchors in an ever-changing natural landscape. Obtain technical expertise via proper training and qualification, as well as appropriate equipment, before venturing onto these more advanced routes in the book.

This book is not an instruction manual. Obtain proper instruction before venturing onto any of these potentially dangerous routes.

The information in this guidebook was compiled over many ascents, and was most likely accurate at the time of publication. However, conditions can change rapidly and the wise explorer expects the unexpected, and is prepared to find or create anchors when necessary, and deal with awkward and unexpected challenges as they are encountered. Where reality and this book disagree, make decisions based on reality.

There are no warranties, expressed or implied, that this guidebook is accurate or that the information contained is reliable. By using this book you assume the risk of descriptive errors and sole responsibility for your safety. In other words, proceed entirely at your own risk. **You are responsible for your own safety.** The author and publisher assume no responsibility for accidents, injury or death incurred as a result of the use or misuse of information contained in this book. Hiking, scrambling and climbing contain inherent risks which no amount of care, caution or expertise can eliminate. The information provided in this book is no substitute for quality topographic maps and a compass, excellent route-finding skills, terrific physical conditioning and good judgment.

Strolling along Bright Angel Trail in Grand Canyon

Contents

Introduction 9
Using This Guide 10

Part 1: Nevada

Red Rock Canyon National Conservation Area 19
SR-159 (Outside of the Scenic Drive) & SR-160 20
SR-159 or the Scenic Drive 39
Scenic Drive 45
Calico Basin & Blue Diamond Hill 67
The Limestone Crest 74
La Madre Range & Environs 76
Spring Mountains National Recreation Area 84
Kyle Canyon 85
US-95 near Corn Creek Road 92
Lee Canyon 93
Cold Creek Road 101
Indian Springs 104
US-95 near the Clark County Boundary 106
US-95 near NV-160 107
NV-160 near Pahrump 108
Lovell Canyon 109
NV-160 near Mountain Springs 113
Goodsprings 115
I-15 117
Lake Mead National Recreation Area 118
Gold Butte Area 120
North Shore 128
West Shore 144
South Shore 150
Colorado River 156
Arrow Canyon Range 160
Desert National Wildlife Refuge 172
US-93 near I-15 173
Corn Creek 175
US-93 near NV-168 182
Beatty 185
Bare Mountains 185
South of the Bare Mountains 189
Beatty Area 190
Valley of Fire State Park 193
South of Las Vegas 202
Cottonwood & Bird Spring Range 202
Sloan & Jean 205
McCullough Range & the Railroad Peaks Area 209

Highland Spring Range 215
Laughlin 219
Searchlight 219
Nelson & Boulder City 220
Northwest of Boulder City 226
Urban Las Vegas 227
North of Las Vegas 234
Apex 234
Muddy Mountains 236
Ute 239
Virgin Mountains 240
I-15 Corridor Between Glendale & Mesquite 241
Coyote Springs & Alamo 245
Pahrump & Crystal 251
Great Basin National Park 253
Scattered 260
Quinn Canyon Range 261
Pioche Area 261
Lida Summit Area 262
Schell Creek Range 263
Ruby Mountains 264
White Pine Range 267

Part 2: Arizona

Northwest Region 271
Hualapai Mountains 271
Bullhead City & Oatman 273
Dolan Springs Area 278
Colorado River 280
Flagstaff & Williams 283
Williams Area 284
Sunset Crater National Monument 285
Flagstaff Area 287
Sedona 290
East & Southeast of Sedona 290
Northwest of Sedona 290
North of Sedona 293
West & Southwest of Sedona 295
Grand Canyon National Park 297
Grand Canyon-Parashant National Monument 306
Scattered 309
Lake Havasu City Area 309
Kofa National Wildlife Refuge 310
Superstition Mountains 316
Tucson Area 318

Part 3: California

Mojave National Preserve 323
Northern Kelbaker Road 323
Southern Kelbaker Road 327
Halloran Springs & Halloran Summit 327
Cima Road 329
New York Mountains 332
Hole-in-the-Wall 338
Providence Mountains 342
Mountain Pass 343
Outlying 346
Death Valley National Park 349
Panamint Range 350
Death Valley Junction 351
Daylight Pass 353
Titus Canyon Road 355
Northern Grapevine Mountains 358
Jubilee Pass & Salsberry Pass 359
Dante's View 361
Towne Pass & Panamint Valley 363
Furnace Creek 364
Stovepipe Wells 367
Middle-of-Nowhere 368
West of Panamint Valley 368
Shoshone Area 369
Shoshone 369
Resting Spring Range 370
Nopah Range 371
Kingston Range 372
Tecopa 373
Scattered 374
Needles Area 374
Blythe Area 376
Yuma Area 377

Appendix 379
CP's 25 Favorite Scrambles 379
The Fifteen 10,000+ foot, P300 Peaks of the Spring Mountains 380
The Clark County P2000 List 380
The Nine P1000 Peaks of Lake Mead National Recreation Area 381
The Fourteen P300 Peaks of Valley of Fire State Park 381
General Ticklist 382
Index 393

A delightful tinaja in the Calico Basin area of Red Rock

Introduction

Moving to Vegas more than a decade ago, I was enamored of the glitter, the neon, the *ding-ding-ding*, the bells and whistles. A month later, the stinking, cigarette smoky novelty wore off and the mountains took hold of me (as they had since I climbed my first one at age 11). I still remember—

Wait. Hold on a second.

What is peakbagging, anyway?

Peakbagging is the act of obsessively endeavoring to hike, climb, crawl or drive to the top of every sand pile, slag heap, hill, crag, pimple, temple, spire or certified "mountain" within the realm of human reach.

And so it was, in true obsessive fashion, that I began to seek out the mountaintops around me—Charleston Peak, Mummy Mountain, Turtlehead Mountain, Bridge Mountain, Gass Peak, Frenchman Mountain, Lone Mountain—the regulars, the good stuff, the local classics. Then I became curious about the lesser-visited peaks, like Sheep Peak, Spirit Mountain and River Mountain. And eventually the never-visited peaks, those anonymous, unnamed ones splashed across the landscape, started to call my name too—Knife-Edge Peak, Playground Peak, and peaks I can't even remember anymore. I stretched my legs, spread out a little, explored the nearby parks—Great Basin National Park, Grand Canyon National Park, started to hit Red Rock hard. I fell in love with all of it.

A friend of mine named Dean Molen, highpointer and prominence peakbagger extraordinaire (a man who runs with the likes of prolific guys like Andy Martin, Ken Jones and Bob Packard) eventually suggested I write a guidebook. So I did.

And here, you'll find minimalist beta (my favorite kind, being an explorer and all) designed to share with you what is possible for nearly 950 peaks across the Desert Southwest—obscure to classic; hikes to climbs. I've found my way up every lump in this book, some by multiple routes on multiple visits, and enjoyed each and every peak here in our vast and often desolate backyard. Quality peaks, amazing scenery, interesting culture, and a fine mixture of sandstone and limestone and even granite. This book is the definitive resource for peakbagging in the Desert Southwest.

I've given a highly subjective "Star Rating" for each peak in the book. The ratings go something like this:

**** A classic
*** Very good
** Good
* Eh, 'twas alright

I hope you enjoy these peaks as much as I have (and continue to do!).

Thanks to one of my favorite people, Harlan Stockman, for the map work and route photos, the wit, and the competence. Thanks also to Andy Archibald, Tracy Foutz, Thich Nhat Hanh, Chris Meyer, Walt Hutton, Jason Pease, and Aron Ralston. My heartfelt appreciation is also extended to my wonderful wife, DB, for her love, support and tireless efforts to make this guide worth having.

Using This Guide

When to Climb

With appropriate preparation, equipment, knowledge and experience, and cooperative weather and conditions, all of the peaks in this guide can be climbed year-round. But, even with all of those things in your favor, common sense must always prevail.

Summers in the desert can be brutally hot; winters can be brutally cold. While doing a mountain such as, say, Hart Peak, in July or August would be flirting with death, a hike up Jeff Davis Peak, the third highest peak in Nevada, during the same month would most likely be a wonderful, and rather comfortable, time in the mountains. In this region, as in others, lower means hotter, while higher means cooler.

The sandstone spots, such as Sedona and Red Rock Canyon National Conservation Area, warrant special mention, I think. Like many of the other areas covered in this book, both of these spots are prone to snow and ice in the colder months. Sandstone slabs covered in snow and/or ice are not safe. Also, avoid these sandstone environments for a good 24 to 48 hours after a rain. Wet sandstone is considerably weaker than dry sandstone. Even with other types of rock, such as granite or limestone, expect it to become much slicker, and therefore more dangerous, when wet.

Flash floods are also a real concern in the desert. Rain falling a dozen miles away can quickly drain without warning into the wash or canyon you're following toward some mountain peak somewhere. Always check the weather locally, as well as regionally, before heading out. Slot canyons, like those found in portions of Red Rock Canyon, are particularly dangerous during a flash flood.

And speaking of falling water, the summer monsoon season can bring heavy rains, and even snow in the high mountains, and lightning. Being high on a mountain, or on a mountain's ridges, is not a place to be during a thunderstorm. If you see a storm approaching, retreat! Gambling with lightning is strongly discouraged, and the risk of hypothermia associated with cold, windy mountains hit by a storm is one that could result in death.

Rockfall is an inherent hazard in climbing mountains, particularly in mid-morning in the high mountains, when freezing temperatures during the night warm, causing rock to break loose and fall. I've seen rocks the size of small cars break loose in the mornings and fall hundreds of feet down a mountain slope or face or chute—not something you want to be struck by while you're climbing through or under that slope or face or chute.

You and your partners are another common source of rockfall. Getting struck by even a small rock falling down on you from hundreds of feet above could be disastrous. Helmets are always a good idea, and extreme care should always be taken to prevent knocking rocks down onto those climbing below you.

Though it should apply only minimally in this context, I might as well mention altitude sickness. While many can climb from sea level to over 14,000 feet in a day without any ill effects, others can experience headaches and nausea at even modest elevations, say, at 9,000 feet. That said, when traveling in the higher mountains covered in this book, be aware of the symptoms of altitude sickness. While a mild headache can frequently be ignored, and the climb can continue, one should be aware that altitude sickness *can* lead to more serious conditions, such as HAPE (High Altitude Pulmonary Edema) or HACE (High Altitude Cerebral Edema). When heading for the high hills, move slowly, drink lots of water, and head down if symptoms of altitude sickness present themselves.

Ratings

Ratings in this guide are based on the Yosemite Decimal System (YDS). Although YDS ratings can be somewhat subjective, when I give a route a rating, your experience should translate to something like this:

Class 1 – a trail or cross-country route that requires nothing more technical than "easy" walking;

Class 2 – a rough cross-country route that requires the occasional use of hands for balance or simple negotiation;

Class 3 – this is scrambling. All four limbs are used, not just for balance, but for actual negotiation of the route. The terrain will frequently be steep, though the hand and footholds should be large and apparent;

Class 4 – this is the most difficult rating to articulate. It is the ground between scrambling and actual climbing. Expect steep terrain with ample, though typically small, hand and footholds.

Class 5 – technical rock climbing. A rope and gear to protect the route in the event of a fall are recommended.

5th class is broken down further from 5.0 to well beyond anything covered in this book. Generally speaking, the higher the number beyond the decimal point, the steeper the climbing and the smaller the holds. In the case of the East Face Crack System route (5.10) on Jumbo Peak, the zero at the end of the rating does not mean that the route is a 5.1 (a "five-one"), but rather, a grade harder than 5.9—a "five-ten".

A couple more things on ratings in this book…

The YDS rating of a route reflects the most technically difficult portion of the entire route. For example, if a route is essentially a walking trail, but it happens to have a 10-foot section of 3rd class scrambling at some point along the way, the route will be rated as being class 3. Some routes rated as class 4, as another example, might entail only a very short section of 4th class scrambling on good rock, while another route of the same rating may be considerably more serious, with sustained, exposed, loose 4th class terrain to be negotiated. My suggestion: Thoroughly read the entire route description to know what you're getting into.

If I rate something as, say, class 2+ (or sometimes "class 2-3"), I mean that the route is primarily class 2 with perhaps a spattering of relatively trivial class 3 here and there. Routes with a "+" after them may also suggest that, while some may feel the route is "merely" class 4, others may rate the route as "easy" 5th class (5.0 or 5.1). Again, YDS ratings can be somewhat subjective.

Although a rope and protective gear are recommended on all 5th class routes in this book (as well as for those folks uncomfortable with routes of a technically "easier" [sub-5th class] nature), most of the class 5 routes covered herein feature only a short amount of "difficult" climbing. That said, I might sometimes refer to a short 5th class section of a route as a "scramble," meaning that I did not feel that *I* needed to rope up or protect that section of the route.

I do not intend to mislead or "sandbag" anyone. I simply mean that I subjectively felt that the section of the route in question was trivial enough that I could simply "scramble" it without any sort of protection. You, however, may want to protect the same section that I or someone else climbed without protection. On the flipside, stronger climbers than I may "scramble" a difficult section that I "climbed" with a rope and protection. Factors such as the quality of the rock and the protection available, the length and difficulty of the climbing section, and the exposure, not to mention the climber's experience and abilities, among others, *must* be taken into consideration when deciding whether or not to "rope up." In other words, you make your own informed decision.

I've assigned a grade rating to each route in the book. Traditionally, grades are used to concisely describe the difficulty and danger of climbing technical routes; however, I've adapted the system in this context to concisely describe the length of time typically required to complete a route (with some lingering emphasis on difficulty and commitment). Like YDS ratings, grades are subjective, but when I give a route a grade, your experience should translate to something similar to this:

I – an hour or two of effort required
II – a half day of effort required
III – most of a day of effort required
IV – a full day of effort required
V – more than a day of effort required

Route Descriptions

While I have made every effort to provide accurate route information, I firmly believe that practicing the art of route-finding is part of the joy of mountain climbing. Rather than hold one's hand all the way to the mountaintop, I try hard to get one started and then point out helpful things one might encounter along the way. Those routes that seem to require more-detailed information *might* offer it. The goal is not to hold your hand; it is to show you what is possible.

You might notice that some of the mountains have quotation marks around their names. Those peaks do not have official names recognized by the USGS. In many of those cases, a local name existing for decades but never recognized by the naming authority, or in some cases, a name I've simply come up with, has been given. Take 'em or leave 'em. While I certainly find unnamed peaks mysterious and appealing, I also feel that naming a peak adds to its character and allows it to stick in the memory a bit more firmly.

Also, near the peak names I've provided a latitude and longitude. Considering the obscure nature of many (most) of the peaks described in this book, I saw it fit to provide approximate coordinates for their summits.

Oh yeah: In the first edition, the emphasis was on providing somewhat detailed beta for most of the peaks described. There were some 260-odd peaks in that edition, a rather manageable number. With this edition covering quite a lot more peaks, I debated whether to publish it as a multi-volume encyclopedia chronicling the histories and nuances of the various peaks and their routes, or as a single volume dictionary that simply defined what is possible. I chose the latter. As such, it seemed silly to remove pre-existing detailed beta from the first edition in order to treat all peaks in the second edition in the same minimalist style. That's why some peaks in this edition awkwardly retain their cumbersome detailed beta, while the vast majority of the others display themselves scandalously bare. Make sense?

Please feel free to contact my well-staffed Customer Service department with your concerns.

Stuff to Bring

It goes without saying that some things should be a standard part of everyone's outdoor packing list. Most of us don't always carry "The 10 Essentials"…but we should.

Things like reliable footwear, an extra layer, such as a windbreaker, sunscreen and a hat, and the like, should always be brought. The colder seasons may require extra layers, and in cases like Great Basin National Park, often times snowshoes, crampons, and an ice axe.

Climbing in the desert, we should always bring plenty of water. Though water can frequently be found in places like Great Basin National Park, you can't always count on it. Bring lots of your own. Water found in the field should be treated or filtered before consumption. Giardia = less time in the mountains.

Topographical maps and compasses (and knowledge of how to read and use them) are two other important elements of desert (or any kind of) mountain travel. GPS units, too. Even the most "friendly" of terrains can occasionally have good route-finders scratching their heads in wonder. The desert is not a good place to get lost. It tends to be unforgiving.

Even with a topo map, places such as the backcountry of Red Rock Canyon National Conservation Area, as examples, will frequently surprise the new visitor with troublesome cliffs and impassable canyons. In other words, have a map but always be prepared for surprises.

And speaking of cliffs and canyons: Don't ever climb up, or go down, steep terrain, such as slot canyons, that one cannot retrace steps on…unless you know what lies ahead and are prepared to negotiate it.

Lastly, some basic assumptions have been made. When I speak of ropes, gear, and whatnot, folks should already know what to do with them…and should have, or at minimum, should be with someone who has, appropriate experience with the stuff. An easily-rated technical route, such as Dove Benchmark on Castle Peak (YDS 5.2), is not the appropriate place for a group of newbies to "try using a rope" to climb.

My suggestions for "Stuff to Bring" are not the end-all be-all, but simply suggestions. You must make your own decision on what you will or will not need.

Native American Artifacts

Though I try not to publish exact locations of Native American artifacts, the fact of the matter is that the area contained within the scope of this book is chock full of Native American stuff. Petroglyphs, pictographs and pottery are found in many locations throughout the desert southwest, including locations on and around the mountains in this book.

My hope is that those who love the mountains also love and appreciate Native American culture and history. Please, if you are fortunate enough to stumble across some artifacts, take only pictures. Leave the artifacts for others to enjoy.

Other Stuff

-Many of the peaks in this book are located in designated or proposed Wilderness Areas. Wilderness is the highest designation by Congress for protection of these rugged but fragile lands. No vehicles, and this includes bicycles, are permitted in Wilderness Areas.

-Pack it in/pack it out. In other words, leave nothing in the mountain but footprints. Trash, human waste, etc should be taken out of the mountains with you. It's not pleasant, but you gotta do it. Please practice *Leave No Trace* ethics.

-If thinking of building a nice campfire in that out of the way, special spot in the mountains, be sure to note any area fire restrictions on the public lands you will be visiting, specifically during summer. Contact the managing agency of the area you will be in for restriction information.

-When looking for a place to camp, stay well away from desert springs and watering holes. Your presence prevents wildlife from accessing these precious spots.

-Don't harass the critters. Don't feed them.

-Hiking in wash bottoms and on durable surfaces (rocks and outcroppings), whenever possible, to minimize impact to soils and vegetation is strongly encouraged. Once the desert crust is broken, causing soil exposure to erosive factors, and when sensitive soils (gypsum, cryptobiotic) are trampled, they take a long time to heal.

-Please do your best to stay on approved roads when doing the approach drive to the peaks in this book.

-If attempting any of the high peaks in this book during times of snow coverage, be aware of the potential for avalanches (and cornices, too). Proper assessment of avalanche hazard is scientific and not the job of beginners. Before venturing out on questionable snow slopes, be sure to have received proper instruction and have appropriate experience in evaluating the safety of the snowpack. Be particularly cautious around steep (greater than 35-degrees) slopes during or shortly after a heavy snowfall, and also on those warm, spring days when wet slides tend to occur!

-And a quick mining safety warning: In a region rich with mines and mining history, please stay out of any abandoned mines you might come across on your journeys. They are unstable and extremely dangerous. Also, desert animals, such as bats, snakes and tortoises, are known to inhabit abandoned mines. Let them do so in peace.

☯ *Nevada* ☯

The author meditating on a chilly morning above Red Rock. Photo by Aron Ralston.

Red Rock Canyon National Conservation Area

Red Rock Canyon National Conservation Area (or RRCNCA or Red Rock Canyon or Red Rocks or whatever you know it as) is world famous for its fantastic and highly aesthetic climbing. With well over a thousand established technical rock climbing routes on its beautiful and typically high quality sandstone faces, this climbing destination has earned its high place among the Joshua Tree's and Yosemite's of the nation.

In addition to being a fine hiking, climbing and sight-seeing destination, Red Rock offers some of the most fantastic sandstone scrambling routes to be found. Dozens of named and unnamed peaks and sub-peaks grace the awe-inspiring escarpment. Obscure, sometimes tricky, and always beautiful routes make hiking, scrambling and climbing to the tops of the NCA's peaks something not to miss.

With massive faces, colorful canyons, hidden waterfalls, charming pools of water, petroglyphs, agave roasting pits, and wildlife such as bighorn sheep, ringtail cats and wild burros, the 197,000 acres of Red Rock is a special place indeed.

Much has been said of Red Rock Canyon…but it's not enough. It is the crown jewel of southern Nevada (if you don't count the fountains at Bellagio).

Camping inside the NCA is only allowed above 4,600 feet, and that requires an overnight permit. From 4,600-6,000 feet, overnight permits are only issued for wall bivouacs and for camping along Rocky Gap Road. Other camping arrangements above 6,000 feet simply require an overnight permit.

A developed campground can be found on Moenkopi Road, just off SR-159 near the main entrance to the NCA. There are also opportunities for primitive camping on Bureau of Land Management (BLM) land outside of the NCA boundary along Lovell Canyon Road (off of SR-160, west of Mountain Springs Summit). Additionally, nearby Las Vegas offers plenty of lodging for those looking to plush-up their stay in the area.

Hiking/climbing permits are not required at RRCNCA, unless the outing is of a multi-day nature.

Hours for the Red Rock Canyon Scenic Drive (the outstanding, 13-mile loop through the NCA) vary by season, but it usually opens shortly after sunrise and closes some time around dark. Be aware that you can be ticketed for parking anywhere along the loop after closing time. Sadly, this means that you'd better get a good, early start on short winter days for those longer peaks along the Scenic Drive, such as Bridge Mountain, Yoga Peak, etc. Be sure to ask the guy/gal at the fee booth what closing time or visit the NCA's web site for (theoretically) up-to-date info! Although Red Rock is most famous for its beautiful sandstone peaks and crags, the NCA also boasts a fine collection of limestone peaks for the adventurer to play upon. Most are described herein.

Objectives in Red Rock along the sandstone escarpment are arranged here roughly south-to-north. Additionally, I've broken down the various parts of the NCA into bite-sized pieces, generally based on access and (hopefully) common sense. For those paying closer attention, don't get bent out of shape when you notice that not all of the peaks in the following sections actually lie within the NCA. Some reside on the fringes, but are close enough neighbors to get lumped in with the other fun stuff.

By the way, the kind BLM folk at Red Rock Canyon discourage swimming or washing in any of the tinajas found in the NCA. Please refrain.

SR-159 (Outside of the Scenic Drive) & SR-160

Note: Vehicles parked along SR-159 for longer than 24 hours could be cited for parking in the Nevada Department of Transportation (NDOT) right-of-way.

Mount Wilson, as seen from the east along SR-159.

"South Peak" (5,870)

South Peak is the southernmost sandstone peak at Red Rock.

Follow the directions given for the alternate route to Hollow Rock Peak to a point shortly after reaching the sandstone where one can easily drop directly south to the saddle connecting Hollow Rock Peak and South Peak. From that saddle, it's a pleasant stroll southeast to the highpoint.

-WGS84 Lat: 36.0045405 deg N Lon: -115.4709356 deg W

*-II, Class 2 via Northwest Ridge **

"Hollow Rock Peak" (5,960+)

Hollow Rock Peak lies just to the south of Windy Peak in the obscure southern portion of southern Nevada's Red Rock Canyon NCA. The peak is easily recognized by the very prominent deep gully splitting the mountain's east face in half.

Presumably named for the large crack in the summit crag, a pleasing mixture of steep faces, stunning buttresses, tempting ridges, alluring cracks and other weaknesses make this peak a fine objective for scrambling and climbing routes alike.

Lying atop the flattish summit area are a few protruding crags, all of them vying for the title of "highest." Edging out the others by a few feet is the easternmost summit crag, a gnarly, cool-looking one, steep-to-overhanging on a couple sides, which requires 20 feet of steep class 3-4 scrambling to surmount.

The sandstone peaks of the NCA, running north up from Hollow Rock Peak to North Peak, are part of the Rainbow Mountain Wilderness.

To approach the peak from the east, take I-15 south from downtown Las Vegas to SR-160 (the road to Pahrump, Nevada). Follow SR-160 west toward the beautiful sandstone bluffs of southern Red Rock Canyon. Before reaching the NCA, you'll pass SR-159, which is an alternate way of reaching the NCA's main entrance at the Red Rock Canyon Scenic Drive. Continue west on SR-160 for 4.9 miles until you come to mile marker 16. Immediately beyond marker 16 (at 5.0 miles from the SR-160/159 junction) is a dirt road on the right. Passing this initial dirt road, turn right onto the next good dirt road, which is 0.7 mile past the first.

Once on the dirt road, follow it initially left (southwest) for a mile then as it bends right and begins to parallel the sandstone escarpment. As you near the bluffs, Hollow Rock Peak should be rather obvious. Continue driving another mile to a point that seems reasonably close and look for one of a number of small pull-outs to put your vehicle in. You should be no more than a mile or two from the paved highway. Pick a spot that suits you.

Though road conditions vary, depending on the season and other factors, I would anticipate that a high clearance vehicle (at a minimum) would be needed for this approach.

On the approach, you'll notice a deep gully splitting the east face of Hollow Rock Peak in half. The craggy/cliffy ridge along the north side of the gully looks rather tantalizing. The ridge/buttress on the south side of the gully looks equally appetizing. I decided to give the ridge/buttress a go…and that's where this route stems from.

From wherever you park along the rough dirt road, hike cross-country for about 0.5 mile to the steep and dirty base of the south ridge on the east face. Although from here the going looks more slope-like than ridge-like the transition occurs soon enough. Stay near the crest as the slope turns into more of a ridge, and work your way upward until scrambling/minor climbing difficulties develop. Although many different lines of ascent are feasible, at a glance it appears that the north side of the ridge presents greater difficulties, while the south presents lesser ones.

After some enjoyable class 3 and 4 scrambling (again, easier/harder variations are possible) on good rock, you should find yourself staring up at increasingly difficult terrain—and soon, at the base of an impressive buttress discouraging further ascent. Though an easier line of ascent may be possible if one looked hard enough, I didn't notice anything easier than a steep chimney (perhaps YDS 5.8) near the southern portion of the buttress.

From the vicinity of the southeast side of the buttress, drop back down onto dirty slopes and descend the ridge a couple hundred feet to the brushy wash to the south below you. If you stay close enough to the cliffs on your right as you descend, you should only have to bushwhack for a hundred feet (or less) in the bottom of the wash before it opens up into a section of boulder hopping, followed by a slickrock watercourse.

Continuing up-canyon in the watercourse for a couple hundred yards, exit as soon as you see a system of steep slickrock ramps, gullies and chutes on your right providing the first obvious 3rd class means of getting back onto the mountain. Get onto the ramp/gully/chute system and head up a couple hundred yards until you encounter a sandstone talus slope near the base of the obvious cliffs above you. Then, hang a right and follow the talus east up along the base of the cliffs until you find that class 2 terrain takes you all the way back to the crest of the ridge you were on earlier… this time just above the top of the troublesome buttress – perfect!

Unfortunately, if you try to climb back onto the crest of the ridge from here, you're immediately back into moderate-to-high 5th class climbing. Instead, backtrack approximately a hundred feet until you see a heavily broken wall. Although steep and comprised of poor rock, this weakness allows a 4th class means of reaching the crest of the upper ridge, which is about 80 or 90 feet up.

(Alternatively, there is a chimney/crack system just to the right (east) of the broken wall that allows a slightly more challenging means of reaching the upper part of the broken wall below the upper ridge. The chimney's less intimidating exposure, sadly, still includes a nice cluster of large cacti to land on if you peel off the rock.)

Once on the crest of the upper ridge, continue up and west, following the path of least resistance. Although I tried to stick to the crest, some variations left or right (usually left) were sometimes necessary. The going is in the class 2-3 (a little light class 4 may be encountered here and there) range.

As you scramble along the upper ridge, you should notice a rather large and conspicuous, roundish boulder above and to the right. This is the summit crag.

Hugh de Q in the Red Rock backcountry

Upon gaining the top of the ridge, exit right and drop down about 10 feet and next to a notch that looks eastward. From there, walk west from the notch a short distance and then cross-country it to the north/northwest for a couple hundred feet over crumbly talus. Work around to the northwest side of the summit crag.

A quick scan of the various small faces of the summit crag allows that the northwest side appears to provide the most reasonable means of ascent. Head up. Though the holds are relatively small, they are plentiful. The rock is high-quality varnished sandstone, and there are only about 20 feet of difficulties.

The roundtrip for this route is 4 or 5 miles, with roughly 1,500 feet of gain.

To approach the peak from the west, follow the directions given for Mountain Spring Benchmark to the crest of the main south-to-north limestone ridge behind the sandstone escarpment of Red Rock. At the crest, leave the main trail (which heads north) and follow a lesser trail heading south along the ridge, which begins to bend to the southeast. After many ups and downs along the ridge, the route eventually reaches sandstone and will require a bit of route-finding and/or working around various obstacles leading to the summit block. Expect nothing harder than a tiny bit of class 2-3 scrambling prior to the summit block.

-WGS84 Lat: 36.0085318 deg N Lon: -115.4690192 deg W
*-II, Class 2-3 from the west ***
*-II, Class 3-4 via South Ridge of East Face (Indirect) ***

"Windy Peak" (6,246)

Windy Peak is a fine desert peak that gets a surprisingly high amount of visitation, no doubt owing to a well-traveled use trail that can be followed virtually all the way from the "trailhead" to the summit. Nestled between Mud Spring Canyon and Windy Canyon, Windy Peak is the first peak south of the well-known Black Velvet Peak, which hosts Epinephrine, one of the classic climbs of Red Rock.

To climb via Windy Canyon: From downtown Las Vegas, take I-15 south to SR-160 (the road to Pahrump, Nevada). Follow SR-160 west toward the sandstone bluffs of southern Red Rock Canyon. Before reaching the NCA, you'll pass SR-159, which is an alternate way of reaching the NCA's main entrance at the Red Rock Canyon Scenic Drive. Instead of turning onto SR-159, continue west on SR-160 for 4.9 miles until you come to mile marker 16. Immediately beyond marker 16 (at 5.0 miles from the SR-160/159 junction) is a dirt road on the right. Passing this initial dirt road, turn right onto the next dirt road, which is 0.7 mile past the first. Once on the dirt road, follow it initially left (southwest) for a mile then as it bends right and begins to parallel the sandstone escarpment. As you near the bluffs, Windy Peak will be the first peak north of Hollow Rock Peak, the beautiful sandstone peak split in half by a deep cleft in its east face. Continue driving two miles to a point that seems reasonably close and look for one of any number of pull-outs to put your vehicle in. Pick a spot that works for you. Though road conditions vary (depending on the season and other factors) I would anticipate that a high clearance vehicle (at a minimum) would be needed for this approach.

From wherever you parked, hike toward the mouth of Windy Canyon (the first major canyon to the south of Windy Peak). I found that staying on the north side of the wash draining from the canyon provides the most reasonable approach, along with the most reliable network of use trails. As you approach, you will notice a very prominent ramp heading west up along the base of the south face of the mountain. You are ultimately aiming for this ramp.

Approaching the mouth of the canyon, you should notice several sub-drainages coming down from the higher reaches of the canyon above. Get into the northernmost one that heads directly up toward the ramp just mentioned. Though brushy if you drop into this northernmost sub-drainage too early, do the short scramble up-canyon until further progress is blocked by a very large band of cliffs. Look to your left for an exit from the drainage and onto the ridge above. Within 50 feet of the cliffs is a short class 3 chute heading up and back left that will dump you off precisely where you want to be. Gain the ridge above and start up, staying near the crest but left of the obvious crags that take the climbing above the class 3 range. Work your way up class 2-3 terrain to the obvious highpoint of the ridge above. Upon reaching the highpoint, you will have the entirety of the aforementioned ramp visible in front of you. Separating you from it are two shallow drainages.

Work your way down slightly to the left and drop into the first shallow drainage, cross a low ridge, then cross the second shallow drainage, before getting onto a loose dirt ridge that heads steeply toward the ramp above. Following a use trail near the crest of this dirty ridge seems the easiest way to go. Upon reaching the head of the dirty ridge, you should find that you are at the edge of some steep slickrock slabs leading up onto the ramp. If you feel comfortable, climb straight up (or utilize any of the weaknesses you can find) to the ramp *or* traverse to the right and down slightly until you see a ledge system that allows reasonable access onto the lower portion of the ramp.

Once on the ramp, head up (class 2-3). The ramp will ultimately lead you to a sort of saddle. From the saddle, drop a short distance to the other side and traverse along the base of the cliffs on your right. The occasional use trail and lots of cairns should keep you on track. Regardless, the route-finding is relatively straightforward. After traversing for a hundred yards (or slightly more) from the saddle, start looking for a likely looking place to head up to the right. If it looks harder than class 3, keep going until you see something easier. Once a feasible-appearing option presents itself, hang a right and head up. There are a number of possible lines of ascent from this point—pick one that suits you. Route-finding from here to the summit is fun, and you should find yourself on the summit within a few minutes.

To descend, retrace your steps. Finding one's way from the summit back to the base of the cliffs above the saddle can present some difficulties. Look for cairns, place your own, or budget some time for trial and error. Alos, a well-traveled trail can be picked up near the base of the ramp on the south side of the mountain—it runs parallel to and about 75 feet south of the route up the ridge you took when you first exited the northernmost sub-drainage on your ascent.

The roundtrip is about 6 miles and 2,000 feet of gain.

Alternatively, Windy Peak can be approached from the west. Following the directions given for Mountain Spring Benchmark, leave the main trail prior to Mountain Spring Benchmark, at a point where a lesser trail heads southeast along the ridge connected to Windy Peak. No major obstacles are encountered.

-WGS84 Lat: 36.0212789 deg N Lon: -115.4698476 deg W
*-II, Class 2 from the West ***
*-II, Class 3 via Windy Canyon ***

A large tinaja at Red Rock

"Global Peak" (5,914)

This minor peak sits near the head of Mud Spring Canyon on the northwest shoulder of Windy Peak. To reach it from the backside, follow the directions given for the alternate route to Windy Peak to a point along the limestone ridge slightly northwest of Global Peak's summit. Leave the trail and head northeast down steep limestone terrain until you can find a way to easily get on the yellow sandstone below. Continue descending to a point perhaps 200 vertical feet below Global Peak's summit, looking for cairns that lead one along a wonderful hidden ledge that travels southeast to the saddle connecting Global Peak and Windy Peak. From here, it's a short scramble north-northeast to the Global Peak highpoint.

-WGS84 Lat: 36.0264009 deg N Lon: -115.4741395 deg W
-II, Class 3-4 from the west *

"Black Velvet Peak" (6,234)
Black Velvet Peak is located in southern Red Rock Canyon NCA, nestled between Windy Peak and The Monument. Black Velvet Wall, the highest vertical wall at Red Rock, comprises the monstrous north face of the peak, as well as the south face of Black Velvet Canyon.

To climb via Black Velvet Canyon: Take I-15 south from Las Vegas to SR-160 (the road to Pahrump, Nevada). Turn onto SR-160 and follow it west toward the beautiful sandstone bluffs of southern Red Rock Canyon. Before reaching the NCA, you will pass SR-159, which is an alternate way of reaching the NCA's main entrance at the Scenic Drive. Continue west on SR-160 for 4.6 miles to a dirt road. The dirt road has a stop sign at its exit and a nearby large parking area for mountain bikers. If you happen to pass mile marker 16, turn around because you passed it. Follow the dirt road for 1.5 miles, ignoring any minor dirt roads that branch off. The road will bend left as it approaches a gate. Soon passing a "Black Velvet" sign, continue a mile as the road gets bumpier, nearing its end. Park in the large area at the end of the road. Black Velvet Canyon will be before you. Though the approach drive is rough, a passenger car driven with care should have no problems making it to the parking area.

From the parking area near the entrance to Black Velvet Canyon, follow the main trail into the mouth of Black Velvet Canyon. When class 4-5 difficulties are encountered just inside the mouth of the canyon as you hit a dry waterfall, work around them to your left (class 3) then drop into the wash and continue up-canyon. (Despite its modest class 3 rating, some may find this first obstacle a little intimidating.) Halfway (or more) into the canyon, you may be tempted to scramble up a prominent and exposed 5th class waterfall (sometimes wet, sometimes dry) leading you into a left fork of the canyon. Instead, stay in the main canyon and follow it almost all the way to where the yellow, orange and red sandstone of the canyon joins the grey limestone of the escarpment ahead. Before reaching the limestone, notice that the angle of the canyon walls on the left side lessens somewhat. As soon as practical, head up these steep sandstone slabs, ramps and slopes leading toward user-friendly terrain above. The sandstone slabs, ramps and slopes will eventually lead to a sort of gully where cairns should start to appear. Follow them upward around obstacles, past a couple of small sandstone arches, and ultimately to the area where the sandstone meets the limestone.

Once the area above the gully is reached, notice that Black Velvet Peak and the ridge leading out to it are to the south/southeast and that you are separated from them by a sort of bowl. Traverse class 2-3 limestone/sandstone terrain to the other side of the bowl, staying high, until you find yourself at the toe of the ridge leading toward the peak.

From this point, your objective is clear and so is the route (kind of). With a little trial and error, you should be able to work through various difficulties (class 2-4), including a cool hidden tunnel that must be found early on along the ridge, crawled through, and exited to continue. Ample cairns and signs of usage make the route-finding reasonable. Follow the ridge all the way to the summit.

Although it's lower, some folks consider a subsidiary peak closely to the NNE to be the true "Black Velvet Peak." It can be reached in about 10-15 minutes via some class 2 scrambling.

Roundtrip numbers are roughly 10 miles with 2,600 feet of gain.

From the summit, you can continue along the ridge in an easterly fashion for a bit, looking for cairns. At a point that is well-marked by foot traffic and cairn population, look for a worn use trail that leaves the ridge and heads down the steep north slope toward Whisky Peak. The meandering foot path will eventually take you all the way to the desert floor, and ultimately back to your approach trail a short distance from the trailhead.

Scrambling toward the summit of Black Velvet Peak

This descent option will shave several miles off your roundtrip.

This option, of course, can also be used as an ascent route, though I found it far less enjoyable than the longer and more challenging Black Velvet Canyon route.

Alternatively, following the directions given for Mountain Spring Benchmark to the summit of that peak, one can easily drop 400' down class 1-2 terrain to reach the toe of the ridge leading out toward Black Velvet Peak.

This route converges with the Black Velvet Canyon route at about 6000 feet. It seems that this much shorter, easier approach has become the new standard route to Black Velvet Peak.

-WGS84 Lat: 36.0346383 deg N Lon: -115.4686674 deg W
*-II, Class 2-3 via East Ridge from Whisky Peak **
*-II, Class 3-4 from Mountain Spring Benchmark ***
*-III, Class 4 via Black Velvet Canyon ****

"Whisky Peak" (5,189)

Whisky Peak is a minor sub-peak of Black Velvet Peak. It has wonderful views from its summit, particularly of nearby Black Velvet Wall, the massive north face of Whisky's parent peak—Black Velvet Peak.

Follow the driving directions given for Black Velvet Peak. From the parking area, make out the prominent gully separating Black Velvet Peak from Whisky Peak, the minor sub-peak detached from and to the right (north) of the main peak. Follow the main trail heading toward Black Velvet Canyon for about 0.5 mile and look for a side trail that branches off left and heads toward the gully between Black Velvet and Whisky. This good trail will take you to the gully and all the way to the saddle between the two peaks. From the saddle, turn right (north) and scramble up class 2-3 terrain toward the top. Expect a little class 3 (short slabs and steps) as you approach the summit.

The roundtrip is about two miles, with less than 1,000 feet of gain.

-WGS84 Lat: 36.0340959 deg N Lon: -115.4628154 deg W
*-I, Class 3 via East Gully **

"Burlap Buttress" (5,598)

By gaining Burlap Buttress's prominent east gully near the mouth of Black Velvet Canyon, one can follow cairns and signs of use up a convoluted and interesting class 3 route that gains the peak's southeast ridge shortly before the summit.

The flat, varnished rocks of the summit are funky.

-WGS84 Lat: 36.0399303 deg N Lon: -115.4687939 deg W
*-II, Class 3 via East Gully and Southeast Ridge *****

"Hidden Peak" (6,280+)

Hidden Peak. I didn't know it existed until I stood on the summit of its close neighbor, The Monument, and wondered what that higher sandstone peak just to the west was. Well, I had to solve that mystery. In about an hour, my partner and I stood on its summit and opened the register…Hidden Peak. Ok, then.

Hidden Peak is a high but minor peak in the deep backcountry of the Rainbow Mountain Wilderness of Red Rock Canyon NCA. It offers great views of the obscure southern portion of the NCA. Surrounded by more eye-catching peaks, this little guy is perhaps the easiest (in terms of physical exertion required) of the lot to get to (with Windy Peak as a strong contender).

Follow the directions given for The Monument to the ridge at the top of the gully, mere minutes from Hidden Peak's summit. From the ridge, hang a right and follow mellow class 1-2 terrain to the summit.

The roundtrip numbers are about 7 miles and 2,200 feet of gain.

-WGS84 Lat: 36.0448083 deg N Lon: -115.4722575 deg W

-II, Class 3-4 via Black Velvet Canyon *

"The Monument" (6,260+)

The Monument is the large, complex massif sandwiched between Sandstone Peak and Black Velvet Peak in the obscure southern portion of Red Rock Canyon NCA. Comprised of three summits, The Monument's western summit (6,260+ feet) is the highest. The central summit lies a bit to the east over rugged terrain, while the low, east summit (East Monument Peak) lies well below, detached somewhat from the main massif. This east summit is clearly visible as you drive along SR-159 toward SR-160.

The Monument's route from Black Velvet Canyon involves a little bit of 4th class scrambling over about 9-10 miles (roundtrip), with about 2,400 feet of gain.

Follow the driving directions given for Black Velvet Peak. From the parking area near the entrance to Black Velvet Canyon, follow the main trail into the mouth of Black Velvet Canyon. When class 4-5 difficulties are encountered just inside the mouth of the canyon as you hit a dry waterfall, work around them to your left (class 3) then drop into the wash and continue on. (Despite its modest class 3 rating, some may find this first obstacle a little intimidating.)

A mile (or so) into the canyon, pass a prominent and exposed 5th class waterfall (sometimes wet, sometimes dry) leading you into a minor left fork of the canyon. As tempting as the scramble up the waterfall may be, don't – it's not the direction you wanna go. Perhaps 0.5 mile beyond the waterfall, the canyon makes an obvious fork. About 75-100 yards before this prominent junction, scramble up the north side of the canyon on class 2-3 slabs and ledges. Try to work up and right, aiming for a shallow gully that will soon come into view. A landmark is a medium-size (25-35 feet tall) tree about 100 feet above the bottom of the canyon on the north side. Head up from the tree on a faint use trail to a cliff a short distance away. A slot in this cliff (you'll know it when you see it) takes you to the left and dumps you onto a sort of ledge. From the ledge, traverse right, climb a short (10-15 feet) class 3+ cliff, and you're in the gully.

Follow the gully up until it starts to bend to the left. A shallower fork of the gully goes somewhat to the right before largely cliffing out. Follow the gully as it bends left and climb (mostly class 2-3) all the way to its end at the ridge above. From the ridge, if you hang a right and follow gentle terrain up for a few minutes you'll soon reach the summit of Hidden Peak, The Monument's slightly higher and easier neighbor. If ignoring that option and intending to head straight for The Monument, hang a left at the ridge and work down a short distance to the saddle between Hidden Peak (to the right) and the high sandstone crags to the left. From the saddle, drop north into a descending wash. Follow the wash for 0.25 mile until you see the steep, roundish cliffs of The Monument to the east. When you are able, leave the wash and traverse easterly toward the base of the cliffs. The going is a bit brushy in places, but not bad.

When you reach the base of the cliffs, traverse north, cross a sort of highpoint near the northwest side of the cliffs, then drop 50-100 feet to the base of an obvious chute. There is a large healthy ponderosa pine at the entrance to this chute. Head up the chute until you come to an awkward class 4 chimney then climb the chimney (20-25 feet), traverse to the right at the obvious exit, and then fight your way up past a bush and over questionably secure chockstones to the flattish area above. Above the chimney, continue up the chute, which widens to a gully, for another 50 feet or so until you can exit to the left and climb onto a wide ledge/platform. There should be a cairn marking this exit point.

From the ledge/platform, head southeast along a narrow ledge, following a couple of cairns, until you see a point where you can drop onto more slopey/slabby terrain. You should be able to see another prominent gully system heading southward a short distance away. Head to the bottom of the next gully and start up. Following the gully all the way to its head, you'll see that it ends at a notch with a nice view of a huge drop-off below. At the head of the gully, climb the short (8 feet) class 3-4 wall to your right. Immediately atop this wall is a large, sweet tinaja—delightful. The summit is a few minutes away from you, atop the crag on your left. Class 2-3 scrambling on the back (south/southwest) side of the summit crag gets you there easiest.

-WGS84 Lat: 36.0453311 deg N Lon: -115.4697296 deg W

-III, Class 4 via Black Velvet Canyon ****

"East Monument Peak" (5,360+)

East Monument Peak (sometimes called East Peak) is a sub-peak of The Monument, the latter's much-lower eastern summit. Despite its small stature, it is quite prominent from SR-159, and it is one of the finest minor peak scrambles to be found in the Red Rock Canyon area.

Follow the driving directions given for Black Velvet Peak. From the parking area looking toward Black Velvet Canyon, The Monument is to the right. East Monument Peak is the prominently detached sub-peak of The Monument on the close (east) end of the massif. There is a prominent chute separating the two entities. You want to head for the chute.

Start down the main trail toward Black Velvet Canyon. Although there is the occasional use trail to be found heading off toward the chute in question, I found that they are often tedious and inefficient. Regardless, soon leave the main trail, work toward the base of the chute, and head up. About halfway up the chute, you will encounter cliffy terrain that prevents further easy passage. About 75 feet below that point, look for a class 3-4 exit consisting of a series of ledges on the right (east) side. Scrambling up the exit, then work up and left to find a hidden ledge that traverses north along the very eastern edge of the chute. This ledge may require a bit of route-finding to locate. It is perhaps 50 feet above the level of the chute bottom. (If you are staring at terrain harder than 4th class, you haven't found the ledge yet.)

Traverse the ledge north a short distance, soon finding yourself above the cliffy terrain in the chute. Past the ledge, work class 2-3 terrain up and to the right, gaining complex but easier terrain. Trending left once easier terrain is found, scramble to the summit a few hundred feet above. It is a very satisfying summit.

The roundtrip is 3 miles with about 1,000 feet of gain.

-WGS84 Lat: 36.0426448 deg N Lon: -115.4600429 deg W

*-II, Class 4 via South Face ****

"Fork Peak" (5,796)

Fork Peak is Sandstone Peak's neighbor. The two can readily be bagged in a day. To avoid any private property hassles, simply pay to enter the state park at the peak's base then hike across BLM land to the peak.

-WGS84 Lat: 36.056183 deg N Lon: -115.478354 deg W

*-III, Class 3-4 via West Face ****

"Sandstone Peak" (5,796)

The least visited major sandstone peak in Red Rock. It is a fun scramble with interesting route-finding. And like most of Red Rock's peaks, it is rugged and the key weakness needed to get up the thing is not apparent. Approach as per Fork Peak. Good luck; I failed on my first attempt too.

-WGS84 Lat: 36.0578189 deg N Lon: -115.4729464 deg W

*-III, Class 3-4 via West Face ****

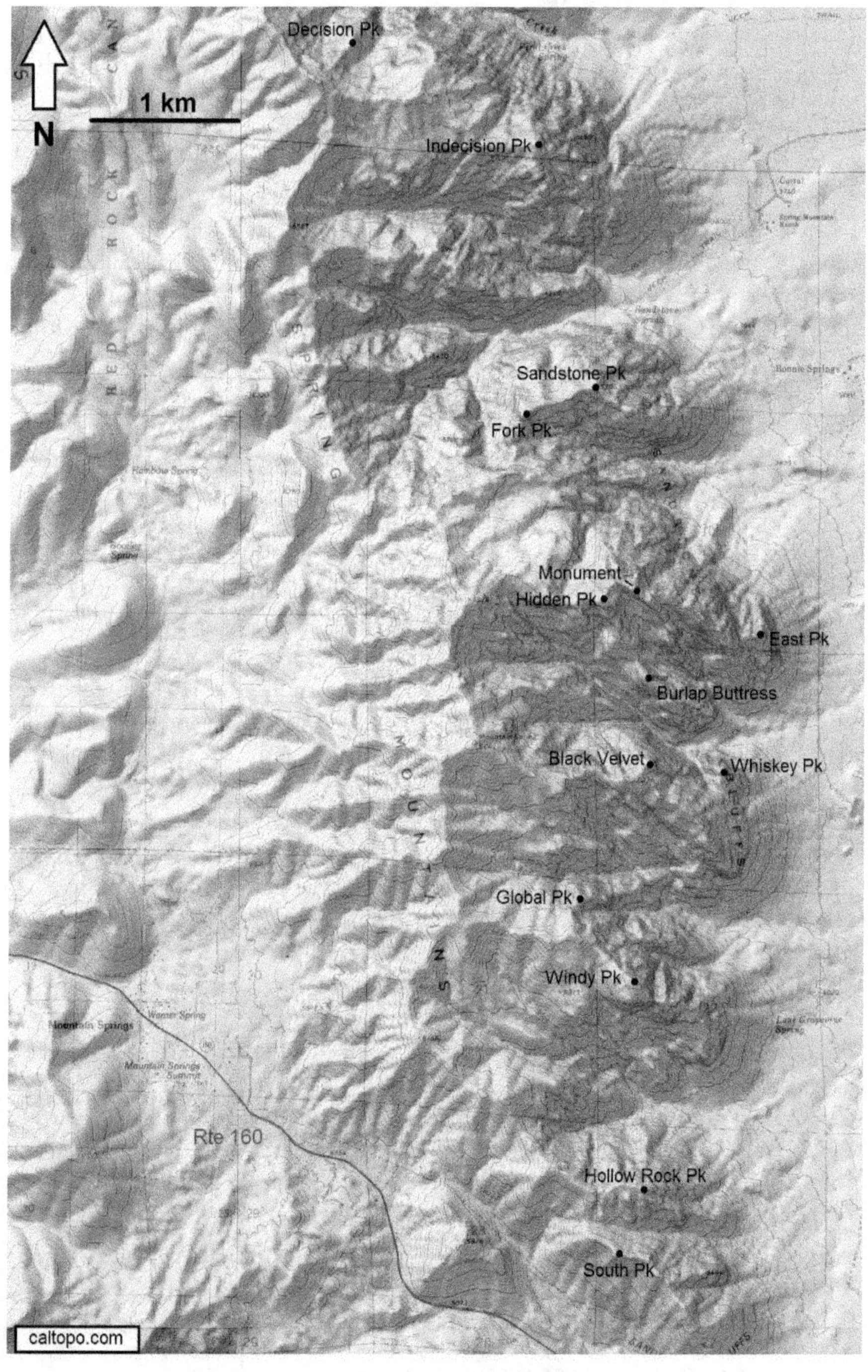
N
1 km
Decision Pk
Indecision Pk
Sandstone Pk
Fork Pk
Monument
Hidden Pk
East Pk
Burlap Buttress
Black Velvet
Whiskey Pk
Global Pk
Windy Pk
Rte 160
Hollow Rock Pk
South Pk
caltopo.com

"Indecision Peak" (6,465)

Indecision Peak is a minor summit on the impressive massif that sits between Mount Wilson and Sandstone Peak in Red Rock Canyon NCA. After a short initial slog, some fun scrambling takes you to the top. Doing this route one early spring, I encountered some beautiful ice formations on the sandstone of the upper mountain.

Head west from Las Vegas on Charleston Blvd (SR-159) toward the RRCNCA Scenic Drive entrance stations. Follow SR-159 for a few miles past the entrance, looking for the dirt pull-out for Oak Creek. This pull-out is a short distance past the *exit* to the Scenic Drive, on the right side of the highway, and immediately in front of the impressive east face of Mount Wilson, the highest sandstone peak in the NCA. Continue for just under a mile past the Oak Creek pull-out, where another pull-out on the right will greet you. This is First Creek, so park here.

From the First Creek trailhead, follow the trail toward the mouth of First Creek Canyon, which is the canyon running between Indecision Peak (on the left) and Mount Wilson (on the right). After about a mile, leave the trail and head cross-country directly toward the base of Indecision Peak. Note an obvious large gully on the east face of the mountain—it is NOT your objective; rather, aim for a much smaller but still distinct gully to the left (south) of the prominent one. This smaller gully is the start of the route.

Once at the gully, start ascending. The gully is steep and the scree portions of the route can be avoided by staying near the center of the gully. Ascend for about 1,000 feet to the top of the gully. Now, look for the southernmost crag in front of you. Its very smooth, 100-foot high east side will stand out distinctly from the other crags nearby. Scramble over class 2-3 boulder terrain to the south side of the smooth-sided crag. Work around to the west side of the smooth-sided crag then start up another gully heading north, keeping your eyes open for cairns steering you westward along the base of the large boulders and cliffs comprising the south side of the mountain. After passing through a sort of natural tunnel in the rocks (or bypassing the tunnel via a short class 3 downclimb) and traversing a short distance more to the west, you should find yourself at the bottom of another large gully. This large gully heads northwestward.

Start up the 1,000-foot gully. As you ascend, the gully becomes more of a series of boulders, ramps and ledges. (Although ascending the gully may sound simple and self-explanatory, those lacking route-finding skills can easily find themselves on some fairly nasty and exposed terrain. If unsure of your route, look for cairns.) Once the top of the gully is gained, the terrain levels out and the summit is the top of the obvious crag ahead to the right.

Roundtrip numbers for this route are about 5 miles and 3,000 feet of gain.

-WGS84 Lat: 36.0727665 deg N Lon: -115.477515 deg W

-III, Class 3 via East Face Gully **

"Decision Peak" (6,200)
Decision Peak is the least prominent peak in this book. It rises perhaps 12" from its saddle with the limestone escarpment next to it. Very *un*impressive! Fortunately, the route to the summit via First Creek (take the south fork at the first major confluence, then take the north fork a hundred yards later) is beautiful and highly enjoyable. The sandstone slabs in the upper portion of First Creek make for some enjoyable scrambling.

-WGS84 Lat: 36.0789652 deg N Lon: -115.4920085 deg W
-III, Class 2 via Traverse from First Creek Peak *
-III, Class 4 via South Fork of First Creek ***

The north face of Indecision Peak from the summit of Decision Peak

"First Creek Peak" (6,100)
First Creek Peak and Decision Peak can be easily combined for an enjoyable half-day out in First Creek, provided one doesn't mind the super-loose, steep and unpleasant sandstone traverse between the two. The summit block of First Creek Peak is steep and fun (class 3), best bagged from its east side. The

peak is most easily approached via the south fork of the north fork of First Creek (class 4).

-WGS84 Lat: 36.0831568 deg N Lon: -115.4930536 deg W
-III, Class 2 via Traverse from Decision Peak *
-III, Class 4 via North Fork of First Creek ***

"White Rock Pinnacle" (5,574)

A feature of Mount Wilson's southeast face, White Rock Pinnacle (sometimes called White Pinnacle Peak) is a very minor sub-peak featuring a fun knife-edge with stimulating exposure. The route is one of the best I've done at Red Rock. A photograph of me on the summit was used as the front cover of the first edition of this guide.

Follow the driving directions given for Indecision Peak. From the First Creek trailhead, head west on the trail toward First Creek Canyon. As you do, make out the southernmost obvious chute on the southeast side of Mount Wilson. I'm referring to the chute as the "east chute," though some call it White Rock Gully. In any case, White Rock Pinnacle is the not-prominent nipple-like feature to the immediate left of the top of the chute.

As the trail approaches a point where the chute/gully in question meets the First Creek drainage (perhaps 1.5 miles from the trailhead), leave the trail, cross First Creek, and hopefully find the decent use trail that improves as it climbs and leads to the chute/gully just as it narrows at the base of Mount Wilson and enters the chute on its right side.

Head up the chute, following cairns and obvious signs of traffic. Notable obstacles/landmarks along the way include:

1) An exposed slab traverse next to a large boulder near the very bottom of the chute;

2) An awkward (and difficult to protect) off-width slab (crux) that sometimes has a fixed rope. The crux (20 feet) is YDS 5.4 if the rope is not used. *(Note: Fixed ropes are not permitted within wilderness areas. White Rock Pinnacle is a part of the Rainbow Mountain Wilderness.)*;

3) A chimney (30-40 feet) with a chockstone in it. Stemming up the chimney, you exit (awkward 4th class) north through a hole. This is one of the more intimidating portions of the route, particularly on the down-climb. Someone has installed a bolt at the top of the hole;

4) About 150 feet of sustained and exposed class 3-4 scrambling on the south side of the chute to reach the notch at the top of the chute.

Above this last section of stiffer scrambling, you'll reach the notch between Mount Wilson (on the right) and White Rock Pinnacle (on the left). Climb onto the spine leading out to White Rock Pinnacle and scramble the fun and exposed knife-edge to the summit. From certain vantage points, a photograph of someone on the summit is particularly impressive.

The roundtrip is 4-5 miles with about 1500' of gain.

-WGS84 Lat: 36.08297 deg N Lon: -115.47961 deg W
-II, Class 4 via East Chute ****

"Dead Horse Point" (5,750)
From the First Creek trailhead, White Rock Gully is the southernmost large gully on the south end of the Mount Wilson massif. The next large gully north of that is known as Dead Horse Gully. Dead Horse Point is the obvious minor summit sitting just left of the top of Dead Horse Gully.

Waiting at the notch below the summit of White Rock Pinnacle

Follow the directions given for White Rock Pinnacle to the notch at the top of White Rock Gully. From there, scramble up a 7' class 2-3 wall and squeeze through a crack that leads to a 15' near-vertical wall on the left. Scramble up the wall (class 3-4) then move right to easier terrain that can be followed up to the notch at the top of Dead Horse Gully. From there, angle right and head toward the north side of the Dead Horse Point summit block. You'll need to traverse a narrow ledge over an abyss to gain a series of wide vertical ledges immediately beyond that lead to the final slab just below the highpoint. The vertical ledges constitute the block's crux; they are steep and exposed but with large holds (some of them loose).

-WGS84 Lat: 36.0837359 deg N Lon: -115.4801811 deg W
-II, YDS 5.0 via White Rock Pinnacle ***

"South Wilson" (6,809)
Mount Wilson's aesthetic twin south summits lie slightly southeast of the main summit. The slighter higher (and easier) eastern of the twin summits is reached by hiking down the parent peak's south ridge, usually just below and west of the crest, until you are at the base of South Wilson, where a bit of class 2 scrambling on the north side leads to the highpoint.

-WGS84 Lat: 36.0870611 deg N Lon: -115.4814895 deg W
-III, Class 2 via Mount Wilson **

Mount Wilson (7,070)
Mount Wilson is the highest peak in Red Rock Canyon NCA. The mountain is situated between First Creek Canyon on its south side and Oak Creek Canyon on its north. Its mighty east face happens to be one of the most prominent and eye-catching sights in Red Rock Canyon.

The finest scrambling route on the peak may be Cleaver Crack, an amazing and improbable class 4-5 route accessed via upper Oak Creek Canyon. For that route, you'll need to approach as per Cactus Flower Tower but head right at the top of the big, beautiful dryfall near the base of Cactus Flower Tower's route proper then follow cairns and signs of use as it works its way to and then up an incredible and improbable pair of slots angling east up Mount Wilson's imposing north face. At the top of Cleaver Crack is a notch, where one needs to scramble 30' up a class 3 weakness to a tree. Next, nastily exposed but easy (class 2-3) ledges lead 30' to the right and then up a shallow groove to easier terrain 40' above. From there, follow cairns and signs of use as you work up and left toward the summit above. The Cleaver Crack route is not suitable for novice scramblers, and many people may wish to have a rope.

To take the Cleaver Crack route to the next level, continue over Mount Wilson to South Wilson then descend via Dead Horse Point and White Rock Pinnacle. Good stuff! But be prepared for tricky terrain and sticky route-finding in spots.

To climb via First Creek: Follow the driving directions given for Indecision Peak. From the First Creek trailhead, follow the trail into First Creek Canyon. Since my earliest visits, a good trail system (and plenty of brush clearing) have made this route much more easy (and pleasant) to follow. Scramble up-canyon, aiming for the head of the canyon branch that runs immediately south of Mount Wilson. Go right at any major fork encountered. Once the head of the canyon is reached, exit right onto the gentle sandstone backside of Mount Wilson. From there, follow signs of use back up and east toward the summit. The terrain becomes a touch convoluted in places, but a bit of trial and error should get you there with minimal difficulties. Just before you decide you don't wanna do this anymore, you'll be on the summit.

The roundtrip is perhaps 10 miles with over 3,000 feet of gain.

-WGS84 Lat: 36.093673 deg N Lon: -115.4839666 deg W

-III, Class 2-3 via First Creek **

-III, Class 4-5 via Cleaver Crack ****

-IV, Class 4-5 via traverse from Cleaver Crack to White Rock Pinnacle ****

Looking north to Mount Wilson from the base of Indecision Peak

SR-159 or the Scenic Drive

All of the peaks in this subsection are in the area of Oak Creek. With easy access to the canyon from trailheads along either the Scenic Drive or SR-159, you can choose which you prefer.

Note: Vehicles parked along SR-159 for longer than 24 hours could be cited for parking in the Nevada Department of Transportation (NDOT) right-of-way.

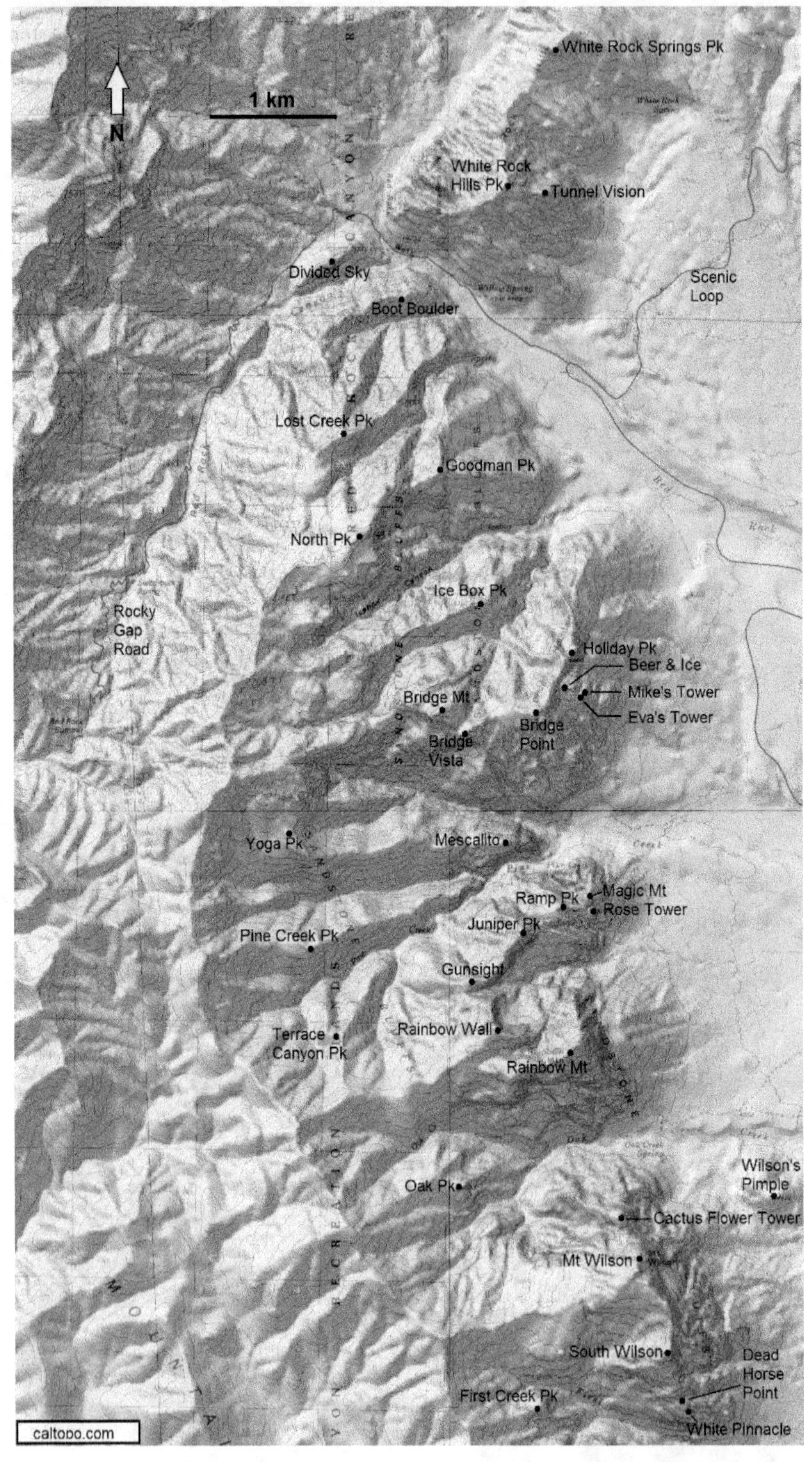
N
1 km
White Rock Springs Pk
White Rock Hills Pk
Tunnel Vision
Divided Sky
Boot Boulder
Scenic Loop
Lost Creek Pk
Goodman Pk
North Pk
Ice Box Pk
Rocky Gap Road
Holiday Pk
Beer & Ice
Mike's Tower
Eva's Tower
Bridge Mt
Bridge Vista
Bridge Point
Yoga Pk
Mescalito
Magic Mt
Ramp Pk
Rose Tower
Juniper Pk
Pine Creek Pk
Gunsight
Rainbow Wall
Terrace Canyon Pk
Rainbow Mt
Wilson's Pimple
Oak Pk
Cactus Flower Tower
Mt Wilson
South Wilson
Dead Horse Point
First Creek Pk
White Pinnacle
caltopo.com

"Cactus Flower Tower" (6,356)

Cactus Flower Tower is a fantastic sub-peak on the north side of Mount Wilson. With awesome scenery on the approach through Oak Creek Canyon (my favorite canyon at Red Rock) and aesthetic scrambling on the peak's west ridge, this is one of the most enjoyable summits in the park.

To get there from Las Vegas, head west on Charleston Blvd. (SR-159) toward the Scenic Drive turn-off. From here, you can either:

1) Follow the Scenic Drive for about 11 miles to the signed Oak Creek dirt road turn-off then take the well-maintained road to its end at the Oak Creek Trailhead;

Or, 2) Continue on SR-159 for a few miles past the entrance to the NCA, looking for the dirt pull-out for Oak Creek on the right side of the road. The pull-out is a short distance past the exit to the Scenic Drive and immediately in front of Mount Wilson.

From either of the two trailheads, follow a well-beaten trail to the mouth of Oak Creek Canyon. Continue up-canyon, taking left forks in the canyon as they come. You may lose the path before getting to a notch, but with vigilance signs of previous heavy usage can be followed all the way to the end of the canyon and to a short class 3 scramble at the base of some cliffs, then up to the notch. Continue east for 50 feet above the notch until you can exit left up a short broken wall (class 3-4; 12-15 feet). Above the wall, the terrain opens again and you should find yourself in a slickrock and boulder field. There should be a couple of cairns prominently placed in this area.

Stay left and head up, once again finding yourself near the crest of the now-narrowing west ridge of the peak. Although easier variations may be found elsewhere, I found that sticking on or very near the crest of the ridge made for an exhilarating scramble all the way to the summit. Expect to encounter an awkward 15-foot chimney (low 5th class) that can be bypassed with very exposed class 3-4 scrambling on its left side. Further up, the crux is a face just below and left of a prominent wide chimney with a couple of chockstones in it. There are a couple of rappel stations here for your return, should you need them. The crux face (about 30-40 feet) is YDS 5.3, following narrow ledges up and right toward easier terrain adjacent to the chimney. The face can also be bypassed with comparable climbing in a wide crack on its left side. Work through the chimney (class 3-4) and continue up easier terrain, soon arriving at the summit. Wasn't that fun?!?

The roundtrip for this baby is 6-8 miles with about 2,400 feet of elevation gain.

-WGS84 Lat: 36.096454 deg N Lon: -115.4854935 deg W

-III, YDS 5.3 via West Ridge ***

"Wilsons Pimple" (4,422)

Great views of Mount Wilson, Sherwood Forest and Cactus Flower Tower. Park as per Cactus Flower Tower.

-WGS84 Lat: 36.0980 deg N Lon: -115.4720 deg W

*-I, Class 2 from any direction **

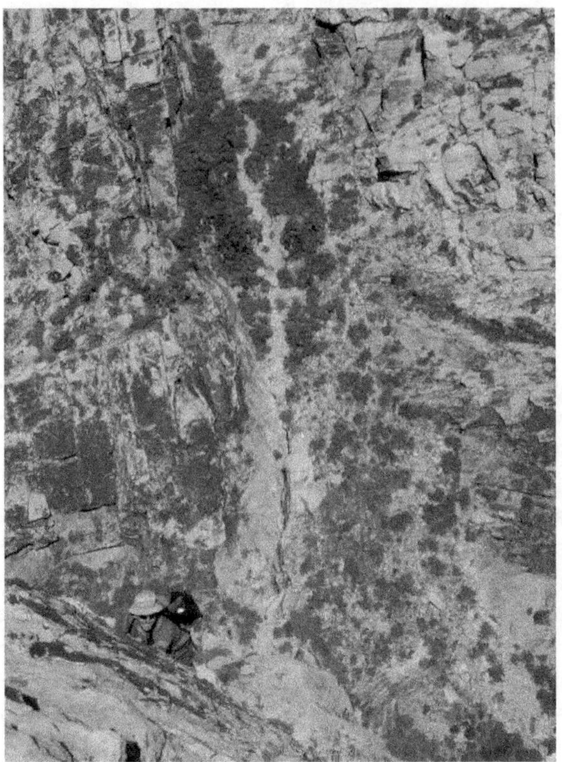

Walt Hutton climbing the west ridge of Cactus Flower Tower

"Oak Peak" (6,033)

Like nearby Yoga Peak, Oak Peak is little more than a sandstone outcropping oozing out from the limestone escarpment behind it. Though easily identified as the small mountain between the north and south forks of Oak Creek Canyon, Oak Peak is completely overshadowed by its higher and more impressive neighbors, Mount Wilson (south) and Rainbow Mountain (north).

Follow the directions given for Cactus Flower Tower into Oak Creek Canyon. The canyon is absolutely gorgeous, particularly in spring in the upper canyon, when the melting snows from the high mountains above send their waters rushing down into the deep sandstone canyon. The result is spectacular cascades and the constant sound of rushing water. Oak Creek runs year-round, but spring is unquestionably the best time of year to be there.

To climb the Northeast Chute: Scramble up-canyon to a prominent fork. Take the right (north) fork. Oak Peak will be immediately above you. Just beyond the fork, make out a very wide chute coming down from the top of the mountain into the north fork of the canyon. The chute, while full of talus on the upper mountain, is largely slickrock and slabby near its bottom. This chute will have been visible during your approach in the main canyon. This is the northeast chute.

Continue hiking up the north fork until come to a section of steep slickrock slabs on your left. There should be a ribbon of water draining the right edge of the slabs where they meet some boulders in the bottom of the canyon. There is a prominent ponderosa pine at the top of this section of slickrock. The spot is also near the right edge of the northeast chute above and to your left.

Scramble up the slickrock (class 2-3) left of the ribbon of water, and once the ponderosa is reached start working your left onto the slickrock of the northeast chute above. Although there are a number of variations possible, I found that working to near the base of the cliffs above and then traversing left 50 feet to the bottom of a steep 4th class chimney (15-20 feet) worked well. Climb through the chimney (mostly good rock) or utilize any other workable route you can find, and scramble into the main body of the northeast chute to your left. Depending on your line, you may need to scramble (3rd class) up some exposed sections of steep dry fall. Work to the top of the chute over progressively easier terrain. The summit is a short distance away, and not hard to find.

To climb the North Chute: Follow the directions given above into the north fork of the canyon. From there, continue up-canyon to another prominent fork near the limestone escarpment. The right fork leads to Rainbow Mountain and Rainbow Wall, and the left fork leads to the base of the limestone escarpment. Instead of taking either fork, bend left and work up beautiful slickrock to the north chute of Oak Peak. Steep in places, you may need to do some route-finding to keep the terrain reasonable. Working the far left or far right sides of the chute presents the easiest opportunities, though heading straight up, while certainly not class 2-3, does make for some stimulating travel. The terrain mellows out considerably as you gain elevation. Once the head of the north chute is gained, follow your nose to the sandstone summit.

Roundtrip numbers for either route are 6-8 miles, with about 1,700 feet of elevation gain.

-WGS84 Lat: 36.0986617 deg N Lon: -115.4999571 deg W

*-III, Class 2-3 via North Chute **

*-III, Class 4 via Northeast Chute ***

Rainbow Mountain (6,810)

Rainbow Mountain is one of the classic peaks of Red Rock. Follow the directions given for Rainbow Wall to the large rock tower not far from Rainbow Wall's summit. Angle right from the tower to gain the west ridge of Rainbow Mountain. Enjoy interesting route-finding on your way to the summit!

-WGS84 Lat: 36.1080348 deg N Lon: -115.4900429 deg W

-III, Class 3 via West Ridge ****

"Rainbow Wall" (6,924)

Rainbow Wall, though arguably a component of the greater Rainbow Mountain massif, is an adjacent big wall feature that is actually 114 feet higher than the officially named Rainbow Mountain. The enormous sandstone wall, visible from nearly all of the Scenic Drive, is a beautiful and beckoning beast, reminiscent of walls seen in Zion, and a worthwhile endeavor for the weekend hiker and big wall climber alike. The views straight down the huge wall to the bottom of Juniper Canyon (about 1,500 feet below) are awesome.

Follow the directions given for Cactus Flower Tower into Oak Creek Canyon. Head up-canyon, taking right forks as they come, ultimately working your way to the end of the main canyon, where the yellow sandstone meets the gray limestone of the higher escarpmet above. You can't miss the geologic transition. It's painfully obvious. Once this area is reached, head north up the yellow sandstone talus slope above. The slope starts out a little steep but mellows out in a short time. As the slope levels off, look for a faint use trail heading easterly. Follow it.

The next part of the route is hard to describe (and while on the mountain a little hard to follow) but good route-finding skills and a little trial and error will get you there nonetheless.

The use trail will continue easterly for a hundred yards or more and then start traversing northward around the edge of a steepening slope on your left. Follow the trail northward a couple hundred feet to the bottom of an obvious ramp/slab. Leave the trail and head up the ramp. From the top of the ramp, you should be able to see Bridge Mountain and the other awesome crags of the northern Red Rock Canyon backcountry. You may be tempted from this point to continue east and up a ledge system to higher ground, but don't; instead, start traversing northeasterly along the north side of the ledge system over class 2-3 terrain (note the route for your return, as it's amazing how class 4-5 terrain seems to materialize out of nowhere) and aim for the base of a prominent cliff that is 0.25 mile ahead of you. From the base of the prominent cliff, follow a use trail on the cliff's west side north for a 0.25 mile to the end of the cliff. The use trail starts to spider web past the cliff and becomes harder to follow. About this time, you should notice a large rock tower to your right. This is an important landmark.

As the use trail starts to spider web, look for one that heads more northerly and away from the rock tower. The use trail should start heading up a talus slope, which will ultimately lead you to the summit, a short distance away. If the route is in question at this point, simply head to higher ground. During the final approach to the summit, there is one difficult section—a short (12-15 feet) and unexposed class 4 wall that must be down-climbed. From the base of the wall, continue north up to the summit.

Roundtrip numbers are around 10 miles, with about 3,100 feet of gain.

Rainbow Mountain's summit is only 45 minutes away. With a little extra time and energy, do them both. Rainbow Mountain's summit requires a bit of exposed class 3 climbing near the end.

-WGS84 Lat: 36.1096268 deg N Lon: -115.4965364 deg W

-III, Class 4 via Oak Creek Canyon ***

Scenic Drive

The peaks in this subsection are accessed from the RRCNCA Scenic Drive. The Scenic Drive, which leaves Charleston Blvd. several miles west of CC-215, is a 13-mile, one-way road through the NCA. A fee is required to access the Scenic Drive.

"Juniper Peak" (6,109)

When viewed from the Scenic Drive, Juniper Peak is the small peak below and just north of the prominent Rainbow Wall. Juniper Peak frames the left edge of beautiful Pine Creek Canyon. Juniper is a fine peak with fantastic scenery.

From the fee station, follow the Scenic Drive for about 10 miles to the signed Pine Creek parking area. It is one of the most popular trailheads along the Scenic Drive, and fills up quickly on weekends. Next, follow the directions given for Gunsight Notch Peak to the worn use-trail in Juniper Canyon leading to Brownstone Wall. Head right up the worn use-trail and then scramble up the slope to the slickrock near the base of Brownstone Wall. The summit of Juniper Peak is at the top of the wall, somewhat to the right. Head north on the slickrock slabs below the base of Brownstone Wall. Although the route is fairly obvious, cairns help keep the difficulty to a minimum (mainly class 1-2). The slabs soon give way to talus, and shortly before the cliffs end to the north you'll encounter a steep class 3 obstacle immediately below a prominent bushy chute that heads steeply up to the left. Follow the chute to its end a couple hundred feet higher. At the top of the chute, follow cairns and signs of foot traffic left., where you'll soon wind around a corner, bend right, and then climb up through a short, fun tunnel/chimney feature. From there, the summit is a short scramble away. Great stuff.

The roundtrip numbers are 5-6 miles with a couple thousand feet of gain.

-WGS84 Lat: 36.1164614 deg N Lon: -115.4942575 deg W
*-III, Class 3 via Juniper Canyon ****

Cruising up the beautiful slabs above Juniper Canyon on the way to Juniper Peak

"Gunsight Notch Peak" (6,200+)

Gunsight Notch Peak is named for the "gunsight" notch separating it from its much higher neighbor, Rainbow Wall. From Juniper Canyon, Gunsight Notch Peak is a fine, short scramble.

Although not described here, a fantastic loop involves bagging Gunsight Notch Peak via a subsidiary fork of Pine Creek near Terrace Canyon, then descending via Gunsight Notch (and Juniper Canyon). With 30m of rope and other appropriate rappelling equipment and expertise, one can also traverse from Gunsight Notch Peak to Juniper Peak (which can then be descended via its standard route). Expect a 40-foot rappel on the traverse between the two peaks.

For the route from Juniper Canyon: Follow the directions given for Ramp Peak to the base of the prominent chute. Rather than climb the chute, continue south on the main trail toward the mouth of Juniper Canyon (the next major canyon south of Pine Creek Canyon). Follow any of several lesser trails that lead to the mouth of Juniper Canyon. Once in the canyon, head west to a use-trail of red dirt on the left (south) side of the canyon that heads steeply up, paralleling the wash below. The trail will eventually lead back down into the bouldery wash. About 30 yards after it does, look for cairns and a worn use-trail on the right leading back out the other side of the wash through some trees and onto a bouldery slope below the base of Brownstone Wall, the prominent big climbing wall above. Do not confuse Brownstone Wall with Rainbow Wall, which is more pastel colorful, higher, and to the left on the opposite side of the canyon.

Looking up-canyon between those two prominent sandstone walls you should see a notch, way up high—the notch is known as Gunsight Notch. You're aiming for it.

Ignoring the side trail that heads up toward Brownstone Wall, continue up-canyon in the bottom of the main watercourse, heading toward Gunsight Notch. As you get deeper into the canyon, not terribly far below the notch, you will encounter the crux of the day—a 12-15 foot chimney (class 4). I'm told that there is also a tunnel nearby that allows you to bypass the crux, though I've never noticed it when I've done the route. Beyond the chimney, continue up over class 2-3 terrain to the notch. From the notch, hang a right (north) and scramble to the summit.

Roundtrip numbers are about 5 miles, with a couple thousand feet of gain.

-WGS84 Lat: 36.1130348 deg N Lon: -115.4987939 deg W
*-III, Class 4 via Juniper Canyon ****

"Terrace Canyon Peak" (6,250)

Like so many of the wonderfully obscure routes to Red Rock's miniscule "summits," this one's really tough to describe. From the south fork of Pine Creek Canyon, get to Terrace Canyon (which is the fork immediately east of the summit) and in its lower reaches gain a crack/chimney feature on the east wall of the canyon. By following cairns, signs of use, the easiest line, and applying plenty of common sense, you'll eventually gain the peak's northeast ridge, which is delightfully scrambled to the unimpressive summit.

-WGS84 Lat: 36.1092089 deg N Lon: -115.5108798 deg W
*-II, Class 4-5 via Northeast Ridge from lower Terrace Canyon *****

"Ramp Peak" (5,400+)

Ramp Peak, also known as Crabby Appleton Peak, is a sub-peak of Juniper Peak. After a short scramble, the summit offers fine views down into Pine Creek Canyon on its north side.

Follow the driving directions given for Juniper Peak.

From the Pine Creek parking area, follow the signed trail as it heads toward Pine Creek Canyon. After about a mile on the main trail, you'll reach the old Wilson homestead. It consists of a foundation—all that remains of a home that once stood in this quaint spot. In case you miss the homestead (which is not signed), immediately after it is a signed junction with the Arnight Trail. Leave the main trail from either the homestead or the junction and follow the Arnight Trail as it heads directly for Pine Creek, crosses it on small boulders 100 yards from the junction, and quickly starts to head up to the south/southeast. Soon, the trail levelsoff again and traverses south along the base of Juniper Peak and one of its subsidiary summits, Magic Mountain, on the north side of the massif. Just left of Magic Mountain is a rose-colored buttress known as Rose Tower, a popular climbing objective. Behind Rose Tower and just out of sight is Ramp Peak.

A prominent chute drains from between Rose Tower and Magic Mountain. Head up the chute. With a little effort, you should be able to pick up a good use trail that leaves the main trail and heads all the way to the saddle at the top of the chute. Magic Mountain is immediately right of the top of the chute. A short scramble to the far left (southeast) will take you to the top of Rose Tower. Instead, scramble up a short (8 feet) band of rock (class 3) on the left side of the saddle. Once atop the band of rock, the summit of Ramp Peak can be seen a few minutes' away up the ridge to the west. Follow the ridge toward the summit. As you approach the summit rocks, traverse west along their north side (a touch exposed) until easier scrambling allows you to climb to the top.

Roundtrip numbers are less than 4 miles, with about 1,200 feet of gain.

-WGS84 Lat: 36.1182698 deg N Lon: -115.4906437 deg W
-II, Class 3 via East Ridge **

"Rose Tower" (5,220)

Rose Tower is another sub-peak of Juniper Peak. It is named for the rose color of the rock on its east face. More a noteworthy feature than a distinct peak, it is home to one of Red Rock Canyon's more famous rock climbs—Olive Oil (YDS 5.7).

Follow the directions given for Ramp Peak to 30 feet below the saddle at the top of the chute. From there, a short scramble to the far left (southeast) will take you to the top of Rose Tower.

The roundtrip is less than 4 miles, with 1,000 feet of gain.
-WGS84 Lat: 36.1178966 deg N Lon: -115.4879678 deg W
-II, Class 3 via East Chute *

"Magic Mountain" (5,350+)

The east face is the preferred ascent route, and most will want to descent via the east chute from the saddle. The south summit block (class 4) is the highpoint. Expect 4 miles and 1,200 feet of gain.

For the east chute route: Follow the directions given for Ramp Peak to the saddle at the top of the chute (class 2). From the saddle, drop 10 feet down the west side and follow cairns and signs of heavy use to the base of the summit block, which is surmounted by 15 feet of class 4 scrambling. Alternatively, one can drop east from the saddle for 50 feet and climb the prominent weakness (YDS 5.2) in the cliffs to easier terrain below the top.

For the east face route: Leave the trail once it levels out above Pine Creek and pick up a good use trail on the peak's northeast side. With plenty of cairns to guide you, follow the beaten route (class 4) to the base of the summit block. Expect fixed ropes in several stiffer sections.

-WGS84 Lat: 36.1189728 deg N Lon: -115.488279 deg W
-II, Class 4 via East Face ****
-II, Class 4 via East Chute **

Gunsight Notch Peak from the upper north fork
of the south fork of Pine Creek

"Pine Creek Peak" (6,265)

The views from the summit of this not-so-prominent peak are splendid, particularly over to Bridge Mountain. Although at least one route has been pieced together via the east ridge (outstanding, by the way: ****), the more mellow approaches via the adjacent canyons are highly scenic and super enjoyable.

-WGS84 Lat: 36.1153482 deg N Lon: -115.5131717 deg W
-III, Class 3-4 via South Fork of Mescalito Canyon ***
-III, Class 3-4 via North Fork of South Fork of Pine Creek ***

Magic Mountain (right) and Rose Tower (left of center from the east. The prominent chute/gully is used to access both peaks.

"Mescalito" (5,440)

Mescalito is the aesthetic, relatively small pyramid splitting the north and south forks of Pine Creek Canyon. It is prominently situated between the Juniper Peak massif and Bridge Mountain. In addition to being a fine scrambling ground, Mescalito is home to a couple of Red Rock Canyon's famous climbing routes—Dark Shadows (YDS 5.8-) and Cat in the Hat (YDS 5.6+).

Follow the driving directions given for Juniper Peak.

To climb via Pine Creek Canyon-North Fork (Fern Canyon): From the Pine Creek parking area, follow the trail toward the mouth of Pine Creek Canyon. Although a number of spider webbing trails start to appear as you get near the canyon entrance, stay on the main trail, looking for a prominent trail which branches off to the right and leads up onto the red, rocky/sandy bench to your right. This is a designated (but unsigned) spur trail that sees many feet. The trail will meander up and down a touch, soon dumping you off just inside the entrance to the north fork of Pine Creek Canyon.

Hike up-canyon for about 0.5 mile to your first obvious major obstacle—a waterfall blocking further easy progress. Immediately before the waterfall, you'll notice a tree on your left next to the cliff wall. The short cliff wall (20 feet) allows a 4th class exit, starting near the tree. Above the waterfall, the canyon splits in about 100 feet. The left fork will dead-end into a spectacular bowl with a large, beautiful waterfall. Instead, follow the right fork for a couple hundred feet until you notice obvious human-caused erosion on the dirty slope on the south side of the canyon. A sandy use trail here can be followed up to the crest of the ridge above.

Once at the crest, continue west until you come to a steep and intimidating face (100 feet) of varnished rock barring further easy progress. Scramble to the top of the intimidating face using crack systems (class 2-3). The holds are large and good; it's hard to imagine that the exposed face is only class 2-3 (be judicial in your route-finding to keep it that way). At the top of the face follow cairns left around a corner then drop into the drainage on the other side. This drainage, incidentally, is the same one atop the large waterfall you would have encountered had you taken the left fork immediately above the first waterfall. Above you to the south/southeast is a sort of bowl below the cliffy crest of the ridge connecting Mescalito and Yoga Peak (west; above it). Scramble to near the top of the bowl then start traversing back east/southeast until you can easily reach the crest of the ridge. Lots of fun scrambling here!

Head east along the crest until you come to a large notch. Downclimb to the notch, following weaknesses (and looking for cairns). It should never be harder than 4th class. From the other side of the notch, work toward the south side of the ridge, doing a delicate step-across move (may intimidate some), then start working your way on an eastward traverse that eventually heads back up toward the summit. The final bit of scrambling is difficult to describe but delightful.

The roundtrip is about 6 miles with around 2,500 feet of gain.

To return via Pine Creek Canyon-South Fork: I recommend ascending Mescalito via the fun and aesthetic north fork of Pine Creek Canyon, so I'll recommend (and provide directions for) this route as a descent option.

From the summit, retrace your steps back through the notch and onto the crest of the ridge. Head back west toward the top of the bowl that you reached from the north fork, and before reaching it keep your eyes open for a small but prominent tree on the ridge crest. There will be a steep chute/gully below it on the south side of the crest. A large cairn usually marks this spot. Head down the chute/gully about 30-40 feet then start working weaknesses down to the west. (Be careful not to drop too low too quickly; if anything, try to stay higher, rather than lower. Look for cairns to assist you in finding the correct route.) Gently traversing ledges and slabs down and west, you'll eventually come to a bouldery gully a couple hundred feet above the bottom of the canyon. Follow this to the canyon bottom. Once in the canyon, head east and follow your nose out. You'll eventually find yourself on familiar terrain near the junction of the north and south forks of Pine Creek Canyon at the base of Mescalito.

-WGS84 Lat: 36.1227312 deg N Lon: -115.4957296 deg W
-III, Class 3 via Pine Creek Canyon (South Fork) ***
-III, Class 4 via Pine Creek Canyon (North Fork) ****

Good hiking and scrambling in Red Rock!

"Yoga Peak" (6,650+)

A part of the same ridge that runs from the summit of Mescalito, Yoga Peak sits due west of and considerably higher than that aforementioned and visually-appealing little pyramid. While gazing up at the easily overlooked Yoga Peak from the NCA's Scenic Drive, the minor summit is one of the highest in the NCA.

Yoga Peak's ascent routes from Pine Creek (described below) are highly aesthetic, and the summit views are among the best in Red Rock Canyon.

Follow the driving directions given for Juniper Peak. From the parking area, Mescalito Peak is the sweet, little pyramid clearly visible at the mouth of Pine Creek Canyon, to the west. Following with your eyes the sandstone ridge rising up from behind Mescalito's summit, Yoga Peak is visible as the highest sandstone point at the top of the ridge.

To climb via Pine Creek Canyon-North Fork (Fern Canyon): Follow the directions for Mescalito via Pine Creek Canyon-North Fork to the drainage above the spectacular bowl with the large waterfall. From there, remain in this main drainage for the remainder of the canyon, following it westward toward the base of an obvious huge vertical headwall at the end of the canyon. The going is typically in the class 2-3 range, and very enjoyable. You are traveling through some infrequently explored terrain. Upon reaching the base of the imposing headwall, stop and look up. Yoga Peak is immediately above you on the left, though you cannot see the summit from here. To your left is an obvious steep watercourse. Get onto the slabs of the watercourse, and following weaknesses, scramble up a couple hundred vertical feet to a likely exit onto a spur ridge/rib on the left. (Note: Although I am confident that an easier exit onto the ridge/rib can be had, I found nothing easier than low 5th class in the quick 5 minutes I spent searching.) Once on the spur ridge/rib, head up class 3-4 terrain (harder climbing is always nearby) to the crest of the main ridge above. The main ridge is the same ridge mentioned earlier that connects Mescalito and Yoga Peak. From the crest of the main ridge, hang a right and continue heading up. Follow the occasional cairn, and look for weaknesses that are very soon encountered in the challenging terrain to come. Other options may exist, but I found a short slot, followed by a class 4+ chimney that worked well to get me back onto class 2-3 terrain above. Once above the major difficulties of the upper ridge, follow your nose to the summit, a short distance away.

To climb via Mescalito Canyon: (Mescalito Canyon is the local name for the prominent north fork of the south fork of Pine Creek Canyon. This is likely the easiest route (of any value) to the summit of Yoga Peak. It is extremely aesthetic.) From the Pine Creek parking area, follow the main trail toward the south fork of Pine Creek, which runs along the left base of Mescalito. Once in the south fork boulder up-canyon to another fork in the canyon. Leaving the main canyon, take the right fork (Mescalito Canyon) and follow it over increasingly spectacular terrain. Even in fall, expect there to be flowing water, several small waterfalls, and many pools of crystal clear water—very pretty. As you get deeper into the canyon, nearly to its end, you'll encounter another fork. Again, take the right fork. Just before the yellow and orange of the sandstone turns to the dull gray of the limestone escarpment it soon meets, leave the canyon and hike cross-country to the right (north) onto yellow sandstone slabs and ledges. Once on the slabs and ledges above the main watercourse, scramble up and to the right. The going is largely in the class 3-4 realm, but harder climbing is always nearby. A little route-finding should get the job done with few difficulties. When you find yourself above the slabs and ledges and on a talus slope of sandstone, follow the slope upward to the right, aiming for the highest point of sandstone ahead of you. Near the top, scramble up class 2-3 terrain to the highest point…only to see that a higher point (the summit) lies a short distance away to the southeast. Easy scrambling will get you to the highpoint.

The roundtrip numbers for either route are roughly 10 miles with 3,000+ feet of gain.

-WGS84 Lat: 36.1234275 deg N Lon: -115.5150514 deg W
*-III, Class 4 via Mescalito Canyon *****
*-IV, Class 4-5 via Pine Creek Canyon (North Fork) *****

Looking west to Mescalito from the hike into Pine Creek.

"Bridge Vista Peak" (6,381)

This is a minor, craggy sub-peak along the ridge connecting Bridge Point and Bridge Mountain. Its summit block, overhanging on its south side, is notable for its views and its funky position next to Bridge Mountain.

To bag Bridge Vista Peak while you're already in the area, drop down from Bridge Point to the saddle at the top of the gully. Crossing the saddle, drop down to its other side a hundred feet or so and then route-find your way left and back up toward Bridge Vista Peak. A number of ribs and chutes will get the job done.

Once the base of the summit block is gained, work your way counter-clockwise around to the southeast side of the block, where a 20-foot class 4 chimney allows access to the top. A nicely-positioned tree at the base of the chimney facilitates matters.

-WGS84 Lat: 36.1303394 deg N Lon: -115.4994184 deg W

*-II, Class 1-2 via Southeast Face ****

"Bridge Point" (6,450)

Bridge Point is a major sub-peak of Bridge Mountain. It is so major, in fact, that the Bridge Point massif is labeled as Bridge Mountain itself on the topo map! From most of the NCA's Scenic Drive, Bridge Point, its wide, horizontal red band, and its pointy summit, are more eye-catching than Bridge Mountain itself.

This scenic route is almost entirely class 1-2, with a couple of short class 3 sections.

Follow the directions given for Juniper Peak to the Pine Creek parking area. Follow the trail toward the mouth of Pine Creek Canyon, although a number of spider webbing trails start to appear as you get near the canyon entrance, stay on the main trail, looking for a prominent trail that branches off to the right and leads up onto the red, rocky/sandy bench to your right. This is a designated (but unsigned) spur trail that sees many feet. The trail will meander up and down a touch, soon dumping you off just inside the entrance to the north fork of Pine Creek Canyon (aka Fern Canyon). Once inside the aesthetic canyon, follow use trails, the path of least resistance and/or occasional cairns for 0.5 mile or so to your first obvious major obstacle – a 25-foot waterfall blocking further easy progress. Just to the right of the waterfall is a steep and brushy chute. Head up the chute and then continue up-canyon either in the wash or staying on the sandstone on your right for a hundred yards or so until you get to a seeping dry waterfall with some white mineral deposits. It will be on your right. The waterfall is almost directly across the canyon from a prominent sandy use trail that heads steeply up the south side of the canyon.

Climbing up to the ledge system (class 2-3) above the dry waterfall in question, start working your way back east, following the path of least resistance (and looking for cairns and/or signs of regular use) as it gradually gains elevation. Over the years, cairns have been liberally placed along most of the route to guide you along. As you near a point almost directly across the canyon from the prominent notch in the Mescalito ridge to the south, look for a very prominent gully that heads up toward the northeast. Heading up the gully, you'll note a prominent rock outcropping partway up that seems to split the gully in half. Go right of the outcropping (left works too, but it's brushy and unpleasant in spots). As you reach the saddle at the top of the gully, hang a right and meander your way (not difficult) to the summit of Bridge Point.

On the descent, it is easy to get off-route but cairns help tremendously. If in doubt, back off and look around carefully for cairns.

-WGS84 Lat: 36.1318529 deg N Lon: -115.4930107 deg W

*-III, Class 3 via South Face ****

"Evas Tower" (5,934)

Evas Tower sits about 35 meters south of the slightly lower Mikes Tower below the imposing east wall of Bridge Point. Evas Tower is a fine outing with cool scrambling.

Follow the directions given for Mikes Tower, but continue to the notch at the head of the north gully. From this notch, angle left and explore one of several options that take you to the summit crag, which is surmounted on its north side. Oddly enough, a slightly higher boulder (without a cairn and summit register) sits 10 yards away from the "summit."

-WGS84 Lat: 36.1328355 deg N Lon: -115.4890407 deg W

*-II, YDS 5.0 via East Gully & North Gully ****

"Mikes Tower" (5,900)

Mikes Tower is an outstanding scramble with relatively easy route-finding. Rappelling equipment is recommended for the return.

Park at a small turn-out big enough for 2-3 cars on the left side of the Scenic Drive just before the Pine Creek trailhead. Make out a large gully to the west. The head of the gully is just north of Mikes Tower, which is a small (largely invisible) crag at the top of the red stone layer visible below the east wall of Bridge Point. Gain the alluvial fan running on the right side of the gully mentioned above and follow it as a use trail materializes (plenty of cairns, too) and eventually leads you into the gully above the initial dry falls. Follow the gully to the obvious headwall above. At the headwall, follow cairns and a use trail to the left into a lesser gully heading to the south. This gully contains the most interesting scrambling of the route, with several short sections in the class 3 to 5.0 range. Mid-way up the gully is the crux, a steep 20' slab/face (YDS 5.6) with little or no protection. An illegal fixed line may be in place to facilitate this portion of the climb. Although it's been downclimbed on the return, a rappel here would be safer.

About 100 feet below the notch at the head of the gully, the use trail splits. Head left toward Mikes Tower just above. The final crag is climbed on its south side.

-WGS84 Lat: 36.1331915 deg N Lon: -115.4887403 deg W

*-II, YDS 5.0 via East Gully & North Gully ****

"Beer and Ice Peak" (6,150)

Beer and Ice is regarded by some as the most difficult of the Red Rock summits to reach. Frankly, it's not particularly difficult, though those attempting it should be prepared to protect (and later rappel) a near-vertical class 4 crack near the top.

Following the directions given for Evas Tower, gain the notch just below Evas and head right (Evas' summit will be 30 yards to the left), following cairns, signs of use, and generally meandering up and around obstacles to the northwest. After crossing a semi-exposed slab near the crest less than 10 minutes above the notch, ignore the yellow crag immediately above and continue northwest toward the summit, which should be visible a short distance away. Continue along the narrowing crest, where the terrain should be no more difficult than easy class 3, until you reach the boulders adjacent to the base of the summit block. Pass through a narrow slot then cut right to climb up a steep, wider slot leading to the base of a near-vertical class 4 crack on the summit block's northeast face. Fifteen feet up the crack, angle left and gain the summit by doing a clockwise scramble the entire way around the summit block, climbing to the highpoint on its north side.

-WGS84 Lat: 36.1335396 deg N Lon: -115.4904935 deg W

*-II, Class 4 via Northeast Face (via Evas Tower) ****

"Holiday Peak" (6,313)

Holiday Peak is but a very minor, fine viewpoint high on the north ridge of Bridge Point. The summit is a small crag at the base of a large vertical wall on the ridge.

For the Southern Route: Park at a small pull-out immediately past mile marker 10 on the Scenic Drive and head west-southwest across the desert to gain a gully with a prominent red pour-off near the bottom of its steeper portion. Follow the gully up, bypassing tougher sections as needed, then look for cairns and a use trail heading left as you near the cliffs above. Cairns should lead to a nifty slot/chimney system that gradually works back north to gain Holiday Peak's north ridge. Expect numerous strenuous chimney climbs along the route, as well as a 20-foot near-vertical class 4 downclimb (or rappel; in case a fixed rope normally there is missing, bring 100 feet of rope and be prepared to establish an anchor in a restricted environment). Once the north ridge is gained, follow cairns south along the interesting and highly varied ridge to the summit above.

For the Northern Route: Park at the pull-out mentioned above and head west across the desert, eventually gaining the peak's north ridge. Although challenging cliffs loom if you head south too early on the approach through the desert, the terrain tends to be easier if you trend a touch right. Once the north ridge is gained, you'll eventually meet the Southern Route, where cairns can be followed south to the summit.

-WGS84 Lat: 36.1359573 deg N Lon: -115.4898712 deg W

*-II, Class 4 via Northern Route ****

*-II, YDS 5.0 via Southern Route *****

The author admiring the lovely form of Bridge Mountain. Photo by Aron Ralston.

Bridge Mountain (6,990)

Named for a large sandstone arch near its summit, Bridge Mountain is one of the most impressive, most imposing and most elusive summits in the entire Red Rock Canyon NCA. Although hidden from view from much of the Red Rock Scenic Drive behind neighboring Bridge Point, a pointy spur summit east of Bridge Mountain, its monolithic summit block invites hikers and climbers alike when they finally see it.

The traditional class 3 route to the summit entails wonderful and stimulating scrambling across incredible limestone and sandstone terrain to the magnificent summit, where wonderful views of the Red Rock Canyon area await. This traditional Bridge Mountain route is a lot of fun and has a sort of playground feel to it.

Near the summit, if one explores around enough or knows where to look, can be found several tinajas, which are natural water catch basins in the sandstone. These tinajas tend to hold water the majority of the year, and one of them, located only a short distance northeast of the "bridge," is of considerable size and depth. Also found near the summit is a hidden forest; the slabs above this small, spectacular grove of ponderosa pines make a great lunch spot.

Getting to the summit of Bridge Mountain via the traditional route from Red Rock Summit requires a high clearance vehicle (in the best of conditions), good route-finding skills, and the ability to travel across exposed class 3 terrain. Despite these deterrents (or perhaps, because of them), Bridge Mountain is, at one time or another, on every Vegas-area hiker's/climber's to-do list.

The mountain can be climbed any time of the year, although winter snows can make the dirt road (Rocky Gap Road) to Red Rock Summit virtually impassable to vehicles. If you hike up Rocky Gap Road to the trailhead, the rest of the route is typically doable in winter, although close attention should be paid for the presence of ice along the more exposed portions of the route. Unfortunately, these more exposed portions are difficult to protect in the event of ice. Potentially treacherous!

To get to the mountain, follow the Scenic Drive for just under 8 miles to the paved Willow Springs turnoff on the right. Turning right, follow the paved road for about 1 mile until it turns into a dirt road. Although passenger cars can usually continue for another 0.25 mile or so, the road quickly deteriorates and a high clearance vehicle will be necessary for the duration. At about the 2.4 mile mark (from the pavement), 4WD will be necessary. Continue on this dirt road (Rocky Gap Road) for about 5 miles until you reach Red Rock Summit, an obvious pass and the highpoint of the road. On the left, you will find adequate parking for 5-6 vehicles and a sign designating the trailhead.

Despite the roundtrip numbers for this route being only about 6 miles and 3,000 (or less) of gain, expect a full-day endeavor.

From the trailhead (6,430 feet) at Red Rock Summit, follow the obvious and well-maintained trail for about a mile as it follows along below the crest of a limestone ridge. At the one-mile mark, the trail reaches the crest of the ridge and a junction with another trail. A sign at that location instructs you to either go left to North Peak or go right for about a mile to Bridge Mountain. From this vantage point, Bridge Mountain is very visible to the east/southeast. Take a minute while at the trail junction to study the remainder of the route, as the majority of it is quite visible from here. When you're done, follow the trail to the right.

The trail continues along or near the crest of the limestone ridge for about 0.5 mile to the south before leaving the crest and heading east toward the sandstone below. Although the condition of the trail deteriorates somewhat upon leaving the crest, it is still obvious. Once on the sandstone, you will note the large and imposing west face of the summit mass to the east. Despite appearing non-technically-impossible from this angle, a crack in the face is visible in the distance and is what you will soon be climbing.

From the sandstone, your objective is quite clear: You need to travel across the sandstone, avoiding the high upper walls of Pine Creek Canyon which drops away abruptly to the south, and soon, another canyon which slopes away steeply to the north, and travel east toward the base of the mountain's west face.

The route across the sandstone is relatively level, although you are gradually losing elevation, and well-marked by trail and cairns, and as awful as it sounds, route markings *painted* directly onto the sandstone. Oh yeah, shortly after gaining the sandstone, you will pass by a platform that looks directly down into the north fork of Pine Creek Canyon. The view into the canyon is incredible – you gotta take a look.

Travel across the sandstone over varying class 1-3 terrain, following the aforementioned trail, cairns and route markings, and you will soon find yourself at the base of Bridge Mountain's huge summit massif. Cairns should steer you toward your next objective—a steep class 3 crack leading directly up the west face of the mountain. The crack is about 100 feet long, and easier terrain is typically found by either staying in the crack itself (most will want to avoid one awkward bulge near the bottom) or just to its right. Near the top of the crack, as it steepens, step left onto a platform. Peek around the corner and discover a class 3-4 slab/crack (15 feet). Follow it up until the terrain eases and you suddenly see a large sandstone arch in front of you. This is the "bridge" for which the mountain is named.

From the arch, you can continue in either of two common ways: Either scurry up onto the sandstone of the arch itself and do a class 3 traverse to the top (far side) of the arch; or, go under the arch and scramble up a steep class 4 slab. No matter which of the two routes you take, you will still be heading in the right direction.

From the top of the ramp or arch, continue east for 15-20 feet over fairly level terrain until you see a ponderosa pine grove nestled at the base of a system of steep sandstone ramps and ledges on the summit mass, to the south. This is the "hidden forest." Stay on the sandstone above (and west of) the hidden forest and work your way to the right (south) along the edge of the forest until you come to a small saddle (or notch) that looks straight down into Pine Creek Canyon. Now work your way south-southeast up a series of steep, left-trending ramps and ledges above the hidden forest. The summit is a short distance away. As the terrain eases up, follow a cairn to the right and walk class 1-2 terrain to the final moves to the top. Yeehaw! Great summit!

For an alternative approach that is way sweeter than the standard approach, follow Rocky Gap Road for 2.4 miles (most vehicles will need to park 1.7 miles in) from the end of the pavement and look for a good use trail on the left side of the road. Follow the trail up the ridge to the crest above. Once on the crest, hang a right (following cairns) and wander a decent but sporadic use trail on the sandstone adjacent to the limestone until you can work left on slickrock (following cairns) to join the standard route as it comes down from the high limestone crest above. From there, follow the directions already given to the base of the long class 3 crack.

-WGS84 Lat: 36.1320009 deg N Lon: -115.5014506 deg W
-III, Class 3 from Red Rock Summit ****

Aaah, Bridge Mountain! This view looks east.

"Ice Box Peak" (6,167)
Ice Box Canyon is a hike in Red Rock Canyon NCA. Sitting high above and immediately south of the end of the tourist-laden route is Ice Box Peak. It is a fine peak with stunning views of Bridge Mountain and North Peak. Ice Box Peak via its north chute is so excellent that I've done it at least 5 times.

Follow the Scenic Drive for about 8.5 miles to the signed Ice Box Canyon parking area. This will be a short distance past the paved turn-off to Willow Springs. From the parking area, Ice Box Canyon is the obvious canyon before you. It is framed by North Peak (to the north) and Ice Box Peak (with the summit just out of sight) to the south below Bridge Mountain and Bridge Point. Follow the trail into Ice Box Canyon. Inside the narrow canyon, just before you reach a prominent fork (the left fork will take you to the end of the Ice Box Canyon hiking route), look for a broken face below a steep chute heading south up the imposing face above on your left. The chute sits approximately due north of Ice Box Peak's summit, though it will not be visible, and is the only apparent and reasonable break in the cliffs.

Work up the chute (class 4-5). As you ascend, expect a couple of short 4th (or low 5th) class obstacles. When you reach the top of the chute, work right, following cairns and/or signs of earlier traffic, until you come to an open slope of brush and slickrock. A dry waterfall should be visible ahead of you. It sits at the bottom of a prominent chute below Ice Box Peak's summit, which is still not visible. Again following cairns and/or signs of earlier traffic, work to the chute above the dry waterfall, which is bypassed on its left. Once in the chute, head straight up, first over slickrock, then over sandstone talus, until you come to the ridge above. Hang a right at the ridge and scramble to the summit a short distance away.

Expect a roundtrip of roughly 4 miles and 1,800 feet of gain.

-WGS84 Lat: 36.139409 deg N Lon: -115.4979785 deg W

*-II, Class 4-5 via North Chute *****

"Willow Springs Overlook" (6,000)

Willow Springs Overlook is but a minor bump (although a nice viewpoint) high on the east shoulder of Goodman Peak. It is reached via a short class 2-3 scramble from the head of the large north-draining gully adjacent to the large headwall on the described Goodman Peak route. Alternatively, the east face can be climbed from midway up the Goodman Peak northeast gully, though folks should anticipate an enjoyable but highly exposed 60-foot class 3 slab 200 feet below the summit.

-WGS84 Lat: 36.1486 deg N Lon: -115.5005 deg W

*-II, Class 2-3 via West Ridge ***

*-II, Class 3 via East Face ***

"Goodman Peak" (6,600)

Turn off the Scenic Drive to head to the Willow Spring Picnic Area and park in the first parking lot on the left (prior to reaching the picnic area). Follow the trail toward the cliffs, noting the peak's prominent, shallow northeast gully. Well north of the bottom of this gully, spot a use trail that leads to a class 3 break in the cliffs. Once the break is found, follow cairns as the route eventually works south toward the northeast gully. From here, you can follow the gully (occasionally leaving it on either side to avoid obstacles) or stay mostly north of the gully, aiming for the giant headwall above. As you reach the headwall, the route funnels you into a narrow, deeper gully heading south. The route becomes more convoluted, though cairns and signs of use should lead you to the summit above.

From the summit, it's a delight to continue west, scrambling up class 3 terrain to the much higher summit of North Peak.

-WGS84 Lat: 36.1487657 deg N Lon: -115.5015923 deg W

*-II, Class 3-4 via Northeast Gully *****

"Deception Peak" (6,200)

Some locals have named this flat and uninspired overlook high on the northeast shoulder of Goodman Peak. It is not a destination of its own via the route described here but makes a sensible bonus peak for obsessed peakbaggers who are headed to Goodman Peak and consumed with padding their stats.

Follow the northeast gully route toward Goodman Peak. When a fun, exposed slab brings one to a prominent tree upon reaching the northeast ridge/face of Goodman, walk 75 feet northeast to the "summit" cairn.

-WGS84 Lat: 36.1493 deg N Lon: -115.5016 deg W

-II, Class 2 via Goodman Peak's Northeast Gully route

"North Peak" (7,056)

North Peak is but a few feet shorter than nearby Mount Wilson, the highest sandstone peak in Red Rock. Despite its imposing 2,000 foot east face and the fact that it is one of the highest peaks in the NCA, the mountain is often overshadowed by its more awe-inspiring neighbors, monolithic Bridge Mountain (to the south) and massive Mount Wilson (which lies a few miles southeast of Bridge Mountain). The extraordinary views from the summit extend across the entirety of Red Rock Canyon and to Las Vegas and Lake Mead beyond.

The route from Red Rock Summit is ideal for those seeking a fun, half-day outing to a high peak with fantastic views. To use it: Follow the directions given for Bridge Mountain to the trail junction a mile from the trailhead. A BLM sign at that location spells it out: Hang a left if you want to go to North Peak. (Note: the sign pointing the way to North Peak is actually referring to a limestone highpoint about 0.2 miles to the north – NOT the sandstone North Peak you're probably more interested in.) Hanging a left, the trail wanders north along or near the crest of the limestone ridge for 0.8 mile and is class 1-2. Although the trail is hard to follow in a couple spots, North Peak's sandstone summit soon comes into view in the distance and the objective is clear. If the route starts to exceed class 2, just look around for an easier way. After about 0.8 mile of following the limestone ridge, you will find yourself rather suddenly on yellow sandstone. From there, follow the path of least resistance cross-country toward the summit. The route across the sandstone is not only obvious but well-cairned. After traveling about 0.4 mile east-northeast then northeast across sandstone slabs and whatnot, the summit crag, which is easily reached via a class 1-2 ramp, is lying in wait. A neighbor crag, which lies perhaps 30 feet to the south of the summit crag, is arguably as high as the summit crag itself and requires only class 2-3 effort to reach the top. The roundtrip distance is about 5 miles and the elevation gain is around 1,000 feet.

For a more direct (class 2) way to reach the summit, follow the alternative approach directions given for Bridge Mountain from the 2.4 mile point along Rocky Gap Road. Upon reaching the main crest at the top of the ridge, the summit of North Peak is only a ten-minute hike away. This is a short, scenic, and steep way to quickly gain the summit of this nice, little peak!

-WGS84 Lat: 36.1441392 deg N Lon: -115.5088154 deg W
-II, Class 2 from Red Rock Summit **

"Lost Creek Peak" (6,800)

Lost Creek Peak is a high but not-so-prominent summit due north of North Peak.

From the Willow Spring Picnic Area, head west into the large canyon to the west. The going is relatively easy and enjoyable. The first major drainage encountered on the left (recognizable by a beautiful dryfall amidst the large trees at its mouth; known to some as Graffiti Canyon) leads to the classic Graffiti Ledges route, while the second major drainage encountered leads to a much less intimidating, easier and less-classic way to the summit.

For the Graffiti Ledges route, work up Graffiti Canyon (avoiding the initial dryfall on the left, and re-entering the drainage just above the initial pour-off) until you encounter a splendid, mostly-level (and sometimes incredibly narrow and exposed; careful!) ledge system that traverses left and around to the next major canyon to the south. Work up this next major canyon, usually via steep, slabby weaknesses to the right of the watercourse, and gain the summit from the south. Considerable care in route-finding must be taken. Cairns and signs of prior human use should be present.

For the route via the second major drainage mentioned above, follow the drainage to its head then angle left to gain the ridge due north of the peak. Harder terrain can generally be bypassed on its left, though the route will eventually bottleneck at an intimidating but easy class 3 arete shortly before the summit.

-WGS84 Lat: 36.1512784 deg N Lon: -115.5101717 deg W
-II, Class 3 via Second Major Drainage **
-II, Class 4 via Graffiti Ledges ****

"Boot Boulder" (5,340)

From the Willow Spring Picnic Area just off the Scenic Drive, Boot Boulder is clearly visible atop the ridge to the west.

Wander up any number of class 2-3 possibilities on the peak's southeastern aspect to the base of the summit boulder. Gain the block's north side and scramble up steep, wide ledges to the final 8' vertical wall. One can either climb the low 5th class wall directly or shuffle west to the spooky northwest corner, which is class 3 but has intimidating exposure. For the descent, a single bolt on the summit facilitates a 40' rappel off the north side of the block.

-WGS84 Lat: 36.1606525 deg N Lon: -115.5049946 deg W

*-I, Class 3 via Southeast Slopes ****

Crossing Graffiti Ledges on Lost Creek Peak

"The Divided Sky" (5,364)

This is a minor, unassuming peak (296' of prominence) north of North Peak and southwest of White Rock Peak. With numerous variations to beef it up, the northeast ridge (class 3 via its easiest variation) is a splendidly fun route with excellent rock. The narrow walk along the final, exposed ridge is most excellent! For a fantastic, very short outing, this one can't be beat.

-WGS84 Lat: 36.1632784 deg N Lon: -115.5111502 deg W

*-I, Class 3 via Northeast Ridge ****

White Rock Peak (6,462)

White Rock Peak (or White Rock Hills Peak, as it's also known) was the first sandstone peak I climbed at Red Rock Canyon. It has always stood out in my mind as a fun scramble with rather enjoyable route-finding (after the initial awful bushwhack!).

White Rock Peak, a stand-alone peak with 1002' of prominence, is a part of the La Madre Mountain Wilderness.

From the fee station, follow the Scenic Drive for 6-7 miles, passing the signed highpoint of the road (with its parking lot and overlook), until you come to the signed dirt road turn-off for White Rock Spring. Hang a right and follow the bumpy dirt road (a passenger car driven with care should be fine) a half-mile to the parking area at the end of the road.

From the parking area, note the closest large sandstone mountain. It is large and pyramidal, with two prominent buttresses on its south face. It is White Rock Peak. A minor peak, locally known as White Rock Spring Peak, is to its northeast. The two are separated by an obvious saddle. You wanna get to the saddle. Although the saddle can be reached via an enjoyable scramble up and over White Rock Spring Peak, the easier but more tedious route is: Follow the signed trail toward White Rock Spring. The trail will shortly fork; go left. After a couple hundred yards, leave the trail and cross-country it toward the saddle. The going is at first reasonably efficient, but soon becomes brush-choked and tedious. Ugh. Grunt up to the saddle.

Now for some good news: The brush is gone, and the rest of the route is fun.

From the saddle, scramble up White Rock Peak's northeast ridge. Although never particularly difficult, there are some fun route-finding challenges.

The roundtrip for this baby is perhaps 4 miles with less than 2,000 feet of gain.

-WGS84 Lat: 36.168548 deg N Lon: -115.4954828 deg W
-III, Class 3 via North Ridge ***

"Tunnel Vision Peak" (6,100)

The YDS 5.4 route up the east face was loose and scary. Not recommended!

-WGS84 Lat: 36.1680526 deg N Lon: -115.4921609 deg W
-III, Class 3 from White Rock Peak ***
-III, YDS 5.4 via East Face **

"White Rock Spring Peak" (5,977)

White Rock Spring Peak is a minor peak that offers a shorter alternative to its more impressive parent peak, White Rock Peak. With some enjoyable class 2-3 scrambling along its southeast ridge, the peak makes for a fine short endeavor.

White Rock Spring Peak lies within the La Madre Mountain Wilderness.

Follow the driving directions given for White Rock Peak. From the parking area, note the closest large sandstone mountain. It is large and pyramidal, with two prominent buttresses on its south face. It is White Rock Peak. White Rock Spring Peak is the minor peak to its northeast. The two are separated by an obvious saddle.

From the parking area, hike cross-country directly to the bouldery southeast ridge of White Rock Spring Peak. You may encounter an agave roasting pit (good stuff!) nearby. If you do, check it out but leave it untouched. Once on the southeast ridge, hike northwest toward the peak. Follow the ridge until it bends to the left a bit on its final approach to the summit. Scramble the final few obstacles to the highpoint. Fun, right?

The roundtrip numbers are less than 2 miles with about 1,000 feet of gain.

-WGS84 Lat: 36.1780258 deg N Lon: -115.4911672 deg W
*-II, Class 2-3 via Southeast Ridge ***

Calico Basin & Blue Diamond Hill

Although some of the peaks in this section, including Red Cap, Turtlehead Mountain and a couple of others, are typically accessed off the Scenic Drive, it seems somehow appropriate to include them here, amongst the peaks and crags above Calico Basin (and generally amidst the flotsam lying on the other side of SR-159, such as Blue Diamond Hill and Red Benchmark). The peaks in this subsection are arranged somewhat randomly.

Blue Diamond Hill (4,956)

Blue Diamond Hill is the large mesa siting directly across SR-159 from the main entrance to Red Rock Canyon NCA's Scenic Drive on the western outskirts of Las Vegas. There is a fine trail leading to the summit area, and the views along the way are stunning. A couple thousand acres of the mesa are under private ownership. That said, please stay on the trail and off private property.

From the intersection of CC-215 and Charleston Blvd/SR-159 in Las Vegas, head west approximately 5.3 miles to the well-signed entrance of Red Rock Scenic Drive/BLM Visitor Center. Continue on SR-159 for 1.1 miles past the entrance to the Scenic Drive to a pull-out with a parking area on the left. There's a gate at the east end of the parking area, with a dirt road continuing on toward Blue Diamond Hill behind it. This is the trailhead—it's known as the Horse Corrals (the BLM refers to this spot as "Cowboy Trails").

Hiking the dirt road a short distance from the gate, it soon bends to the right and heads for Fossil Canyon, the obvious canyon that can be seen beyond road's end. On the left side of Fossil Canyon is a prominent ridge. Leave the dirt road as it heads for Fossil Canyon and head cross-country toward the left side of the base of the ridge mentioned. Pick up a good trail there. You should be able to make out the trail as you hike toward it. Follow the trail up onto the ridge and all the way to the summit area of the mesa. The roundtrip is 6-7 miles, with about 1,400 feet of gain.

-WGS84 Lat: 36.1020 deg N Lon: -115.3967 deg W

*-II, Class 1 from the horse corrals **

"Kraft Mountain" (4,714)

Kraft Mountain, lying within the La Madre Mountain Wilderness, is a small, red sandstone peak in Calico Basin. Known mostly for the fine bouldering opportunities on its south side and some climbing opportunities in Gateway Canyon on its north side, there are also a number of fine scrambling and climbing options for those looking to tackle Kraft Mountain's summit. With a half-mile on the approach and less than 1,000 feet of gain, Kraft Mountain can be knocked off by any route in a relatively small amount of time. Views from the summit are incredible, including nearly all of Red Rock Canyon, the sprawling mass of Las Vegas, and countless limestone peaks all around.

From Charleston Blvd. and CC-215 in Las Vegas, take Charleston Blvd/SR-159 west for 3.8 miles to the signed Calico Basin Road on the right. This will be 1.5 miles before the entrance to the Red rock Canyon Scenic Drive. Follow Calico Basin Road (watch for wild burros!) for a mile until it makes a sharp right bend at the entrance to a park (Red Springs). Take the sharp right for 400 feet then turn left on Assisi Canyon Road. Follow Assisi Canyon Road for 400 feet then bend right onto Sandstone Drive, following it 0.75 mile to its end at a large parking lot. Kraft Mountain will be the red mountain in front of you.

To climb the South Chute: From the parking lot, follow one of the trails toward the base of Kraft Mountain, noting a prominent chute on the left side of the south face. Leave the trail at the bottom of the chute and head up. The going is largely class 2-3, though it can be spiced up here and there. As the chute starts to peter out at its top, exit to the right and follow more class 2-3 terrain to the flattish summit area above. A short walk from there takes you to the highpoint. For trivia's sake, from the summit the higher, mostly limestone peak to the immediate north is Greycap, while the slightly higher, mostly limestone peak to the immediate west is New Peak (which is sometimes called El Hijo). Kraft Mountain is sometimes called La Hija.

For the Northwest Face (as a descent option): Follow the ridge-like area west/northwest of the summit drop down into the first prominent drainage encountered. You should eventually encounter a slot-like dry waterfall (class 3-4) near the bottom. A bit more scrambling below the slot leads to the floor of Gateway Canyon. Once in Gateway Canyon, hang a left (northwest) and follow it to a fork. Gain the terrain above and in between the two forks and pick up a trail that heads west then abruptly south. Follow the trail to the Kraft Mountain-New Peak saddle. Continue along the trail over the saddle and back to the parking lot.

To climb from the Kraft-New saddle: From the parking lot, follow one of several well-used trails that lead to the Kraft Mountain-New Peak saddle. New Peak, which is immediately west of Kraft Mountain, is primarily limestone but features some brightly colored red and orange sandstone near the base of its south face. The route-finding from the saddle is enjoyable, and countless variations are possible.

To climb via the East Slopes: From the parking lot, take the trail that works east past a popular bouldering area at the base of Kraft Mountain. Once the base of the east slopes are reached, pick a line and head up. Countless variations are possible. This route allows one to conveniently bag Big Bird Peak along the way.

-WGS84 Lat: 36.1641 deg N Lon: -115.4217 deg W
*-II, Class 2-3 from the Kraft-New saddle ****
*-II, Class 2-3 via East Slopes ***
*-II, Class 3 via South Chute ***
*-II, Class 3-4 via Northwest Face ***

"Big Bird Peak" (4,650)

This is not much of a peak, though I suppose one could argue that it is the very minor east-ish summit of Kraft Mountain. A register on the summit gives the "peak" its name. The summit can be approached a number of ways, with the east slope or directly from the summit of Kraft Mountain being the most logical ways. A fun class 3-4 slab on the northeast face of the summit crag will be encountered just below the top. Due to exposure, many may wish to avoid downclimbing this. On the south side of the summit crag is a funky, slick face that may feel a bit better.

-WGS84 Lat: 36.1623 deg N Lon: -115.4159 deg W
*-II, Class 3-4 via Northeast Face **

"New Peak" (4,987)

New Peak (or El Hijo, as it's also known) is a minor limestone peak situated between Kraft Mountain and Red Cap in the Calico Basin area. Approached from the east or southeast, the upper mountain is surprisingly rugged, offering some enjoyable class 2-3 scrambling along a narrow spine.

New Peak lies within the La Madre Mountain Wilderness.

Follow the driving directions given for Kraft Mountain.

To climb the East Slope: From the designated parking lot at the base of Kraft Mountain, follow one of several well-used trails that lead to the Kraft Mountain-New Peak saddle. New Peak, which is immediately west of Kraft Mountain, is primarily limestone but features some brightly colored red and orange sandstone near the base of its south face. Leave the trail at the saddle, hang a left, and head directly up the east slope of the peak. Gain the rugged ridge at the top of the face and continue a few minutes longer to the summit.

To climb the Southeast Face: Follow the directions given above toward the Kraft-New saddle. Before reaching the Kraft-New saddle, leave the trail and work up the red and orange sandstone of New Peak's southeast face. Choose a line that looks good (variably class 2 to class 4+, depending on the line taken) and work up the southeast face of the mountain. There are opportunities to make the route as straightforward or as difficult as desired. Intersecting the rugged ridge at the top of the east slope, follow your nose to the summit.

Roundtrip numbers for either route around 2 miles, with less than 1,000 feet of gain.

Alternatively, the northwest ridge is a straightforward endeavor from the New Peak-Red Cap saddle. The saddle can be reached from a variety of points, most obviously upper Gateway Canyon or the canyon separating the Red Cap massif from New Peak.

-WGS84 Lat: 36.1653 deg N Lon: -115.4326 deg W
*-II, Class 2-3 via East Slope **
*-II, Class 2-3 via Northwest Ridge **
*-II, Class 2-4 via Southeast Face **

Red Benchmark (3,998)

This is the mesa northeast of Blue Diamond Hill. It is best approached, perhaps, from the cattle guard on SR-159 a few miles before the Red Rock entrance.

-WGS84 Lat: 36.1323 deg N Lon: -115.3641 deg W
*-I, Class 2 via NW Ridge ***

"Red Cap" (4,925)

Red Cap (also known as Turtlehead Junior) is the highpoint of Calico Hills, the sprawling cluster of aesthetic sandstone slabs and boulders one first encounters when entering Red Rock Canyon NCA on the Scenic Drive. Calico Hill's highest point can be reached via a short but highly enjoyable class 3-4 scramble circuitously traversing the small peak. The route is surprisingly fun. Over the years, numerous other high-quality routes have been put together on this small peak, including at least two excellent scrambles on Red Cap's western aspect. The route described here has many variations. As one might expect, the views from the top are grand. There's even a beautiful tinaja (frequently full of water) just below the summit!

From Las Vegas, head west on Charleston Blvd. to the RRCNCA Scenic Drive. Follow the one-way Scenic Drive to the third pull-out, which is signed for Sandstone Quarry.

From the spacious Sandstone Quarry parking area (restrooms, even), get on the signed trail that starts at the north end of the lot. Although the trail branches off on several occasions, follow the main one for less than 0.5 mile until you can see the yellow Red Cap monolith to your right about 0.5 mile away. The mass is capped by red sandstone; it is the only one of its kind in the area. Picking up one of a few trails heading toward the base of Red Cap (or simply scrambling cross country on your own) find yourself at an area of red sandstone near the base of Red Cap's west-southwest face. Difficult to describe in any real detail, the rest of this route will require a bit of route-finding of your own. Fortunately, that's part of the fun.

Starting at the red sandstone near the west-southwest base of Red Cap, work up for approximately 150-200 vertical feet. Depending on the line taken, the first part of the route may be anywhere from class 2 to low class 5. The terrain above you should become considerably more cliffy. Once below the cliffs, work your way to your right (south) by traversing over easier ground. Soon coming to flattish ground, continue traversing around to the peak's south (almost southeast) side where you will encounter a pair of parallel chutes coming down from the upper mountain. The first chute, its toe a steep dry waterfall, is immediately followed by a second chute that provides the easiest and most obvious way higher that you will have yet seen. Scramble up the second chute (class 3) and follow it to what appears to be the base of the summit block. It's not; rather, it is a subsidiary crag perhaps five feet lower than the highpoint. The highpoint is 40 feet to the west. Hike around the east side of the subsidiary crag for about 20 feet and drop into a chute on the other (north) side. Descend 50-60 feet. Just before you reach a vegetated section in the chute, step left (class 3) around a corner and work up another prominent chute that heads back up in a roughly parallel fashion. Follow this chute to a small saddle or notch between the main summit block (right) and the subsidiary crag you were recently at. From here, drop down the south side for about 10-15 feet until you find a weakness (a steep 8-foot face with small edges) on your right that allows you up the otherwise unhelpful terrain. The weakness is class 4. Climb up and work your way clockwise around the base of the summit block above you. Near its northwest side you'll encounter a class 4 crack (8-10 feet) that will allow you to climb higher. Above the crack, scramble left up a short slab to the summit.

The roundtrip on this little guy is a bit over 2 miles, with about 600 feet of elevation gain.

-WGS84 Lat: 36.1661 deg N Lon: -115.4426 deg W
-II, Class 3-4 from Sandstone Quarry ****

"Tinaja Peak" (4,760)
A local name for a short, fun scrambling summit below Turtlehead Mountain and Red Cap. Some route-finding is required to keep the route non-technical. In the spring, several summit tinajas are filled with clear water.

-WGS84 Lat: 36.1696 deg N Lon: -115.4515 deg W
-I, Class 3-4 via Southeast Face **

Turtlehead Mountain (6,323)
Crowded, crumbly and incredibly popular. A trail leads to the summit from the Sandstone Quarry parking lot off the Scenic Drive.

-WGS84 Lat: 36.1802 deg N Lon: -115.4459 deg W
-II, Class 2 via trail **

"Calico Hills – South" (4,322)
This is the southeasternmost peak in the Calico Hills massif. With countless route options available, it is the ideal starting point for a multi-peak traverse of the entire massif.

-WGS84 Lat: 36.1467 deg N Lon: -115.4247 deg W
-II, Class 3 via East Face ***
-II, Class 3 via Northwest Ridge ***

"Red Book Point" (4,608)
This is the eye-catching red summit southeast of Calico Peak and Tank Peak. Like all of the sandstone peaks in Calico Hills, this one has numerous potential routes, each with numerous potential variations. The routes listed below generically state two routes I've commonly done.

-WGS84 Lat: 36.1558 deg N Lon: -115.4336 deg W
-II, Class 3 via western ledges **
-II, Class 3 via Southeast Ridge ***

"Tank Peak" (4,900)
This minor peak and its neighbor, Calico Peak, are obvious bonus objectives for the motivated hiker looking for more fun stuff from the summit of nearby Red Cap. Just north of the summit is a fine overlook of Calico Basin (and a great place to nap!).

-WGS84 Lat: 36.1620 deg N Lon: -115.4374 deg W
-I, Class 2 from Calico Tanks *
-II, Class 3 from Red Cap **

On the edge of Calico Tanks during an awesome loop of Red Cap, Tank Peak and Calico Peak. The view looks southeast out toward Blue Diamond Hill.

"Calico Peak" (4,890)

Although this peak can be easily bagged from Calico Tanks, the northwest slickrock makes for a wonderfully enjoyable exercise in route-finding and awesome scrambling. There's a cool, deep tinaja just below the summit.

-WGS84 Lat: 36.1602 deg N Lon: -115.4387 deg W

-II, Class 3 via northwest slickrock **

-I, Class 3-4 via Southeast Gully ***

-I, Class 4 from Calico Tanks *

"Greycap" (5,443)

Greycap, a part of the La Madre Mountain Wilderness, is the peak lying immediately northwest of Kraft Mountain. The two mountains are separated by Gateway Canyon, a popular hiking area in the Calico Basin area adjacent to Red Rock Canyon NCA. With a portion of the upper mountain consisting of limestone, and the rest of sandstone, this funky peak offers some fun scrambling opportunities for those interested in exploratory routes.

The full southeast ridge (class 2-3) of Greycap is a surprisingly rugged and enjoyable scramble, with a few interesting towers and craggy features to negotiate. Along the way, one passes over the minor but interesting summit of Goat Bed Peak.

Follow the driving directions given for Kraft Mountain.

To climb from Gateway Canyon: From the designated parking lot at the base of Kraft Mountain, follow one of several well-used trails that lead to the Kraft Mountain-New Peak saddle. New Peak, which is immediately west of Kraft Mountain, is primarily limestone but features some brightly colored red and orange sandstone near the base of its south face. Follow the trail over the saddle and into Gateway Canyon. Greycap will be to the north. Choose any line that looks tasty and work up the sandstone on the north side of Gateway Canyon. Routes as easy as class 2 can be found as readily as class 5. It's typically straightforward working around any difficulties encountered. Have fun, and explore your way up. Nearing the top, the terrain mellows out considerably and becomes lame and tedious. Once the summit ridge is gained, scramble to the highpoint. Roundtrip numbers are variable, but expect four miles, with nearly 2,000 feet of gain.

-WGS84 Lat: 36.1788 deg N Lon: -115.4277 deg W
*-II, Class 2-3 via Southeast Ridge from Goat Bed Peak ****
*-II, Class 2-5 from Gateway Canyon ***

"Goat Bed Peak" (5,200)
This minor summit sits along the southeast ridge of Greycap. The traverse between the two peaks is remarkably interesting.

-WGS84 Lat: 36.1698 deg N Lon: -115.4138 deg W
*-II, Class 2-3 via Northwest Ridge ****
*-II, Class 3-4 via South Face ***

The Limestone Crest

These limestone summits are adjacent to the sandstone escarpment above the Red Rock Scenic Drive. They are arranged here roughly south-to-north.

Mountain Spring Benchmark (6,641)
Historically, this peak is most easily approached from Mountain Springs. Be careful not to cross private property, though.

More recently, a fine trail has developed from the antennas visible 0.25 mile off the highway just before reaching the highpoint of the road (if coming from Vegas). As you approach the highpoint and the road starts to narrow to a single lane in that direction, turn off onto a dirt road and a large parking area on the right. From there, either walk or drive the steep dirt road to the antennas. Immediately behind, a good trail wanders up to the limestone crest paralleling the sandstone peaks of Red Rock. Once the crest is gained, hang a left and follow it to the summit of Mountain Spring Benchmark, which sits immediately behind Black Velvet Peak.

-WGS84 Lat: 36.0359 deg N Lon: -115.4824 deg W
*-II, Class 1 via trail from antennas ***
*-II, Class 2 via West Slope **

"First Creek Overlook" (6,945)
This is a nice peak with excellent views of the backside of Red Rock. The peak lies at the head of First Creek, closely southeast of Oak Creek Overlook.

-WGS84 Lat: 36.0882 deg N Lon: -115.5016 deg W
*-II, Class 1-2 via the Northwest or South Ridges ***

"Oak Creek Overlook" (7,211)
With good dirt road access from the west via Lovell Canyon road, pleasant pinyon/juniper forest walking leads to the summit of this peak at the head of Oak Creek.

The west-southwest ridge can also be used as an ascent or descent route, though very interesting, narrow ridge scrambling should be expected near the bottom.

-WGS84 Lat: 36.0961 deg N Lon: -115.5100 deg W
*-II, Class 2 via Southwest Slopes ***

"Crest Peak" (7,244)
This minor summit has 404' of prominence. Follow the approach directions given for Bridge Mountain to Red Rock Summit.

-WGS84 Lat: 36.1345 deg N Lon: -115.5184 deg W
*-II, Class 1-2 via Red Rock Summit **

Moonset over the mountains. Photo by Aron Ralston.

La Madre Range & Environs

In recent years, much of this area fell into the management of Red Rock Canyon National Conservation Area. Although lacking the glory of the colorful goodness of the red and yellow and orange sandstone crags of the more favored portion of the NCA, some fine, grey-hued desert adventures away the intrepid traveler here.

Access is scattered, quality of roads is highly varied, and a map, compass and GPS are recommended. Peaks in this section are arranged alphabetically.

"Barricade Peak" (6,161)

Approached via the same network of decent dirt roads one uses to get to the north side of El Bastardo.

-WGS84 Lat: 36.2347 deg N Lon: -115.4809 deg W
*-II, Class 1-2 via Northwest Ridge **
*-II, Class 2 via West Slope **

"Burnt Peak" (7,900)

This minor peak sits along the limestone crest between El Padre and El Bastardo. There's really no good reason to go here unless you're heading to (or coming from) one of the others.

Approach in your vehicle as per El Bastardo.
-WGS84 Lat: 36.2074 deg N Lon: -115.4750 deg W
*-III, Class 2 from El Padre ***
*-II, Class 2 via Northeast Ridge **

"Damsel Peak" (6,977)

Also locally known as Pincushion Peak and Manta Ray Mountain, Damsel Peak, lying within the La Madre Mountain Wilderness, is the nice-looking, twin-peaked mountain one sees above the Little Red Rocks area just north/northeast of the Scenic Drive in Red Rock Canyon NCA. Though Damsel Peak sits considerably lower than its nearby neighbor, the aesthetic La Madre Mountain, the views from this impressive mountain are excellent. The western of the two summits is the highpoint.

Development in this area is complicating matters. Once upon a time, one could take 4WD roads all the way in to Little Red Rocks and beyond from the vicinity of Summerlin Parkway and CC-215 in northwestern Las Vegas to get a running start from the base of the mountain. Now, access requires a much longer cross-country approach from the Red Rock Canyon NCA Scenic Drive, Calico Basin, or from the complex terrain around Box Canyon and Summerlin Peak. Refer to the approach information for Red Cap, Greycap and Summerlin Peak for options.

However one must do it, work your way by hiking cross-country to the base of the north slope of the mountain, below the western summit. From there, simply head up. The going is enjoyable, and there are no significant route-finding issues to speak of. Views over to the lower eastern summit (6,792 feet) are excellent.

-WGS84 Lat: 36.2025 deg N Lon: -115.4248 deg W
-III, Class 2 via North Slope **

"East La Madre Peak" (7,033)

East La Madre Peak is a fine desert peak that sees few visitors. Its impressive south face is awesome as one traverses along the narrow terrain above it on the way to the summit. The mountain is situated between Mount Gottlieb and La Madre Mountain, in the dry eastern fringes of the Spring Mountains. La Madre Mountain and East La Madre Peak both lie within the La Madre Mountain Wilderness.

Like its nearby neighbor, Damsel Peak, development has complicated access to this mountain. Refer to the information given for Damsel Peak for access considerations.

However one must do it, work your way to the saddle at the base of East La Madre's east ridge. An old 4WD road crosses this saddle. From the saddle, start hiking up the ridge, following the easiest line of ascent. Some minor route-finding difficulties may be found near the bottom of the route. Negotiating through a couple short scrambling spots, make your way to the summit. The views down the south face from the upper portion of the route are breathtaking.

-WGS84 Lat: 36.2260 deg N Lon: -115.4276 deg W
-III, Class 2-3 via East Ridge ***

"El Bastardo (7,986)

A big, obscure peak with awkward views into the sandstone glory of Red Rock. El Bastardo has two north ridges; the west one is slightly more enjoyable. Despite its meager 406 feet of prominence, this is a dominating peak when approaching from the north.

For the northern approaches on this and the other peaks in its vicinity, leave SR-157 (Kyle Canyon Road) 8.6 miles from I-95 and follow the network of dirt roads (some quite good; some not so much) to points that seem reasonable.

-WGS84 Lat: 36.2045 deg N Lon: -115.4853 deg W
-III, Class 2 via either North Ridge **

"El Padre" (8,093)

La Madre's close neighbor, the two can be readily combined in a day.

For the routes listed here, approach as per El Bastardo.

-WGS84 Lat: 36.2052 deg N Lon: -115.4648 deg W

-III, Class 2 via Northeast Ridge from La Madre **

-III, Class 2 via West Ridge from Burnt Peak *

The limestone crest above Rocky Gap Road

"Gateway Peak" (6,530)

This forgotten peak is nestled between La Madre Mountain and Damsel Peak. Not visible from any road, its summit is a charming perch from which to view all of Red Rock, most of Las Vegas, and even glimpses of such faraway peaks as Jumbo Peak and Spirit Mountain. Although most of the upper south face is cliffy, a loose, class 2 chute directly below the summit is the easiest line from the south.

There's no easy way to get to this peak. We started from the Kraft Mountain parking lot, and it was an outstanding and highly enjoyable day out!

-WGS84 Lat: 36.2105 deg N Lon: -115.4353 deg W

-III, Class 2 via South Face ***

La Madre Mountain (8,154)

Although this mountain can also be approached from the RRCNCA Scenic Drive, it is most easily climbed from the north. Decent dirt roads bring you quite close to the peak's north side. This approach also allows an up-close view of the "La Madre Scar."

For the route mentioned here, approach as per El Bastardo.

-WGS84 Lat: 36.2124 deg N Lon: -115.4591 deg W
-III, Class 2-3 via North Slope **

"Lonely Pinon Mountain" (4,897)

Lonely Pinon Mountain is named for the *single* tree living on the mountain.

To get there: From the intersection of CC-215 and Ann Road in northwestern Las Vegas, get off at Ann and head west toward the mountains. Immediately coming to an intersection near the highway, hang a right on Shaumber Road, then a left a couple hundred yards later onto West La Mancha Avenue. Follow this good dirt road west for a mile, passing a small, twin-peaked mountain ("Mount Golden Eagle") on the left, until you come to a large, open area of sand and spider webbing, rough dirt roads. Lonely Pinon Mountain is the relatively large mountain ahead in the near distance. A long northeast-ish ridge runs down from its summit to near the sandy area you're at. Park at the open sandy spot and start hiking toward the northeast slopes of the mountain, staying left of and below the ridge. Once near the base of the northeast slopes of the mountain, make your way to the top.

Roundtrip numbers are roughly 4 miles, with a little over 1,000 feet of elevation gain.

-WGS84 Lat: 36.2498 deg N Lon: -115.3786 deg W
-II, Class 2 via Northeast Slopes *

"Mount Golden Eagle" (3,704)

The first of many times I climbed this small mountain, I arrived on the summit and startled a pair of golden eagles resting there. Approach as per Lonely Pinon Mountain. A good road, gained from Ann Road and CC-215, runs along the north side of the peak.

-WGS84 Lat: 36.2587 deg N Lon: -115.3440 deg W
-I, Class 2 via North Face *

"Mount Gottlieb" (5,830)

Mount Gottlieb is situated between Mount Woody and East La Madre Peak in the dry eastern fringes of the Spring Mountains, north of all the sandstone glory found in much of Red Rock Canyon NCA. It is an obscure summit that sees few visitors.

To climb the East Col from the North: Follow the directions given for Mount Woody via its north slope route. As you head up Woody's north slope, traverse right (west) a couple hundred feet below the summit, aiming for the col connecting Woody and Mount Gottlieb. Ascend from the col in a westerly fashion to the summit of Mount Gottlieb. Expect a roundtrip of 7-8 miles, with about 3,000 feet of gain.

To climb the East Col from the South: Follow the directions given to Summerlin Peak via its southeast ridge route. Climb to the "saddle" near the base of Summerlin's southeast ridge. Drop to the other side and work west across the desert along the base of the mountains. Passing below Summerlin Peak and Mount Woody, you'll soon come to a drainage heading up to the col connecting Mount Woody and Mount Gottlieb. Follow the drainage to the col. Anticipate some class 3-4 scrambling in the bottom of the drainage. Easier passage is available. Hang a left from the col and walk to the top of Mount Gottlieb. Expect a roundtrip of 6-7 miles, with about 3,000 feet of gain.

-WGS84 Lat: 36.2211 deg N Lon: -115.3862 deg W
*-III, Class 2 via East Col from the North ***
*-III, Class 3-4 via East Col from the South ***

"Mount Woody" (5,356)

Mount Woody is the parent of its lower but more aesthetic sub-peak, Summerlin Peak. When traversing to the summit of Mount Woody from Summerlin Peak, staying high along the crest of the summit ridge, one encounters a surprisingly nice and narrow, knife-like ridge.

To climb the North Slope: Follow the directions given for Summerlin Peak via its northeast ridge route. As you head that way, passing around the south ridge of Cheyenne Mountain, a wide wash will open up on the right. Follow an old dirt road into the wide wash. Shortly after the wash tightens into a short stretch of narrow canyon, go right at a fork. After a brief scramble, the canyon opens up considerably again. Continue for 0.25 mile along the base of the steep terrain on your left, until the terrain mellows out and you can easily work your way left. The gentle north slope of Mount Woody should present itself on the left. Head to the top. The roundtrip for this route will involve about 6-7 miles, with roughly 2,500 feet of gain.

To climb the Southeast Slope from Summerlin Peak: Follow the directions given to the summit of Summerlin Peak. (The easiest route for Summerlin Peak described in this book involves a small amount of class 3 scrambling.) From the summit of Summerlin Peak, drop a couple hundred feet to the saddle between it and Mount Woody to the west. From there, head up to Mount Woody. Aiming left as you ascend will take you to the crest of the summit ridge (and its noteworthy knife-like crest). The roundtrip involves roughly 4-5 miles, with about 2,900 feet or so of gain.

-WGS84 Lat: 36.2220 deg N Lon: -115.3695 deg W
*-III, Class 2 via North Slope **
*-III, Class 2 via Southeast Slope from Summerlin Peak ***

"Nony Peak" (4,897)

A minor peak, rather detached from the La Madre Range but close enough to be lumped in with it, it has nice views of the surrounding area. The mountain is named here for a friend's brother, who went missing without explanation in spring 2010.

Park on the shoulder of SR-157 (Kyle Canyon Road) 8.4 miles from I-95 and start hiking. It'll only take a few minutes.

-WGS84 Lat: 36.2854 deg N Lon: -115.4467 deg W

-I, Class 1 via South Slope *

"Pondview Peak" (6,302)

From the top, the triumphant summiteer can view one of only *two* semi-significant bodies of water in the Spring Mountains! The other is Clark Pond, near McFarland Peak. Pondview Peak is approached via the same network of dirt roads that lead to the north side of El Bastardo.

-WGS84 Lat: 36.2308 deg N Lon: -115.5018 deg W

-II, Class 2 via Northeast Ridge **

"Rainy" (6,850)

Rainy is northeast of Windy and southwest of Pondview Peak. The peak has 469' of prominence.

-WGS84 Lat: 36.2177 deg N Lon: -115.5185 deg W

-II, Class 2 via East Slope *

"Summerlin Peak" (5,089)

Summerlin Peak, really a sub-peak of Mount Woody, is an aesthetic summit close to Cheyenne Mountain. The two fight for the title of "Most Eye-Catching" when one drives west toward the mountains on Cheyenne Avenue in northwestern Las Vegas.

Follow the driving directions given for Cheyenne Mountain to the equestrian park.

To climb the Northeast Ridge: From the park, follow a trail toward the gap between Cheyenne Mountain (to the right) and the very small mountain (this lump has been sometimes referred to as Flag Mountain) to the left. Summerlin Peak will be the high mountain in the gap between them. Summerlin Peak's northeast ridge should be visible dead ahead. Note the high cliff band of the upper mountain and try to make out the weakest spot in the cliff band—it should be apparent. You want to head for that weakness; it's at the top of the northeast ridge. Hike across the desert for about a mile to the base of the northeast ridge. Using any number of possible variations, start working your way up the ridge, aiming for the weakest spot you saw in the cliffs above. Gaining it, you should find that the otherwise 100-foot cliffs can be climbed through at this weakness by merely scrambling up a short 6-foot section of class 3 dry waterfall. Easier terrain follows, so follow your nose to the summit a few hundred feet above. Roundtrip numbers are about 3-4 miles with 2,200 feet of gain.

To climb the Southeast Ridge: After initially following the directions given for the Northeast Ridge route through the gap adjacent to Flag Mountain, hike through open desert for about a mile toward the southeast ridge. Gain the ridge near a "saddle" near its left edge and start up. Minor difficulties are found here and there, with the greatest difficulties found at an obvious cliff band a couple hundred feet below the summit. This cliff band can be climbed directly (YDS 5.4-5.6) or bypassed (class 4) by dropping to the right about 150 feet and working the first obvious weakness one comes to on the left. Finding yourself again near the crest of the ridge, head up easier terrain to the summit. Expect roundtrip numbers around 4 miles with 2,300 feet of gain.

-WGS84 Lat: 36.2176 deg N Lon: -115.3605 deg W
*-II, Class 3 via Northeast Ridge ***
*-III, Class 4 via Southeast Ridge ****

"Ugly Brown Lump" (6,080+)

Next to La Madre and behind Lonely Pinon, the 'ugly, brown lump' that is this long and meandering ridge doesn't draw many visitors. It is most easily hiked directly from SR-157 (Kyle Canyon Road), 7.7 miles from I-95.

-WGS84 Lat: 36.2596 deg N Lon: -115.4083 deg W
*-III, Class 2 via NW Slope **

Willow Benchmark (8,335)

While the summit views are somewhat better than those from nearby, higher Wilson Ridge, this too is a brush-laden exercise in tolerance. This peak is unpopular for a reason. Approached from near the end of Lovell Canyon Road.

-WGS84 Lat: 36.1911 deg N Lon: -115.5393 deg W
*-II, Class 2 from Wilson Ridge **

Wilson Ridge (8,467)

The only thing interesting about this ascent is the brilliant optional knife-edge ridge one can utilize from immediately above The Narrows. The rest is little more than a heinous bushwhack. The summit offers no views. Approach as per Willow Benchmark.

-WGS84 Lat: 36.1948 deg N Lon: -115.5545 deg W
*-III, Class 2 via The Narrows ***
*-III, Class 2 from Willow Benchmark **

"Windy" (7,650)

The summit of this obscure peak near Pondview Peak and El Bastardo is marked by strange, arrow-shaped rocks.

-WGS84 Lat: 36.2046 deg N Lon: -115.5298 deg W

*-II, Class 2 via Northeast Slope **

The author admiring the scenery at Red Rock. Photo by Aron Ralston.

Spring Mountains National Recreation Area

The Spring Mountains, quite possibly the most well-known mountain range in the entire state of Nevada, a state absolutely loaded with mountain ranges (314 of them), is a fine range of diversity. It is named for the many springs found throughout its length. Running roughly south to north (as virtually every mountain range in the Great Basin does) the Spring Mountains stretch all the way from the California/Nevada border near Primm, Nevada to Amargosa Valley between Cactus Springs and Beatty, Nevada—a distance of some seventy miles.

Topped by Charleston Peak (11,915), a very popular year-round hiking and climbing objective, the Spring Mountains also offer more than a dozen officially (and locally) named peaks above 10,000 feet. Lofty enough to gather plenty of snow in the winter, these high mountains provide excellent winter mountaineering challenges to the dedicated and experienced snow climber.

The sandstone playground of Red Rock Canyon NCA also resides within this primarily limestone mountain range of both high, alpine mountains and low, desert peaks. With Red Rock Canyon providing world class trad and sport climbing on beautiful sandstone, the Mount Charleston area also hosts world class sport (and some trad) climbing in and around its many limestone caves and crags. Climbs in the Mount Charleston area range from relatively easy (*Sylvias Slab* – YDS 5.4) to very difficult (*Hasta La Vista* – YDS 5.14c).

Beyond the high limestone mountains and the lower sandstone crags of Red Rock, the range hosts a whole bunch of absolutely obscure lesser peaks that only a few locals even notice. Many of these mountains are fine objectives. Lonely canyons, surprising knife edges, and hundred-mile vistas are just a few of the things that make these lesser known peaks of the Spring Mountains worth exploring.

Developed campgrounds (particularly in the Mount Charleston area), as well as primitive camping opportunities, abound in this sprawling, diverse area. Primitive camping within the Mount Charleston Wilderness requires a wilderness permit.

The subsections contained within the Spring Mountains group of peaks in this guide are geographically arranged in a roughly counter-clockwise fashion, starting in Kyle Canyon (northwest of Las Vegas) and working up along US-95 to the northern tip of the range. The subsections then bend south along Pahrump off of NV-160, and eventually work back toward Mountain Springs. From there, the subsections address the southern peaks of the range, including those around Goodsprings and off I-15 outside of Jean, Nevada.

Charleston Peak (left of center) and Lee Peak (bump to its right) from the vicinity of Mummy's Chin (looking southwest)

Kyle Canyon

The peaks in this subsection are accessed from Kyle Canyon Road (NV-157). They are arranged generally south-to-north.

La Madre Mountain Wilderness Highpoint (9,422)

You know you're an obsessed peakbagger when you embark on a 16-mile, 5300' gain day in order to stand on the summit of a feature with less than 90' of prominence. Such is my life. (In full disclosure, some of that elevation gain comes from bagging the unimpressive and im-prominent Sexton Ridge as a bonus on the way to/from.)

Approach as per Griffith Peak, as you nearly go over the higher summit twice traveling to and from the wilderness highpoint.

-WGS84 Lat: 36.2007 deg N Lon: -115.6373 deg W

*-III, Class 1-2 via North Ridge **

Sexton Ridge (10,088)

It's sort of a longish (but pleasant and scenic, before the big fire) slog to this minor bump on the south ridge of Griffith Peak. While you're out there, you may as well grab the La Madre Mountain Wilderness Highpoint further south too.

-WGS84 Lat: 36.2146 deg N Lon: -115.6423 deg W

*-III, Class 1-2 via North Ridge ***

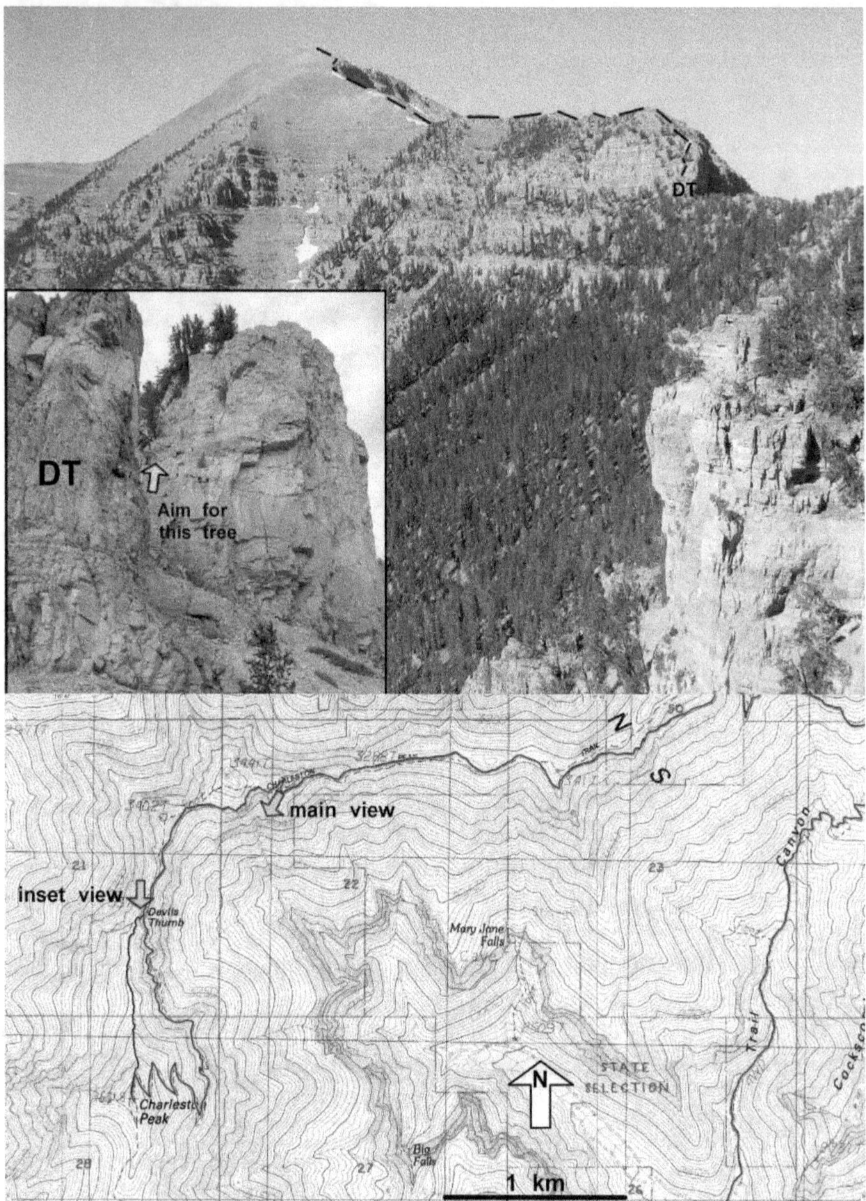

This displays the Devil's Thumb Shortcut from the North Loop Trail. To utilize this shortcut, follow the North Loop Trail to Devil's Thumb (DT). Once at DT, look around the right side of the thumb to view the tree shown in the inset. Work left then up to the tree, surmounting a 7'-high crease below the tree (class 4). Continue straight up (south), then cut right (west) to a notch. Cross over south from the notch, then right (west) up a wall. From the top of the wall, continue south over the ridge to the summit.

Griffith Peak (11,059)

Approach as per the directions given for Charleston Peak. From the trailhead, follow the South Loop Trail up to the high crest above. There, rather than hang a right to head to Charleston Peak, hang a left and make the short hike up to Griffith Peak.

-WGS84 Lat: 36.2323 deg N Lon: -115.6462 deg W

-III, Class 2 via South Loop Trail ***

Harris Mountain (10,014)

Although Harris Mountain has never struck me as appealing as a summer objective, I've climbed it several times in winter. As such, both routes detailed for this peak reflect my experiences climbing it in snow.

Harris Mountain is one of the higher peaks in the Spring Mountains. Although appearing relatively small next to its much higher neighbors, Griffith Peak, Charleston Peak, and Mummy Mountain, its steep and imposing north face grabs the attention of those visiting the popular Kyle Canyon area of the Mount Charleston region, as it is the first large mountain encountered as one enters the upper canyon.

Due to the mountain's lack of designated trails and its position as the "little sister" of the group of giants surrounding it, Harris Mountain does not see many visitors. Those who do visit generally do so via a class 1-2 use trail from the Harris-Griffith saddle (accessed from the signed Harris Springs Road off Kyle Canyon Road, 12.6 miles from I-95).

From Las Vegas, take US-95 north to the Kyle Canyon (SR-157) exit. Turn left and follow the paved road for 18 miles in the direction of the small community of Mount Charleston. You will pass through the desert scrub lands of the lower part of Kyle Canyon, into the Joshua tree lands of the middle section (be sure to check out the La Madre Mountain "scar" to the south), then into the pinon/juniper woodlands of the upper middle portion, and ultimately to the ponderosa forests of the upper canyon. Upon reaching the ponderosa forests of the upper canyon, you will notice Harris Mountain's north face on the left (south) side of the road. Shortly after the old (a new one is being built several miles down-canyon) Kyle Canyon Visitor Center (about 18 miles from US-95), which is on the left side of the road, look for a prominent, cliffy ridge towering above the road as it sweeps down from Harris Mountain. This is the north ridge. Just below the toe of the ridge is a small parking area on the side of the road. Park here.

To climb the North Ridge: From the parking area along Kyle Canyon Road, you can see the prominent and cliffy toe of the north ridge looming a thousand feet above the road to the south. From this vantage point, the summit is not visible. Heading cross-country toward the toe of the ridge, the terrain steepens quickly and considerably. Aim straight for the cliffs (a sort of headwall) visible ahead of you on the north ridge. The route-finding is simple as your first objective is hard to miss. Once the base of the cliffs at the toe of the north ridge is reached, traverse easterly and slightly upward until you reach a sort of chute leading up to a notch. Assuming that you follow these directions and hug the cliff base, you should not miss the "notch." Once at the notch, cross through and continue traversing in a more southerly direction, still hugging the base of the cliffs as you follow the ridge itself toward the summit. The summit itself should finally come into view in the distance. You should find that once past the notch staying a little below the base of the cliffs will give you easier, though still steep, ground on the traverse. Continue traversing south, looking for terrain suitable for your skills and desires that will allow you to finally scramble up the rocky cliffs and to the ridge crest above you. The further you traverse along the base of the cliffs, the lower the cliffs get and the easier the scramble to the crest. A couple hundred yards after the notch, you will find that the cliffs have shrunken enough to make a class 3 scramble up to the crest a quick and painless venture. Though still steep in places, once the ridge crest is reached the remainder of the route is at a moderate angle and the remaining objective is clear: Follow the ridge, fighting the frequent brushy areas and attempting to stay near the crest, all the way to the summit.

To climb the North Ridge Direct: Follow the directions given for the North Ridge route to the headwall. Once the headwall is reached, rather than traverse to the east toward the notch mentioned for the north ridge route, look for a nearby 20-foot chimney leading to a ledge above you. The mixed climbing found in this semi-exposed chimney (and the terrain just beyond it) is the crux. Once the top of the chimney is reached, it appears that easier ground is to the left (east)—wrong! Traverse to the west (right) on a narrow and exposed snowy rock ledge and then down-climb a short but exposed class 3 section until you come to a wide chute leading you upward on easier ground to your left. Once the chute is found, head up on whatever terrain seems comfortable. The climbing in the chute is class 2 and 3, though you should expect it to be mixed with rock and ice and fairly exposed. Work your way up the chute as it steers you toward the west-southwest. Once the top of the chute is gained, head back east and up on easier ground toward the ridge crest above. While doing so, some marvelous vistas of Kyle Canyon open up below you. Though still steep in places, once the ridge crest is reached, the remainder of the route is at a moderate angle and the remaining objective is clear: Follow the ridge, fighting the frequent brushy areas and attempting to stay near the crest, all the way to the summit.

The roundtrip stats for either route are around 5 miles with a little over 3,000 feet of gain.

-WGS84 Lat: 36.2414 deg N Lon: -115.6115 deg W
*-III, Class 3 via North Ridge (Winter) ***
*-III, YDS 5.3 via North Ridge Direct (Winter) ****

Cathedral Rock (8,597)
A pleasant (mostly-)trail hike to a nice viewpoint over Kyle Canyon. Start from the trailhead near the end of Kyle Canyon Road (SR-157).

-WGS84 Lat: 36.2546 deg N Lon: -115.6498 deg W
-II, Class 2 via Cathedral Rock Trail **

Charleston Peak (11,915)
The highest peak around Las Vegas—and a classic. Just ask the dozens of people you'll be sharing the summit with on any summer Saturday afternoon. Charleston Peak also happens to be the most prominent peak in the state of Nevada, with nearly 8,300 feet of rise. Take SR-157 (Kyle Canyon Road) about 21 miles to the South Loop trailhead near the end of the road. Alternatively, the peak can be climbed via the North Loop Trail (most easily accessed from Trail Canyon; see Cockscomb Peak driving directions), a number of off-trail routes from Kyle or Lee Canyons, or even from the Pahrump side of the range. Be particularly careful on the off-trail routes, as folks have died from falls.

Oh yeah, please don't refer to the mountain as Mount Charleston. Or more annoyingly, Mount Charlie.

-WGS84 Lat: 36.2715 deg N Lon: -115.6956 deg W
-III-IV, Class 1 via South Loop Trail ****
-III-IV, Class 1 via North Loop Trail ****
-III-IV, Class 4 via Devil's Thumb Shortcut ****

"Cockscomb Peak" (9,692)
Plenty of loose rock on this one, so be sure to pick your route carefully.

From I-95, take SR-157 (Kyle Canyon Road) 20.5 miles to where the main road bends left. Here, stay straight and follow Echo Road for 0.5 mile to the Trail Canyon trailhead (7,900 ft.). From there, hike the trail to its junction with the North Loop Trail. Here, hang a hard right and follow the initially easy ridge on your approach to the awesome summit crag of Cockscomb Peak, which is clearly visible in front of you. As the terrain stiffens, snoop around, dropping down a bit on the left side of the crest, and work around obstacles to gain the final scramble leading to the top.

-WGS84 Lat: 36.2792 deg N Lon: -115.6486 deg W
-II, Class 3 via South Face ***

Fletcher Peak (10,252)
Most easily approached from SR-158 (Deer Creek Highway) and the North Loop Trail, though it's also often approached via the Trail Canyon trailhead (7,900 ft.) off of Echo Road and SR-157 (Kyle Canyon Road).

Follow the Cockscomb Peak directions to get to the Trail Canyon trailhead. To find the Deer Creek Highway, leave I-95 outside of Las Vegas and follow SR-157 (Kyle Canyon Road) for 17.6 miles. There, hang a right and follow the paved road as it winds its way toward the North Loop trailhead (which will be on your left). In either case, the North Loop Trail passes within 0.5 mile of the summit. Leaving the trail near Raintree (a giant bristlecone pine along the trail), easy cross-country travel takes one to the summit.

-WGS84 Lat: 36.2867 deg N Lon: -115.6216 deg W
-II, Class 1-2 via North Loop Trail **

"Lee Peak" (11,312)
From either the Trail Canyon trailhead (see Cockscomb Peak) or the North Loop trailhead (see Fletcher Peak), follow the North Loop Trail to a point where it cuts below the summit of Lee Peak. Leave the trail and cruise up to the summit. The peak can also be bagged while looping up and over Charleston Peak via a North Loop-South Loop tour. I've also done a couple of routes from Lee Canyon.

-WGS84 Lat: 36.2874 deg N Lon: -115.6896 deg W
-III, Class 2 via Southeast Ridge from North Loop Trail ***

"Mummys Toe" (10,926)
The north gully is accessed from Mummy Spring (gotten to via a side trail next to The Raintree, a large bristlecone found along the North Loop Trail) via the North Loop Trail (see Fletcher Peak).

-WGS84 Lat: 36.2921 deg N Lon: -115.6384 deg W
-III, Class 2-3 via West Ridge from North Gully ***

Mummy Mountain (11,527)
Although a touch shorter than Charleston, Mummy is a much more interesting mountain. It has five principal summits. This, the highest, is commonly called "Mummys Tummy."

Follow the directions given for Cockscomb Peak to the Trail Canyon trailhead (7,900 ft.). Follow this trail to its junction with the North Loop Trail. There, hang a left and follow the trail past Cave Spring to a large scree slope (10,300 ft.) just as you exit a large grove of aspen trees. Leave the North Loop Trail and head up the scree slope (to the right) at a tree with a large 'M' scratched on it, following a significant erosion trail to the crest straight above (10,900 ft.). From there, turn right and follow a decent use trail (and cairns) initially up the crest then just left of it, eventually bending left and working easily to a large break (a chute on the right) in the final summit cliffs. The chute, which is choked with annoying talus, leads to mellow terrain 50 yards from the highpoint.

Expect about 3,800 feet of elevation gain on the roundtrip.

-WGS84 Lat: 36.2993 deg N Lon: -115.6495 deg W

-III, Class 2 via North Loop Trail from Trail Canyon ****

The Mummy massif from the east. Mummys Toe (left), Mummys Forehead (right) and the Mummy Mountain highpoint (center), as seen from US-95 northwest of Las Vegas

"Snow King" (8,067)

A wonderful, mellow snow climb during the winter season. It takes (some people) 3-4 hours roundtrip from Kyle Canyon Road. A good starting point for the hike is found along a dirt road leaving Kyle Canyon Road (SR-157) 11.8 miles from I-95.

Six miles, 2,800 feet of gain on the hike.

-WGS84 Lat: 36.3106 deg N Lon: -115.5447 deg W

-II, Class 2 via Southeast Ridge **

"Grapevine Spring Point" (5,383)

To get to this obscure peak, one starts as per Snow King, hiking the old road directly from Kyle Canyon Road to Grapevine Spring and beyond, gaining the southwest ridge at its base and following it easily to the top. Grapevine Spring, as it happens, is a rather tranquil place to meditate on the return from the summit.

-WGS84 Lat: 36.3347 deg N Lon: -115.4826 deg W

-II, Class 1 via Southwest Ridge **

US-95 near Corn Creek Road

Peaks in this subsection are west of US-95, generally opposite Corn Creek Road (graded dirt). A bumpy powerline road provides easy, high clearance access to most of the peaks in this area. The area is sandwiched between NV-156 and NV-157. The peaks are arranged here generally south-to-north.

"Bee Canyon Peak" (4,858)
Bee Canyon Peak lies a few miles west of US-95, south of Lucky Strike Canyon and north of the Kyle Canyon turn-off. The southern of the long and elegant twin northeast ridges of this peak is a two-mile long enjoyable scramble. From the summit, we dropped into the prominent and highly intriguing canyon draining east between the twin ridges. This canyon is technical, featuring a few rappels, none longer than 50 feet. We dubbed it Bee Canyon.

-WGS84 Lat: 36.3718 deg N Lon: -115.4547 deg W
-II, Class 2-3 via Northeast Ridge **

Kyle Benchmark (5,751)
Approached as per Dull Mountain. Don't be tempted to follow the dirt road over the pass (beyond the mountain) and down to Kyle Canyon Road when you're done. It gets super nasty and committing.

-WGS84 Lat: 36.3500 deg N Lon: -115.4834 deg W
-I, Class 2 via Southwest Ridge *

"Lucky Strike Mine Peak" (6,610)
A 4WD dirt road leads one close to the west side of the peak. This route, while not particularly interesting, is less sloggy than the gravel found in the canyon on the east side of the mountain.

-WGS84 Lat: 36.3486 deg N Lon: -115.5319 deg W
-I, Class 2 via West Slope *
-II, Class 2 via East Canyon *

Edge Benchmark (6,322)
This obscure peak north of Lucky Strike Mine Peak in upper Lucky Strike Canyon is approached via the primitive dirt road that leads past the base of the south ridge.

-WGS84 Lat: 36.3776 deg N Lon: -115.5252 deg W
-II, Class 2 via South Ridge **

"Graduation Peak" (5,220)
A forgettable peak in Lucky Strike Canyon.

-WGS84 Lat: 36.3741 deg N Lon: -115.4719 deg W
-I, Class 1-2 via Northwest Slope *

"Burro Peak" (5,603)

The north ridge of this peak is easily accessed via the bumpy Lucky Strike Canyon road off of US-95 opposite the Corn Creek turn-off.

-WGS84 Lat: 36.3607 deg N Lon: -115.4739 deg W

-II, Class 2 via North Ridge **

"Dull Mountain" (4,800)

As its name implies. It is approached via a decent dirt road across US-95 from Corn Creek Road.

-WGS84 Lat: 36.3942 deg N Lon: -115.4591 deg W

-I, Class 2 via Southwest Ridge *

"Mount Pumpkin" (4,563)

This small peak sits across Lucky Strike Canyon from Lucky Strike Peak. Its neighbor is Dull Mountain. Approach as per Dull Mountain.

-WGS84 Lat: 36.4031 deg N Lon: -115.4535 deg W

-I, Class 2 via Northwest Ridge *

"Lucky Strike Peak" (4,974)

The peak sits on the north side of Lucky Strike Canyon on the eastern edge of the Spring Mountains. Approach as per Dull Mountain.

-WGS84 Lat: 36.4251 deg N Lon: -115.4815 deg W

-II, Class 2 from the Southeast **

Lee Canyon

The peaks in this subsection are accessed from Lee Canyon Road (NV-156). They are arranged here generally south-to-north.

"Amargosa Overlook" (10,154)

Best approached from the end of Lee Canyon. From the Upper Bristlecone Trailhead at road's end, follow the trail 0.9 mile to a decommissioned trail on the left. Follow the old trail up to a minor saddle with 3 wilderness boundary signs and a yellow-orange survey monument sign. There, look for a faint game trail heading up the steep slope to the left. Follow the game trail to the ridge crest above then follow the ridge west to the indistinct highpoint.

-WGS84 Lat: 36.3010 deg N Lon: -115.7241 deg W

-III, Class 1-2 via East Ridge **

Pioneer Rock (9,035)

The summit of this seldom noticed named feature above upper Lee Canyon requires exposed class 4 scrambling (about 30-40 feet) to reach its summit. Fortunately, there are adequate bushes (and even a single bolt/hanger) available to protect the route. The crux is found in the first eight feet of the route, with most of the route being 3rd class.

-WGS84 Lat: 36.3057 deg N Lon: -115.6687 deg W

*-II, Class 4 via Southeast Arete ***

"Mummys Chin" (11,043)

The Chin has the same stunning approach as the Forehead. The traverse between the two summits is semi-interesting. Approach from Lee Canyon Road.

-WGS84 Lat: 36.3123 deg N Lon: -115.6531 deg W

*-III, Class 2-3 via Mummys Forehead *****

"Mummys Forehead" (11,037)

This is a nice summit. The approach is interesting, including a short bit of class 4 face climbing, an exposed traverse, a bit of a chimney and then a walk through a stunning grove of bristlecone pines. Have a blast exploring your way to the top of this one…that's what I did.

-WGS84 Lat: 36.3150 deg N Lon: -115.6542 deg W

*-III, Class 4 via Northeast Slope *****

Approaching the summit of Mummys Forehead.
Mummys Nose is in the background. The view looks northeast.

"Mummys Nose" (10,751)

Although easier routes certainly exist, we utilized an aesthetic hidden slot on the mid-east face that led to a short, steep class 4-5 wall in order to gain the easy upper north face on the ascent. The south ridge from the north gully was used on the descent. The north gully drains from the Mummys Nose-Mummys Chin saddle. Both routes are approached from Lee Canyon Road. The northeast face route, approached from SR-158, is quite pleasant.

-WGS84 Lat: 36.3204 deg N Lon: -115.6456 deg W
-III, Class 2 via Northeast Face ***
-III, Class 2-3 via South Ridge from North Gully ***
-III, Class 4-5 via North Face ***

The author below the summit of Mummys Nose (photo by Tracy Foutz)

The Sisters (10,177)

The Sisters is an impressive mountain consisting of two summits—two "sisters." The southern Sister is the highest. South Sister (10,177) also has a minor, subsidiary summit to its south—some might call this one Little Sister; some might not. Although North Sister is the more striking of the two Sisters, it is lower and lies a bit further north along the massif and away from the higher South Sister. It is therefore less frequently visited, though a traverse of the two summits is a wonderful outing with interesting route-finding. Even better is a link-up of the Macks Peak traverse and the Sisters traverse.

Follow the driving directions given for Macks Peak toward the ski resort at the end of Lee Canyon Road. The Sisters, although visible from far down the road, first come nicely into view on the right side of the road at around 15 miles from US-95.

For the Macks Canyon approach or the Sisters Traverse: Follow the driving directions given for Macks Peak to the end of the road in Macks Canyon.

To climb from upper Macks Canyon: From the end of the road, an obvious wide track continues into Macks Canyon. Follow the route into the canyon for about a mile. From time to time, small side canyons will branch off, but stay in the main canyon. After a mile or so, the canyon narrows and a thin, non-designated dirt trail continues on. Follow the trail as it crosses and re-crosses a small stream. In springtime, the columbines and hummingbirds along the stream make it rather charming. After following the trail along the stream for about 0.5 mile, both the trail and the stream start to die out and become hard to follow. Continue up the main drainage on steepening scree slopes to the east-west trending ridge above. (This is the same west ridge referred to in the winter route.) Once at the crest of the east-west ridge, follow it east as it travels up toward The Sisters, which is obvious at this point. As you progress, the ridge turns into a chute between South Sister (on the left) and South Sister's subsidiary summit (on the right). Travel up into the chute on progressively loosening scree and steepening class 2 terrain. Along the way, there are excellent specimens of the fabulous Bristlecone Pines that can be seen in the higher elevations throughout much of the Great Basin. At the top of the chute, you will come to the saddle between South Sister and her sub-peak. From this point, the sub-peak can be gained by hanging a right and scrambling up class 2 terrain to the top. South Sister is gained by heading left from the saddle to the base of a class 3 chimney. Climb up the chimney for about 10 feet (some exposure) to a small, somewhat narrow and exposed ledge. From this point, it is only about 10 vertical feet to the summit. Follow the ledge around the corner and up to the summit. (In winter, this snow-covered ledge is attention-getting.) The highpoint is 100 feet to the north along the narrow and exposed summit ridge. The traverse to the highpoint is class 2. This route involves about 1,500 feet of elevation gain and six miles roundtrip.

For the Winter Route: While traveling on Lee Canyon Road (SR-156) toward the ski resort, you will come to a snow play area (a large, open meadowy area) on the right at about mile 16. The Sisters is the prominent mountain towering above the snow play area. Park along the road, making sure that NDOT is not removing snow that day. If they are, your vehicle could be ticketed. Walk back down the road less than 0.25 mile to the entrance to the Old Mill Picnic Area, on the same side of the road as The Sisters. Enter the Picnic Area (8,300 feet) and follow the road (the area is closed in winter and the road is not plowed) for about 0.5 mile. You will pass a few minor ridges and drainages. At about 0.5 mile, pick a route up one of the ridges on the right and start up. The Sisters should be obvious to the north/northeast. Although it may be tempting to head straight for the mountain, trend westward a little to avoid cliffs and rocky obstacles, and ultimately aim for a prominent east-west ridge heading up to the mountain. This is the west ridge of The Sisters. Once you gain the west ridge, head east toward the top, where the ridge turns into a wide chute leading to a minor saddle. South Sister will be on the left and her minor sub-peak on the right. Toward the top of the chute, the angle can sharpen to around 45-50 degrees in places, depending on the snowpack. At this point, you can either stay to the left side of the chute and negotiate typically iced-over rock or move a little to the right and work your way upward through typically deep snow. Once the saddle is gained, climb a class 3 chimney (snow/ice/rock) on the north side of the saddle. The chimney's about 10 feet high, and at the top is an exposed snowy ledge about two or three feet wide. Traverse the ledge for a few feet and then work your way up a short slab on the left to the narrow summit ridge just above you. On my most recent winter climb of this route, the narrow summit ridge sported a 100' long cornice along the traverse to the highpoint. The exposure along the summit ridge can be attention-getting. This route involves approximately 1,900 feet of elevation gain and five miles roundtrip.

-WGS84 Lat: 36.3297 deg N Lon: -115.6831 deg W
*-II, Class 3 from Upper Macks Canyon ****
*-III, Class 3 via Winter Route ****
*-III, Class 3 via Sisters Traverse ****

"North Sister" (10,042)

In addition to the northeast ridge route, North Sister can be traversed to from its higher, parent peak. The traverse is class 3, and requires careful route-finding.

-WGS84 Lat: 36.3356 deg N Lon: -115.6801 deg W
*-III, Class 2-3 via Northeast Ridge ****
*-III, Class 3 via Sisters Traverse ****

"Black Rock Sister" (9,646)

I'd noticed this small, black protrusion on the ridge north-northeast of North Sister, but it wasn't until I thumbed through the register that I found someone had dubbed the little thing "Black Rock Sister." So I headed off to do it next!

-WGS84 Lat: 36.3407 deg N Lon: -115.6742 deg W
*-II, Class 2 via West Face **
*-II, Class 4 via East Arete ****

"Divide Peak" (10,068)

This minor peak sits along the Spring Mountains crest south of McFarland Peak. To get there, follow the Bristlecone Trail to the Bonanza Trail, which eventually passes very close to the summit. An easy off-trail walk leads to the highpoint. A MacLeod/Lilley register on the summit gives the peak its name.

-WGS84 Lat: 36.3305 deg N Lon: -115.7099 deg W

-II-III, Class 1 via Bonanza Trail **

McFarland Peak (10,744)

A really nice backcountry mountain. A classic, actually. Take SR-156 (Lee Canyon) to its end at a cul de sac above the ski resort. Follow the Bristlecone Trail to the Bonanza Trail, which is taken to a point below McFarland Peak. Find the gully in question (the correct one, that is) and carefully head up.

-WGS84 Lat: 36.3414 deg N Lon: -115.7256 deg W

-III-IV, Class 2-3 via South Gully from Bonanza Trail ****

"Mud Hole Mountain" (7,654)

This obscure mountain lies south of Mud Hole Spring. With a good dirt road leading all the way to the base of the mountain from Lee Canyon Road, it is a fine winter objective. Just enough snow to make it extra-pretty!

-WGS84 Lat: 36.3465 deg N Lon: -115.5578 deg W

-II, Class 2 via Northwest Ridge **

"Macks Peak" (10,036)

Though not far off the beaten path, this often-overlooked mountain, tucked away behind its neighbor, The Sisters, in the more obscure northern portion of the Spring Mountains, is seldom noticed and infrequently climbed. By its easiest route, this well-fortified peak, surrounded on all sides by limestone cliffs, is class 3, requiring a roundtrip jaunt of four miles with approximately 1,400 feet of elevation gain. Although Macks Peak's standard route is short, it doesn't disappoint. There's a nice (though short) bit of exposure toward the end of the route and the summit views are expansive.

From Las Vegas, take US-95 north past the Kyle Canyon (SR-157) exit to the Lee Canyon (SR-156) exit to Charleston Peak. The exit is about 45 minutes' drive from downtown Las Vegas, and there is obvious signage for Lee Canyon and the ski resort. Turn left onto Lee Canyon Road and keep driving—it's 17.3 miles to the ski resort, but you'll be turning off a few miles before that. After 13.6 miles on Lee Canyon Road, look for the dirt turn-off to Macks Canyon on your right (north). There is a sign, but it is not obvious. If you reach the junction of Lee Canyon Road and Deer Creek Road (SR-158; paved, on the left), you've gone too far. Turn around and backtrack about a mile. Turn right onto Macks Canyon Road and follow it for 4.3 miles to its end at a parking area. Toward the end, the condition of the road deteriorates.

A high clearance vehicle is recommended. In winter, the dirt road will be snowed in and very likely impassable.

From the end of the road, an obvious wide track continues on into Macks Canyon. You may have noticed that the vegetation has changed from pinon/juniper to ponderosa pine, that there is a small (protected) spring on the left as you approached, and there are many fine spots to camp near the mouth of canyon. It's a nice area.

From the parking area, follow the wide track (an old road) west into Macks Canyon for about 0.5 mile. From time to time, small side canyons and drainages will branch off from the main canyon. You are looking for a small drainage branching off to the north (right) and marked by a cairn. If you find it—great; if not—no worries. Whether you're successful or not in finding the correct drainage to leave Macks Canyon and head north, know that around 0.5 mile from the parking area you can safely work your way out of Macks Canyon and to the crest of the ridge above you on the right. Fortunately, the north side of Macks Canyon tends to be slopey (if steep) rather than cliffy. Work your way to the crest above. From the crest, Macks Peak may or may not be visible, depending on your vantage point, but rest assured that it is just a short distance to the north.

Travel cross-country (there aren't any trails to be easily found at first) to the north over undulating terrain until Macks Peak comes into view. Work your way to the base of the cliffs near the southwest side of the peak. As you near the southwest side, the occasional use trail and/or cairn should come into view. Follow them to and/or look for the only apparent way up the cliffs—a sloping narrow ledge heading west up the face of the mountain. This ledge, covered in loose scree and only 18-inches or so wide in places, is about 50 feet long and somewhat exposed. Head up the ledge. Once the top of the ledge is gained, follow sloping, scree-covered terrain upward toward obvious terrain allowing you to continue on. Further description is not really necessary, as there's only one practical way to proceed and it's spelled out for you when you're there. Continue up class 2 and occasional class 3 terrain to the right (north) around a bend and follow it up to the summit.

From the summit, one can make the sweet (class 4) traverse to North Macks Peak, although I think it's better done from North Macks Peak. Regardless, the route features knife edges, exposure, sketchy climbing, lots of scrambling, and requires careful route-finding. Beware loose rock!

-WGS84 Lat: 36.3506 deg N Lon: -115.6973 deg W

*-III, Class 3 via Macks Canyon to Macks Peak ****

*-III, Class 4 via Macks Peak Traverse *****

"North Macks Peak" (9,975+)

This is a fun one. The knife-edge at the top of the bristlecone slab on the northeast ridge is short but dramatic, and the bristlecone slab itself (which is gained via a 40-foot, class 4 slabby groove) features 200+ feet of sustained class 3-4 slab climbing with nice exposure.

Perhaps the finest alpine(ish) adventure in southern Nevada is a traverse from North Macks Peak to its parent peak. The route is class 4, features knife edges, exposure, sketchy downclimbs, lots of scrambling, and requires careful route-finding. Beware loose rock!

Refer to the driving directions for Macks Peak, as both routes are initially approached from the end of the road in Macks Canyon.

-WGS84 Lat: 36.3557 deg N Lon: -115.6938 deg W

-III, Class 4 via North Face to Northeast Ridge ****

-III, Class 4 via Macks Peak Traverse ****

The author signing one of his trademark bogus names in the register atop North Macks Peak. Photo by Aron Ralston.

"Seldom Seen Peak" (5,082)

This minor peak is northeast of Traction Benchmark. It is perhaps best approached from NV-156 (Lee Canyon Road) to the east.

-WGS84 Lat: 36.4607 deg N Lon: -115.5565 deg W

-II, Class 1-2 via East Slopes **

Cold Creek Road

The peaks in this subsection are accessed from Cold Creek Road (highway 172). They are arranged here generally south-to-north.

"Mount Everest" (9,868)
Mount Everest lies about a mile north-northeast of McFarland Peak. The peak's long north ridge is an enjoyable hike, and a loop can be completed by working down to the saddle south of the summit and then descending the canyon (class 3) on the west side of the peak. Some interesting caves can be seen from the lower canyon. Approach via a good dirt road leading south from the Cold Creek Road near the south end of Indian Ridge.

-WGS84 Lat: 36.3540 deg N Lon: -115.7191 deg W
-III, Class 2 via North Ridge **

Bonanza Peak (10,396)
Follow the directions given for Willow Peak to Cold Creek. On the edge of the small community, locate the developed trailhead at the base of the mountain and follow the good trail to the top.

-WGS84 Lat: 36.3594 deg N Lon: -115.7472 deg W
-III, Class 1 via Bonanza Trail **

Willow Peak (9,977)
Lying just north/northwest of Bonanza Peak in the northern portion of the Spring Mountains, Willow Peak is seldom visited. It just barely misses out on being another of the esteemed 10,000+-foot peaks of the range.

During the summer months, Willow Peak's steep northeastern face, visible from US-95 as one travels north from Las Vegas, appears as a nothing sort of mountain a few hundred feet shorter than its aforementioned and beautifully forested neighbor to the south. During the winter months, however, Willow Peak steals the show. After suffering a large fire some years back, most of the mountain is treeless, giving the snow-laden high desert peak a very white, alpine appearance. The peak makes a fine snow climb during the wintry months.

Take US-95 north from Las Vegas past the Kyle Canyon (SR-157) and the Lee Canyon (SR-156) exits. Your exit, the Cold Creek exit, will be the third turn-off on the left, about an hour north of downtown Las Vegas and five miles north of SR-156. There are huge prison facilities on both sides of the Cold Creek road, immediately off the highway.

Turn onto the signed and paved Cold Creek road and follow it for 13.1 miles toward the small community of Cold Creek (no services). Just as the outskirts of Cold Creek are reached on the Cold Creek road, look for a dirt road (Forest Road 601) leaving the paved road and heading off to the north (right). There are several dirt roads in the area heading off to the north, but this one is well-traveled, in the vicinity of the Cold Creek Picnic Area, has a small pond and some ruins of old buildings near the junction with the paved road, and should be signed for Wheeler Pass. Wheeler Pass will be visible to the west, just north of Willow Peak.

Although the dirt road branches off occasionally, it's not too difficult to stay on track; stick with the main dirt road, aiming for the pass. The pass is about 7.5 miles from the pavement, and the road deteriorates extensively. A 4WD vehicle is often necessary to negotiate the last couple of miles, and a high clearance vehicle is recommended well before that.

For the Northwest Ridge: After hiking or driving to Wheeler Pass, gain the northwest ridge of Willow Peak (to the south) and start hiking up. Staying near the crest of the ridge, follow it to the summit.

Roundtrip numbers from Wheeler Pass are 3 miles, with no more than 1,700 feet of gain.

The north face route is brushy and uninteresting.

-WGS84 Lat: 36.3856 deg N Lon: -115.7738 deg W

*-II, Class 2 via Northwest Ridge from Wheeler Pass ***

*-II, Class 2 via North Face **

"Mine Peak" (7,739)

This obscure peak sits west of Wheeler Benchmark in the northern Spring Mountains. Although it could be more easily approached from the west (Pahrump) side of the range, I chose to slog up to Wheeler Pass from Cold Creek then make a tedious traverse first through obnoxious brush then through pinyon/juniper woodland, ultimately reaching the saddle east of the peak. Delightfully, the final summit rocks feature about 200 feet of sustained class 2-3 scrambling with interesting route-finding en route to the highest, overhung block.

-WGS84 Lat: 36.3941 deg N Lon: -115.8252 deg W

*-III, Class 3 via Southeast Aspect ***

Wheeler Benchmark (8,967)

Though not particularly high, Wheeler Benchmark (also called Wheeler Peak) is one of the prominent, high peaks of the northern Spring Mountains. It is easily seen from US-95 north of Cactus Springs, Nevada. The peak lies just north of Wheeler Pass.

Follow the driving direction given for Willow Peak. From Wheeler Pass, head north up the ridge. Some class 3 terrain may be encountered, though easier travel can be found. Once the crest of the ridge is gained, follow it north/northeastward toward Wheeler Peak, which will be obvious in the distance. The route steepens after about a mile as it begins its final ascent to the summit. Follow the easiest line of ascent (class 2) to the top.

Note: If your vehicle did not make it all the way to Wheeler Pass, you may be tempted to head cross-country from the peak (or the approach ridge) directly back to your vehicle. I do not recommend this; though it can be done, an unpleasant bushwhack will be necessary.

Roundtrip numbers from Wheeler Pass are fewer than 5 miles, with about 1,400 feet of gain.

-WGS84 *Lat: 36.4215 deg N Lon: -115.8105 deg W*

-II, Class 2 via South Ridge from Wheeler Pass *

The summit rocks of Mine Peak

Traction Benchmark (6,496)

A very obscure peak above the prison near Indian Springs, Nevada. There are fine views of the greater Spring Mountains from the summit. Approach as per Ison Peak.

-WGS84 *Lat: 36.4511 deg N Lon: -115.5964 deg W*

-II, Class 2 via North Ridge (from Ison Peak) **

"Ison Peak" (5,856)

A sub-peak of Traction Benchmark. Approach directly from the paved Cold Creek Road near the prison.

-WGS84 Lat: 36.4652 deg N Lon: -115.6027 deg W

-II, Class 2 from Traction Benchmark **

-I, Class 3 via North Ridge **

Indian Ridge (5,498)

An otherwise uninteresting mountain, I will say that the winter views from the summit toward the snow-clad north face of Willow Peak are something special to behold. Oh, and wild horses roam all over the slopes of this mountain! The peak is readily approached directly from the pavement outside of Cold Creek.

-WGS84 Lat: 36.4643 deg N Lon: -115.6717 deg W
*-I, Class 2 via Southeast Face **
*-II, Class 2 via North Ridge **

Indian Benchmark (5,371)

Nice views from the top. The traverse here from Indian Ridge is enjoyable. Expect to see wild horses to and fro! Approach as per Indian Ridge.

-WGS84 Lat: 36.4825 deg N Lon: -115.6606 deg W
*-II, Class 2 via Southwest Ridge ***
*-II, Class 2-3 via South Ridge ***

Indian Ridge – North (5,051)

A dirt road leaving Cold Creek Road south of the peak works around to the interesting-looking south side of the peak. Steep, enjoyable scrambling up the face leads straight to the top.

-WGS84 Lat: 36.5067 deg N Lon: -115.6379 deg W
*-II, Class 2-3 via South Face ***

Indian Springs

The peaks in this subsection are accessed off of US-95 at Indian Springs. They are arranged here generally south-to-north.

Peak 5,475 (5,475)

This peak is a couple miles south of Smith Benchmark. Very pleasant ridge walking encounters one who decides to connect the two.

-WGS84 Lat: 36.4825 deg N Lon: -115.7397 deg W
*-II, Class 1-2 via North Ridge ****
*-II, Class 2 via Northeast Wash **

Peak 5,035 (5,035)

A lot of wild horses and bighorn sheep live in this neat area. The mountain is easily accessed from a dirt road that runs along its western base.

-WGS84 Lat: 36.5052 deg N Lon: -115.7131 deg W
*-II, Class 2 via East Face **
*-II, Class 2 via Northwest Ridge ***

Peak 4,839 (4,839)

This minor peak near Indian Springs can be combined with several others in the area for a pleasant day out.

-WGS84 Lat: 36.5078 deg N Lon: -115.6920 deg W
*-II, Class 2 via Southwest Ridge **

Smith Benchmark (5,267)

This peak is easily accessed from a decent dirt road running along its eastern base.

-WGS84 Lat: 36.5107 deg N Lon: -115.7331 deg W
*-II, Class 2 via South Ridge ***
*-II, Class 2-3 via Northeast Canyons ***

Peak 4,945 (4,945)

The peak has a large circle of dark rocks with an inner circle of white rocks on the flat summit slab.

The northwest slope route is steep, loose and unpleasant. Instead, a traverse to/from Peak 4930 might be recommended. Desert tortoises roam this area.

-WGS84 Lat: 36.5196 deg N Lon: -115.7037 deg W
*-II, Class 2 via Northwest Slope **
-II, Class 2-3 from Peak 4930

Peak 4,930 (4,930)

Interesting route-finding is required to reach the summit of this rugged, well-protected peak. If approaching from the north, a neat broken arch might be encountered. Additionally, a funky "male" symbol constructed from rocks is on the summit.

-WGS84 Lat: 36.5258 deg N Lon: -115.6923 deg W
*-II, Class 2 via Northern Aspect ***
*-II, Class 2-3 via Southwest Ridge ***

"Indian Springs Peak" (4,019)

This is a small, rugged mountain immediately southeast of Indian Springs. A short hike from the dirt access road on the south side of the peak leads one to the top.

-WGS84 Lat: 36.5523 deg N Lon: -115.6614 deg W
*-I, Class 2 via Southeast Ridge **

US-95 near the Clark County Boundary

The peaks in this subsection are accessed via a bumpy dirt road heading south-southwest from US-95, very close to the Clark County boundary. The peaks are arranged here generally south-to-north.

Chris M. nearing the summit of Mount Bulworth, along the east ridge route

"Dead Horse Mountain" (8,579)

With care and good road conditions, a high clearance vehicle can be driven all the way to Big Timber Spring at the base of the peak's north ridge. From there, expect a roundtrip of 5 miles and nearly 3,800 feet of elevation gain. Keep your eyes peeled for wild horses! This is a beautiful and lonely part of the Spring Mountains!

-WGS84 Lat: 36.4165 deg N Lon: -115.9158 deg W
-III, Class 2 via North Ridge **

"Mount Bulworth" (7,755)

Mount Bulworth, as named by a fellow who placed a register on its summit, receives quite a bit more visitation than one might expect. Perhaps that's due to the aesthetic cliffs on the mountain's upper east face which can be clearly seen from US-95 near the Clark/Nye county line.

The east ridge route features some wonderful broken class 3-4 scrambling if you stay on the crest of the upper ridge. As the ridge bends toward the final cliff below the summit, there's an obvious cleft (class 4) that allows access to the top. The northeast ridge, as a descent route, is tedious and uninteresting.

-WGS84 Lat: 36.4525 deg N Lon: -115.9442 deg W

*-II, Class 2 via Northeast Ridge **

*-II, Class 4 via East Ridge ****

Looking northwest to Mount Stirling (distant left) while traversing the long north ridge of Dead Horse Mountain from north of the main summit.

Mount Stirling (8,218)

Lots of petroglyphs can be seen amongst the rocks below the summit. Not only that, but one can catch a glimpse over into Area 51's S-4 facility (at Papoose Lake) from not far below the summit. Compare these views with those from closer Tikaboo Peak! Approach via a forest access road directly off US-95 near the Clark County boundary sign.

-WGS84 Lat: 36.4531 deg N Lon: -115.9687 deg W

*-II, Class 2 via Northeast Ridge ***

Jaybird Benchmark (6,565)

Approach as per Mount Stirling by utilizing the rough-ish forest access road near the county line along US-95.

-WGS84 Lat: 36.4992 deg N Lon: -115.9476 deg W

*-I, Class 4 via Direct Southeast Face ***

US-95 near NV-160

The peaks in this subsection inhabit the northernmost portion of the Spring Mountains. They are arranged generally south-to-north.

"Point of Rocks Peak" (3,550)

At the northern end of the Spring Mountains. Approach directly from US-95.

-WGS84 Lat: 36.5595 deg N Lon: -116.0765 deg W

*-I, Class 2 via Northwest Slope **

"Freddie Peak" (4,032)

An otherwise dull mountain, the last hundred yards to the summit are surprisingly rugged and interesting. This peak is easily bagged directly from Chase Mountain or from US-95 by skirting around Chase Mountain.

-WGS84 Lat: 36.5689 deg N Lon: -116.0495 deg W

*-II, Class 2-3 via North Ridge ***

"Chase Mountain" (3,910)

This is the northernmost peak in the Spring Mountains. It is approached directly from US-95.

-WGS84 Lat: 36.5802 deg N Lon: -116.0514 deg W

*-I, Class 2 via North Gully **

*-I, Class 2 via South Slope **

NV-160 near Pahrump

The peaks in this subsection are arranged south-to-north.

"Mount Reagan" (10,187)

This might be the most obscure high peak in the Spring Mountains. Approach as per Clinton Peak.

-WGS84 Lat: 36.2634 deg N Lon: -115.7187 deg W

*-III, Class 1 via North Ridge ***

"Clinton Peak" (10,160)

Clinton Peak is a fantastic backcountry romp. Parking at road's end in Wallace Canyon, simply head up the steep north slope while aiming for a semi-prominent notch in the cliffs of the upper face. Gain the easy summit ridge (route-finding is key!) via 200 feet of class 3 staircase ledges just east of the notch and then wander to the highpoint. There are lots of cliffs and loose rock on the upper face, so if you're confronted with something harder than class 3, look harder for a better way! For the descent, one can hike down to the Clinton-Reagan saddle and then drop east down a loose gully (two short class 3 spots) into the south fork of Wallace Canyon. Follow Wallace Canyon back to the car.

-WGS84 Lat: 36.2725 deg N Lon: -115.7258 deg W

*-III, Class 3 via North Face ****

Horse Benchmark from the summit of Spring Peak. The view looks south.

Horse Benchmark (8,490)
An obscure peak with surprisingly pleasant views from the top, it sits quite prominently above Pahrump, Nevada.

-WGS84 Lat: 36.3287 deg N Lon: -115.8692 deg W
-II, Class 2 via East Ridge **

"Spring Peak" (8,756)
This obscure peak, easily approached via the Wheeler Well Road off of the Wheeler Pass Road outside of Pahrump, is, at 1,785 feet of prominence, the 13th most prominent peak in Clark County. Despite its obscurity, the commanding views from the aesthetic, bare north summit are even better than the views from the slightly higher, tree-covered south summit.

-WGS84 Lat: 36.3703 deg N Lon: -115.8716 deg W
-II, Class 2 via East Ridge ***

Lovell Canyon

Most of the peaks in this subsection are accessed from Lovell Canyon Road (via NV-160). They are arranged here roughly south-to-north, then west-to-east.

Mesa Benchmark (6,031)

This sprawling mesa is just off the highway near Mountain Springs, Nevada. Leave the highway at Lovell Canyon Road and drive to a point below the mountain's east face. Start from there.

-WGS84 Lat: 36.0401 deg N Lon: -115.5712 deg W

*-I, Class 2-3 via East Face **

On the north summit of Spring Peak,
with the camera looking north through the gap out toward US-95

Peak 4,773 (4,773)

This very obscure peak southwest of Lost Cabin Springs and northwest of Mesa Benchmark is a pleasant, meandering hike by starting at the springs and going up and over the higher ridge on the way to and from the summit.

-WGS84 Lat: 36.0706 deg N Lon: -115.6695 deg W

*-II, Class 2 via East Slope ***

Peak 6,742 (6,742)

This and Peak 6830 (to the east) can be easily combined after driving up (or down) Trout Canyon near Lovell Summit.

-WGS84 Lat: 36.1544 deg N Lon: -115.6604 deg W

*-I, Class 1 via East Slope **

*-I, Class 1-2 via North Slope **

Peak 6,830 (6,830)

This treed peak in upper Trout Canyon is a short and easy hike from the dirt roadway on its north side. The summit doesn't offer much in the way of views.

-WGS84 Lat: 36.1563 deg N Lon: -115.6454 deg W
*-I, Class 1-2 via Northeast Face **
*-I, Class 1-2 via West Slope **

"Mount Alexander" (7,424)

More wild than smaller Mount Hualapai to the north, Mount Alexander (with 617 feet of prominence) is the last high mountain of the southern Spring Mountains until you get to the Potosi Mountain area. With tedious brush, a small, hidden spring, fantastic seasonal wildflowers and pretty decent summit views, this obscure peak is a seldom-visited non-classic. Approached as per Dead Badger Peak.

-WGS84 Lat: 36.1485 deg N Lon: -115.6141 deg W
*-II, Class 2 via Northeast Ridge from Mount Hualapai **
*-II, Class 2 via North Ridge **

"Mount Hualapai" (7,194)

Mount Hualapai and Mount Alexander lies due south of Harris Mountain. The massif forms the south end of the "high peaks" region of the Spring Mountains. This wilderness-laden portion of the range is relatively pristine and certainly less visited. Approach as per Dead Badger Peak.

-WGS84 Lat: 36.1621 deg N Lon: -115.6048 deg W
*-II, Class 1 via trail from Lovell Summit **

"Dead Badger Peak" (7,417)

The name of this peak was inspired by a dead badger I saw on US-93 across from the Arrow Canyon Range the morning after hiking up this small peak. Although the peak is minor (roughly 400 feet of prominence) the views from the top, as well as while hiking along the brushy-at-times south ridge, are nice. A good dirt road leads to Lovell Summit from Lovell Canyon Road.

-WGS84 Lat: 36.1740 deg N Lon: -115.6064 deg W
*-I, Class 1-2 via South Ridge from Lovell Summit **

"Bootleg Spring Peak" (5,954)

This peak sits just south of Bootleg Spring and northwest of Mountain Spring Benchmark, due north of Mountain Springs.

-WGS84 Lat: 36.0438 deg N Lon: -115.5104 deg W
*-I, Class 1-2 via Northwest Slope **

"The Roasting Pit" (6,427)

The decent dirt road that ends at the northwestern base of the peak is accessed directly from Lovell Canyon Road. The northeast slope route is the more pleasant of the two routes mentioned here.

-WGS84 Lat: 36.0703 deg N Lon: -115.5187 deg W
*-II, Class 1-2 via Northeast Slope ***
*-II, Class 1-2 via Northwest Slope **

"Peak Four" (6,902)

From the dirt road used to access The Roasting Pit, it's a simple affair to continue up the wash to the southeast slope and slog up. This and The Roasting Pit can be combines in a casual half-day.

-WGS84 Lat: 36.0831 deg N Lon: -115.5237 deg W
*-II, Class 2 via Southeast Slope **

"Profile Point" (6,893)

This not-great peak (with not-great views) has its summit hidden in a clump of trees. South Spring, west of the summit, flows most of the year.

-WGS84 Lat: 36.0964 deg N Lon: -115.5290 deg W
*-II, Class 2 via North Ridge * /*
*-II, Class 2 via South Slope **

"Cactus Flower Point" (7,493)

This highpoint of a minor subrange behind Red Rock has 1047' of prominence and a summit register placed by the prolific John Vitz. From the summit, there are good views of the backside of Red Rock.

-WGS84 Lat: 36.1128 deg N Lon: -115.5378 deg W
*-III, Class 2 via Northeast Ridge from Rainbow Point ***
*-III, Class 2 via South Ridge ***

"Rainbow Point" (7,444)

This peak has excellent views. The north ridge can be gained directly from the segment of Rocky Gap Road west of Red Rock Summit. From the summit, it's easy and pleasant enough to traverse the ridge south and bag Cactus Flower Point and Profile Point.

-WGS84 Lat: 36.1213 deg N Lon: -115.5393 deg W
*-II, Class 2 via North Ridge ***
*-II, Class 2 via Southeast Ridge ***

"Pepper Peak" (7,557)

This minor peak sits just north of the western segment of Rocky Gap Road, west of Red Rock Summit. The summit has a register and nice views.

-WGS84 Lat: 36.1364 deg N Lon: -115.5400 deg W

*-II, Class 2 via Southwest Slope & Ridge ***

"Tio Grande" (7,703)

This nice peak lies slightly northwest of Red Rock Summit and can be climbed via the south ridge from Pepper Peak (to the south). Access is via the western segment of Rocky Gap Road, west of Red Rock Summit.

A pleasant loop can be done by descending the southwest ridge of the subpeak south of the main summit. This ridge has short bits of excellent trail (and a nice dry camp spot for several tents at the 6900-ft level).

-WGS84 Lat: 36.1465 deg N Lon: -115.5405 deg W

*-II, Class 2 via South Ridge from Pepper Peak ***

*-II, Class 2 via Southwest Ridge ***

NV-160 near Mountain Springs

The peaks in this subsection are arranged here generally south-to-north.

Potosi Mountain (8,514)

Though the described route doesn't take you past it, the remnants of the Carol Lombard plane crash of 1942 isn't far below the summit of the mountain. Lombard was Clark Gable's fiancé at the time of her death.

-WGS84 Lat: 35.9656 deg N Lon: -115.5015 deg W

*-III, Class 2-3 via West Ridge ***

"North Potosi Peak" (7,418)

This, the detached north summit of Potosi Mountain, has 598 feet of prominence and excellent views of the region stretching from Castle Peaks to Telescope Peak to Charleston Peak and portions of Red Rock. The peak has two east ridges. A roundtrip via the northern of the two east ridges, which is approached at its toe just off SR-160, entails an effort of 3.5 miles, 2,900 feet of gain and some class 3 scrambling.

-WGS84 Lat: 35.9804 deg N Lon: -115.4890 deg W

*-II, Class 3 via East Ridge ****

"Bluebird Peak" (7,188)

This is Pas Rump's neighbor to the south. It is an impressive peak that is well guarded by steep cliff bands. Bluebird Peak is most easily approached via a dirt road and short off-trail hike to the saddle between it and Pas Rump (from the east), then by following the rugged and sometimes tedious northeast ridge over several false summits to the highpoint. Cliffs guard the highpoint, but a convenient ledge system works left of the cliffs and angles up to easier ground (via a short class 3 face) leading to the summit.

-WGS84 Lat: 35.9783 deg N Lon: -115.5552 deg W

*-II, Class 3 via Northeast Ridge ****

On the east ridge of North Potosi Peak.
The visible road is SR-160, snaking its way toward Las Vegas.

"Pas Rump" (7,291)
I once climbed this peak during a late winter snow storm, allowing for a dreamy whiteout experience on the higher, north summit.

-WGS84 Lat: 35.9881 deg N Lon: -115.5455 deg W
-II, Class 3 via Southeast Slope & Face **

"Claret Peak" (6,653)
This quick peak is southwest of Mountain Springs and northeast of Pas Rump. The south ridge is easily accessed from the dirt road east of Potosi Pass. Be mindful of some private property in this area.

-WGS84 Lat: 35.9989 deg N Lon: -115.5220 deg W
-II, Class 2 via South Ridge **

"Gap Peak" (5,826)
A minor peak with a touch of fun scrambling and good views. It is approached directly from the shoulder of NV-160.

-WGS84 Lat: 36.0053 deg N Lon: -115.4833 deg W
-I, Class 2 via Northwest Face **

Bluebird Peak's slightly lower south summit from immediately below the main summit

"Misty Mountain" (6,456)
Above Mountain Springs and close to Pas Rump. Approach directly from the highway.

-WGS84 Lat: 36.0107 deg N Lon: -115.5137 deg W
*-I, Class 2 via North Ridge **

"Shaft Peak" (5,954)
Named for a mine tunnel midway up the mountain.

-WGS84 Lat: 36.0260 deg N Lon: -115.5122 deg W
*-II, Class 1-2 via West Ridge **

Goodsprings

The peaks in this subsection are accessed via Goodsprings, Nevada (highway 53). They are arranged here generally south-to-north.

Bonanza Hill (3,777)
Out there by Little Devil Peak.

-WGS84 Lat: 35.7758 deg N Lon: -115.5441 deg W
*-I, Class 2 via West Face **

"Whale Peak" (4,448)

Whale Peak is named for the mine on its southwest side. The peak, short but steep and crumbly, is easily accessed from the paved Sandy Valley Road. Beware of rattlesnakes in spring!

-WGS84 Lat: 35.8103 deg N Lon: -115.5253 deg W
-I, Class 2 via East Ridge **

"The Wild Horse" (4,500)

Named for the two dozen wild horses I saw near the base of the mountain one August morning as I set out to hike it.

-WGS84 Lat: 35.7818 deg N Lon: -115.4340 deg W
-I, Class 2 via East Ridge *

Table Mountain (5,152)

Hike the service road directly from the pavement just outside of Goodsprings.

-WGS84 Lat: 35.8054 deg N Lon: -115.4862 deg W
-I, Class 2 from service road *

Shenandoah Peak (5,864)

This is a lame peak with a rather tranquil summit. The mountain is easily approached from just outside of Goodsprings.

-WGS84 Lat: 35.8503 deg N Lon: -115.5095 deg W
-I, Class 2 via Northeast Ridge **

Ragged Peak (5,036)

For whatever reason, some maps show this as a named peak and others don't. The peak is most easily reached beyond Goodsprings, where a marginal dirt road passes along the northern base of the mountain.

-WGS84 Lat: 35.8730 deg N Lon: -115.5842 deg W
-I, Class 2 via Northwest Ridge *

Green Monster Benchmark (4,851)

This is a rugged peak near Sandy Valley and above the Green Monster Mine.

-WGS84 Lat: 35.9011 deg N Lon: -115.6291 deg W
-II, Class 2 via SW Gully *
-II, Class 2-3 via West Ridge **

"Jagged Peak" (5,167)

Jagged Peak, a few miles northeast of Green Monster Mine, is a nice peak with possibilities for interesting scrambling routes. The peak has 591' of prominence.

-WGS84 Lat: 35.9024 deg N Lon: -115.5855 deg W

*-II, Class 2 via South Ridge ****

"Ridge View Peak-East" (6,352)

This minor peak with excellent views sits a few miles south of Potosi Mountain. The summit is just a short stroll from the end of a good service road outside of Goodsprings, Nevada.

-WGS84 Lat: 35.8954 deg N Lon: -115.4967 deg W

*-I, Class 1-2 via South Slope ***

"Ridge View Peak" (6,715)

After hiking (or driving) to the end of the service road which accesses some antennae immediately south of Ridge View Peak – East, a very pleasant ridge walk leads to this nice, sublime highpoint.

-WGS84 Lat: 35.9066 deg N Lon: -115.5251 deg W

*-II, Class 2 via Southeast Ridge from Ridge View Peak-East ****

Potosi Mountain – South (8,170)

A nice, steep hike up the service road starting outside of Goodsprings leads to a great overlook of the Goodsprings/Sandy Valley area.

-WGS84 Lat: 35.9440 deg N Lon: -115.4972 deg W

*-II, Class 1 via Service Road ***

I-15

The peaks in this subsection are accessed off of I-15, south of Jean, Nevada. They are arranged south-to-north.

Devil Peak (5,881)

What first intrigued me about Devil Peak was *Desert Summits* author Andy Zdon commenting that the register hadn't been signed in years when he'd visited. Of course, by the time I got there it was jam-packed full of names!

-WGS84 Lat: 35.6976 deg N Lon: -115.4538 deg W

*-II, Class 2 via Southeast Ridge ***

Lead Mountain (4,614)

I imagine more imaginable folks are utilizing an easier way to get to the summit than the way I found. My route was extremely rugged, rather exposed in places, and involved intricate route-finding to keep it reasonable. On the summit of this seldom-visited peak, I found a cairn but no register.

-WGS84 Lat: 35.7183 deg N Lon: -115.4986 deg W

*-II, Class 3-4 via East Ridge ****

Little Devil Peak (5,576)
Once spent some time watching a large tarantula in a canyon on the north side of the peak. Approach via the road to the Christmas Mine. In recent years, it has been in pretty decent shape.

-WGS84 Lat: 35.7378 deg N Lon: -115.4920 deg W
*-I, Class 2 via East Face ***
*-I, Class 2 via South Ridge ***

Pearce Ferry Rapid, at the far eastern edge of Lake Mead's south shore

Lake Mead National Recreation Area

The Lake Mead area is a wonderful, raw desert environment that receives far less hiking attention than it deserves. Then again, that's a major part of its appeal.

Lake Mead, a sprawling manmade lake (the largest reservoir in the United States, incidentally) above Hoover Dam, which is outside of Boulder City, Nevada, offers 550 miles of shoreline. Below Hoover Dam, the Colorado River and Lake Mohave offer 250 miles of shoreline. The relatively seldom-visited peaks guard the shorelines and offer motivating solitude and inspiring, intense scenery.

Beyond the mountains, the area offers wonderful geologic displays with incredible coloration, fantastic spring wildflowers, magical canyons (such as the tight and twisting Anniversary Narrows), lush oases, and lots of mining history, including the St. Thomas ghost town, which was flooded under the rising waters of the then-newly-created Lake Mead. The remains of the town have now surfaced due to the lake's receding water caused by a sustained drought situation. The National Park Service has since constructed a fine trail to explore the foundations of the old town. Lake Mead National Recreation Area (NRA) hosts a number of developed and backcountry camping and lodging opportunities along the lakeshore, as well as countless sweet spots for primitive camping outside of the Lake Mead area.

This section not only covers peaks within Lake Mead NRA, which falls under the management of the National Park Service, but also those peaks, such as Jumbo Peak and Bonelli Peak, that lie outside the park on Bureau of Land Management land but are close enough to the lake to be considered in the "Lake Mead area."

Matthew H. downclimbing the south chimney of Jumbo Peak

What you find here is just the tip of the iceberg. This area has countless high-quality, obscure peaks waiting to be climbed. I've climbed many dozens of them. The views and the solitude draw me back time and again.

Gold Butte Area

To get to Gold Butte from Las Vegas (or points north along I-15), head toward Mesquite, Nevada. Eight miles south of Mesquite, you will come to the signed Riverside/Bunkerville exit (exit 112). Exit, and follow the paved road (NV-170) south three miles, passing over a bridge spanning the Virgin River in the process. Immediately after the bridge, turn right onto a paved road heading west/southwest. This road is known as Gold Butte Road. It heads to Whitney Pockets. A network of (mostly-) good dirt roads beyond Whitney Pockets takes you deep into the middle-of-nowhere.

The peaks are arranged here generally south-to-north, by point of access from the main drag through the Gold Butte area.

As it turns out, most of the peaks in this subsection are *not* within Lake Mead National Recreation Area. I have chosen to include it in the Lake Mead section due to its proximity to the greater Lake Mead area.

Gold Cross Peak (3,414)

This obscure and hard to access, interesting peak boasts nearly 1500' of prominence. On our visit, the register hadn't been signed in nearly a decade.

While a cross-country approach could be utilized after miles of rough dirt roads from Gold Butte, a far easier approach is from Scanlon Bay via boat. From there, route-finding can get you to the summit via class 2-3 terrain. More difficult terrain lurks nearby!

-WGS84 Lat: 36.0721 deg N Lon: -114.1727 deg W

*-II, Class 2-3 via Northern Aspect ****

Scanlon Hill (1,400)

If you've already dragged yourself all the way out here (for Gold Cross Peak, presumably), you might as well grab Scanlon Hill as an easy bonus. It takes all of five minutes of hiking from the shores of Scanlon Bay.

The hill is just northeast of Gold Cross Peak.

-WGS84 Lat: 36.0908 deg N Lon: -114.1487 deg W

*-I, Class 1 via South Slope **

Bonelli Peak (5,334)

Bonelli Peak is an otherwise uninteresting peak that happens to have stunning (some describe it as "classic") views from its summit. The views extend across the eastern edge of Lake Mead, to the Spring Mountains, into the sandstone wonderlands at the edge of the Colorado Plateau of northwestern Arizona at the Grand Wash Cliffs, and beyond. They are really quite magnificent.

In a very obscure area, Bonelli Peak is one of the most remote peaks to be found. It lies about six miles southwest of Jumbo Peak, on the edge of Lake Mead near Gold Butte. Upon leaving the pavement and getting onto dirt road on the drive in to this peak, expect it to take considerably longer just to make it to Ruby Spring, at the base of the mountain, than the roundtrip hike to the peak will take. The *drive* to this peak is a desert classic. A good approach map is highly recommended.

Follow the directions given for Mica Peak to the site of Gold Butte. Once at Gold Butte, continue south on the main road (Scanlon Road) past the corrals to a fork at 3.5 miles. Stay left and continue 5.3 miles to a minor side road on the right. Take the minor road into Garnet Valley (and ultimately, Bonelli Peak). After a mile or less, most will want to park. The brush is bad and vehicles tend to get scratched up badly.

Whether by foot, wheel or burro, continue toward Ruby Spring. Vehicles fortunate enough to make it to the spring will need to park somewhere around there in a previously disturbed area or wash bottom. When I was there one spring, the approach roads were badly washed out around Garnet Valley, requiring several interesting stream crossings in a Jeep Wrangler.

Hike south from Ruby Spring on an old dirt track. At a point roughly north of Bonelli Peak, leave the dirt track and head south up to the ridge above. From the ridge, continue south a bit, gaining another minor ridge leading to the summit.

The roundtrip from Ruby Spring is about 3 miles, with perhaps 1,000 feet of elevation gain.

-WGS84 Lat: 36.1488 deg N Lon: -114.2492 deg W

-II, Class 2 via Garnet Valley to Bonelli Peak **

Rattlesnake Peak (4,931)

This is a remote peak deep in the Gold Butte backcountry. Oddly enough, it gets a fair amount of visitation, as evidenced by the summit register.

With a high clearance 4WD vehicle, one can drive to the Nevada Mica Mine on the southwest slopes of the peak, making for a very short outing.

-WGS84 Lat: 36.1951 deg N Lon: -114.2154 deg W

-I, Class 2 via Southwest Slope **

"Packard Peak" (5,604)

Named in honor of Bob Packard. This is an easy bonus after Jumbo Peak.

-WGS84 Lat: 36.2017 deg N Lon: -114.1733 deg W

-II, Class 2 via Northwest Slope **

The dashed line is where the route is in view, while the dotted line is where the route goes out of view behind rocks. Note the GPS track on the map.

Jumbo Peak (5,761)

Seen by some desert peak enthusiasts as unclimbable and by some alien enthusiasts as promising (there's a story there), Jumbo Peak is an intriguing mountain indeed.

Though the slopes of Jumbo Peak are class 2, the summit block, a huge, sheer-to-overhanging mass of granite, is intimidating and appears to be impenetrable. As it turns out, there are several possible, and feasible, routes to the top.

Follow the directions given for Mica Peak to the 50-gallon drum in Cedar Basin. Turn onto the dirt road adjacent to the 50-gallon drum and head south. Jumbo Peak first comes into view about now; it is to the south and the summit block can easily be seen. From a distance, the summit block appears quite a bit smaller than it actually is.

Follow the road two miles until you find yourself near the base of the peak. There is no established parking area, so park wherever you can find room in a previously disturbed area or wash bottom. In good, dry conditions, Jumbo Peak's base can be reached in a passenger car. In less than optimal conditions, a 4WD with high clearance will probably be needed.

For any of the routes described here, roundtrip numbers are about 2 miles, with 1,000 feet of gain.

From the base of the peak, head straight up class 2 slopes to the summit block. Some heavy brush will probably be encountered near the base of the block.

For the West-Northwest Chimney route, ascend an 80-foot class 4 chimney with loose chockstone obstructions to the top. From the top of the chimney, follow the obvious exit under an overhang and around a corner then do an exposed step-across move and immediately move right into a slot. Climb 15 feet up the slot (class 3) then cut left up another slot (also class 3) for 15 feet. Above you is a short but exposed (and rather unprotectable) face (YDS 5.3). Scramble 10 feet to the diagonal-right across the face to easier ground leading to the summit ridge.

Note: A class 2-3 variation can be found by seeking out a tunnel under the rocks at the top of the initial chimney. The tunnel can be crawled and scrambled through for about 30 feet before it dumps you out in the open slot mentioned below in the S Chimney route. I have not personally done this variation, however, partners of mine did. This variation makes the WNW chimney route class 4 overall.

For the West Chimney route: From the base of the West-Northwest Chimney, traverse about 50 feet over class 2-3 terrain to the west side of the summit block. Do not drop onto lower terrain. Look for a strange, short, little chimney and head up. The chimney is class 4, and requires a couple of acrobatic moves, followed by short tunnel "stomach-slide" move to an exposed ramp on the other side. Traverse south a short distance along the ramp to an exposed YDS 5.3 moderately high-angle face. The face can be protected by anchoring a couple of nearby small trees (brush, really), or you can bypass the face altogether and fight through the nagging, thick brush on the right side of the face and struggle your way to the top. (You should know what I'm talking about when you get there.) From the top of the aforementioned face, follow the path of least resistance upward and to the left over varying class 1-3 terrain to the summit. Though the brush is a drag and the exposure on parts of this route is worse than on some of the other routes, this is the least technical way to the summit.

For the South Chimney route: Look for a 100-foot chimney on the south side of the summit block. The chimney is steep, but reasonably unexposed, and loaded with a few flakey, awful chockstones requiring gymnastics or excellent stemming techniques to surmount. Like much of the rock on the summit block, the granite is of poor quality and I would not trust it. The crux of this chimney is found 20 feet from the bottom, where a YDS 5.1 acrobatic move is required to get around a weird, tilted, and untrustworthy chockstone. Questionable handholds can be found on the flaky, crumbling, hollow-sounding rock making up the chimney. Once above the crux, the remainder of the chimney is class 3-4. From the top of the chimney, you'll find yourself in an open slot with walls on either side. The left (west) wall requires 3rd class scrambling to surmount. The east wall is much more difficult. Once the west wall is surmounted, follow the path of least resistance upward and to the right (north) over varying class 1-3 terrain to the summit. Due to the large number of huge boulders lying all around the base of much of the summit block, this route is probably the easiest and fastest to approach from the base of the mountain.

For the East Face Crack System route: On the northeast side of the summit block, look for a crack system. Looking at the summit block from the approach at the base of the mountain, this crack system is apparent and appears (from a distance, at least) to be a possible and viable route. Possible, yes; viable, yes; easy, no. Use common sense to work through the route. The crux is found at the top of a sort of dihedral where a tricky left (southeast) traverse requiring holding onto a narrow groove in the rock above you, hand-to-hand inching your way over to a ledge, then pulling yourself up onto the ledge is required. Once the ledge is gained, head southeast over class 1 terrain, then look for a class 3-4 move bringing you up to the summit ridge, which is to your immediate right. Follow the summit ridge to the top.

Note: A variation exists that makes this route quite a lot easier (YDS 5.6-5.7). From the top of the obvious dihedral-like feature on the route, avoid the crux (on the left) and head to the right instead. An exposed 5th class move or two will put you at the base of the YDS 5.3 crux move on the West-Northwest Chimney route.

-WGS84 Lat: 36.2065 deg N Lon: -114.1808 deg W

*-II, Class 4 via West Chimney ***

*-II, YDS 5.1 via South Chimney ***

-II, YDS 5.3 via West-Northwest Chimney ****
-II, YDS 5.10 via East Face Crack System **

"Playground Peak" (5,054)
Two crags battle for the title of "highest." One's somewhat hard to get up; the other's harder. Park at the base of the peak and have a blast figuring your way to the top.

-WGS84 Lat: 36.2325 deg N Lon: -114.1619 deg W
-II, YDS 5.2 via Southwest Face ****

The summit rocks of Jumbo Peak. Here, you're looking up at the east face.

Mica Peak (5,760)
Mica Peak sits a few miles north of Jumbo Peak in the obscure, seldom-visited Gold Butte area of southern Nevada. Unlike its classic neighbor, Mica Peak is a straightforward ascent from any direction.

To get to the peak, follow Gold Butte Road for 20 miles as it winds its way toward the south. Along the way, you will note Virgin Peak, the large peak that towers over the southern end of Mesquite, toward the east. At around 20 miles, you will reach an area known as Whitney Pockets, a very interesting spot characterized by an abundance of Aztec sandstone formations. On weekends, the area is frequented by RV's and ORV enthusiasts.

Just past Whitney Pockets, the paved road ends and there is a fork. The left fork will take you toward the Virgin Peak trailhead, while the right fork (a Backcountry Byway in surprisingly good shape) takes you into the Gold Butte area. Take the right fork 9.3 miles to another fork. Staying right, continue 7.2 miles to yet another fork. Again staying right, continue 2.6 miles to a road junction and the remnants of the old mining community of Gold Butte.

The remains of Gold Butte lie along the northern base of a small mountain also called Gold Butte. Continue on the main road past the corrals, etc. Just past Gold Butte, as you pass the west/northwest ridge of Gold Butte (the small mountain), you'll cross a cattle guard. Continuing on the main road from the cattle guard, turn onto the third dirt road on the left.

Follow this decent dirt road about 3 miles into Cedar Basin until you come to a sort of dirt road intersection. From the intersection, look for a landmark white 50-gallon drum. From this point, Mica Peak should be visible as the highest peak about two miles to the north/northeast.

Ignore the adjacent dirt road that heads to the south (and toward Jumbo Peak) from the 50-gallon drum, and work your way in and left to a point close to Mica Peak. There are a number of minor roads throughout this area. Park in a previously disturbed area or wash bottom when you feel you're reasonably close.

In good, dry conditions, this approach can be done in a passenger car. In less than optimal conditions, a 4WD with high clearance will probably be needed.

From wherever you parked, head north cross-country to the peak.

Roundtrip mileage and gain will vary, depending on starting location, but expect no more than 3-5 miles, with roughly 1,000 feet of gain.

-WGS84 Lat: 36.2662 deg N Lon: -114.1563 deg W

*-II, Class 2 via South Slope ***

Gold Butte (5,049)

Approach this peak directly from the old Gold Butte town site for either route. See the Mica Peak driving directions.

-WGS84 Lat: 36.2730 deg N Lon: -114.1847 deg W

*-I, Class 2 via old mining road ***

*-II, Class 4 via Direct Northwest Face ****

Peak 5,003 (5,003)

This is the southernmost major peak in the high and imposing Tramp Ridge massif. The north ridge is narrow and exposed in places.

-WGS84 Lat: 36.3144 deg N Lon: -114.1899 deg W

*-II, Class 2 via North Ridge ****

Five years after my first visit to Jumbo, I returned with Matthew Holliman, Adam Helman and Bob Packard (seen here on the summit in December 2009). The view looks north.

"South Tramp Point" (5,194)

South Tramp Point is the rugged and interesting peak between Tramp Ridge and Peak 5003. A seldom-signed register is found in the summit cairn.

-WGS84 Lat: 36.3239 deg N Lon: -114.1909 deg W
*-II, Class 2-3 via Northeast Gully from Northeast Saddle ***
*-II, Class 2-3 via Southeast Ridge ***

Tramp Ridge (5,262)

Although there are many cliff bands guarding access to the summit from the east, it's not difficult from a distance to piece together a reasonable line that heads directly up the face toward the summit. The views from the top are righteous.

Tramp Ridge has 1408' of prominence.
-WGS84 Lat: 36.3345 deg N Lon: -114.1813 deg W
*-II, Class 1-2 via East Face ****
*-II, Class 2 via South Ridge ***

"Iceberg Peak" (2,365)

This delightful and interesting peak, accessed from Devil's Cove after miles of rough dirt roads, hovers above Iceberg Canyon. One in our party nearly stepped on a baby rattlesnake on the descent from this peak.

-WGS84 Lat: 36.1634 deg N Lon: -114.0863 deg W
*-II, Class 2 via North Slope ***

"Condor Peak" (4,334)
Condor Peak lies just north of the good dirt road north of Summit Spring (worth a visit, by the way) and Summit Pass. As my partner and I approached the summit one winter afternoon, we startled two condors sitting on the highpoint.

-WGS84 Lat: 36.2971 deg N Lon: -114.1157 deg W
*-I, Class 2 via South Ridge ****

Peak 3,068 (3,068)
This minor ridge is northeast of Red Rock Springs and southeast of Black Butte, from which the peak is quickly approached. Anticipate some route-finding to keep any routes up the west face reasonable.

-WGS84 Lat: 36.4807 deg N Lon: -114.1836 deg W
*-II, Class 2-3 via North Ridge ***
*-II, Class 3-4 via West Face ***

Peak 3,123 (3,123)
This is the next peak northeast of Peak 3068. The two can be combined for a nice couple of hours of hiking and scrambling. The fastest route to the summit is up and over the many small bumps east of Falling Man.

-WGS84 Lat: 36.5030 deg N Lon: -114.1665 deg W
*-II, Class 2 via South Ridge ***
*-II, Class 2-3 via West Face ***

Black Butte (2,772)
From the designated parking area and trailhead on the southwest side of the peak (accessible by high clearance vehicle), any route will do.

-WGS84 Lat: 36.4979 deg N Lon: -114.1982 deg W
*-I, Class 2 via South Face **

North Shore

The peaks in this subsection are accessed from Northshore Road (NV-167). They are arranged here roughly west-to-east, by point of access from Northshore Road.

Boxcar Rock (1,212)
Good dirt road access from the north makes this a short (but unpleasant) hike along the shore to the tiny summit on the edge of the lake.

-WGS84 Lat: 36.1191 deg N Lon: -114.7819 deg W
*-I, Class 2 from the north **

Black Mesa (2,210)

Grab this one right from Northshore Road. The basalt talus hopping on the mesa is a touch tedious but the views are nice.

-WGS84 Lat: 36.1566 deg N Lon: -114.7655 deg W
*-I, Class 2 via Northwest Face **

"Mud Tower" (2,420)

Mud Tower is the lowest and westernmost of the trio of aesthetic and colorful mud crags north of northwest of Black Mesa.

-WGS84 Lat: 36.2106 deg N Lon: -114.8039 deg W
*-II, Class 2 via Northeast Face ***

"Mud Crag" (2,492)

Mud Crag is the southeastern of the three mud crags in this area. The entire cluster is comprised of loose but interesting rock features.

-WGS84 Lat: 36.2043 deg N Lon: -114.7866 deg W
*-II, Class 2 via Northwest Ridge ***
*-II, Class 2 via Southeast Ridge ***

"Mud Hill" (2,540)

Mud Hill and the other two nearby mud crags form an interesting cluster north of Northshore Road, northwest of Black Mesa. Parking along the highway, the cluster is quickly approached via the wash that runs along the east side of the peaks.

-WGS84 Lat: 36.2183 deg N Lon: -114.7950 deg W
*-II, Class 2 via Southeast Ridge ***
*-II, Class 2 via Southwest Slope ***

"Blowing Peak" (2,171)

This minor peak can be hiked directly from Northshore Road. You *can* park in the gated parking area at the base of the peak too, though you might find yourself locked in, as I once was!

-WGS84 Lat: 36.1764 deg N Lon: -114.7452 deg W
*-I, Class 1-2 from Northshore Road **

"After-Work Peak" (2,358)

Just one of dozens of short, easy peaks off Northshore Road that can be tackled in a quick afternoon after one gets off work (or play) in Las Vegas.

-WGS84 Lat: 36.1875 deg N Lon: -114.7266 deg W
*-I, Class 2 via North Slope **

"Knife Peak" (2,564)

This and Knob Peak can be combined in a short afternoon outing. Perfect for an after-work hike.

-WGS84 Lat: 36.2041 deg N Lon: -114.7500 deg W
*-I, Class 3 via East Ridge ****

"Knob Peak" (2,558)

This and nearby Knife Peak are fun, short scrambles near Northshore Road.

-WGS84 Lat: 36.2028 deg N Lon: -114.7216 deg W
*-I, Class 3-4 via West Ridge **

"Slabs Peak" (2,492)

A short hike with some fun scrambling.

-WGS84 Lat: 36.2098 deg N Lon: -114.7334 deg W
*-I, Class 3-4 via Southeast Face ***

Peak 2,159 (2,159)

This is a nice peak with good views of Callville Bay Marina. The peak is just south of After-Work Peak, sandwiched between West End Wash and Callville Wash. It's a worthwhile bonus peak after doing nearby Peak 1804.

-WGS84 Lat: 36.1765 deg N Lon: -114.7225 deg W
*-II, Class 2 via East Slopes ***

Peak 1,804 (1,804)

From the primitive dirt road that follows Callville Wash south from Northshore Road, the peak is just a short hike.

-WGS84 Lat: 36.1755 deg N Lon: -114.7050 deg W
*-I, Class 1-2 via Northeast Slope **

"Capuchin Peak" (2,831)

It has been suggested that this peak be called 'Anniversary Mine Peak'. Initial approach is as per Endless Peak and Anniversary Narrows.

-WGS84 Lat: 36.2227 deg N Lon: -114.7082 deg W
*- II, Class 2-3 via Northeast Slope ***
*-II, Class 3-4 via East Face and Ridge (with numerous variations possible) ***

"Anniversary Narrows Peak" (3,073)

Hike through Anniversary Narrows and look for a suitable place to start up on your right. Choose carefully.

-WGS84 Lat: 36.2284 deg N Lon: -114.6838 deg W
*-II, YDS 5.0 via West Face Direct ***

Sustained, steep scrambling on the east face and ridge of Capuchin Peak.

"Endless Peak" (3,414)

Fun hiking and scrambling on good limestone slabs. You might as well visit Anniversary Narrows while you're right there too. The peak is best approached via a weakness found just inside the Narrows on the left (as you look up-canyon).

-WGS84 Lat: 36.2312 deg N Lon: -114.7076 deg W

-II, Class 2 via Southeast Ridge ***

The view east to Anniversary Narrows Peak from the slopes of Capuchin Peak

"Bowl View Peak" (2,290)

This forgettable peak offers a good view of Bowl of Fire from its summit.

-WGS84 Lat: 36.2250 deg N Lon: -114.6509 deg W

*-I, Class 2 via Southwest Slope **

"Polytick Peak" (2,661)

This minor but good-looking peak is immediately north of Mine View Peak. We picked up three ticks while hiking the small mountain.

-WGS84 Lat: 36.2176 deg N Lon: -114.6827 deg W

*-I, Class 2 via Northeast Face ***

"Mine View Peak" (2,132)

This trivial lump (262' of prominence) is just southeast of Anniversary Narrows and approached from the same dirt road (staying right when the road bends left toward the Narrows).

-WGS84 Lat: 36.2110 deg N Lon: -114.6841 deg W

*-I, Class 2 via Southeast Face **

Peak 2,421 (2,421)

This peak is closely northeast of Bowl View Peak. This and the several other minor lumps in this vicinity can be linked-up for a highly enjoyable lumpbagging fest!

-WGS84 Lat: 36.2296 deg N Lon: -114.6430 deg W

*-I, Class 2 via East Slopes **

Peak 2,474 (2,474)

This anonymous peak has a register on the summit. The peak makes for a worthwhile objective while heading in or out of Bowl of Fire.

-WGS84 Lat: 36.2269 deg N Lon: -114.6611 deg W
*-I, Class 2 via South Slope **
*-I, Class 2 via North Slope ***

Peak 3,537 (3,537)

This, one of the highest peaks in the Bowl of Fire area, is a largely loose and unpleasant hike. Approach the peak via the valley to the southeast then head up via a weakness on the east face, south of the summit. Expect some steep and exposed scrambling on the way up to the south slope.

-WGS84 Lat: 36.2507 deg N Lon: -114.6750 deg W
*-II, Class 3 via South Slope & East Face **

"Murphys Peak" (2,696)

A nice-looking peak right off Northshore Road. Vegas locals named it for local hiker Susan Murphy. Poor DB got sick once while climbing this thing on a hot summer afternoon.

-WGS84 Lat: 36.2187 deg N Lon: -114.6730 deg W
*-II, Class 3 via full Southeast Ridge ***

Hamblin Mountain – West (3,294)

This is Hamblin Mountain's more rugged west summit. That are equally good views from here, and there's some fun scrambling to be had just before the top.

-WGS84 Lat: 36.1761 deg N Lon: -114.6517 deg W
*-III, Class 2 via North Ridge ***
*-III, Class 2-3 from Hamblin Mountain ***

Hamblin Mountain (3,310)

Hamblin Mountain is a locally prominent peak that happens to have stunning views of Lake Mead from its summit. The mountain is within the Pinto Valley Wilderness of Lake Mead NRA.

Follow the directions given for Hamblin Butte. From the parking pull-out, cross the highway and drop into the prominent wash on the other side. Follow the wash up-stream for about a mile until you encounter Cottonwood Spring. There may or may not be water, but expect to find two large cottonwood trees there…they'll stand out.

Continue up the wash past the spring, scrambling up a short obstacle just past the trees. Continuing along, you'll see a ridge dead ahead. Aim for its northwest toe. Reaching the toe, continue along in the wash, which is known as Cottonwood Wash, heading south while following the western side of the ridge. Just past a narrow portion of the wash, you'll encounter a fork near the southwestern toe of the ridge. Take the right (west) fork. Aim for a low saddle on the skyline, about a half mile away.

From the saddle, work your way into a prominent wash to the west. Continuing up-stream, taking right forks as encountered, after about 0.3 mile you'll encounter a box canyon and a fork. Climb a short dry waterfall on the right side of the box and continue on a good use trail to a saddle on the summit ridge above. From the saddle, head west along the summit ridge for a few minutes until you reach the summit. Great views await the intrepid traveler!

The roundtrip involves about 1,400 feet of elevation gain over 6-8 miles.

-WGS84 Lat: 36.1787 deg N Lon: -114.6451 deg W
-III, Class 2 from Cottonwood Wash ***

"Hamblin Butte" (2,833)

Not to be confused with nearby Hamblin Mountain, Hamblin Butte is a minor volcanic peak that overlooks Northshore Road in Lake Mead NRA. It sits about a mile northwest of Hamblin Mountain and lies within the Pinto Valley Wilderness Area.

Follow the directions given for Cathedral Peak to the SR-147 entrance to Lake Mead NRA. Entering the NRA, continue along 3 miles until you come to the obvious T-intersection with North Shore Road. Hang a left and follow North Shore Road for 18.2 miles. Here you'll find a paved pull-out on the left side of the road.

From the parking pull-out, Hamblin Butte is the prominent butte a mile or so to the south/southwest. Cross the highway and head toward it. As you reach the base, simply pick a line and head up. A touch steep in places, the going should never exceed 2nd class.

Expect fewer than 1,000 feet of elevation gain on the roundtrip.

-WGS84 Lat: 36.1920 deg N Lon: -114.6648 deg W
-I, Class 2 via North Slope *

"Basalt Peak" (2,761)

Approached as if you're going to Cottonwood Spring/Hamblin Mountain.

-WGS84 Lat: 36.1971 deg N Lon: -114.6505 deg W
-I, Class 2 via Southeast Slope *

Bearing Peak (2,520)

This remote peak is an enjoyable hike from mile marker 18 along the paved Northshore Road. The roundtrip involves about 12 miles of awesome hiking through beautiful terrain. And the views of Lake Mead from the summit are outstanding!

-WGS84 Lat: 36.1619 deg N Lon: -114.6192 deg W
*-III, Class 2 via North Ridge ****
*-III, Class 2 via Northwest Gully ***

Boulder Peak (3,093)

Another remote peak. The very shortest land-based route is a solid 12 miles or so on the roadtrip. The way we went was 18 miles, via Cottonwood Spring.

-WGS84 Lat: 36.1721 deg N Lon: -114.5803 deg W
*-III, Class 2 via North Ridge ****

"Harlan Peak" (2,530)

Local hiking legend Harlan WS deserves to have a *real* peak named after him. Instead, he got this one.

-WGS84 Lat: 36.1898 deg N Lon: -114.5974 deg W
*-III, Class 3-4 via Northwest Face ****

"Northshore Peak – West" (2,874)

This is an awful peak, littered with loose scree. The north face is a treacherous, supremely dangerous route.

-WGS84 Lat: 36.2125 deg N Lon: -114.6371 deg W
*-I, Class 2 via Southeast Face **
*-I, Class 2-3 via North Face **

"Northshore Peak" (3,329)

Northshore Peak is the nice-looking peak towering above Northshore Road near Northshore Summit in Lake Mead NRA. Its east ridge route, which falls within the Pinto Valley Wilderness Area, is a fun 3-mile roundtrip hike with about 1,000 feet of gain. The summit views are awesome.

Follow the directions given for Cathedral Peak to the SR-147 entrance to Lake Mead NRA. Enter the NRA and continue along 3 miles until you come to the obvious T-intersection with North Shore Road. Hang a left and follow North Shore Road for 20.6 miles to a paved and signed pull-out on the left side of the road. This is North Shore Summit. Park here.

Northshore Peak is prominent from the parking area.

Cross the highway and head south to the toe of the east ridge. Negotiate your way onto the ridge, and continue up along or near the crest. As you near the summit, you'll encounter a couple short sections of class 2-3 scrambling.

-WGS84 Lat: 36.2160 deg N Lon: -114.6281 deg W
*-II, Class 2-3 via East Ridge ***

Razorback Ridge (2,920)

Razorback Ridge parallels Pinto Ridge, both south of Northshore Road. The two peaks can be combined in a pleasant half-day. The northeast ridge of Razorback Ridge is interesting and enjoyable.

-WGS84 Lat: 36.2137 deg N Lon: -114.6085 deg W
*-I, Class 2 via East Slope **
*-I, Class 2-3 via Northeast Ridge ***

Pinto Ridge (3,051)

Pinto Ridge forms a dramatic wall along Northshore Road. The peak is just a short hike from where the highway makes a lazy U north of the summit.

There is a neat cave not far from the summit, entered by a squeeze leading to a small interior room.

-WGS84 Lat: 36.2159 deg N Lon: -114.5852 deg W
*-I, Class 2 via North Slope ***

"Mount Graybeard" (3,051)

This otherwise forgettable mountain has significant to me because of the 20 minutes I once spent watching in close proximity a very elderly bighorn ram who was completely unaware of my presence.

-WGS84 Lat: 36.2327 deg N Lon: -114.5595 deg W
*-I, Class 1-2 via East Slope **
*-I, Class 2 via Northeast Ridge **

"Glyph Point" (2,592)

Glyph Point is west of Echo Hills and immediately north of where Pinto Valley meets Northshore Road.

-WGS84 Lat: 36.2487 deg N Lon: -114.5389 deg W
*-I, Class 2 via South Slope **

"Ram Skull Peak" (2,825)

Unofficially named Ram Skull Peak is essentially the higher north summit of officially named Guardian Peak. The peak is about a 14-mile roundtrip hike via Pinto Valley and Boulder Wash.

-WGS84 Lat: 36.1661 deg N Lon: -114.5613 deg W
*-III, Class 2 via North Ridge ***

Guardian Peak (2,818)

Although Guardian Peak is about a 15-mile roundtrip hike via Pinto Valley and Boulder Wash, the going is fast (thanks in part to an old road in upper Pinto Valley). Quicker types can roundtrip this baby in about 3.5 hours.

-WGS84 Lat: 36.1592 deg N Lon: -114.5595 deg W

-III, Class 2 from Ram Skull Peak **

"Sentinel Peak" (3,207)

Some might argue that Sentinel Peak is the best peak in the Lake Mead area. The east ridge is more interesting than the west ridge, though they're both high-quality. The east ridge features some 200 feet of class 3 scrambling on good, sharp limestone. Going up the east ridge and down the west ridge makes for an outstanding outing.

-WGS84 Lat: 36.2059 deg N Lon: -114.5548 deg W

-III, Class 3 via East Ridge ****

-III, Class 3-4 via West Ridge ***

Hugh de Q on the summit of Sentinel Peak. Above his head to the west, Lava Butte can be seen. Potosi Mountain is also visible in the distant-left.

"South Crag" (3,168)

This is the southern of two fang-like crags just southeast of Little Pyramid. It is a fine scramble.

-WGS84 Lat: 36.2125 deg N Lon: -114.5156 deg W

-II, Class 3 via North Ridge to West Face ***

"North Crag" (3,158)

This, the northern of two fang-like crags just southeast of Little Pyramid, is a short, enjoyable scramble via its northwest face.

-WGS84 Lat: 36.2135 deg N Lon: -114.5133 deg W
-II, Class 2 via Northwest Face **

"Little Pyramid" (3,363)

It's interesting that *Little* Pyramid is actually taller than Pyramid Peak, a mere two miles or so away. Little Pyramid is a short, pleasant hike from the pavement of Northshore Road. Speedy types can reach the top in well under an hour.

-WGS84 Lat: 36.2202 deg N Lon: -114.5219 deg W
-II, Class 2 via Northwest Face **

"Land's End Peak" (2,536)

This unofficially named peak lies between Pyramid Peak and Boulder Peak, and is separated from the latter by Boulder Wash. The summit gives up an interesting view of Lake Mead. This peak is very seldom climbed. I built a small cairn on the top.

-WGS84 Lat: 36.1869 deg N Lon: -114.5593 deg W
-III, Class 2 via Northeast Ridge **
-III, Class 2-3 via Northwest Face **

Bitter Ridge Highpoint (3,474)

The highpoint of the long and meandering Bitter Ridge, this summit offers stunning views of the Lake Mead NRA backcountry.

-WGS84 Lat: 36.2893 deg N Lon: -114.6457 deg W
-III, Class 2 via Northwest Slope ***
-III, Class 2-3 via West Bitter Peak ***

"West Bitter Peak" (3,340)

One of the summits of Bitter Ridge. Approach as you would the others in the group.

-WGS84 Lat: 36.2972 deg N Lon: -114.6417 deg W
-III, Class 2 from Bitter 3 **
-III, Class 2-3 via South Ridge **

"Bitter 3" (3,236)

This summit along the pleasant Bitter Ridge traverse has fine views across the open desert at its feet.

-WGS84 Lat: 36.307 deg N Lon: -114.632 deg W
-III, Class 2 from Middle Bitter Peak ***
-III, Class 2 via South Ridge ***

Exposure on Bitter Ridge

"Middle Bitter Peak" (3,307)

Part of the Bitter Ridge traverse.

-WGS84 Lat: 36.3092 deg N Lon: -114.6260 deg W
-III, Class 2 from East Bitter Peak ***
-III, Class 2 via Southwest Ridge ***

"East Bitter Peak" (3,309)

This is the first (easternmost) peak in a fine 5-peak traverse that can be made of Bitter Ridge.

-WGS84 Lat: 36.3126 deg N Lon: -114.6137 deg W
-I, Class 2 via Northeast Slope **
-II, Class 2 via Southwest Ridge ***

"Vista Peak" (3,350)

Vista Peak is another summit in the Redstone Peaks group. It lies just southeast of Mystery Cairn Peak.

-WGS84 Lat: 36.2282 deg N Lon: -114.5062 deg W
-II, Class 2 via Southeast Slope from Mystery Cairn Peak *

"Mystery Cairn Peak" (3,390)
Like all the Redstone Peaks, approach this one from the general vicinity of the Redstone Peaks picnic area along Northshore Road.

-WGS84 Lat: 36.2298 deg N Lon: -114.5080 deg W
-II, Class 3 via Northeast Slope from Redstone Peak **

"Redstone Peak" (3,510)
The loose and rugged Redstone Peaks make for a nice half-day wander around the Lake Mead area.

-WGS84 Lat: 36.2337 deg N Lon: -114.5038 deg W
-II, Class 2 via Northeast Face from East Redstone Peak **

"East Redstone Peak" (3,330)
Approach this minor summit as you would the others in the Redstone Peaks group.

-WGS84 Lat: 36.2361 deg N Lon: -114.5011 deg W
-I, Class 2 via West Face **

The Redstone Peaks complex, to the northeast, from the top of Little Pyramid

"Tall Cairn Peak" (3,017)
Part of the Redstone Peaks group. Approach as you would the others in the group. This summit is immediately east of East Redstone Peak.

-WGS84 Lat: 36.2360 deg N Lon: -114.4952 deg W
-II, Class 2 via West Ridge from East Redstone Peak **

Echo Hills (3,008)

Amidst flashes of lightning, we were *almost* chased off this thing by a quickly approaching storm. Approach directly from Northshore Road or the Redstone Peaks picnic area.

-WGS84 Lat: 36.2510 deg N Lon: -114.5102 deg W
-I, Class 3 via South Face **

Pyramid Peak (3,069)

Booth Pinnacle's neighbor, this is a fine, remote peak that offers some loose, exposed scrambling as one approaches the summit.

-WGS84 Lat: 36.1863 deg N Lon: -114.5403 deg W
-III, Class 2 via North Slope ***
-III, Class 2-3 from Booth Pinnacle ****

Saddle Mountain (2,595)

This isolated peak is in the neighborhood of Pyramid Peak and Booth Pinnacle. It is seldom visited.

-WGS84 Lat: 36.1827 deg N Lon: -114.5442 deg W
-III, Class 2 via Northeast Slope from Pyramid Peak **

"Booth Pinnacle" (2,988)

This is an enjoyable remote peak. There is a bit of loose, exposed scrambling near the top. The peak is commonly approached from either Boathouse Cove Road or directly from Northshore Road near the Redstone Peaks picnic area.

-WGS84 Lat: 36.1858 deg N Lon: -114.5304 deg W
-III, Class 2 from Pyramid Peak ****
-III, Class 2-3 via Northwest Ridge from Northeast Face ****

"Manganese Peak" (3,042)

Nice views of Lake Mead from the summit. Approach from the dirt Boathouse Cove Road off of Northshore Road.

-WGS84 Lat: 36.2158 deg N Lon: -114.4684 deg W
-II, Class 2-3 via South Ridge ***

"Stock Ridge" (2,604)

This fun ridge has a number of interesting crags to climb and clamber about on. It lies northeast of Manganese Peak, and the two can be easily combined in a half-day.

-WGS84 Lat: 36.2264 deg N Lon: -114.4625 deg W
-II, Class 2-3 via East Ridge **

Peak 2,674 (2,674)

This ordinary peak southwest of Cathedral Peaks can be hiked in less than an hour car-to-car.

-WGS84 Lat: 36.2499 deg N Lon: -114.4539 deg W
*-I, Class 2 via Northwest Slopes **

"Pellet Peak" (2,644)

This short hike can be completed in well under an hour from Boathouse Cove Road.

-WGS84 Lat: 36.2597 deg N Lon: -114.4622 deg W
*-I, Class 2 via Northwest Slope **

Cathedral Peak (2,851)

Cathedral Peak is an obscure, infrequently visited peak in the Jimbilnan Wilderness Area. The area surrounding the peak sports some enjoyable cragging on volcanic spires, and the views from the mountain's summit, which looms over Lake Mead a mere 0.25 mile away, are particularly stunning.

From I-15 north of downtown Las Vegas, exit at Lake Mead Boulevard (SR-147) and head east. Continue through town and over the pass north of Frenchman Mountain, the prominent twin-peaked mountain on the eastern edge of Las Vegas, and at 16.5 miles you'll come to the entrance booth for Lake Mead NRA. Enter the NRA and continue for 3 miles until you come to the T-intersection with North Shore Road. Hang a left and follow North Shore Road for a touch over 20.5 miles until you come to a paved and signed pull-out on the left side of the road. This is North Shore Summit. Continue past North Shore Summit for 9.5 miles, looking for Boathouse Cove Road (AR-97), a park approved dirt road on the right. Boathouse Cove Road is just before mile marker 30. Turn onto Boathouse Cove Road and continue down the good dirt road for 0.5 mile and park in a previously disturbed location or wash bottom. A low ridge blocks your view of Cathedral Peak to the east/northeast.

From Boathouse Cove Road, scramble to the top of the low ridge to the east. From here, Cathedral Peak can be seen three miles away across the open desert. The true summit is just out of view behind a sub-peak. Dropping from the ridge, head cross-country toward the base of Cathedral Peak. There are many minor ups and downs along the way as you cross through a number of washes. They are a bit tedious, particularly on the return. As you near the peak, get into the canyon that is due west of the summit. Heading up-canyon (roughly east-southeast) for a few hundred yards, exit left and scramble to the upper mountain. It's not hard to keep the going in the class 2 realm. Once the upper mountain is gained, follow your nose toward the apparent summit, passing by a couple of tasty-looking spires along the way. (My partner and I climbed a couple of these nasty, volcanic features—spicy, but fun.) Upon reaching the apparent summit, you'll see that the true summit is another 0.3 mile away to the east. Dropping slightly from the false summit, follow your nose to the true summit. A small bit of enjoyable scrambling can be found as you approach the top. Working your way counter-clockwise around the summit mass gives itself up class 2. Admire the views—they are considerable.

The roundtrip involves about 8 miles, with roughly 1,000 feet of elevation gain.

-WGS84 Lat: 36.2701 deg N Lon: -114.4277 deg W

*-II, Class 2 via West Slopes ***

Peak 2,890 (2,890)

This short peak, an outlier of the Muddy Mountains northwest of Longwell Ridge, can be approached via dirt roads coming in from the southeast. There is some semi-interesting scrambling along the exposed ridge near the top.

-WGS84 Lat: 36.3633 deg N Lon: -114.5498 deg W

*-I, Class 2 via Southeast Ridge ***

West Longwell Ridge (3,186)

Approach West Longwell Ridge as per East Longwell Ridge South. None of the three peaks in this cluster had a register or summit cairn.

-WGS84 Lat: 36.3358 deg N Lon: -114.5322 deg W

*-II, Class 2 via East Face **

East Longwell Ridge South (3,065)

This is an enjoyable hike with nice views. The summit ridge becomes interesting toward the top.

With a high clearance 4WD vehicle, one can drive to the end of the road just north of the summit, allowing one in a half-day to bag all three peaks in this tight cluster.

-WGS84 Lat: 36.3195 deg N Lon: -114.5235 deg W

*-II, Class 2-3 via Northeast Ridge ****

East Longwell Ridge (3,100)

Approached as East Longwell Ridge South.

-WGS84 Lat: 36.3314 deg N Lon: -114.5166 deg W

*-II, Class 2 via Southwest Ridge **

*-II, Class 2-3 via Northwest Face **

"The Raven (3,561)

A nice, rarely-visited summit on the north side of Northshore Road. The north-northeast canyon features a semi-keeper pothole, an unusual feature in this neck of the woods.

-WGS84 Lat: 36.3419 deg N Lon: -114.5112 deg W

-III, Class 2-3 via Northwest Ridge from Fire Benchmark ***
-III, Class 4-5 via North-Northeast Canyon ***

Fire Benchmark (3,928)
Another fine and seldom-visited peak. This is The Raven's higher neighbor. For either route, approach directly from Northshore Road.
-WGS84 Lat: 36.3632 deg N Lon: -114.5127 deg W
-III, Class 2-3 via East Slope & Ridge ***
-III, Class 2-3 from The Raven ***

"Bighorn Peak" (3,742)
This is North Fire Peak's much more rugged neighbor. We saw about 20 bighorn sheep during this day's adventure.
-WGS84 Lat: 36.3859 deg N Lon: -114.5018 deg W
-III, Class 2-3 from North Fire Peak ***

"North Fire Peak" (3,743)
Awesome views into Valley of Fire from the summit. Approach from Northshore Road.
-WGS84 Lat: 36.3899 deg N Lon: -114.4949 deg W
-III, Class 4 via south-draining canyon west of summit ***
-III, Class 4 via south-draining canyon east of summit ***

"North Fire Peak - East Summit" (3,654)
The east summit of North Fire Peak is actually more like a *north*east summit.
-WGS84 Lat: 36.3932 deg N Lon: -114.4895 deg W
-III, Class 4 via south-draining canyon west of summit **

Blue Point (2,096)
Blue Point Spring is a stunning oasis along Northshore Road. From the spring, simply hike up the peak's east ridge to the summit.
-WGS84 Lat: 36.3909 deg N Lon: -114.4406 deg W
-I, Class 2 via East Ridge **

West Shore

The peaks in this subsection have a variety of access points, from Boulder City to Las Vegas. The peaks are arranged here generally south-to-north.

"Red Mountain" (3,654)
This minor but colorful summit sits above Boulder City, Nevada. The true summit is a closed facility, so you'll have to settle for the slightly lower sub-bump. Approach as per River Mountain Peak.
-WGS84 Lat: 35.9957 deg N Lon: -114.8637 deg W

-I, Class 1 via trail *

Black Mountain (3,628)

With a nice trail approach, Black Mountain can be easily combined with Red Mountain for a good after-work hike. The trailhead is just off the left side of US-93 as you leave Boulder City on the way to Hoover Dam (see the approach to River Mountain Peak).

-WGS84 Lat: 36.0064 deg N Lon: -114.8521 deg W

-I, Class 2 from trail **

"River Mountain Peak" (3,642)

River Mountain Peak is a part of the River Mountains, a locally popular range that offers stunning views of Lake Mead from its crest. The peak sits along the crest 0.75 mile north of Black Mountain and about 0.5 mile south of River Mountain Benchmark (3,789), the highpoint of the range. With maintained trails to nearby Black Mountain and Red Mountain, one can link up several peaks in this range in an afternoon.

From Boulder City, Nevada, travel east on US-93 toward Hoover Dam. A mile outside of Boulder City, as an awesome (though obscured by power lines) view of Lake Mead unfolds, look for the signed River Mountain Trail on the left. There's a large parking area there. This is the trailhead.

From the parking area, follow a well-maintained trail to a saddle in the distance. Arriving at the saddle, you can either hang a left and follow a trail to the top of Red Mountain (the true summit is off-limits, though a subsidiary point you *are* allowed on is only a few feet lower), or hang a right (ignoring a side trail that heads to the left a hundred yards or so later) and hike up to the summit of Black Mountain. Head to Black Mountain. From the summit of Black Mountain, drop to the ridge to the north. Negotiating the occasional minor obstacle, sometimes encountering a use trail, work you way over a minor peak and to the summit of River Mountain Peak. The views of Lake Mead and down the peak's cliffy east face are awesome.

If you have extra energy, consider continuing north and dropping down into the saddle between River Mountain Peak and River Mountain. River Mountain is a short class 2 scramble away.

The route from the trailhead to River Mountain Peak and back is roughly 6-7 miles, with about 1,800 feet of elevation gain.

-WGS84 Lat: 36.0140 deg N Lon: -114.8548 deg W

-II, Class 2 via South Ridge *

River Mountain Benchmark (3,789)

This peak can be approached directly from Lake Mead (the lake itself, I mean) by following the powerlines to the saddle just below the peak, or from a traverse across Black Mountain and River Mountain Peak.

-WGS84 Lat: 36.0175 deg N Lon: -114.8589 deg W
-III, Class 2 from the big blue lake **

Peak 2,740 (2,740)
This minor peak near (but west of) River Mountain Benchmark is easily approached from the west, where a paved road leads within a mile of the peak's base.

-WGS84 Lat: 36.0361 deg N Lon: -114.9117 deg W
-II, Class 2 via West Slope **

"Falls Peak" (2,580)
Parking along the paved park roadway (NV-166) immediately east of the peak, one can quickly begin scrambling up progressively steeper and more interesting terrain on the east face. Care must be taken to avoid harder scrambling and climbing in spots. The views from the summit are terrific.

A fine descent is had by dropping down the east canyon, where all but the two lowest dryfalls can be downclimbed with class 3-4 scrambling. The lowest dryfall is bypassed on its right (looking down-canyon) and the one just above that on its left.

-WGS84 Lat: 36.0422 deg N Lon: -114.8339 deg W
-II, Class 2-3 via East Face ***
-II, Class 3-4 via East Canyon ***

Peak 2,500 (2,500)
This minor peak, due west of Saddle Island, is one of the northernmost dominant summits of the range. As such, it affords fine views of the area. Approach as per Pipeline Hill.

-WGS84 Lat: 36.0637 deg N Lon: -114.8503 deg W
-II, Class 1-2 via North Slope **

"Pipeline Hill" (1,980)
This small peak is a short hike directly from the paved road, slightly northwest of Saddle Island. Park on the paved shoulder of NV-166 to its east, drop into the wash and follow it to the base of the northeast slope. Then head up!

-WGS84 Lat: 36.0740 deg N Lon: -114.8392 deg W
-I, Class 1 via Northeast Slope *

"Long View Peak" (2,584)
Park at the Long View Overlook along NV-166 northwest of Saddle Island. From there, a nice walk up a couple washes leads to steep rubble and basalt talus to a break in the upper cliffs. The final, exposed (at times) walk to the summit affords truly exceptional views of both Lake Mead and Las Vegas.

-WGS84 Lat: 36.0830 deg N Lon: -114.8670 deg W
-II, Class 2 via East Face **

"Mount Mangreed" (2,135)

Mount Mangreed is currently being converted into a housing development and golf course. The summit, while it survives, offers interesting views of Henderson and Lake Mead. You can park along NV-146 at the peak's southeast base and head up decomposing slopes to the depressing summit.

-WGS84 Lat: 36.0951 deg N Lon: -114.9211 deg W
-I, Class 1 via Southeast Aspect *

Pinnacle (2,020)

Pinnacle and its even more striking neighbor, Red Needle, are two amazing summits in the Rainbow Gardens area. Both are accessed via the dirt Lava Butte Road (see approach directions for Lava Butte). Red Needle is dangerous. Pinnacle, on the other hand, is an enjoyable, relatively safe scramble to a nice, exposed summit. We climbed it once on a slippery, rainy day. Be aware of loose rock!

-WGS 84 Lat: 36.1225 deg N Lon: -114.9493 deg W
-I, Class 3 via East Face from North Ridge ***

Red Needle (1,957)

Red Needle is a striking and improbable overhung tower closely southwest of Red Butte and just north of Pinnacle. It's not reasonable to climb the feature without the use of aid, and my partner and I did so by using an extension ladder to overcome the initial crumbly overhang on the upper north face. To get to the ladder "crux" will require about 20 feet of spooky class 3-4 scrambling up the northeast corner to reach a ledge. Above the 15-foot ladder crux is a squeeze through an awkward chimney leading to a notch, where one steps around the corner to the right and then climbs an exposed 15-foot loose and shallow gully that leads to the highpoint.

With a 4WD vehicle, one can drive to the base of Red Needle from the north.

-WGS84 Lat: 36.1269 deg N Lon: -114.9468 deg W
-I, Class 4 A0 via North Face ***

"Red Fox Peak" (2,020)

A small mountain with a precipitous southwest face, Red Fox Peak sits across the valley from Red Needle and near the shoulder of Lava Butte. Approach as if you're driving to Pinnacle.

-WGS84 Lat: 36.1309 deg N Lon: -114.9405 deg W
-I, Class 2 via Northwest Ridge **

Lava Butte (background) and Red Needle from the summit of Pinnacle. The view looks north.

"White Eagle Peak" (2,445)

White Eagle Mine sits at the east-southeast base of the mountain. The views from the top are rather nice. The mountain is approach directly from the dirt Rainbow Gardens Road (off of NV-147).

-WGS84 Lat: 36.1316 deg N Lon: -114.9681 deg W

*-I, Class 2 via East Slopes **

Lava Butte (2,871)

Lava Butte is a small but prominent mountain situated between Frenchman Mountain and Lake Mead. It is located just outside the boundary of Lake Mead NRA.

In addition to a number of class 1-2 options along the peak's ridges, there is a semi-stimulating and steep class 2-3 route directly up the northwest face.

From I-15 north of downtown Las Vegas, exit at Lake Mead Boulevard (SR-147) and head east for 13.3 miles to a prominent dirt road on your right. There is a sign that says "Lake Mead Remediation Area" at the junction. Getting onto the rough(ish) dirt road (passenger cars driven with care should be okay, though a high clearance vehicle is recommended), follow signs for 'Lava Butte' (and ignore signs for 'Rainbow Gardens') about 2 miles to the base of the northwest face of the mountain. Find a place to park near the base of the face. From the road, head cross-country a short distance to the base of the steep northwest face. From there, head up; any line will take you to the top. The going can be steep, but shouldn't exceed class 2-3. Beware of loose rock and unstable talus.

The roundtrip should be less than 2 miles with under 1,000 feet of elevation gain.

-WGS84 Lat: 36.1486 deg N Lon: -114.9372 deg W

-II, Class 2-3 via Northwest Face *

"Walts Ridge" (2,685)

On the way to Rainbow Gardens, and easily approached from the good dirt Middle Wash Road (off of NV-147; initially approached as per Lava Butte).

-WGS84 Lat: 36.1657 deg N Lon: -114.9645 deg W

-I, Class 2-3 via East Face *

"Knife-Edge Peak" (3,085)

Not as exciting as it might sound, but still a pretty decent desert peak with a fun bit of knife edge along the top. Park along Lake Mead Boulevard (NV-147), east of the pass.

-WGS84 Lat: 36.1896 deg N Lon: -114.9774 deg W

-I, Class 2-3 via North Ridge **

"Hanging Valley Peak" (2,947)

This peak is just northeast of Knife-Edge Peak. Park along Lake Mead Boulevard (NV-147), east of the pass.

-WGS84 Lat: 36.1937 deg N Lon: -114.9688 deg W

-I, Class 2 via South Ridge from Knife-Edge Peak *

-I, Class 2-3 via Northwest Face *

"Division Peak" (2,980)

The east ridge is a surprisingly delightful, sustained class 2-3 scrambling route with nice exposure in places. There are three summits, two of which claim highest – bag 'em both! For a pleasant descent, the gully between the three summits can be followed to the south (class 3), bypassing a 30-foot dryfall on the right. Approach both routes directly from the pavement of Lake Mead Boulevard (NV-147).

-WGS84 Lat: 36.2083 deg N Lon: -114.9745 deg W

-I, Class 2-3 via East Ridge ***

-I, Class 3 via South Gully **

"Unity Peak" (3,012)
Being so close to Las Vegas, there's been a history of vehicle break-ins near the base of this peak. If you're a gambler, park along Lake Mead Boulevard (NV-147) a bit east of the pass.

-WGS84 Lat: 36.2131 deg N Lon: -114.9719 deg W
*-I, Class 2-3 via Southeast Face **

"The Minefield" (2,498)
Approach directly from the pavement of Lake Mead Boulevard (NV-147) to the south of the peak. When you go there, you'll find out why the peak is so named.

-WGS84 Lat: 36.2141 deg N Lon: -114.9433 deg W
*-I, Class 2 via West Slope **
*-I, Class 2-3 via South Face **

"The Triple" (2,568)
Approach from the paved shoulder of NV-147.

-WGS84 Lat: 36.2199 deg N Lon: -114.9427 deg W
*-I, Class 2 via East Slope **
*-I, Class 2 via Southeast Face **

"Coyote Skull Peak" (2,740)
Short, loose, decent views. The peak is approached directly from Lake Mead Boulevard (NV-147) to the south.

-WGS84 Lat: 36.2200 deg N Lon: -114.9540 deg W
*-I, Class 1-2 via Northeast Slope **
*-I, Class 2 via East Face **

"The Double" (2,580)
The peak is situated east of The Triple and Coyote Skull Peak. Approach all of them directly from the shoulder of NV-147.

-WGS84 Lat: 36.2207 deg N Lon: -114.9342 deg W
*-I, Class 2 via West Face **
*-I, Class 2 via Southwest Slope **

South Shore

The peaks in this subsection have a variety of access points, from the vicinity of Hoover Dam to Arizona itself. They are arranged here roughly south-to-north.

Mount Wilson (5,445)
Mount Wilson, located just inside the Arizona border near Hoover Dam, is the highpoint of the long and prominent Wilson Ridge, which falls within the

Mount Wilson Wilderness Area. Mount Wilson can be clearly seen from nearly all of Las Vegas.

From Boulder City, Nevada, take US-93 toward Hoover Dam. Crossing over the dam bypass bridge into Arizona, continue along US-93 for 8 miles to a dirt turn-out on the right side of the road. The turn-out is just past mile marker 8. Park here.

From the turn-out, Mount Wilson is the obvious high mountain to the northeast, a couple miles across the open desert. Cross the highway and head into the desert. Though you'll likely have to cross in and out of a few washes, easily make your way to the base of the south ridge of the mountain. It will be visible during the entire approach. Once at the base of the south ridge, head up gentle, sloping terrain. As you get higher, the ridge becomes craggier. You may be required to do some light scrambling in and around a few obstacles here and there. Generally speaking, staying on the left (west) side of the ridge provides easiest travel. At the top of the ridge, do a couple more scrambling moves to gain the summit. The views of Lake Mead, the Colorado River Basin, and lots and lots of aesthetic lonely mountains around them, are surreal.

Expect a roundtrip of about 8 or 9 miles and 3,200 feet of gain.

Alternatively, Mount Wilson can be approached via an official trailhead on AR130, accessible by highway 143 (to Temple Bar Road). The route via that approach is not described here.

-WGS84 Lat: 35.9967 deg N Lon: -114.6119 deg W

*-III, Class 2-3 via South Ridge ****

Rough Benchmark (2,248)

The northeast slope is gained directly from the Lakeview Overlook parking lot along US-93 near Hoover Dam. Some good scrambling can be found in spots but watch for loose rock.

-WGS84 Lat: 36.0128 deg N Lon: -114.7662 deg W

*-I, Class 2-3 via Northeast Slope ***

*-II, Class 2-3 via West Slope ***

"Uranus" (2,170)

I dubbed it 'Uranus' and its close neighbor 'Pluto' after summiting this peak and seeing that someone had arranged talus blocks to spell out the words 'PLUTO' and 'URANUS' near the summit. Interesting (or at least cultured) types seem to visit the place, as also evidenced by my finding a Mozart CD high on the mountain.

-WGS84 Lat: 36.0136 deg N Lon: -114.7782 deg W

*-II, Class 2 via East Slope **

*-I, Class 2 via North Gully **

"Pluto" (2,138)

There are extraordinary views of Lake Mead from the summit. Assuming one traverses to Pluto from Rough Benchmark (via the Lakeview Overlook along US-93), a nice loop can be completed by dropping down the west slope of Pluto to the Pluto-Uranus saddle and then descending north to the Railroad Tunnel Trail. Follow the trail east to just below the Lakeview Overlook parking lot. Class 2 terrain left of the trail takes you to the parking lot.

-WGS84 Lat: 36.0146 deg N Lon: -114.7734 deg W
*-I, Class 2 via West Slope **
*-II, Class 2-3 via Southeast Slope from Rough Benchmark ***

Peak 1,876 (1,876)

This minor peak, with only so-so summit views, is just off Kingman Wash Road, northeast of Hoover Dam. A boulder on the east slope carries an inscription dated to 1964.

-WGS84 Lat: 36.0188 deg N Lon: -114.7154 deg W
*-I, Class 1 via East Slopes **

"Dam View Point" (2,020)

This peak, northeast of Hoover Dam and closely northwest of Peak 1,876, has an awesomely outstanding view from its top. The peak is easily accessed from Kingman Wash Road.

-WGS84 Lat: 36.0273 deg N Lon: -114.7178 deg W
*-I, Class 2 via Northeast Slope ****

Promontory Point (2,230)

Approached from the Lakeview Overlook parking lot along US-93 near Hoover Dam, a rugged ridge leads northeast up and over a multitude of bumps and crags (including one that requires route-finding to locate a class 3-4 weakness through significant cliffs) to the highpoint. Count on seeing dozens of bighorn sheep!

-WGS84 Lat: 36.0294 deg N Lon: -114.7376 deg W
*-II, Class 3-4 from Lakeview Overlook ***

"Cove Peak" (1,575)

Approached via Kingman Wash Road (via US-93), just over the dam in Arizona.

-WGS84 Lat: 36.0337 deg N Lon: -114.7082 deg W
*-I, Class 2 via East Face **
*-I, Class 3 via West Ridge **

Classic Lake Mead scenery along the south shore,
near the park's shared border with Grand Canyon National Park

Fortification Hill (3,718)

Fortification Hill is the prominent mesa above Hoover Dam. It can be clearly seen from much of Las Vegas. The mountain is located just inside of Arizona and is within a proposed wilderness area. With a nice trail going to the top, this peak gives up what I believe to be the best views from any peak in the area.

To get there: From Boulder City, Nevada, take US-93 toward Hoover Dam. Continue along US-93 over the bridge bypassing the dam then turn onto Kingman Wash Road (AR-70). Follow AR-70 for 3.3 miles until you come to a junction. You should see a restroom here. Hanging a right onto AR-70C, continue along the rough road for another 2.7 miles until you come to a signed trailhead and small parking area below Fortification Hill.

A high clearance vehicle is recommended for this approach.

From the trailhead, pick up a good trail that heads up the crest of a minor ridge leading toward the mesa above. This ridge will be to your immediate right when viewed from the trailhead. Continuing along the trail up and over a few bumps along the ridge, you will eventually find yourself at the base of the cliffs of Fortification Hill. The trail bends north and soon disappears. When it does, look for passage through the cliffs. Signs of prior traffic should lead you to a short (20-30 feet) class 2-3 weakness above.

Follow the easiest terrain you can find to the top of the cliffs. Young children have been known to do this route.

Above the cliff band, you'll see that you're on top of the mesa. Pick up the good trail that materializes again and follow it to the summit on the other side of the mesa. The views become spectacular as soon as the summit is reached.

Expect a roundtrip of about 6 miles, with about 1,000 feet of gain.

For the trail variation, follow the directions already given to the point where the trail bends north at the base of the cliffs of Fortification Hill. At that point, instead of heading north to look for the class 2-3 weakness, head directly up the cliffs. I found the easiest line to be 4th class, not on the best rock. Climb about 50-60 feet up the cliffs until you reach the top of the mesa. From there, cross-country it a bit south/southwest until you pick up the trail taking you to the summit.

-WGS84 Lat: 36.0443 deg N Lon: -114.6811 deg W
-II, Class 2-3 via Trail ***
-II, Class 4 via Trail Variation ***

Paint Pots (1,709)

Paint Pots is a funky little peak surrounded by steep cliffs. Two convenient breaks are found on the backside, once the peak is approached from the cove adjacent to Kingman Wash Road.

-WGS84 Lat: 36.0435 deg N Lon: -114.7051 deg W
-I, Class 2 from the south **

Arch Mountain Highpoint (3,763)

This is an isolated mountain. It lies a bit south of the named Arch Mountain, but in truth, this unnamed summit is the highpoint of the Arch Mountain massif. It is best approached from the vicinity of the paved Temple Bar Road, out where Chris McCandless once abandoned his car shortly before embarking for Alaska. This summit is just barely in Arizona.

-WGS84 Lat: 36.1166 deg N Lon: -114.5620 deg W
-III, Class 3 from southeast ***
-III, Class 3 via North Ridge from Arch Mountain ***

Arch Mountain (3,375)

An all-day walk-in-the-park, so to speak. This and several other peaks in this section actual reside in Arizona. Approach via the paved Temple Bar Road in Arizona.

-WGS84 Lat: 36.1353 deg N Lon: -114.5590 deg W
-III, Class 2-3 from southeast ***

Tracy F. nearing the summit of Salt Spring Mountain

"Salt Spring Mountain" (3,973)

Salt Spring Mountain, which was named by John Vitz, has 1113' of prominence.

From Dolan Springs, continue north on Pearce Ferry Road toward Pearce Ferry. Turn left onto the signed Greggs Hideout Road (graded dirt) and follow it for 11 miles to the signed Temple Bar Back Road (good dirt; ESE of the peak). Turn left onto Temple Bar Back Road and follow it to a large wash southwest of the peak, where you'll park and hike up the wash to its head then follow the ridge north to the summit.

-WGS84 Lat: 35.9334 deg N Lon: -114.2214 deg W

*-I, Class 1-2 via Southwest Wash **

"Golden Mine Peak" (3,580)

This minor peak sitting across the valley from Salt Spring Mountain is just above Golden Mine.

Follow the directions given for Salt Spring Mountain to about 10 miles up Greggs Hideout Road. Turn right onto Golden Mine Road (4WD; high clearance), pass through three unlocked gates, and park at the saddle northeast of the summit. Hike the northeast ridge for 0.3 mile to the top.

-WGS84 Lat: 35.9148 deg N Lon: -114.1426 deg W

*-I, Class 2 via Northeast Ridge **

Colorado River

The peaks in this subsection are accessed via a variety of points. They are arranged here generally south-to-north.

Little Peak (4,812)

Although the entire Little Peak-North Peak massif is covered in antennae, the views from the top of Little Peak are extraordinary.

-WGS84 Lat: 35.2469 deg N Lon: -114.7433 deg W

-II, Class 2 via Traverse from North Peak **

North Peak (4,917)

North Peak can also be climbed directly from Christmas Tree Pass to the north.

-WGS84 Lat: 35.2511 deg N Lon: -114.7472 deg W

-II, Class 2 via Southwest Ridge **

"Iguana Peak" (4,019)

This fun, boulder-covered peak is southeast of Spirit Mountain. Park in a pull-out just northwest of Willow Spring and head for the mountain. Interesting scrambling and route-finding should be expected, particularly as the final summit blocks are reached.

-WGS84 Lat: 35.2426 deg N Lon: -114.7042 deg W

-II, Class 3-4 via Northeast Face ***

"Christmas Tree Peak" (4,380)

This peak is located due north of Christmas Tree Pass and just outside of Lake Mead NRA, west of Spirit Mountain. The summit views are nice.

-WGS84 Lat: 35.2709 deg N Lon: -114.7451 deg W

-I, Class 1 via South Slope *

Spirit Mountain (5,639)

Spirit Mountain is a rugged, granitic Zen garden. It is sacred to the Indians, and a very special place.

The peak is relatively popular amongst hiking types, and since nearly everyone uses the same route a use trail exists for the bulk of the route. The peak is obvious from the nearby comunity of Cal-Nev-Ari, and the nicely graded Christmas Tree Pass road leads right past the southern base of the mountain.

-WGS84 Lat: 35.2749 deg N Lon: -114.7234 deg W

-III, Class 3 via South Slope ****

Devils Thumb (5,189)

Rugged and remote, this peak can also be climbed from the southeast.

-WGS84 Lat: 35.2908 deg N Lon: -114.7147 deg W
*-III, Class 2 via West Slope **
*-III, Class 3-4 via Traverse from Spirit Mountain ***

Peak 3,153 (3,153)
This small peak is just northeast of the Pipe Spring Trailhead near Christmas Tree Pass. This is a wonderful area with plenty of interesting objectives.
-WGS84 Lat: 35.2719 deg N Lon: -114.6793 deg W
*-I, Class 2 via Southwest Slopes ***

Mount Newberry (3,624)
Mount Newberry has awesome summit views. Approach from the trailhead at the end of Pipe Spring Road. The peak has 964' of prominence.
-WGS84 Lat: 35.2931 deg N Lon: -114.6625 deg W
*-II, Class 2 via Southwest Face ***
-II, Class 2 via Northwest Slope

Bill Gays Butte (1,975)
Just south of Black Mountain, a short drive on a dirt road dumps one off at the western base of this tiny mountain. Approach via Cottonwood Cove Road (NV-164) from Searchlight, Nevada.
-WGS84 Lat: 35.4524 deg N Lon: -114.7616 deg W
*-I, Class 2 via West Slope **

Black Mountain (2,210)
Right off the paved Cottonwood Cove Road (NV-164) east of Searchlight, Nevada.
-WGS84 Lat: 35.4899 deg N Lon: -114.7519 deg W
*-I, Class 2 via South Ridge **

"Indigo Peak" (1,874)
Near Indigo Road, and just east-southeast of Copper Mountain, Indigo Peak can be shortly bagged from the dirt road.
-WGS84 Lat: 35.5256 deg N Lon: -114.7372 deg W
*-II, Class 2 from the road **

Copper Mountain – West (3,022)
This lesser but still dominant sister to Copper Mountain is a logical bonus peak.
-WGS84 Lat: 35.5304 deg N Lon: -114.7761 deg W
*-II, Class 2 via Southeast Ridge ****
*-II, Class 2 via West Face ***

Copper Mountain (3,214)

Well hidden behind entire mountain ranges in the backcountry of Lake Mead NRA, and only visible from a single paved road (NV-164), it's no wonder that Copper Mountain had only two recorded ascents before I wandered my way to its top. I'd never even heard of the mountain, but quickly noticed its striking, pointy mass and its serrated, winding south ridge in the distance to the northeast as I headed down Cottonwood Cove Road on my way to check out Lake Mohave for the first time. With a little exploration, I found a park approved dirt road (AR32) heading off the paved road that took me quite near the base of the mountain. Deciding on a whim to check it out, I found my way up to the crest of the enjoyable south ridge, narrow and somewhat knife-edgy in not one, not two, but perhaps six different spots, and followed it northward and up. Along the way, the views grew ever-expansive: A neat old mine, a striking hidden cactus garden of preternatural coloration, an awesome arch showing views of Lake Mohave through it, and of course, the winding, craggy ridge stretching all the way to the top.

Mostly class 2 with the occasional morsel of 3rd class, the crux of the route is a 4th class notch about halfway up that requires about 15 feet of 4th class downclimbing, followed by about 25 feet of 4th class up-climbing to continue.

To get to the mountain: From US-95 in tiny Searchlight, Nevada (between Las Vegas, Nevada and Needles, California), head east on the paved Cottonwood Cove Road. Following the road for 7.9 miles toward Lake Mohave, you'll encounter a minor dirt road heading northeast from the paved road. Copper Mountain should be plainly visible as the most striking peak to the northeast. Get onto the dirt road (high clearance suggested, though probably not necessary) and follow it for 2.0 miles to a fork. The left fork is signed for park approved road #35; the right fork is signed for park approved road #32. Park just off the road at the fork in a previously disturbed area or wash bottom, or continue a short distance more down the left fork to a place that seems about right. The south ridge of Copper Mountain will be close at hand to the north.

This route requires an effort of about four miles roundtrip with roughly 1,500 feet of gain.

From wherever you parked your vehicle, head for the base of the obvious south ridge (or any of a few spur ridges that ultimately connect with the south ridge above). Gaining the ridge should require nothing more than a bit of sandy slogging. Once on the south ridge, head north along the winding crest. Although sticking to the crest is quite enjoyable, you may encounter the occasional use trail below the crest that certainly speeds up the process in its efficiency.

Enjoying the several knife-edgy portions of the ridge crest along the way, you'll soon come to a notch in the ridge. Downclimbing about 15 feet of

4th class rock (so-so quality), climb up the other side (about 25 feet of 4th class on slightly better rock) and continue on. You'll eventually pass a small hidden bowl near the upper third of the ridge, in which resides a cozy spattering of perhaps 500 brightly-colored chollas.

As you ascend, the going gets steeper. You'll notice increasing exposure on the east side of the upper ridge, and some may choose to drop below the crest on its west side and follow the easier terrain found there. Regardless, continuing up, if you don't climb over the top of it, you'll pass by a very impressive arch on its west side. Take a peak through and check out the nice, framed vista of Lake Mohave.

A few minutes' more effort should land you on the summit.

To descend, retrace your steps *or* drop back down to the cholla garden, which is just above and east of the saddle between Copper Mountain and Copper Mountain-West. Work your way down to the saddle, drop into the canyon on the south side of the saddle and follow it to the level wash at the bottom. Dry waterfalls may be encountered, but can be avoided with a little care. Once in the wash, follow it to the left until you near the base of the south ridge then make for your vehicle! This alternate descent can be done class 2.

-WGS84 Lat: 35.5306 deg N Lon: -114.7639 deg W

*-II, Class 4 via South Ridge ****

"Talus Mound" (2,291)

Talus Mound is the peak immediately southeast of Salt and Pepper Mountain. It's easily approached from the dirt road running along its southwestern base.

-WGS84 Lat: 35.5423 deg N Lon: -114.7394 deg W

*-I, Class 2 via West Slopes **

*-I, Class 2 via Northwest Face **

"Salt and Pepper Mountain" (2,700)

Salt and Pepper Mountain, sporting 1011' of prominence, is just northeast of Copper Mountain. The summit has a register.

-WGS84 Lat: 35.5487 deg N Lon: -114.7469 deg W

*-II, Class 2 via Southwest Slope ***

"Midway Peak" (3,140)

Midway peak is a minor summit across the rough dirt Yucca Camp Road from Pilot Mesa.

-WGS84 Lat: 35.8178 deg N Lon: -114.7875 deg W

*-I, Class 2 via Northeast Slope **

*-I, Class 2 via Northwest Slope **

"Yucca Camp Mountain" (3,114)

I once nearly stepped on a baby rattlesnake while descending the rugged north ridge.

-WGS84 Lat: 35.8227 deg N Lon: -114.7937 deg W

-I, Class 2-3 via Southeast Face **

-I, Class 3 via North Ridge **

"Pilot Mesa" (3,300)

Pilot Mesa, Midway Peak and Yucca Camp Mountain lie just inside Lake Mead NRA off of the mega-obscure, rough dirt Yucca Camp Road.

-WGS84 Lat: 35.8375 deg N Lon: -114.7883 deg W

-I, Class 2 via Southwest Slope *

-I, Class 2-3 via South Face *

Arrow Canyon Range

The Arrow Canyon Range is one of the most impressively rugged desert ranges in the state. Its west face, when viewed from US-93 between Las Vegas and Alamo, is eye-catching. The range hosts Arrow Canyon, an impressive, high-walled canyon containing Native American art. The deep, narrow canyon is located within the Arrow Canyon Wilderness.

Primitive camping opportunities are readily found in this area, though you should be sure to bring plenty of your own water. Don't expect to find any here! Also, don't forget to bring a topo map along on your explorations of this fine range. The topography is complex.

While once exploring the range on a multi-peak traverse, I bumped into a baby bighorn sheep running blindly along the north ridge of South Arrow Peak. I saw him coming but he didn't see me, so he nearly ran into me before he took notice and ran off in the other direction. It was a magical moment.

The peaks in this section are arranged here roughly south-to-north. The bulk of them are approached directly from US-93 or SR-168, which connects Moapa/Glendale and Coyote Springs.

"South Arrow Cone" (3,116)

South Arrow Cone is the southernmost peak in the Arrow Canyon Range. It is a forgettable scree dome.

-WGS84 Lat: 36.4374 deg N Lon: -114.9415 deg W

-I, Class 2 via Southwest Slope *

"Dry Lake Peak" (3,060)

Dry Lake Peak is easily approached via a decent dirt road heading west from the frontage road north of the I-15/US-93 junction (west of I-15).

-WGS84 Lat: 36.4699 deg N Lon: -114.9226 deg W
-I, Class 2 via Northeast Slope **

"Bedrock Peak" (2,865)
Approached as per Dry Lake Peak, which is to the south. Dig the awesome dry lake driven over on the way to either peak.
-WGS84 Lat: 36.4943 deg N Lon: -114.9070 deg W
-I, Class 2 via Southeast Ridge **

Dry Benchmark (3,994)
This is the largest peak in the southern Arrow Canyon Range. Approach it directly from US-93 west or southwest of the peak.
-WGS84 Lat: 36.5091 deg N Lon: -114.9250 deg W
-II, Class 2-3 via West Face or Southwest Slope **

"Trench Peak" (3,455)
If traversing from Painted Prow to Trench Peak, you must drop into an interesting trench-like formation between the two peaks.
-WGS84 Lat: 36.5233 deg N Lon: -114.9072 deg W
-II, Class 2 via Northwest Face **
-I, Class 2 via West Face *

"Gunshot Peak" (3,020)
This is a minor lump in the desert just north of Dry Benchmark. You can drive a decent dirt road right to the base of it from US-93.
-WGS84 Lat: 36.5348 deg N Lon: -114.9197 deg W
-I, Class 2 via Southeast Face *
-I, Class 2 via North Face *

"Mount of Caves" (3,215)
The north face of the mountain is spackled with caves. The southwest ridge is a delightful class 4 scramble.
-WGS84 Lat: 36.5420 deg N Lon: -114.9115 deg W
-I, Class 3-4 via Northeast Face **
-I, Class 4 via Southwest Ridge ***

"Painted Prow" (3,468)
The peak is named for an interesting prow-like feature on the mountain's west face. There is fun scrambling on the west-northwest ridge, which can be cruised directly to the highpoint.
-WGS84 Lat: 36.5504 deg N Lon: -114.9051 deg W
-I, Class 3 via the long South Ridge **
-I, Class 3-4 via West-Northwest Ridge ***

Traversing the crest of the Arrow Canyon Range

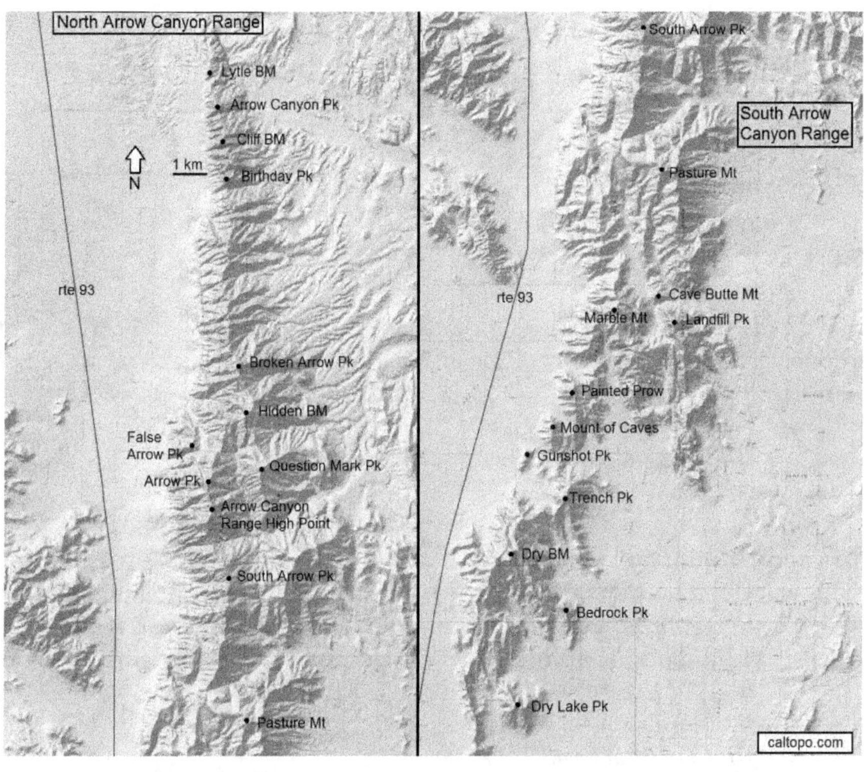
North Arrow Canyon Range
Lytle BM
Arrow Canyon Pk
Cliff BM
1 km
N
Birthday Pk
rte 93
Broken Arrow Pk
Hidden BM
False Arrow Pk
Question Mark Pk
Arrow Pk
Arrow Canyon Range High Point
South Arrow Pk
Pasture Mt
South Arrow Pk
South Arrow Canyon Range
Pasture Mt
rte 93
Cave Butte Mt
Marble Mt
Landfill Pk
Painted Prow
Mount of Caves
Gunshot Pk
Trench Pk
Dry BM
Bedrock Pk
Dry Lake Pk
caltopo.com

"Landfill Peak" (4,082)

This impressive peak was the third in an awesome 4-peak loop I once did in this part of the range. Careful route-finding is necessary to keep the going reasonable.

Landfill Peak has 862' of prominence.
-WGS84 Lat: 36.5689 deg N Lon: -114.8711 deg W
*-III, Class 2-3 via Northwest Ridge ****
*-III, Class 2-3 via South Ridge & West Face ****

"Marble Mountain" (4,139)

This was the final peak of a stellar 4-peak loop I once did in this portion of the range. Descending the west face can be tricky, due to some steep terrain in spots.

-WGS84 Lat: 36.5721 deg N Lon: -114.8912 deg W
*-III, Class 2-3 via southeast canyon ****
*-II, Class 2-3 via West Face ****

"Cave Butte" (3,398)

Cave Butte is south of Pasture Mountain and north of Landfill Peak, east of the main crest of the Arrow Canyon Range. There's no quick way to access this minor peak.

-WGS84 Lat: 36.5758 deg N Lon: -114.8765 deg W
*-III, Class 2 via North Slope **
*-III, Class 2 via South Face **

"Pasture Mountain" (4,837)

This graceful mountain became the first in an outstanding 4-peak loop I once did. The loop, which linked up Pasture Mountain, Cave Butte, Landfill Peak and Marble Mountain, covered some 13 miles and 6,600 feet of gain.

-WGS84 Lat: 36.6085 deg N Lon: -114.8753 deg W
*-II, Class 2 via West Slope ***
*-III, Class 2 via South Ridge ***

"South Arrow Peak" (5,219)

Being seven feet lower than Big Arrow Peak, South Arrow Peak just barely misses out on being the highest peak in the Arrow Canyon Range. At a glance, its complex north cliffs look virtually impassable.

From the intersection of US-95 and I-15 in downtown Las Vegas, take I-15 north for 21 miles to the US-93 (Great Basin Highway) exit. Follow US-93 north for 20 miles and park on the right (east) side of the road. The Arrow Canyon Range will be immediately east. Depending on where you parked, you should be roughly east of Big Arrow Peak, the highpoint of the range. Just south of Big Arrow Peak is a prominent wash draining from the crest. The head of the wash is at the saddle between Big Arrow Peak and South Arrow Peak.

Hike toward the wash leading to the saddle between the two peaks. Once the saddle is reached, work slightly up and eastward below the peak's north cliffs for a few hundred yards (the going over shifty talus and scree is tedious) and you'll come to a prominent break in the north-facing cliffs—a wide chute. This chute, with many variations possible, allows passage as easily as class 2-3. Work your way to its top. Easiest escape appears to be near its left (east) side. Atop the chute, you'll find yourself on a gentle slope. Head south up the slope toward higher ground. A minor ridge begins to form as you near the summit. Walk to the top. The views down the precipitous west face of the mountain are excellent.

The roundtrip is 7-8 miles, with perhaps 3,000 feet of elevation gain.

-WGS84 Lat: 36.6453 deg N Lon: -114.8816 deg W

*-III, Class 2-3 via North Cliffs from the West ****

Descending steep, grippy limestone slabs in the Arrow Canyon Range

Arrow Canyon Range Highpoint (5,226)

This peak is also known as Big Arrow Peak. It is a fine peak that once boasted an eight-foot summit cairn.

Follow the driving directions given for False Arrow Peak.

To climb via the North Ridge from Arrow Peak: Follow the hiking directions to Arrow Peak's summit via its west face or the prominent saddle north of the peak. Drop from the summit to the saddle between it and Big Arrow Peak then work up Big Arrow Peak's north ridge to its summit. The ridge connecting the two peaks is surprisingly rugged and serrated. With lots of scrambling and ups and downs, expect a solid hour to negotiate 0.5 mile of terrain. The route-finding is stimulating, but fairly straightforward.

The roundtrip if doing this route as an out-and-back is 9-10 miles with about 3,500 feet of gain.

To climb via the South Face from the West: From the road, note the large, prominent wash draining from the crest just south of Big Arrow Peak and hike toward it. Once the crest is reached at the head of the wash, you'll find yourself at the saddle between Big Arrow Peak and South Arrow Peak (which is just barely the 2nd highest peak in the range). Hang a left and wander up the south face of Big Arrow Peak. The going should never be harder than class 2-3, and even more mellow (scree) terrain can be found if one works toward the right (east) side of the face. The summit is not far away.

The roundtrip if doing this route as an out-and-back is 7-8 miles, with perhaps 3,000 feet of gain.

-WGS84 Lat: 36.6632 deg N Lon: -114.8873 deg W
-III, Class 2-3 via South Face from the West **
-III, Class 3 via North Ridge from Arrow Peak ****

"Arrow Peak" (5,205)

Arrow Peak is one of the most impressive high peaks of the Arrow Canyon Range. Though not officially named, it typically appears as "Arrow" on topographic maps. The peak's west face and south ridge are high quality, rugged routes. Arrow Peak is a desert classic.

Follow the driving directions given for False Arrow Peak.

To climb via the West Face from False Arrow Peak: Follow the hiking directions to the summit of False Arrow Peak via its north ridge. From the summit looking due east, the west face of Arrow Peak is steep, rugged and intimidating. Drop a few hundred feet to the saddle between False Arrow Peak and Arrow Peak. From the saddle, work back up and east toward Arrow Peak's west face. Although the going is quite mellow for some time, you'll soon find yourself confronted with steep, cliffy terrain a few hundred feet below the crest of the range. Although several options provide 4th and low 5th class opportunities, make for a 4th class weakness at a point directly above (that is, due east of) the saddle between the two peaks. Depending on the specific line chosen (and there are many to choose from), you might expect to climb up a steep chimney and then traverse right into a steep chute leading to a notch above. The rock is relatively good, the scrambling is enjoyable, and the views are great. Climbing to the notch, you'll be surprised (as I was) to find yourself on the crest of the range. Once the crest is gained, head south over rugged terrain and a false summit to the true summit.

To descend, either a) retrace your steps; b) continue north past the notch to a saddle (the top of the canyon you originally aimed for on the approach to False Arrow Peak) then drop into the canyon and work your way back to the car; or c) head south and loop back to the car via Big Arrow Peak.

To climb via the South Ridge from Arrow Canyon Range Highpoint: Follow the hiking directions to Big Arrow Peak's summit via its south face. Drop from the summit to the saddle between it and Arrow Peak then work up Arrow Peak's south ridge to its summit. The ridge connecting the two peaks is surprisingly rugged and serrated. With lots of scrambling and ups and downs, expect a solid hour to negotiate 0.5 mile of terrain. The route-finding is stimulating, but fairly straightforward.

The roundtrip for either route as an out-and-back is roughly 8-9 miles with about 3,500 feet of gain.

-WGS84 Lat: 36.6702 deg N Lon: -114.8887 deg W
-III, Class 3 via South Ridge from Arrow Canyon Range Highpoint ****
-III, Class 4 via West Face from False Arrow Peak ***

"Question Mark Peak" (5,008)

This is my dumb name for an ultra-obscure peak sitting on a spur ridge east of the crest of the Arrow Canyon Range. The summit affords phenomenal views of the bulk of the range, including interesting perspectives of Arrow Peak and the Arrow Canyon Range Highpoint.

Follow the driving directions given for Broken Arrow Peak. Once there, follow the hiking directions given to Hidden Benchmark via the Southwest Ridge from the West route (class 2). Once the saddle at the crest of the range atop the prominent canyon is gained, drop a few hundred feet east into the canyon on the other side of the crest. From there, Question Mark Peak is the obvious peak to the immediate east. Pick a line on Question Mark's west slope and head up.

Anticipate roundtrip numbers of about 10 miles and 3,200 feet of gain.

-WGS84 Lat: 36.6736 deg N Lon: -114.8707 deg W
-III, Class 2 via West Slope *
-III, Class 2 via North Ridge from Hidden Peak *

"False Arrow Peak" (3,943)

False Arrow Peak is a minor peak lying just west of the crest of the Arrow Canyon Range. The peak offers fine views of the rugged escarpment above. Though this is a minor peak, it makes for a nice bonus peak while working toward the west face of Arrow Peak.

From the intersection of US-95 and I-15 in downtown Las Vegas, take I-15 north for 21 miles to the US-93 (Great Basin Highway) exit. Follow US-93 north for 22 miles and park on the right (east) side of the road. The Arrow Canyon Range will be to the east. Depending on where you parked, you should be roughly east of Arrow Peak, or just to the south, Big Arrow

Peak, the highpoint of the range. A bit north of Arrow Peak is a prominent canyon coming down from the crest of the range. It drains to the northwest. Just south of Big Arrow Peak is a prominent wash draining from the crest. Ignoring the many minor washes and canyons between them, these two prominent drainages are important landmarks in this range.

Hike northeast across the desert toward the major canyon coming down from the crest north of Arrow Peak. As you approach, False Arrow Peak is the small peak sitting west of the crest, northwest of Arrow Peak. Reaching the mouth of the canyon, either gain False Arrow's north ridge as it appears on your right, or follow a minor wash just west of the ridge. Either way, you'll eventually need to gain the ridge and follow it to the top.

The roundtrip is about 4-5 miles with 1,500 feet of gain.

-WGS84 Lat: 36.6797 deg N Lon: -114.8941 deg W

*-II, Class 2 via North Ridge **

Hidden Benchmark (5,026)

Hidden Benchmark (also known as Hidden Peak) is a so-so peak located on the crest of the Arrow Canyon Range between fantastic Broken Arrow Peak and also-fantastic Arrow Peak.

Follow the driving directions given for Broken Arrow Peak.

To climb the Southwest Ridge from the West: From wherever you parked, hike across the desert to the mouth of the very prominent canyon draining northwest from the range crest above to the desert floor. Once there, wander up to the saddle at its head. The saddle sits on the crest of the range. Hang a left and follow the crest of the range northeast up to the summit of Hidden Peak.

Roundtrip numbers are about 2,500 feet of gain over 7-8 miles.

To climb the North Ridge from Broken Arrow Peak: Follow the directions given to Broken Arrow Peak via the West Face Chute (class 3). Rather than climb the class 3-4 cliffs at the base of the apparent false summit of Broken Arrow Peak, traverse right until you find yourself on the crest of the range between Broken Arrow Peak (left; north) and Hidden Peak (the less-impressive, rounded hump to the south). Once on the crest between the two peaks, drop to the saddle separating them and then follow undulating terrain to the summit of Hidden Peak.

Expect about 3,000 feet of gain over roughly 10 miles (roundtrip) for this route.

-WGS84 Lat: 36.6884 deg N Lon: -114.8762 deg W

*-III, Class 2 via Southwest Ridge from the West ***

*-III, Class 3 via North Ridge from Broken Arrow Peak ****

"Broken Arrow Peak" (5,146)

Broken Arrow Peak might be the finest peak in the excellent Arrow Canyon Range. 'Course, the title is not readily given up by Arrow Peak to its south.

With a number of potential routes up the peak's west face, all of them likely rather interesting, the route detailed here is quite good.

From the intersection of US-95 and I-15 in downtown Las Vegas, take I-15 north for 21 miles to the US-93 (Great Basin Highway) exit. Follow US-93 north for 22.5 miles and park on the right (east) side of the road. The Arrow Canyon Range will be to the east. Depending on where you parked, you should be roughly east (or slightly north) of Arrow Peak. A bit north of Arrow Peak is a prominent canyon coming down from the crest of the range. It drains to the northwest. This is an important landmark to remember.

From wherever you parked, hike across the desert toward the mouth of the very prominent canyon draining northwest from the range crest above to the desert floor. Once there, rather than enter this major canyon, hike north a few yards to the mouth of the next canyon. This canyon is big, but more minor. Head into the canyon, which forks after 0.5 mile. Take the left fork. In the distance, note a deep cleft (a chute, really) on the left side of the left fork of the canyon. It runs just about all the way to the crest of the range above. This cleft (chute) is your next objective. To the trained eye, it will have been visible since you left the highway.

Shortly after entering the left fork (a hundred yards or so), exit left out of the wash and work scree-covered slopes to the mouth of the chute. Head northeast up the chute (class 2 and 3) for several hundred feet until it dumps you off at a flattish spot near the base of a "ridge" running up to what appears to be a cliffy, minor summit just south of the true summit, which has just come into view. Work along the base of the "ridge" to the toe of the steep terrain immediately below the apparent false summit and head straight up the cliffs (30 feet of class 3-4 poor-quality rock) to the top. The exposure is nice. Alternatively, one can traverse right at the base of the cliffs and then work counterclockwise around to the feature's north side to avoid the steep, loose climbing of the cliffs. Regardless, once through this section head north a short distance to the base of the summit mass. A chute (class 3) near the right (east) side of the mass leads to the top. To descend, retrace your steps or traverse over to Hidden Benchmark and then descend that peak's southwest ridge route.

Roundtrip numbers for the out-and-back are roughly 8 miles and 2,600 feet of gain.

-WGS84 Lat: 36.7005 deg N Lon: -114.8784 deg W

*-III, Class 3-4 via West Face Chute *****

"Spider Peak" (3,396)

Spider Peak is a part of the northeast arm of the Arrow Canyon Range, wherein lies the funky and impressive Arrow Canyon itself. Starting from the Arrow Canyon trailhead, this is a pleasant jaunt into an obscure mountain area.

-WGS84 Lat: 36.6915 deg N Lon: -114.8057 deg W
*-II, Class 2 via North Ridge ***
*-II, Class 2 via East Slope ***

"Tortoise Peak" (3,237)

Tortoise Peak, named for the tortoise I encountered near the summit, is northeast of Spider Peak.

-WGS84 Lat: 36.6964 deg N Lon: -114.7907 deg W
*-II, Class 2 via West Slope ***
*-II, Class 2 via North Slopes ***

"Red Barrel Peak" (3,024)

Red Barrel Peak, northeast of Spider Peak, is a nice peak with excellent views. It is easily approached by heading south up the canyon on the peak's east side from the Arrow Canyon trailhead.

-WGS84 Lat: 36.7145 deg N Lon: -114.7956 deg W
*-II, Class 1-2 via Northwest Slope ***
*-II, Class 2 via East Slope ***

"Reale Peak" (2,876)

Reale Peak is a short but pleasant peak near the mouth of the Arrow Canyon narrows.

-WGS84 Lat: 36.7154 deg N Lon: -114.7532 deg W
*-II, Class 1-2 via North Slopes ***

"Fossil Peak" (2,737)

This small peak is due north of the entrance to the Arrow Canyon narrows. The views from the top are very nice.

-WGS84 Lat: 36.7360 deg N Lon: -114.7661 deg W
*-I, Class 1-2 via Northwest Slope ***
*-I, Class 2 via South Slope ***

"Hidden Wash Peak" (2,565)

Hidden Wash Peak sits north of and across the gulf of Arrow Canyon from Red Barrel Peak. The peak is above the head of the Arrow Canyon narrows, where a dam prevents one from walking the length of the canyon.

-WGS84 Lat: 36.7452 deg N Lon: -114.7940 deg W
*-II, Class 1-2 via East Slopes ***
*-II, Class 2 via West Ridge ***

"Birthday Peak" (3,897)

Thinking we were climbing Cliff Benchmark, we ended up on this one instead. There's an awesome arch that one gets close to as the summit is approached. With a keen eye, the arch can be seen from the highway. There were no signs of prior visitation on the summit. Approach the peak directly from US-93 to the west.

-WGS84 Lat: 36.7489 deg N Lon: -114.8828 deg W
*-III, Class 3-4 via South Face ****

Cliff Benchmark (3,598)

A small, nice-looking peak in the Arrow Canyon Range, between Lytle Benchmark and Birthday Peak.

-WGS84 Lat: 36.7584 deg N Lon: -114.8840 deg W
*-III, Class 2-3 via North Ridge ***

Dead Man Hill (2,136)

Dead Man Hill, hiding timidly behind 80' of prominence in the midst of obscurity, requires but a 2-minute effort from the jeep road along its southern base.

-WGS84 Lat: 36.7591 deg N Lon: -114.8361 deg W
*-I, Class 1-2 from the jeep road **

Table Mountain (2,283)
For a tiny mountain with only 200' of prominence, Table Mountain is remarkably well protected on most sides by minor but efficient cliff bands. The peak is easily approached from the jeep road running along its southern base.

-WGS84 Lat: 36.7594 deg N Lon: -114.8295 deg W
*-I, Class 2-3 from jeep road **

"Arrow Canyon Peak" (3,282)
Between Lytle Benchmark and Cliff Benchmark.

-WGS84 Lat: 36.7674 deg N Lon: -114.8858 deg W
*-I, Class 2 via North Slope **
*-II, Class 2 via South Slope **

Lytle Benchmark (2,776)
The northernmost peak in the Arrow Canyon Range.

-WGS84 Lat: 36.7763 deg N Lon: -114.8885 deg W
*-I, Class 2 via North Ridge **
*-I, Class 2 via South Ridge **

Desert National Wildlife Refuge

The DNWR, established in 1936, is the largest wildlife refuge in the lower 48 states. The arid region is home to six major mountain ranges. These mountain ranges, particularly the Sheep Mountains, are very rugged, the peaks often separated by deep, complex canyons and high limestone cliffs.

Lots of primitive camping spots can be found in the DNWR. A fine spot near a spring (Wiregrass Spring) can be found at Hidden Forest, a lush, pine forest below Hayford Peak. The Hidden Forest camp is a relatively long drive (and a five mile hike, to boot) from most of the peaks described in this book. Hidden Forest, incidentally, is one of the few places in the southern portion of the DNWR where water can be found during the summer. Water can be acquired from the cast iron tub next to the Hidden Forest cabin. All water should be treated before consumption. Also, camping next to springs or other water sources is strongly discouraged because it can prevent wildlife use of the water.

As with many of the remote areas covered in this book, come prepared with an adequate spare tire, water, anti-freeze (especially in summer) and food. No facilities are available beyond Corn Creek.

US-93 near I-15

The peaks in this subsection are arranged roughly south-to-north.

Dike Benchmark – East Summit (3,430)

The west summit appears to be higher. Approach as for Dike Benchmark.

-WGS84 Lat: 36.3426 deg N Lon: -114.9840 deg W
-II, Class 2 via North Ridge **

Dike Benchmark – Middle Summit (3,671)

I once had the pleasure of seeing six bighorn sheep on this mountain—three on the summit plateau and thre on the northeast ridge. Approach as for Dike Benchmark.

-WGS84 Lat: 36.3437 deg N Lon: -114.9890 deg W
-II, Class 2 via East Slope *
-II, Class 2 via Northeast Ridge **

"Mount Freedom" (3,770)

This is a pristine and beautiful mountain with awesome views of the region. A winter ascent on a calm, clear day can yield unbelievable views of the snowy Spring Mountains, Lake Mead, and even Signal Peak in Utah.

-WGS84 Lat: 36.3472 deg N Lon: -115.0240 deg W
-II, Class 1 via North Ridge ***

Dike Benchmark (4,109)

Huge canisters of something-or-other, a fallen structure, an old lamp and other odds and ends reside on the summit. To access the peak, leave US-93 where it bends southeast at the southern tip of the Arrow Canyon Range, and follow a decent dirt road to a point just northeast of the Dike massif.

-WGS84 Lat: 36.3472 deg N Lon: -114.9977 deg W
-II, Class 2-3 via Southeast Slope **

Marble 2 Benchmark (5,379)

While lacking any significant signature to make it "extra special," Marble 2 is a fine peak that is seldom visited. My December 2009 sign-in was only the 4th since the register was placed in 1986. The relatively long east ridge route is an enjoyable romp.

As of fall 2009, signage declaring 'Unauthorized Entry Prohibited' has been placed along the base of The Tri-Lambs, Marble 2 Benchmark, Mount Freedom, Fleur de Lis Peak and Elbow Range Highpoint. Per folks at the BLM, *hiking* into these areas is still permitted.

-WGS84 Lat: 36.3920 deg N Lon: -115.0501 deg W
-III, Class 2 via East Ridge **

Slogging up Dike Benchmark

"The Tri-Lambs – Dudley" (3,844)

As of fall 2009, signage declaring 'Unauthorized Entry Prohibited' has been placed along the eastern base of The Tri-Lambs, Marble 2 Benchmark, Fleur de Lis Peak and Elbow Range Highpoint. Per folks at the BLM, *hiking* into these areas is still permitted.

-WGS84 Lat: 36.3924 deg N Lon: -114.9922 deg W
*-II, Class 2 via North Slope ***
*-II, Class 2-3 via Northeast Ridge ***

"The Tri-Lambs – Louis" (4,085)

Can anyone guess what one of my favorite movies is?

-WGS84 Lat: 36.4042 deg N Lon: -114.9925 deg W
*-II, Class 2 via Northwest Slope ***
*-II, Class 2-3 via South Ridge ***

"Little Smokey" (3,190)
This small peak lies on the eastern edge of the DNWR. It is best approached from the powerline road to its east.

-WGS84 Lat: 36.4059 deg N Lon: -114.9789 deg W
*-I, Class 2 via Northeast Slope **

"The Tri-Lambs – Gilbert" (4,313)
A highly enjoyable north-to-south loop of the Tri-Lambs can be done in 3-5 hours car-to-car. The Tri-Lambs are approached directly from US-93.

-WGS84 Lat: 36.4161 deg N Lon: -114.9948 deg W
*-II, Class 2 via North Ridge ***
*-II, Class 2 via South Ridge ***

Peak 4,608 (4,608)
This and Peak 4300 (just to the northeast) are easily accessed as described for the latter peak.

-WGS84 Lat: 36.4373 deg N Lon: -115.0403 deg W
*-II, Class 1-2 via Northeast Ridge ***

Peak 4,300 (4,300)
This obscure peak is slightly northeast of Marble 2 Benchmark. The peak and its neighbor to the southwest, Peak 4608, are easily accessed via a good west-east dirt road that leaves Highway 93 and terminates just southeast of the summit.

-WGS84 Lat: 36.4531 deg N Lon: -115.0313 deg W
*-II, Class 1-2 via South Slopes ***

Corn Creek

The peaks in this subsection are accessed from Corn Creek, off of US-95. They are arranged here roughly south-to-north.

From the intersection of US-95 and I-15 near downtown Las Vegas, head north on US-95. Leaving the city, you'll eventually pass the Kyle Canyon (SR-157) exit on your left and the Snow Mountain exit (exit 95) on your right. The next turn-off is the signed Corn Creek Road. It is a well-graded dirt road on your right in the neighborhood of mile marker 101.5. Once on Corn Creek Road, follow it four miles to a beautiful new visitor center, restrooms and some interpretive signage (on the left). Behind the visitor center is a small pond and some endangered fish (the Pahrump poolfish) in a refugium (similar to an aquarium) in an interpretive area.

Castle Rock (4,365)

Castle Rock is the small peak immediately west of the much higher Gass Peak (the latter rises nearly 2,600 feet higher than the former). Not only can semi-interesting routes be found on the mountain, but the views from the summit are absolutely terrific.

Follow the driving directions given for Yucca Benchmark to Gass Peak Road. Turn onto Gass Peak Road and continue for 2.5 miles to a turn-out and parking spot on the right. There will be a wilderness boundary sign just inside the turn-out. Vehicles are not permitted beyond this area. Although I once got this far in a Toyota Corolla, I'd recommend a high clearance vehicle (or better, a 4x4).

From the turn-out, Castle Rock is the obvious small mountain immediately south across the open desert. Hike cross-country a little over a mile to the base of the mountain. From there, pick a line that looks good and head up. The summit is not far away. Largely class 2, some short stretches of class 3 (and higher) can be found (and avoided, too).

The roundtrip is about three miles, with only a few hundred feet of elevation gain.

-WGS84 Lat: 36.3987 deg N Lon: -115.2458 deg W

*-I, Class 2 via North Slopes ***

Gass Peak (6,943)

Gass Peak is the prominent and pyramidal mountain forming the northern edge of the Las Vegas Valley. Although a number of routes have been established on the mountain, most approach it via a hike up the back (north) side. The large mountain is a part of the Las Vegas Range.

Follow the driving directions given for Yucca Benchmark to Gass Peak Road. Turning onto Gass Peak Road, jar your vehicle for 8.1 miles to a turn-out (and parking area) on the right. There, you'll also encounter a service road heading south toward Gass Peak. Vehicles are not permitted beyond this parking area. Although I once got this far in a Toyota Corolla, I'd recommend a high clearance vehicle (or better, a 4x4).

From the parking area adjacent to Gass Peak Road, hike the access road to a fork. Head up the left fork until it ends. At that point, head cross-country and gain a ridgeline that can be followed to the summit. From the summit, the views looking south toward Las Vegas are unusual. Try to ignore the manmade debris growing out of the mountaintop.

Plan on 6-7 miles roundtrip with a bit over 2,000 feet of elevation gain.

-WGS84 Lat: 36.4007 deg N Lon: -115.1804 deg W

*-II, Class 2 via North Slopes ***

"Cow Camp Peak" (5,327)

Take Cow Camp Road and park a short bit beyond Black Hills Gap. From there, a short but steep hike up the southeastern aspect leads to the top, where a MacLeod/Lilley register is found under a cairn.

-WGS84 Lat: 36.5822 deg N Lon: -115.3514 deg W

-II, Class 2 via Southeastern Aspect **

"First Peak" (5,676)

This rugged peak is sandwiched between First Canyon and Yucca Gap. The views along the ridge and from the summit are nice.

-WGS84 Lat: 36.4625 deg N Lon: -115.2733 deg W

-II, Class 2 via South Ridge **

Fossil Ridge (5,449)

This is a nice peak. There are three nearby springs one can visit while in the area.

-WGS84 Lat: 36.4440 deg N Lon: -115.2089 deg W

-I, Class 2 via South Face **

"Naked Peak" (5,428)

Naked Peak is the low, blocky mountain one passes to the east of while traveling the Mormon Well Road a mile or two past Yucca Gap. Its west face, not entirely visible from the road, is impressively cliffy.

Follow the driving directions given for Yucca Benchmark to Yucca Gap. Pass through Yucca Gap and continue for another three miles to a pull-out on the left, roughly a mile northeast of Naked Peak. The road is rough, and though passenger cars can often reach this point with little difficulty, a high clearance vehicle (or better yet, a 4x4) is recommended.

From the pull-out, hike toward the base of Naked Peak's northeast slope. Once there, work your way up class 1-2 terrain to the summit. This is the easiest route on an otherwise surprisingly rugged little mountain.

The roundtrip requires a little over two miles of effort, with less 1,000 feet of elevation gain.

-WGS84 Lat: 36.4608 deg N Lon: -115.2548 deg W

-I, Class 1-2 via Northeast Slope *

"Lost Yucca Peak" (6,665)

Lost Yucca Peak sits 0.5 mile south of Yucca Benchmark in the southeastern portion of the Sheep Mountains. On my only visit, I didn't find any evidence of earlier visitation. Like many in this desolate range, it is a lonely peak.

To get to the mountain, follow the driving directions given for Yucca Benchmark.

To use the Southeast Slope from Naked Peak: From either parking area (the first one works better), head cross-country, following directions to Naked Peak via its northeast slope. Rather than head for Naked's summit, when you get within 200 feet of the top traverse to the right below Naked's north cliffs. You'll soon come to a saddle between Naked Peak and a highpoint on the ridge connected to it on the north/northwest. From the saddle, start heading north, following the left side of the ridge below the crest. As you progress, the cliffs on the left side of the ridge grow tall. Continue to skirt along them until you can climb onto the ridge crest just before a large rocky outcropping resembling a battleship on the ridge. Climbing over the battleship outcropping (class 2), you'll see Lost Yucca Peak dead ahead of you. Continue along the ridge crest, bend left, and then work your way to a minor saddle directly below Lost Yucca's summit. From there, follow your nose to the top. The terrain gets a bit steep as you near the flattish summit area.

The roundtrip is about five miles with roughly 2,400 feet of elevation gain.

To climb via the Northeast Ridge: Due to potential route-finding complications in this rugged area, this route works better as an ascent route than a descent route. On a descent of this route, be prepared for high, unexpected, and impassable dry waterfalls blocking your progress. Consider a loop of the southeast slope route instead.

From either parking area (the second one works better), head cross-country for the prominent canyon just south of the large shelter cave (Shaman Cave) below Yucca Benchmark. Despite major obstacles (dry waterfalls) in the canyon that you must negotiate (always working left to bypass them) you eventually want to work to the head of the canyon. It will end at the saddle between Yucca Benchmark and Lost Yucca Peak. Once in the canyon, continue up-canyon, exiting left once you see the first high dry waterfall ahead that blocks your progress. Negotiate the terrain above (class 2-3), aiming for the gully below a battleship-like formation on the ridge crest above to the left. From below the battleship-like formation, work your way back into the canyon or the terrain just above it on the left. Eventually gaining the saddle at the head of the canyon, scramble 10 feet of 3rd class rock on the left to gain the northeast ridge of Lost Yucca Peak. Once on the northeast ridge, follow class 2 terrain to the flattish summit area.

Expect a roundtrip of about 4 or 5 miles, with about 2,500 feet of gain.

-WGS84 Lat: 36.4749 deg N Lon: -115.2659 deg W

*-II, Class 2 via Southeast Slope from Naked Peak **

*-II, Class 3 via Northeast Ridge ***

Yucca Benchmark (7,103)

Yucca Benchmark is a fine but lonely peak in the Sheep Mountains. It lies close to Lost Yucca Peak and Naked Peak near the southeastern portion of the rugged range.

While visiting Yucca Benchmark, be sure to stop by the large shelter cave (locally known as Shaman Cave) below its east face. It is massive, and massively worth seeing.

From the junction immediately after the Corn Creek visitor center, get onto the signed dirt Mormon Well Road and follow it 4.3 miles to the signed Gass Peak Road. Continue straight past Gass Peak Road and drive for another 1.2 miles to Yucca Gap, the gap between Fossil Ridge (on the right) and the Sheep Mountains (on the left). Pass through Yucca Gap and continue for another three miles to a small parking pull-out on the left, roughly a mile northeast of Naked Peak, the nearby low blocky mountain. Alternatively, a short bit beyond pull into another small pull-out on the left side. From this second turn-out, Shaman Cave can be clearly seen across the desert. Either pull-out will work just fine.

The road is rough, and though passenger cars can often reach this point with little difficulty, a high clearance vehicle (or better yet, a 4x4) is recommended.

To use the Southeast Cave Route: From either parking spot, head cross-country across the desert toward the wash directly below Shaman Cave. As you approach the cave, leave the wash and climb up onto the scree slope on its left side. Follow the scree slope up until you can traverse back right and onto gentle terrain just left of another wash immediately above the cave. Paralleling the wash for a bit, follow your nose generally westward and up toward the summit, soon encountering a ridge. Follow the ridge to the summit.

This roundtrip involves perhaps five miles of effort, with around 2,500 feet of elevation gain.

To climb the East Slopes: Due to potential route-finding complications, this route works better as an ascent route than a descent route. Unfortunately, it's not that great of a route. It best serves as the ascent portion of a loop with the southeast cave route.

Approaching from the second turn-out described, head cross-country toward Shaman Cave. A half-mile or so before you reach it, start angling to the right, looking for a short (15-20 foot) class 3 break in the cliffs near the bottom of Yucca's east slopes, perhaps 0.25 mile north of the cave. Everything else is considerably harder, so the break should be apparent when you get to it. You'll likely need to cross through a couple of minor washes before you get to the break. Once through the break, head up the east slope through minor washes and ridges toward the summit above. You should meet up with the southeast cave route near the base of the ridge below the summit.

This roundtrip involves roughly 5-6 miles of effort, with about 2,500 feet of elevation gain. If looping the two routes, expect comparable numbers.

-WGS84 Lat: 36.4842 deg N Lon: -115.2585 deg W
*-II, Class 2 via Southeast Cave Route ***
*-II, Class 3 via East Slopes ***

The snow-clad Las Vegas range in winter

Peak 6,252 (6,252)

An enjoyable hike from Quail Spring. We found the top to a military airplane cockpit, and later, a radar sighting target on the ridges near the peak.

-WGS84 Lat: 36.4720 deg N Lon: -115.1558 deg W
*-II, Class 2 via Southeast Wash **
*-II, Class 2 via Northeast Ridge ***

Peak 6,610 (6,610)

Although the official road is blocked at Quail Spring a few miles southwest of the peak, one can still walk the road to the eastern base of the peak then head easily to the summit. A MacLeod/Lilley register is found under a summit cairn. I have a history of using bogus names in summit registers, and in this register I signed in as 'Juan Densmore' after having met the legendary Doors drummer the evening before.

-WGS84 Lat: 36.4810 deg N Lon: -115.1229 deg W
*-II, Class 2 via East Slope **

-II, Class 2 via West Slope **

Sheep Peak (9,750)

A fine summit. While often approached from the west, I thought the eastern approach was rather enjoyable.

-WGS84 *Lat: 36.5829 deg N Lon: -115.2488 deg W*

-III, Class 2-3 via East Ridge ****

Hayford Peak (9,912)

Me and a buddy climbed this one in wintry conditions one late spring after a blizzard had slammed the desert the evening before. Leaving US-95 at Corn Creek Road, follow the graded dirt road to the visitor center and then hang a left onto a graded but less smooth dirt road. The drive is long and bumpy. Eventually, Deadman Canyon Road comes in on the right. Follow it for as long as you're comfortable. It's more bumpy.

On the hike, leave some time to hang out and enjoy Hidden Forest, the trees, the cabin, and the small spring there.

-WGS84 Lat: 36.6578 deg N Lon: -115.2008 deg W

-III, Class 2 via Southwest Ridge from Deadman Canyon ****

Bald Knob (6,681)

This nice, obscure peak is a mile or so southeast of Twin Buttes. If approaching from Twin Buttes, expect to do a bit of route-finding up and over several subsidiary lumps.

-WGS84 Lat: 36.5559 deg N Lon: -115.1200 deg W

-II, Class 1-2 via Southwest Wash *

-II, Class 1-2 via Northwest Slopes **

Twin Buttes (7,208)

If approaching via the north ridge, expect some route-finding and scrambling up the final east face.

-WGS84 Lat: 36.5793 deg N Lon: -115.1440 deg W

-II, Class 2 via Southeast Ridge *

-II, Class 2-3 via North Ridge & East Face **

Peak 7,265 (7,265)

This pleasantly obscure peak sits just north of Twin Buttes.

-WGS84 Lat: 36.5952 deg N Lon: -115.1422 deg W

-II, Class 1-2 via West Slope **

-II, Class 1-2 via South Ridge **

Banded Ridge South (5,449)
From the primitive dirt road that passes the southern base of this peak, a short but unpleasant hike leads to this decent overlook of the area.

-WGS84 Lat: 36.7204 deg N Lon: -115.2751 deg W
*-I, Class 2 via East Slope **
*-I, Class 2 via North Ridge ***

Banded Ridge North (5,356)
A lot of miles of bumpy dirt roads are required to get to this minor peak. The summit has a seldom-signed register.

-WGS84 Lat: 36.7379 deg N Lon: -115.2753 deg W
*-I, Class 2 via South Ridge ***
*-I, Class 2 via Northeast Slope **

US-93 near NV-168

The peaks in this subsection are arranged here from south-to-north.

Quartzite Mountain (7,111)
The highpoint of the Las Vegas Range. Traditionally approached from the south, this northern approach is an easy, scenic alternative.

-WGS84 Lat: 36.5021 deg N Lon: -115.0875 deg W
*-II, Class 2 via North Ridge or Northwest Slopes ****

Fossil Benchmark (7,084)
Easily approached from the dirt Mormon Well Road in Peek-A-Boo Canyon by following an old road halfway to the summit.

-WGS84 Lat: 36.5169 deg N Lon: -115.0782 deg W
*-I, Class 1 via Northwest Ridge ***

"Gumby Peak" (9,374)
Although not the highest peak in this part of the DNWR, it is certainly one of the more interesting in appearance. From the east, its huge, dark-gray cliffs are imposing and eye-catching. The north ridge is a pleasant hike leading to an easy scramble through an interesting boulder field set amongst a forest of ponderosa pines, white firs and bristlecone pines. The south ridge is rugged and brushy. From the junction of Mormon Well Road and Sawmill Canyon Road, follow Sawmill Canyon Road (left fork) past a locked gate and for several miles (watching for a minor left fork, which you take, below Gumby Peak). Leave the road at the base of the north ridge to follow that route to the summit. A GPS is handy. Expect a 12.5 mile/4,200+ foot day.

-WGS84 Lat: 36.6679 deg N Lon: -115.1698 deg W
*-III, Class 2 via North Ridge ****
*-III, Class 2-3 via East Ridge-to-South Ridge ****

The Arrow Canyon Range (distant) from the summit of Gumby Peak. Gumbo Peak can be seen (white spot at the summit) just above and left of the Gumby Peak summit cairn. The view looks east.

"Gumbo Peak" (7,775)

Although nearly 2,000 feet lower than nearby Gumby Peak, Gumbo Peak is actually the more prominent of the two (with roughly 100 feet more prominence). While the hike to the summit is nothing remarkable, the summit rocks are a pleasant spot to enjoy a beverage and take in the views. The peak is approached as per Little Sawmill Peak and Gumby Peak, leaving the road at a point between the two and pushing toward the summit up steep but largely forgiving slopes.

-WGS84 Lat: 36.6713 deg N Lon: -115.1373 deg W
-II, Class 1-2 via West Slope **
-II, Class 1-2 via Northwest Slope **

Johns Peak (9,401)

Being the lowest of the trio of 9,000-foot peaks in this part of the Sheep Range, it's interesting to me that it's the only one with an official name. Johns Peak is just a minor bump, with about 60 feet of rise from its saddle with Iko Iko Peak to the north. To get here, follow the directions given for Gumby Peak to the base of Gumby's north ridge. From there, keep following the old road all the way to Sawmill Spring (there was water when I visited in mid-September 2010). From the spring, gain the ridge to the right of the water trough (looking up-canyon) and follow it to the high crest above. Once there, hang a right and follow gentle terrain to the 4-foot tall protruding summit block.

-WGS84 Lat: 36.6832 deg N Lon: -115.1878 deg W
-III, Class 1-2 via East Ridge **

"Little Sawmill Peak" (6,561)

I heard about this small "peak" after a friend mentioned seeing it on Jim Boone's excellent outdoor site (www.birdandhike.com). Although the summit rocks were described as class 4, they were unfortunately only class 2. Nice views of Gumby Peak from the top. The peak is easily approached directly from Sawmill Canyon Road, about 1.4 miles past the locked gate (which is just beyond the junction of Sawmill Canyon Road and Mormon Well Road).

-WGS84 Lat: 36.6869 deg N Lon: -115.1202 deg W
-I, Class 2 from the old road *

Gumby Peak, to the west, from the summit of Little Sawmill Peak, nearly 3,000 feet below.

"Iko Iko Peak" (9,676)

This peak is a short hike from the summit of Johns Peak. A bit of sloggy talus must be dealt with as one approaches the summit from the south.

-WGS84 Lat: 36.6882 deg N Lon: -115.1852 deg W
-III, Class 1-2 via South Slope **
-III, Class 1-2 via North Ridge **

"Big John" (9,787)

This is the 2nd highest peak in the Sheep Range. It is isolated and not easily reached. Its easiest route (class 1-2) follows the Sawmill Canyon Road (east of the peak) before leaving it at Sawmill Spring and heading up and over Johns Peak and Iko Iko Peak to its own lofty summit. It requires a roundtrip of about 15 miles with nearly 5,000 feet of elevation gain. A mostly pleasant (but sometimes loose and tedious) short-cut *can* be used, though I'd suggest it be reserved for the descent. To pick up the short-cut from the summit, find the head of a rubbly draw draining southeast just southeast of Big John's summit. Follow this drainage (class 2-3) until it meets the road shortly below Sawmill Spring.

-WGS84 Lat: 36.6960 deg N Lon: -115.1836 deg W
-III, Class 1-2 from Iko Iko Peak ***
-III, Class 2-3 via Southeast Draw **

Jason P admiring the western view from the summit of Big John

Beatty

Bare Mountains

The Bare Mountains is the small, colorful range of dry, rugged beauty seen along US-95 as one approaches Beatty, Nevada from Las Vegas. The range's striated coloration is striking, particularly when viewed from the ghost town of Carrara at its western base. The peaks of the range are seldom-visited, and thus lonely.

Primitive camping can be found on BLM land on and along the mountains. Additionally, comfortable lodging and gas/food can be readily scored in nearby Beatty, seven miles distant.

The peaks in this subsection are arranged south-to-north.

Wildcat Peak (5,052)

This is the southernmost peak in the Bare Mountains. A well-graded dirt road heads northeast from US-95 south of Beatty, passing to the immediately south of the mountain.

-WGS84 Lat: 36.7881 deg N Lon: -116.6447 deg W
-II, Class 2+ via South Ridge **
-II, Class 2+ via East Gully *

Bare Mountain (6,317)

Bare Mountain is a striking desert mountain of fantastic striated coloration. The highpoint of an impressive and rugged range of inhospitable terrain, the peak's west ridge, approached from the nearby ghost town of Carrara, is a fantastic, direct route that features fun scrambling along a long knife-edge high on the mountain.

From Las Vegas, follow US-95 north toward Beatty, Nevada (115 miles away). Seven miles before Beatty, as you pass by the obviously colorful and striking Bare Mountains to the east, keep your eyes peeled for the ruins of Carrara. They are plainly visible a mile off of the highway and consist of several building remnants. (A mile or so before Carrara, much closer to the highway, are a couple of ruins (foundations and whatnot). Carrara is much more prominent.) A good dirt road heads east from the highway directly toward Carrara. Head up the dirt road toward the mountains as far as you feel comfortable, passing Carrara along the way. The road becomes rough but is typically passable in a passenger car. The road ends after 3 miles in a canyon directly below Bare Mountain.

From the end of the road, hike east into the canyon. Bare Mountain's west ridge is immediately above you to the left. At any point that seems reasonable, start working your way up to the ridge crest. Depending on where you head up, the going could be anywhere from class 2 to class 5. As an alternative, you can continue deeper into the canyon, soon coming to a series of dry falls. A couple of the dry falls require a short bit of class 4 scrambling to surmount. They can also be bypassed by working around them, typically on their left. After the last dry fall, continue deeper into the canyon for another hundred yards then head up to the crest of the west ridge on class 2 terrain. Once the crest of the west ridge is gained, continue up. Gentler terrain can almost always be found by looking to either side of the ridge crest, though it's far more fun to stick to the crest. With several short sections of class 3-4 scrambling along the way, the west ridge features a solid 150 yards or more of knife-edge terrain, one section being particularly airy and narrow. Follow the west ridge to the crest of the range above. From there, a short scramble to the northeast will take you to the summit.

Roundtrip numbers are about 6 miles and 2,500 feet of gain.

-WGS84 Lat: 36.8429 deg N Lon: -116.6745 deg W

-III, Class 4 via West Ridge ***

"Barely Peak" (6,050+)

Barely Peak is a minor summit along the Bare Mountains crest between Bare Mountain and Bare Mountain Peak. The peak appears far more prominent when viewed from US-95 south of Beatty, Nevada than it does when actually standing on it. Hardly an objective of its own, Barely Peak does make for a worthwhile (and necessary) stop-over on a traverse of the range.

To climb the North Ridge: Follow directions to Bare Mountain Peak via its south ridge. From the summit of Bare Mountain Peak, drop down the gentle east/northeast slope until you can attain the crest of the range. Following the crest south/southeast, work around the west side (working directly over it, as well as around the east side, works as well) of a prominent feature at the southwest end of Razorback Ridge until you can regain the crest of the range. From here, Barely Peak is the next peak to the south, perhaps 0.5 mile away. Follow class 1-2 terrain south to the summit. As an out-and-back, this route involves about 9 miles, with perhaps 2,500 feet of gain.

To climb the South Ridge: Follow directions to Bare Mountain via its west ridge. From the summit, Barely Mountain is the next peak north/northwest along the range crest. Drop to the range crest and head northwest. You'll soon arrive at Barely's summit. As an out-and-back, this route involves about 8 miles and roughly 2,900 feet of gain.

-WGS84 Lat: 36.8530 deg N Lon: -116.6877 deg W

-III, Class 2 via North Ridge *

-III, Class 2 via South Ridge *

Razorback Ridge (6,060)

Razorback Ridge is a ridge spurring to the northeast off the crest of the Bare Mountains between Barely Peak and Bare Mountain Peak. Unfortunately, the summit is less interesting than a prominent feature directly on the range crest at the southwest end of the ridge.

Follow the directions given for Barely Peak or Bare Mountain Peak to either of the summits. From either summit, head along the crest of the Bare Mountains toward the prominent feature at the southwest end of Razorback Ridge. Work around to the northeast side of the prominent feature and gain the crest of Razorback Ridge a few minutes' walk from the summit. It offers great views of the Bare Mountains.

The roundtrip is variable, depending upon the approach. A generic ballpark figure is 8 miles with perhaps 3,000 feet of elevation gain.

-WGS84 Lat: 36.8649 deg N Lon: -116.6900 deg W

-III, Class 2 via West Ridge from Bare Mountain *

-III, Class 2 via West Ridge from Bare Mountain Peak *

Bare Mountain Peak (6,030)

Lying a couple miles northwest along the range crest from Bare Mountain, the range's highpoint, Bare Mountain Peak, is an obscure, prominent mountain that sees little visitation. Approachable from a number of directions, including from the vicinity of the nearby ghost town of Carrara, or better, if one wants a loop, via a haul along the crest from Bare Mountain and its west ridge, Bare Mountain Peak is certainly an adventure worth undertaking. Desert solitude and far-reaching vistas are the rewards for taking the time to scramble up this nice peak.

Follow the directions given for Bare Mountain. This approach works well for the south ridge route and the optional traverse along the crest from Bare Mountain.

To climb the South Ridge: From wherever you parked your car, head northwest across desert terrain toward the base of Bare Mountain Peak's south ridge. (Depending on where you parked, the mountain may not be visible and you may have to first follow an old mining road up to a saddle near the base of Bare Mountain's west ridge. The mountain should come into view in the distance once the saddle is gained.) The cross-country slog across the desert on the way to the base of the south ridge involves a number of ups and downs—tedious, but not too long. Once the base of the south ridge is gained, head up gentle terrain to the point where it obviously steepens and becomes more craggy. Route-find your way up interesting terrain to the summit. Although it's certainly possible to find something easier, the going is largely in the class 3-4 realm. Class 5 terrain can be found as easily as it can be avoided.

As an out-and-back, this route involves about 5 miles with a couple thousand feet of gain.

To traverse from Bare Mountain: Follow the directions given for Bare Mountain's west ridge route to the summit of that peak. From the summit, Bare Mountain Peak is the large and prominent mountain a couple miles northwest along the crest. Drop to the range crest and head northwest. Passing over Barely Peak along the way, then later around a prominent feature at the southwest end of Razorback Ridge, work your way across progressively easier terrain to the northeast slope of Bare Mountain Peak. Once there, follow class 1-2 terrain to the summit.

If doing this route as a closed loop, expect about 7-8 miles and 4,500+ feet of gain.

-WGS84 Lat: 36.8660 deg N Lon: -116.7071 deg W
*-III, Class 2 via traverse from Bare Mountain ***
*-III, Class 3-4 via South Ridge ***

Meiklejohn Peak (5,940)
An obscure peak on the eastern edge of the Bare Mountains. A network of good dirt roads leads from the southern end of Beatty to the vicinity of Secret Pass. Start hiking from there.

-WGS84 Lat: 36.8830 deg N Lon: -116.6632 deg W
*-I, Class 2 via West Face **

South of the Bare Mountains

The peaks in this subsection are located just off (and usually east of) US-95, south of the Bare Mountains. They are arranged here roughly south-to-north.

Skeleton Hills – West (3,672)
It's easy to drive right on past this rugged desert peak just off US-95 on the edge of Amargosa Valley. The peak hosts a fun scramble to its flat, tabletop-like summit. A good north-south dirt access road runs just west of the base of the peak.

The peak has 827' of prominence.
-WGS84 Lat: 36.6109 deg N Lon: -116.3578 deg W
*-II, Class 2 via West Face ****

"Foundation Peak" (3,466)
Foundation Peak is north of Skeleton Hills and US-95, near Amargosa Valley. The peak is easily accessible via a run-down but still drivable road leading to the summit.

-WGS84 Lat: 36.6446 deg N Lon: -116.3380 deg W
*-I, Class 1 via service road ***

Black Marble (3,662)
This small mountain is just south of Wildcat Peak. Use the same graded dirt road used to access Black Cone, Little Cones, Red Cone and Wildcat Peak.

-WGS84 Lat: 36.7511 deg N Lon: -116.6253 deg W
*-I, Class 2 via Southwest Ridge **

Little Cones (3,083)
Little Cones, Black Cone and Red Cone are easily approached from the graded dirt road between Wildcat Peak and Black Marble.

-WGS84 Lat: 36.7711 deg N Lon: -116.6062 deg W
*-I, Class 1 from any direction **

Red Cone (3,414)
This cone is approached as per Black Cone and Little Cones.

-WGS84 Lat: 36.7937 deg N Lon: -116.5794 deg W
*-I, Class 1 from any direction **

Black Cone (3,688)
A graded dirt road (the same one used to approach Wildcat Peak) from US-95 leads out to the bases of Black Cone, Little Cones and Red Cone.

-WGS84 Lat: 36.8136 deg N Lon: -116.5651 deg W
*-I, Class 1 via West Slope **

Beatty Area

The peaks in this subsection are accessed via a variety of points. They are clustered around the small (and not very charming) town of Beatty, Nevada. The peaks are arranged here alphabetically.

Beatty Mountain (4,282)
This peak, hovering nicely to the east of Beatty, can be approached from a number of directions. The same dirt road used to access Meiklejohn Peak works well.

-WGS84 Lat: 36.9066 deg N Lon: -116.7390 deg W
*-I, Class 2 via Southwest Ridge **

Black Peak (4,653)
Approached from Rhyolite, the cool, little ghost town just outside of Beatty off of NV-374.

-WGS84 Lat: 36.9190 deg N Lon: -116.8128 deg W
*-I, Class 2 from Rainbow Mountain **

Bonanza Mountain (4,300)
A lame and indistinct "summit" outside of Beatty, Nevada, it's really more of a shoulder of Sutherland Mountain. Approached from the ghost town of Rhyolite.

-WGS84 Lat: 36.8971 deg N Lon: -116.8359 deg W
*-I, Class 1-2 via NW Ridge **
*-I, Class 2 via East Face **

Burton Mountain (4,365)
The colorful peak northwest of Beatty, Burton Mountain was the 5th of 8 named peaks I climbed one day while in the Beatty area.

-WGS84 Lat: 36.9180 deg N Lon: -116.7885 deg W
*-I, Class 2 via West Face **

Busch Peak (5,070)
The highest peak hovering directly over the ghost town of Rhyolite. The summit is sublime.

-WGS84 Lat: 36.9151 deg N Lon: -116.8389 deg W
*-I, Class 2 via SW Ridge ***
*-I, Class 2 via SE Face ***

Coba Mountain (4,638)
Coba Mountain is an interesting north-south ridge with a steepish west face and a mellow east slope. The peak is on the south side of US-95, north of Springdale Mountain and Beatty.

-WGS84 Lat: 37.1522 deg N Lon: -116.9215 deg W
*-I, Class 1 via North Ridge ***

"Elizabeth Peak" (3,660)
Elizabeth Peak was named for young lady who violently lost her life the day before our ascent. The peak is easily accessed via the graded dirt road that heads west from US-95 south of Beatty and adjacent to the fishing pond next to the highway.

-WGS84 Lat: 36.8804 deg N Lon: -116.7625 deg W
*-I, Class 1 via Northwest Slope **

Ladd Mountain (4,132)
Above Rhyolite, a very neat ghost town with ruins of a jail, a bank, a hotel, a brothel, and even a house made of bottles. Approached from the townsite itself, the ascent will prove to be short, steep, loose, and barely worth making.

-WGS84 Lat: 36.8958 deg N Lon: -116.8212 deg W
*-I, Class 2 via Northwest Face **

Montgomery Mountain (4,334)
An easy bag with Paradise Mountain. Approached from Rhyolite.

-WGS84 Lat: 36.9106 deg N Lon: -116.8085 deg W
*-I, Class 2-3 via Southeast Slope **

Paradise Mountain (4,295)
The mountain has two summit crags of comparable elevation. Bag them both (class 2-3).

-WGS84 Lat: 36.9086 deg N Lon: -116.8018 deg W
*-I, Class 2+ via Southwest Ridge **
*-I, Class 2+ via Northwest Ridge from Montgomery Mountain **

"Pioneer Mine Peak" (4,991)

Pioneer Mine Peak is just east of Donovan Mountain. At the northwestern base of the peak is Pioneer Mine Peak, from which a steep service road can be hiked to the summit.

-WGS84 Lat: 37.0078 deg N Lon: -116.7938 deg W

-I, Class 1 via service road **

Rainbow Mountain (4,662)

Approached from Rhyolite. Black Peak and Rainbow Mountain can be easily done together in less than an hour. Tough stuff! Train hard.

-WGS84 Lat: 36.9205 deg N Lon: -116.8166 deg W

-I, Class 2 from Black Peak *

-I, Class 2+ via Southwest Face *

Sawtooth Mountain (6,005)

If one chooses, a service road can be driven nearly to the top. From there, some fun scrambling ensues. There is probably an easier way to the top than the south chimney; I simply picked a fun-looking line and went for it!

-WGS84 Lat: 36.9367 deg N Lon: -116.8494 deg W

-I, Class 4 via South Chimney ***

Sharp Benchmark (4,790)

Super obscure. Use the system of good dirt roads heading off left from the vicinity of the entrance to Rhyolite.

-WGS84 Lat: 36.8857 deg N Lon: -116.9063 deg W

-I, Class 2 via North Slope *

Springdale Mountain (4,941)

A paved service road leaves US-95 north of Beatty and goes straight to the top.

-WGS84 Lat: 37.0817 deg N Lon: -116.8184 deg W

-I, Class 1 via service road **

"Springdale Mountain – Northeast" (4,735)

Follow the paved service road leading to the top of Springdale Mountain then start hiking from the saddle between the two peaks. There's some weird, wooden contraption on the summit.

-WGS84 Lat: 37.0937 deg N Lon: -116.8113 deg W

-I, Class 2 via South Ridge *

Sutherland Mountain (4,500)

An easy bag on the way from Bonanza Mountain and to Busch Peak.

-WGS84 Lat: 36.9057 deg N Lon: -116.8447 deg W

-I, Class 2 via Southeast Ridge *

-I, Class 2 via North Slope *

Velvet Peak (3,918)

Velvet Peak sits just southwest of Beatty. It is not particularly interesting. The loose ascent takes perhaps five minutes. Could this be the easiest peak in the book??? (It's not.)

-WGS84 Lat: 36.8965 deg N Lon: -116.7768 deg W

-I, Class 2 via Northeast Slope *

"West Sawtooth Peak" (5,920+)

Chossy, but a fun scramble. Approached as per Sawtooth Mountain, leaving NV-374 southwest of Beatty then taking the Rhyolite turn-off. Rather than continuing to Rhyolite, turn left on a good dirt road before the townsite and explore your way back in there.

-WGS84 Lat: 36.9365 deg N Lon: -116.8584 deg W

-I, Class 3 via East Face **

Valley of Fire State Park

All things being relative, not many people have heard of Valley of Fire. But those who have rant and rave! Fabulous, surreal fire-red sandstone crags and cliffs and vistas of trippy ice cream swirls of yellow and peach and purple slickrock—yum! The place is a must-see.

From Las Vegas, follow I-15 north toward Mesquite and St. George. About a half-hour outside of Las Vegas, get off at the well-signed Valley of Fire exit (exit 93; route 169) and head south on the paved road for 15 miles to the entrance to the state park. Although there is a fee booth, it seems to be infrequently staffed in the morning. There's a self-pay set-up here; it's an outrageous ten bucks (eight for locals) to get in.

If short scrambles to sweet sandstone peaks are your thing, this might be your place! Beware of crumbly rock, and ticks. There are lots of both!

Although the majority of the peaks in this section lie within the actual boundaries of this small state park, a few are *not* technically a part of Valley of Fire. I tossed them in because of their proximity to the park, as well as the fact that their access is generally the same as for those peaks within the park.

The peaks in this subsection are arranged here alphabetically.

These two photos show key route-finding components in climbing Valley of Fire Summit. The top photo displays a groove near the upper-right corner that is used to access the slab leading out of the frame. The bottom photo shows a notch you pass through, cutting left around a corner on the backside. Both photos by Harlan Stockman.

"The 5-Arch" (2,313)

This striking horn, the most aesthetic sandstone peak in Valley of Fire State Park, can be approached from a number of directions. The easiest route to the summit gains a chute on the north side. At the base of the chute is a highly unusual rock cluster containing five arches. Follow the chute to its head at the base of the summit crag. From there, work up and left (when you hit a vertical cliff), looking for an exposed 100-foot slabby ramp. From the top of the ramp, an exposed face (class 4; 8 feet) leads to an outrageously exposed arête (class 3) that dumps you off at the base of the final face (class 3-4; 12 feet) leading to the highpoint. A nice summit!

-WGS84 Lat: 36.4328 deg N Lon: -114.4728 deg W
-II, Class 4 via North Gully ****

Peak 2,431 (2,431)

This peak is a short distance northwest of The Orphan. Although a route to the top appears improbable, a fun bit of route-finding at the top of the south gully unfolds a summit route that is quite easy. From the top of the prominent south-side gully west of the summit, follow an exposed slab/ledge on the right to a hidden weakness that allows one to step around a corner to the right and get into a chimney that leads to the top. Pretty nifty, actually.

-WGS84 Lat: 36.4922 deg N Lon: -114.5474 deg W
-II, Class 3 via South Gully ***

Peak 3,077 (3,077)

Although technically a part of Valley of Fire State Park, this limestone peak resides on the northwest fringe of the park and has none of the glorious taste of the rest of the area. Still, a morsel of fun scrambling can be found near the top.

Approach this peak via the Ute exit off of I-15.
-WGS84 Lat: 36.5271 deg N Lon: -114.5820 deg W
-I, Class 2-3 via Northwest Face **

Baseline Mesa (2,378)

This is a short hike from the Fire Canyon overlook. The flattish summit gives up very nice views of The 5-Arch.

-WGS84 Lat: 36.4482 deg N Lon: -114.4773 deg W
-I, Class 2-3 via West Face *

"Boneyard Peak" (2,312)

We named this peak for the scattering of sheep bones in a slot we passed through on the way to the summit. Like virtually all of the peaks in this area, expect interesting route-finding en route to the top. We descended via a south-draining slot east of and below the summit.

-WGS84 Lat: 36.4962 deg N Lon: -114.5424 deg W

*-II, Class 4 via Northeast Slopes ****

"Cairn Peak" (2,497)

This small peak, a short hike from the Rainbow Vista parking lot, provides nice views of the park. The flat summit sports four or five cairns!

-WGS84 Lat: 36.4468 deg N Lon: -114.5124 deg W

*-I, Class 3 via North Face **

On the top of Cairn Peak, as Valley of Fire Summit beckons in the background. The view looks southwest.

"Crimson Staircase" (2,454)

From the Mouse's Tank trailhead, follow the trail to Mouse's Tank. Carefully bypass the tank on the left and work down into Fire Canyon. Follow the canyon through two tricky downclimbs (some may want a handline; even trickier as upclimbs on the return) and a rappel (bypassable on the left), and then walk the beautiful, sandy wash to a wash coming in on the right near the western base of Crimson Staircase. Follow this lesser wash to a point on the southwest side of the mountain. Here, locate a small, boulder-choked canyon coming in on the left. Follow this canyon up past several obstacles (class 3-4) until you see a brilliant red staircase on the left just short of the canyon head.

Follow the staircase (and occasional adjacent cracks/chimneys; class 4) up to a notch at its head. Gain the slabs to the right and work up to an apparent dead-end at a steep crag. Follow an excellent narrow ledge up and to the left, and step around a blind corner to a hidden class 3-4 open book that allows access to easier walking. Continue up, weaving around obstacles, climb a short face (class 3; 20 feet) and then boulder-scramble to the summit a short distance away. This is a really nice peak.

-WGS84 Lat: 36.4369 deg N Lon: -114.4936 deg W

-II, Class 4 via Southwest Aspect ****

On the hard-earned summit of Crimson Staircase.
In this view north, Silica Dome can barely be made out left-of-center.

"Duane Peak" (3,002)

This is a limestone peak near the sandstone highpoint of the park, which the two somewhat connected by this peak's south ridge. It's a decent peak with good views.

-WGS84 Lat: 36.4564 deg N Lon: -114.5535 deg W

-II, Class 2 via Southwest Face *

Gibraltar Rock (2,172)

Surprising for such a short, little peak, very interesting and convoluted route-finding is required to reach the summit. I am aware of at least three class 4 routes up this thing. Look around, and have fun finding a way up.

-WGS84 Lat: 36.4880 deg N Lon: -114.5252 deg W

-I, Class 4 by its easiest route ****

"Gregg Peak" (2,999)

Unfortunately, this forgettable limestone peak lacks flavor, just like its brother Duane. There are nice views of The Pinnacles from the summit, though.

-WGS84 Lat: 36.4368 deg N Lon: -114.5765 deg W

*-II, Class 2 via East Face **

"The Orphan" (2,280)

This is an incredibly interesting looking spire not far from the end of the Scenic Drive, due south of Boneyard Peak, with Magnesite Wash running along its southeastern base. The route, likely the only feasible way, was interesting and much easier than expected, though the route-finding was somewhat tricky. We encountered a very young bighorn sheep in a slot not far below the summit.

-WGS84 Lat: 36.4900 deg N Lon: -114.5407 deg W

*-II, Class 3 via weaknesses in the northeast aspect *****

Looking east from the top of Valley of Fire Summit

"Prospects Peak" (3,366)

This minor peak is approached directly south from the Valley of Fire road, just outside the park boundary.

-WGS84 Lat: 36.4182 deg N Lon: -114.6129 deg W

*-I, Class 2 via South Slopes **

Silica Dome (2,349)

Not so much a mountain as a prominent feature of the state park, Silica Dome is a short scramble that provides stunning views of much of the park (and of Lake Mead in the distance).

Once inside the park, follow the main road for three miles, keeping your eyes peeled for signage for the visitor center, which will be on your left. Hanging a left at the visitor center turn-off (Mouses Tank Road), follow the road for another 1.9 miles to the signed Fire Canyon turn-off on the right. It will be immediately after the "Rainbow Vista" pull-out. Follow the graded Fire Canyon road for a mile to its end. Silica Dome will be the yellow sandstone dome before you. The views from the trailhead are already immense. They get better.

From the trailhead, a well-traveled dirt path wanders over to a lookout above Fire Canyon. Following the path for about 50 feet, pick up a smaller foot trail branching off to the left. From there, meander over slickrock and desert terrain, following the occasional use trail, and work your way to the base of the steepish terrain immediately below Silica's northeast face. From there, pick a line (class 2) and head up to the summit.

Expect a roundtrip of well under a mile and less than 300 feet of gain.

-WGS84 Lat: 36.4516 deg N Lon: -114.4989 deg W
*-I, Class 2 via North Slopes ***

Silica Dome from the west. The recommended route essentially follows the left skyline.

"Sitting Monkey" (2,260)

This striking peak is clearly seen from near the end of the Scenic Drive, just as the road makes its final bend toward White Domes. The two routes we used were interesting and enjoyable. Some may want a belay for a couple <20' crux-y sections along the south ridge route.

The peak is named for a crag to the south that resembles a crouched monkey.

-WGS84 Lat: 36.5081 deg N Lon: -114.5382 deg W
*-II, Class 4 via South Ridge *****
*-II, Class 3 from the east saddle ****

"Thin Peak" (3,694)

Thin Peak's narrow profile is striking when viewed in the distance from I-15 at exit 75. Unfortunately, the much more impressive Muddy Peak is also visible and steals most of Thin Peak's thunder. The peak is quickly scrambled directly from the pavement just inside the Valley of Fire boundary. The exposed limestone summit affords incredible views of the red sandstone that dominates the state park.

-WGS84 Lat: 36.4159 deg N Lon: -114.5814 deg W
*-I, Class 2 via Southwest Face ***

According to the park, this picnic table is for wedding parties that get helicoptered to the summit plateau.

"Valley of Fire Summit" (2,972)

This is the highpoint of Valley of Fire (but not of the state park itself). The route to the top is a highly enjoyable exercise in route-finding. Fantastic! And as you can imagine, the views from the slickrock summit are outstanding.

But can someone explain the significance of the picnic table and umbrellas on the slickrock just below the summit???

-WGS84 Lat: 36.4393 deg N Lon: -114.5310 deg W

-II, Class 4-5 via South Ridge from the East ****

"Weekapaug Mountain" (2,674)

Situated south of Valley of Fire Summit and southeast of Atlatl Rock, Weekapaug Mountain is a fun scramble with most excellent scenery. Among the views from the top, one can clearly see what I call 'Weekapaug Groove'—a large, vertical groove across the way on Valley of Fire Summit's south face. Finding Weekapaug Groove is the ticket to the upper south ridge that leads to the top of Valley of Fire Summit!

-WGS84 Lat: 36.4150 deg N Lon: -114.5388 deg W

-I, Class 3-4 via Northeast Face ***

Looking north across the valley at Valley of Fire Summit from near the top of Weekapaug Mountain. Weekapaug Groove can be made out as the shaded vertical groove leading to the visible highpoint. The true summit is the bump left of that.

"West White Dome" (2,220)
Not only is the scrambling exposed and fun near the top but there are two arches that can be found on the peak, one of which has an attached tunnel that can be squeezed through. This little dome can be roundtripped in 10 minutes from the end of the paved park road. As elsewhere in the park, be careful of loose rock, and plenty of exposure up high.

-WGS84 Lat: 36.4842 deg N Lon: -114.5330 deg W
*-I, Class 3 via North Face ****

White Dome (2,234)
Somewhat harder but less aesthetic than its western next-door neighbor. Do 'em both—it'll only chew up about a half-hour of your day. Like West White Dome, approach from the parking lot at the end of the paved park road.

-WGS84 Lat: 36.4846 deg N Lon: -114.5319 deg W
*-I, Class 4 via North Slope ***

South of Las Vegas

Cottonwood & Bird Spring Range

The peaks in this subsection are accessed from a variety of points. The peaks are arranged here somewhat randomly.

"Joshua Peak" (4,300)
A short, pleasant hike via the west face. Accessible off the powerline road from the paved Jean-to-Goodsprings road (NV-161).

-WGS84 Lat: 35.8343 deg N Lon: -115.3649 deg W
*-I, Class 2 via West Face ***

"Cottonwood Peak – North" (5,200)
Outstanding views from the top. This is a short, quick traverse from Cottonwood Peak. Bighorn sheep have been seen on the south ridge.

-WGS84 Lat: 35.9661 deg N Lon: -115.4300 deg W
*-I, Class 1-2 via South Ridge ***
*-I, Class 2-3 via North Face ***

"Cottonwood Peak" (5,300)
Nice views from the top. The peak is easily approached from Cottonwood Pass or from a number of dirt roads near its base.

-WGS84 Lat: 35.9522 deg N Lon: -115.4283 deg W
*-I, Class 1 via Southwest Ridge **
*-I, Class 1-2 via South Slope **

This little guy was playing dead just below the summit of The Jingle Bells.

"Escarpment Peak" (5,020)
An easy hike to an excellent viewpoint of the city of Las Vegas and the sandstone glory of Red Rock. Fantastic scenery! Approach the peak from NV-160, to the north.

-WGS84 Lat: 35.9943 deg N Lon: -115.4142 deg W
*-I, Class 1-2 via Northwest Ridge ***

"Trident" (4,180)
Named for its three parallel north ridges, all of which can be used to easily gain the summit. Sitting just across NV-160 from Hole-in-the-Top, this small mountain is an easy leg-stretcher, requiring only about 30 minutes roundtrip from the pavement.

-WGS84 Lat: 36.0139 deg N Lon: -115.4158 deg W
*-I, Class 2 via any of the north ridges **

"Hole-in-the-Top" (4,072)
Named for a curious arch at the very top of the mountain. This small peak, while just off NV-160, can also be approached from some of the Cottonwood mountain bike trails.

-WGS84 Lat: 36.0237 deg N Lon: -115.4219 deg W
*-I, Class 2 via South Slope **

"Flowered Peak" (4,182)
There are interesting views of Red Rock from the summit. As a bonus, the intrepid hiker approaching from the northeast gets to step around a quarter-mile of broken glass and stumble past long-forgotten, valueless relics (aka *a half-mile of trash, old cars and the like*) in the otherwise glorious, spring flower'd desert.

Approach the peak from NV-159, to the northeast.
-WGS84 Lat: 36.0454 deg N Lon: -115.4313 deg W
-I, Class 1-2 via Northeast Slope *
-I, Class 1-2 via U-Ridge **

"Bird Peak" (5,672)
Bird Peak can be readily combined with the Bird Spring Range Highpoint in a mellow, couple hour affair. A decent dirt road from Goodsprings (or a bit rougher, from Cottonwood Pass) leads to a lesser road heading right to the base of the peak.
-WGS84 Lat: 35.8840 deg N Lon: -115.3862 deg W
-I, Class 2 via Northwest Ridge **
-I, Class 2 via North Face **

Bird Spring Range Highpoint (5,695)
A surprisingly nice little hike to an obscure highpoint with interesting views.
-WGS84 Lat: 35.8926 deg N Lon: -115.3899 deg W
-I, Class 2 via mining road from north *
-I, Class 2 via Southeast Ridge **

"Mount Roses Are Free" (4,951)
Found 1.5 miles south of Cottonwood Peak, this is an easy hike from a number of dirt roads near its base.
-WGS84 Lat: 35.9254 deg N Lon: -115.4209 deg W
-I, Class 1 via West Slope *
-I, Class 1-2 via Northwest Ridge *

"Joshua Tree" (4,553)
Although the meandering northwest ridge is a nice walk, a more efficient way to reach the summit is by approaching the southwest face via primitive dirt roads and mountain bike trails going over the low pass west of the summit.
-WGS84 Lat: 35.9117 deg N Lon: -115.3192 deg W
-II, Class 1-2 via Northwest Ridge **
-II, Class 2 via Southwest Face *

"Christmas Gift" (4,241)

Accessed from a system of primitive dirt roads that comes in northwest of the peak, Christmas Gift and its neighbor, Joshua Tree, to the southeast, make for a nice desert outing.

-WGS84 Lat: 35.9378 deg N Lon: -115.3289 deg W
*-II, Class 1-2 via North Ridge ***
*-II, Class 2 via Southwest Face **

"Peacock Mountain" (4,052)

This is a nice peak with good views. Although the peak sits due east of Christmas Gift, it is perhaps best approached from the good north-south dirt road running along its eastern base.

-WGS84 Lat: 35.9386 deg N Lon: -115.2932 deg W
*-II, Class 2-3 via East Face ***

"The Jingle Bells" (5,020)

A decent little peak in the Bird Spring Range, its summit offers good views of the Cottonwood Pass area. The Jingle Bells is easily approached via decent dirt roads south the pass.

-WGS84 Lat: 35.9280 deg N Lon: -115.4101 deg W
*-I, Class 1 via Northwest Slope **
*-I, Class 1 via West Slope **

"Joshua Peak" (4,231)

A long but decent dirt road leaves Blue Diamond Road and eventually passes along the southern base of the peak. From there, a short but enjoyable hike leads to the top.

-WGS84 Lat: 35.9624 deg N Lon: -115.3876 deg W
*-II, Class 2 via South Slope ***

Sloan & Jean

All of the peaks in this subsection are initially accessed from I-15. They are arranged here roughly south-to-north.

Sheep Mountain (4,184)

Not to be confused with the bigger, badder Sheep *Peak* outside of Las Vegas, this mountain's on the east side of bustling Jean, Nevada.

-WGS84 Lat: 35.7608 deg N Lon: -115.2961 deg W
*-I, Class 3-4 via West Face ***

"Bad Hill" (3,644)

Bad Hill is east of Sheep Mountain and south of Sloan, Nevada, near I-15. A network of mostly good dirt roads leads close to the peak.

Just below the summit, we found a basalt boulder with "Bad Hill" scratched into it.

-WGS84 Lat: 35.7714 deg N Lon: -115.2160 deg W

*-II, Class 1-2 via North Ridge ***

Hiking up The Jingle Bells.
Potosi Mountain, to the northwest, forms the backdrop.

"Tortoise Foot Hill" (3,613)

Tortoise Foot Hill is closely northeast of Bad Hill. I named the peak for a broken tortoise shell with a foot still attached found in a rugged, boulder area just below the summit.

-WGS84 Lat: 35.7861 deg N Lon: -115.2085 deg W
*-II, Class 2 via Southwest Face ***

"South Twin" (3,940)

Despite its close proximity to I-15 and a network of good dirt roads in the vicinity, this peak seems to get little traffic.

-WGS84 Lat: 35.8437 deg N Lon: -114.2133 deg W
*-II, Class 2 via Northeast Slope **
*-II, Class 2 via North Slope **

"North Twin" (3,957)

North Twin and South Twin are obscure, basaltic peaks tucked away behind Dog Skull Mountain near Sloan and Hidden Valley. Although I didn't realize it when I visited (having hiked directly from I-15), there is a good dirt road that starts out near the highway and ends at the northern base of the mountain.

-WGS84 Lat: 35.8490 deg N Lon: -115.2041 deg W
*-I, Class 2 via North Slope **
*-I, Class 2 via Southwest Slope **

"Dog Skull Mountain" (4,024)

I found a canine skull on the north slopes of this mountain. Later that morning, I placed the skull on the summit of nearby Canine Crag.

-WGS84 Lat: 35.8581 deg N Lon: -115.2023 deg W
*-I, Class 1-2 via North Slopes **

Sutor Benchmark (4,186)

Sutor Benchmark, a gentle-sloped peak within Sloan Canyon National Conservation Area, is part of the McCullough Range. Hardly a climbing objective, Sutor's big draw, aside from the nice views from its summit, is a nearby canyon that is home to about 1,700 documented petroglyphs. This area is protected, and is sacred to Native Americans. Tread lightly—it should be treated with respect.

With the possibility of new development as the NCA prepares itself for increased visitation and the City of Henderson continues to sprawl, my approach directions are tentative. In the meantime, from Las Vegas or Henderson, Nevada, follow I-15 south toward Los Angeles. As you leave Henderson, get off at the Sloan exit (exit 25), pass under the highway, and hang a left on the two-lane highway running parallel to I-15. Head back toward Las Vegas for 0.5 mile then hang a right on a prominent dirt road. Follow the dirt road in for about two miles until you come to a powerline road behind a large energy structure. Follow the rough powerline road for approx. 2.5 miles until you come to a minor dirt road on your right heading toward a cluster of small peaks to the south. Just before this minor dirt road is a power pole with a metal tag marked #X12084. Sutor Benchmark is the highest of the peaks in the distance. Hang a right on the minor dirt road, continue to the road's end about 1.1 miles away (passing a Sloan Canyon sign midway down) and park at a fence at the mouth of Sloan Canyon. High clearance will likely be needed to reach road's end.

Camping is not allowed inside the NCA, though primitive camping can be found on the BLM land outside of it.

From road's end, Sutor Benchmark is the highest mountain to the south. Hike cross-country toward it. There are no significant difficulties.

-WGS84 Lat: 35.8836 deg N Lon: -115.1198 deg W
-II, Class 2 via North Slopes ***

"Canine Crag" (3,982)
This is the most aesthetic peak in the Sloan Canyon area. The easiest route is a very loose class 2 ramp on the northwest face. Approach this peak via Sloan Canyon, as per Sutor Mountain.

-WGS84 Lat: 35.8838 deg N Lon: -115.1339 deg W
-II, Class 2 via Northwest Face Ramp **
-II, Class 3-4 via West Ridge ***

"Feline Fang" (3,980)
Canine Crag's twin summit. An easier ascent though. Drive in as per Sutor Mountain.

-WGS84 Lat: 35.8838 deg N Lon: -115.1358 deg W
-II, Class 2 via Southeast Face **
-II, Class 2 via Northwest Face **

"Ecru Peak" (3,975)
Two of the most aesthetic desert towers in the region are found on the peak's northeast face. I've scrambled to the base of them, and they are not climbable by the sane! Drive in as per Sutor Mountain.

-WGS84 Lat: 35.8839 deg N Lon: -115.1427 deg W
-II, Class 2 via Northwest Slope **
-II, Class 3 via East Ridge **

"Sloan Peak" (3,900)
This is a nice hike with fantastic views of the Vegas Valley. Approach from the pavement south of Sloan, Nevada.

-WGS84 Lat: 35.8909 deg N Lon: -115.1976 deg W
-I, Class 2 from the Old L.A. Highway **

On the summit of Canine Crag

Peak 3,970
This rather unintererstng bump is out by Sloan Canyon. The driving approach is as per Sutor Mountain.

-WGS84 Lat: 35.8972 deg N Lon: -115.1420 deg W
-I, Class 1 via East Slope *

"Pleasant Peak" (3,375)
The east ridge and east face routes offer enjoyable (though very easy) scrambling on good limestone.

-WGS84 Lat: 35.9134 deg N Lon: -115.1783 deg W
-I, Class 2 via East Ridge **
-I, Class 2 via East Face **

McCullough Range and the Railroad Peaks Area
The peaks in this subsection are arranged here generally south-to-north.

"Fishhead Peak" (6,184)

This peak, named for the two fish heads we found on a ridge not far from the summit, requires a tedious hike up and over several higher bumps to get to the obscure highpoint. With a sturdy 4WD vehicle, one can cut down on the slog factor by following a steep dirt subsidiary road from the powerline road to the radio tower northeast of the summit. This subsidiary dirt road leaves the powerline road just north of the nearby Wee Thump Joshua Tree Wilderness Highpoint.

-WGS84 Lat: 35.5255 deg N Lon: -115.1786 deg W
*-II, Class 2 from the radio tower **

Wee Thump Joshua Tree Wilderness Highpoint (5,140)

This minor summit is located just off NV-164, west of Searchlight, Nevada. It is easily accessed from the powerline road on its west side.

-WGS84 Lat: 35.5207 deg N Lon: -115.1366 deg W
*-I, Class 1 via West Slope **

"McCullough Point" (6,557)

This is a minor peak (297' of prominence) south of McCullough Mountain. There's not much reason to visit it. Driving directions are the same as for McCullough Mountain.

-WGS84 Lat: 35.5834 deg N Lon: -115.1749 deg W
*-II, Class 2 via East Ridge ***
*-II, Class 2 via Northeast Ridge ***

McCullough Mountain (7,026)

Granted this is one of the most prominent summits in southern Nevada, but it's really nothing interesting. Get off I-15 at the Nipton Road exit (south of Primm, Nevada) and follow that road 18.1 miles to a dirt road on the left. Follow the dirt road less than a mile to a decent powerline road, which you'll turn right onto and follow 3.9 miles to another dirt road on the left. Follow that dirt road 4.5 miles to good camp spots at a corral. From there, you'll need a GPS and/or a good topo map for the hike.

-WGS84 Lat: 35.6029 deg N Lon: -115.1800 deg W
*-III, Class 2 from the East-southeast ***

"Indian Point" (4,530)

Indian Point is an isolated summit southwest of North McCullough Peak. It doesn't seem to have any quick point of access, and the logical way to climb it is on a multi-peak outing starting with Black Mountain.

-WGS84 Lat: 35.8916 deg N Lon: -115.0537 deg W
*-III, Class 2 via East Slope **

"North McCullough Peak" (5,058)

This, the peak south of Fracture Ridge Peak, has excellent views of the spine of the North McCullough Mountains. The most logical way to approach this and its neighbor peaks is by going up and over Black Mountain via the excellent maintained trail to that peak's summit.

-WGS84 Lat: 35.9051 deg N Lon: -115.0447 deg W
-III, Class 2 via North Ridge **
-II, Class 2 via South Ridge **

"Fracture Ridge Peak" (4,928)

Fracture Ridge Peak is the next summit south of Black Mountain. Despite some tedious basalt boulder walking in spots, it is a pleasant peak with a remote feel.

-WGS84 Lat: 35.9186 deg N Lon: -115.0454 deg W
-II, Class 2 via North Ridge from Black Mountain saddle **
-III, Class 2 via South Ridge **

Black Mountain (5,092)

This is the big peak south of Henderson, Nevada and roughly east of Sloan Canyon. A good trail has been developed on the west side of the mountain.

-WGS84 Lat: 35.9311 deg N Lon: -115.0441 deg W
-II, Class 2 via west trail **

"Maid of Rubble" (2,709)

Though the summit can be reached via a number of "easy" routes, this might be the loosest and most dangerous class 2 peak in the area. The northeast ridge, while aesthetically littered with gendarmes, requires steep and exposed scrambling traverses in multiple sections. The northwest face is safer (though much less aesthetic). Few visit this summit; I built a small cairn next to the bush jutting out of the highest rocks.

Get here by following a decent dirt road straight west from highway 95, just a few miles south of its junction with highway 93 in Boulder City. Drive to a point north of the peak and start hiking.

-WGS84 Lat: 35.9179 deg N Lon: -114.9645 deg W
-I, Class 2 via Northeast Ridge **
-I, Class 2 via Northwest Face *

"Railroad Peak" (4,142)

Railroad Peak, with 1526' of prominence, is the highpoint of the fine and striking sub-range of the McCullough Mountains one sees just west and southwest of Railroad Pass when traveling along US-93/US-95 between Las

Vegas and Boulder City, Nevada. A four-peak traverse of the "Railroad Peaks" is a worthwhile and satisfying endeavor. It is described here.

Development in the area is complicating access. At the time of this writing, one can approach the peak from the north from the area of Nevada State Drive (take I-515/US-93/US-95 to exit 56) and Paradise Hills Drive in Henderson, Nevada. Following Nevada State Drive a mile south to Paradise Hills Drive, one can then pick up any of several dirt roads heading south for less than a mile off of Paradise Hills Drive toward the Railroad Peaks. How long this easy access will last is not known.

Alternatively, from either Las Vegas or Boulder City, get on US-93/US-95 and head toward Railroad Pass, the mountain pass between the city of Boulder City and the city of Henderson. The Railroad Peaks, as the cluster of nice-looking peaks to the west and southwest of the pass are known, will be obvious from the pass. Exploring around for the best legal access, your ultimate goal will be to gain the north ridge of Peak 4,089, which is three small peaks to the north of Railroad Peak. If you can't gain access to the ridge directly from the area of Nevada State Drive/Paradise Hills Drive, you may have to cross-country it a bit around the small peaklets to the northeast of Peak 4,089 to get there.

From the base of Peak 4,089's north ridge, head up to the summit on a rough use trail. The trail disappears near the summit. The going is class 1-2. This is the easiest of the four peaks in the traverse.

From the summit of Peak 4,089, continue south along the crest to the summit of Black Hill. The going is class 2 but the traverse gets tougher after this. Dropping fro the summit of Black Hill, continue south near the crest toward Peak 3,954. It's amazing how rugged the terrain becomes, though it is no harder than class 2-3. Work your way to the summit of this, the lowest peak of the traverse.

Descend from the summit of Peak 3,954 and make your way south to the saddle between it and Railroad Peak. From there, any number of lines can be followed southward to Railroad's summit. Sticking on or near the crest provides the most interesting climbing. The basalt is typically of good quality, and class 2-3 routes can be found.

To descend, either retrace your steps or drop back to the saddle between Railroad Peak and Peak 3,954 and follow steep chutes (class 1-2) down either east or west (depending on where you parked) to the desert below. From there, wander your way to your vehicle.

Roundtrip numbers (assuming an out-and-back) from the base of Peak 4,089's north ridge are in the ballpark of 2 miles and 2,000 feet of gain.

-WGS84 Lat: 35.9478 deg N Lon: -114.9473 deg W

-II, Class 2-3 via Railroad Peak Traverse ***

Peak 3,954 (3,954)

Peak 3,954 is south of Black Hill and north of Railroad Peak, separated from the latter by a distinctive saddle. Rather than treat Peak 3,954 as an objective of its own, I suggest it as part of a traverse of the four Railroad Peaks. Refer to Railroad Peak for the description of the traverse.

-WGS84 Lat: 35.9523 deg N Lon: -114.9464 deg W
*-II, Class 2-3 via Railroad Peaks Traverse ****

Black Hill (4,092)

Black Hill is immediately south of Peak 4,089. It is one of two peaks in the Railroad Peaks with at least 300' of prominence. Rather than treat Black Hill as an objective of its own, I recommend it as part of a traverse of the four Railroad Peaks. Refer to Railroad Peak for the description of the traverse.

-WGS84 Lat: 35.9564 deg N Lon: -114.9444 deg W
*-II, Class 2-3 via Railroad Peaks Traverse ****

Peak 4,089 (4,089)

Peak 4,089 is the northernmost of the four Railroad Peaks. Although it could be hiked as an objective of its own, it's greater value lies in being the first stop on a traverse of all four peaks. Refer to Railroad Peak for the description of the traverse.

-WGS84 Lat: 35.9585 deg N Lon: -114.9430 deg W
*-I, Class 1-2 via North Ridge ***
*-II, Class 2-3 via Railroad Peaks Traverse ****

"The Fortress" (4,168)

I had no idea that this peak had already been given a local name until I climbed to the summit and found a register in an Altoids tin. The person placing the register had dubbed the rugged peak "The Fortress." On my descent, I downclimbed a steep face and then stepped around an exposed ledge, startling a bighorn sheep that was resting there.

There might be easier routes than those mentioned here, but I haven't taken the time to look for them.

-WGS84 Lat: 35.9563 deg N Lon: -115.0343 deg W
*-II, Class 4 via East Face ****
*-II, YDS 5.6 via North Face ****

"The Jack" (3,517)

The Jack, The King, The Queen, White Gold #7 and Quo Vadis Peak (3,440) can all be looped in a semi-enjoyable couple hours of effort.

-WGS84 Lat: 35.9627 deg N Lon: -114.9880 deg W
*-I, Class 2 via South Ridge **

*-I, Class 2-3 via North Slope **

"Railroad Hill" (3,162)

A small, easy peak that makes an ideal after-work 1-2 hour roundtrip leg stretcher.

-WGS84 Lat: 35.9625 deg N Lon: -114.9559 deg W
*-I, Class 2 via Northwest Face **
*-I, Class 2 via North Ridge **

"White Gold #7" (3,600+)

This peak sits just west of The Queen.

-WGS84 Lat: 35.9665 deg N Lon: -114.9927 deg W
*-I, Class 2 via East Ridge **
*-I, Class 3-4 via Southwest Face **

"The Queen" (3,620+)

This is the highest of the five peaks in its massif.

-WGS84 Lat: 35.9669 deg N Lon: -114.9902 deg W
*-I, Class 2 via North Ridge **
*-I, Class 2 via West Ridge **

"Rattlesnake Mountain" (3,916)

Technically, I didn't *summit* this mountain; as I arrived at the top one spring afternoon, I found a rattlesnake coiled atop the highest rock.

-WGS84 *Lat: 35.9682 deg N Lon: -115.0338 deg W*
*-II, Class 2 via Northeast Ridge ***

"The King" (3,572)

-WGS84 Lat: 35.9723 deg N Lon: -114.9883 deg W
*-I, Class 2 via East Ridge **
*-I, Class 2 via South Ridge **

"Tortoise Shell Peak" (3,753)

I found a desert tortoise shell once while descending the east slope. This peak is approached as per Henderson Benchmark.

-WGS84 *Lat: 35.9948 deg N Lon: -115.0173 deg W*
*-I, Class 2 via Northeast Ridge **
*-I, Class 2 via East Slope **

Henderson Benchmark (3,358)

Lame, and strewn with ball bearing scree, many Henderson locals mistakenly think this small peak is called Black Mountain. A friend of mine used to tell me stories of how she and her friends would drop acid on the summit as teenagers.

-WGS84 *Lat: 36.0073 deg N Lon: -115.0072 deg W*
*-I, Class 2-3 via Southeast Ridge **

Highland Spring Range

The Highland Spring Range is located west of US-95, northwest of Searchlight, and southwest of Boulder City. It is a fine and rugged place to visit. The peaks are arranged here south-to-north.

"Mount Tappen" (4,900)

Mount Tappen is an easy bonus peak from the saddle between it and Peak 4,540.

-WGS84 Lat: 35.5676 deg N Lon: -115.0480 deg W
*-II, Class 2 via Northeast Ridge ***

Peak 4,540 (4,540)

This minor peak sits just northwest of Cow Spring. A 4WD vehicle can drive a rough dirt road to the saddle southwest of the summit, from which a short hike leads to the top.

-WGS84 Lat: 35.5795 deg N Lon: -115.0209 deg W
*-I, Class 2 via Southwest Ridge **

"Highland Peak" (4,940)

A summit register calls this peak, which is only 40 feet lower than the range highpoint, Highland Peak. While the approach from the south is mostly straightforward (though some steep terrain needs to be worked through as one nears the southeast ridge), the north ridge is more complex, particularly on the descent.

-WGS84 Lat: 35.6117 deg N Lon: -115.0327 deg W
*-II, Class 3 via South Slope to Southeast Ridge ***
*-II, Class 3 via North Ridge ***

"Highland Juniper Peak" (4,900)

This peak was named for a rare-in-this-range grove of junipers encountered not far below the summit. Hiking this peak once in winter, we encountered large mountain lion tracks in the snow.

-WGS84 Lat: 35.6152 deg N Lon: -115.0543 deg W
*-II, Class 2 via East Slope ***
*-II, Class 2 via Southeast Wash ***

"Sleeping Indian Peak" (4,860)

The traverse here from Highland Peak is surprisingly complex and interesting, though the rock is dangerously loose. Fifty feet below the summit on the east side is a figure that in the wintry morning light looks striking like a reclining Indian woman.

-WGS84 Lat: 35.6237 deg N Lon: -115.0446 deg W
*-II, Class 2-3 via South Ridge ***

Highland Spring Range Highpoint (4,980)

The highpoint of an otherwise very rugged and impressive range, this summit is a chossy and unpleasant lump. Exit I-15 at the Nipton Road exit and follow that road 18.1 miles to a dirt road on the left. Follow the dirt road less than a mile to a powerline road, where you'll turn right and follow it 5.5 miles to a dirt road on the right. Turn onto the dirt road and follow it less than two miles toward Highland Spring until it becomes extremely rough. Park well before a point of commitment. The peak is a short hike away.

-WGS84 Lat: 35.6007 deg N Lon: -115.0603 deg W
*-I, Class 2 via South Face ***

"Possible Mesa" (4,045)

This improbable peak is well-guarded on all sides by massive cliffs and crumbly faces. Fortunately, an interesting weakness (surmountable by stacking rocks to climb a dry fall on its left side) near the peak's north saddle allows a reasonable way to the top.

-WGS84 Lat: 35.6479 deg N Lon: -115.0352 deg W
*-II, Class 3 via North Saddle ****

"Castle Peak" (4,900+)

The crown jewel of the obscure Highland Spring Range, Castle Peak is a striking, rugged and colorful desert peak without an easy route to its summit. Part of a seldom-visited range of rugged canyons, impressive cliffs, and unclimbed towers and pinnacles, Castle's 80-foot summit tower requires a short bit of exposed class 4 climbing on awful rock. In recent years, a chain has been installed to aid through the crux.

For those less adventurous, a sub-peak (Point 4,879) just north of the true summit, is a walk-up. The views are as good, especially down the precipitous west face of the mountain.

A number of routes could be used to attain the base of the summit tower, but most reasonable from the standard approach described below would be either the east ridge or the east wash. The east ridge is more enjoyable and aesthetic, though those who avoid the east wash route will miss out on a close encounter with "Monkey Fist," a striking fin of rock clearly visible from the highway and during much of the approach. The Monkey Fist, most likely unclimbed, resembles a monkey's fist when viewed from the east.

From Las Vegas, take I-515/US-95/US-93 south toward Boulder City, Nevada (and Hoover Dam). Before you get to either of them, you'll pass the Railroad Pass Casino (20 miles southeast of downtown Las Vegas). Continuing south from the casino another mile and take US-95 as it exits the main highway and heads toward Searchlight, Nevada. Heading south toward Searchlight from the exit, in 21.2 miles you'll come to a powerline road on your right. Follow the powerline road west for 2.9 miles then hang a left and head south/southeast for about 1.5 miles to a secondary dirt road. Turn right onto this secondary road and follow it for a mile or less and park at a point south/southeast of Mount Alex (Point 3,485 on the map). A high clearance vehicle should do the trick. Castle Peak will be due west of you, though it is obscured by Possible Mesa.

To climb the East Ridge: From your parking spot, head west cross-country or follow the obvious wash that travels west toward the mountain. As you approach the base of the mountain (or what *appears* to be the mountain but is actually Possible Mesa) after about a mile, follow the wash around the southeast tip of Possible Mesa and into the washy canyon that heads somewhat northwesterly toward Castle Peak. Continue up-canyon and aim for the saddle between Possible Mesa (on your right) and Castle Peak (straight ahead). Once at the saddle, hang a left and head up the east ridge of Castle Peak. Though harder variations can readily be found, the ridge can be done class 2-3. Shortly above the saddle, you'll come to a prominent arête. You can avoid the arête by moving around to its right and heading up a steep, loose slope. Once on the slope, follow along the base of the cliffs on your left until you reach an obvious break (and a notch) in the cliffs above. Scramble up to the notch (class 2-3). The east ridge mellows out considerably above the notch. From here, the summit tower can be seen to the west/northwest. Hike up class 2 terrain to the base of the summit tower. Sub-peak 4,879 is just a short hike away to the north.

To climb the East Wash: Follow the directions given above to the washy canyon heading somewhat northwesterly toward Castle Peak. Next, instead of aiming for the saddle, continue up-canyon as it bends to the left and heads west below the cliffs of Castle's east ridge. As the wash approaches the crest of the range above (west), the Monkey Fist will be in view. Aim for the Monkey Fist. As you work to the crest above, you'll encounter a number of ways to leave the wash and work the steepening and somewhat convoluted terrain above. A steep chute on the far right side (near the base of the cliffs on Castle's south face) appears to be easiest and most direct. With careful route-finding, you should be able to reach the crest with nothing harder than class 3 scrambling. Once on the crest, the Monkey Fist should be obvious. Looking north to the south face of Castle Peak from around the Monkey Fist, note an obvious, large weakness in the form of a steep drainage. Head for it. Work your way up a couple of short dry falls (class 3) in the drainage, noting a large cave to your left. At the top of the drainage, further progress is blocked by cliffs. Angle right (east) a short bit near the base of the cliffs, then scramble up the first section of cliffs that looks reasonable (class 3 can be found, if one looks hard enough). Once above the cliff band of the south face, head north cross-country for 0.25 mile to the base of the summit tower.

To climb the summit tower: The summit tower is steep, and comprised of loose rock. Although a number of possible lines could be chosen, by far the most obvious, safe and easy line appears to be a ramp system on its east face. Starting near the northeast corner of the tower, get onto the ramp system, which follows a ledge across the east face, climbs a short headwall, ramps steeply back northwest, then surmounts a very short but loose and exposed face (crux; class 4), and scramble easily a few feet more to the highpoint.

Anticipate a roundtrip of 8 miles and 2,500 feet of gain for either route.

-WGS84 Lat: 35.6488 deg N Lon: -115.0489 deg W
*-III, Class 2-3 via East Ridge (with class 4 summit block) *****
*-III, Class 3 via East Wash (with class 4 summit block) *****

"Mount Alex" (3,485)

Mount Alex is east of the Highland Spring crest. It is an unexciting, minor objective.

-WGS84 Lat: 35.6523 deg N Lon: -115.0139 deg W
*-I, Class 1-2 via East Face **

"North Castle Peak" (4,584)
North Castle Peak lies just north of Castle Peak. It is most easily climbed by ascending the eastern drainage just south of the summit then angling north toward the top.

-WGS84 Lat: 35.6557 deg N Lon: -115.0500 deg W
*-II, Class 2 via Eastern Drainage ***

Laughlin

The peaks in this subsection are closely clustered just off (and to the south) of NV-163, west of Laughlin.

Center Benchmark (2,844)
This can be combined with Conical Peak and Hiko Point for a fun, half-day loop scramble. I roundtripped the trio in 80 minutes.

-WGS84 Lat: 35.1542 deg N Lon: -114.6866 deg W
*-I, Class 2 via East Slope **
*-I, Class 2-3 via North Slope from Hiko Point ***

Conical Peak (2,771)
This minor peak came to my attention after reading a write-up about it online some years back. It was a fun enough hike.

-WGS84 Lat: 35.1550 deg N Lon: -114.6772 deg W
*-I, Class 2 via West Slope ***
*-I, Class 2-3 via Northwest Slope ***

"Hiko Point" (2,862)
Although the peak can be easily reached from mostly any direction, a single class 4 move on the north side of the summit block is required to reach the highpoint. Mine was the first sign-in the register had seen in 11 years.

-WGS84 *Lat: 35.1587 deg N Lon: -114.6891 deg W*
*-I, Class 4 via North Ridge (class 2) ***
*-I, Class 4 via South Slope (class 2) from Center Benchmark ***

Searchlight

The peaks in this subsection are located northeast of the junction of US-95/NV-164, in and around Searchlight, Nevada. They are arranged here south-to-north.

Doherty Mountain (3,940)
Hovers over Searchlight, Nevada. A service road can be followed to the top.

-WGS84 *Lat: 35.4712 deg N Lon: -114.9192 deg W*
*-I, Class 1 via service road **

"Morning Glory Mountain" (4,340)

This small mountain next to Light Benchmark makes for a very pleasant early morning stroll. I once hiked up to the summit before dawn to a cool breeze, encountering outstanding lighting on the Joshua trees and small granite outcroppings on the descent. Zen!

-WGS84 Lat: 35.4859 deg N Lon: -114.9138 deg W
*-I, Class 2 via Northwest Face ***

Light Benchmark (4,327)

When I hiked up to the summit of this little peak in March 2007, it had been 30 years since someone had last signed the register.

-WGS84 Lat: 35.4898 deg N Lon: -114.9080 deg W
*-I, Class 2 via East Ridge **

Nelson & Boulder City

Some of the peaks in this subsection lie along the Colorado River, outside of Lake Mead NRA. A variety of access points are used. The peaks are arranged here generally south-to-north.

"Bard Peak" (4,969)

Ireteba's neighbor to the south.

-WGS84 Lat: 35.5898 deg N Lon: -114.8271 deg W
*-I, Class 2 via West Slope **
*-I, Class 2 via North Ridge from Ireteba Benchmark **

Ireteba Benchmark (5,060)

Ireteba can be easily linked with Bard Peak for a nice, short loop.

-WGS84 Lat: 35.5946 deg N Lon: -114.8291 deg W
*-I, Class 2 via South Ridge from Bard Peak **
*-I, Class 2 via Southwest Slope **

Knob Hill (4,547)

This uber-obscure little peak was a touch more fun than I might have guessed. Good dirt roads lead to the southern base of the thing from US-95 in Eldorado Valley.

-WGS84 Lat: 35.6627 deg N Lon: -114.8516 deg W
*-I, Class 3 via Southeast Face ***

"Keyhole Peak" (4,416)

Approached from the Keyhole Canyon parking area, the northwest ridge can be followed directly via some outstanding class 3-4 scrambling. Easier variations can be found to keep the route class 3. Halfway up the mountain, the terrain eases substantially and the final walk to the summit is mellow.

Note: Although I mention the class 1-2 north slope route, be aware that it's only recommended as a *descent* route for those with technical gear (and appropriate expertise) intending to pass through Keyhole Canyon on their way to the car. Folks should bring a 60-meter rope, a pull cord, and rappelling gear (don't forget helmets!) for the descent through Keyhole Canyon.

-WGS84 Lat: 35.7005 deg N Lon: -114.9163 deg W
*-II, Class 1-2 via North Slope **
*-II, Class 3-4 via Northwest Ridge ****

"Little Hands Peak" (3,989)
This nice peak, located near Aztec Wash, has a pleasant flavor.

-WGS84 Lat: 35.6483 deg N Lon: -114.8063 deg W
*-II, Class 2 via North Ridge ***
*-II, Class 2 via West Slope ***

"Aztec Mountain" (4,153)
Aztec Mountain and Little Hands Peak are prominent to the south as one descends into Nelson along the paved highway.

-WGS84 Lat: 35.6473 deg N Lon: -114.8156 deg W
*-II, Class 2 via East Slope ***
*-II, Class 2 via North Ridge ***

"Eagle Peak" (3,602)
This minor peak sits above Aztec Wash near Nelson.

-WGS84 Lat: 35.6693 deg N Lon: -114.8075 deg W
-II, Class 1-2 via South Slope
*-II, Class 2 via Northeast Slope **

Mount Duncan (2,790)
Just above Nelson, Nevada. Covered in barbaric cacti. With 99 feet of prominence, it's a bit embarrassing to call it a "*Mount.*" Apparently the USGS felt otherwise.

-WGS84 Lat: 35.7058 deg N Lon: -114.8049 deg W
*-I, Class 2 via West Ridge **

"Neslon Peak" (2,575)
A small peak above Nelson, the rocky summit of Neslon Peak gives up nice views of the area. The 15-minute scramble is approached directly from the pavement.

-WGS84 Lat: 35.7096 deg N Lon: -114.7907 deg W
*-I, Class 2 via South Face **

Nelson Benchmark (1,165)

There's a bit of fun scrambling required to reach the tippy-top of this small peak lying just north of Nelson.

-WGS84 Lat: 35.7186 deg N Lon: -114.8211 deg W

-I, Class 3 via West Face ***

An unusual feature—a keeper pothole—encountered in the backcountry near Nelson

"Mount Stocker" (3,854)

This peak lies northeast of the small, semi-interesting community of Nelson. The peak has a prominence of slightly more than 500'.

-WGS84 Lat: 35.7302 deg N Lon: -114.8068 deg W

-I, Class 3 via West Face Chute *

"Pigs in Zen Peak" (3,832)

Just southeast of Arch Back, this short, easy peak has nice views of the area. Approach directly from NV-165, north of Nelson.

-WGS84 Lat: 35.7351 deg N Lon: -114.8216 deg W

-I, Class 2-3 via upper North Ridge from the west **

"Lonesome Peak" (3,858)

This obscure peak, the highpoint of the Eldorado Mountains Wilderness, has simply awesome views from its small summit. Having spent a few days ticking off peaks in the rugged lands immediately north of Nelson, I was completely surprised to find a register on the summit (the only register I'd yet found in the area)—with a sign-in from the very same day!

The original sign-in from 2003 was by Howard Booth and Ursula Wilson-Booth, who were the same two folks to revisit on the day of my fine visit in April 2010. They dubbed the peak "Lonesome Peak" for Lonesome Wash, which starts to the west and then bends around north of the peak to the confluence of Oak Creek Canyon, before they turn due east to drain to the Colorado River. The peak lies immediately west of Oak Creek Canyon and can be easily combined with Pigs in Zen Peak for a mellow, 2-hour car-to-car from the pavement.

This area is stunningly wild and beautiful. Those digging the area might want to take more time to check out the really cool upper portion of Lonesome Wash immediately west of Lonesome Peak's summit and due north of Pigs in Zen Peak.

-WGS84 Lat: 35.7418 deg N Lon: -114.8148 deg W

-I, Class 2-3 via South Ridge **

-I, Class 4 via West Face (class 2, except for the final 30 feet) ***

"Arch Back" (3,660)

A short hike to a fine viewpoint directly from the pavement just outside of Nelson, Nevada. It is accessed from NV-165, north of Nelson.

-WGS84 Lat: 35.7504 deg N Lon: -114.8344 deg W

-I, Class 2 via North Ridge from the West **

"Techatticup Peak" (3,225)

The north ridge is a pleasant stroll from a good dirt road nears its base. This is desert tortoise country. The peak is approached from NV-165, to its north.

-WGS84 Lat: 35.7969 deg N Lon: -114.8990 deg W

-I, Class 2 via North Ridge **

Peeper Benchmark (3,513)

This obscure peak requires miles and miles of dirt road driving to get anywhere near it. Fortunately, about half the miles are on excellent roads. If you're lucky, you might even stumble across the old, unmarked cemetery hiding away near there…

-WGS84 Lat: 35.8010 deg N Lon: -114.7961 deg W

-I, Class 1-2 via West Slope **

"The Ignorant Fool" (2,506)

With 356' of prominence, this small peak offers really nice views of the expansive desert near Nelson. It can be readily combined with nearby Point of Redemption for a short, 1-2 hour loop from NV-165. The northwest face is loose and unpleasant.

-WGS84 Lat: 35.8050 deg N Lon: -114.9280 deg W
-I, Class 1-2 via North Ridge *
-I, Class 2 via Northwest Face *

"Point of Redemption" (2,290)

This is a minor summit just southeast of the US-95/NV-165 junction near Nelson and Boulder City.

-WGS84 Lat: 35.8135 deg N Lon: -114.9335 deg W
-I, Class 2 via North Ridge *
-I, Class 2 via South Ridge *

Pilot Cone (3,045)

A tranquil and seldom-visited summit.

-WGS84 Lat: 35.8580 deg N Lon: -114.8059 deg W
-I, Class 2 via Soouth Ridge **
-I, Class 2 via Southeast Face **

The Knoll (2,231)

This is the lamest summit in the book. I *should* be embarrassed for even including it. A dirt road out of Boulder City lands one within a 5-minute walk of the barely discernible highpoint.

-WGS84 *Lat: 35.9369 deg N Lon: -114.7761 deg W*
-I, Class 1 from any direction *

"Windbreak Peak" (2,583)

This small peak, just south of Pass Benchmark, is a short hike from the parking area at the end of North Boy Scout Canyon Road.

-WGS84 Lat: 35.9819 deg N Lon: -114.7784 deg W
-I, Class 1-2 from the Northwest **

"Gold Strike Mountain" (2,410)

This peak is bordered by Gold Strike Canyon to the north, Boy Scout Canyon to the south, and the Colorado River to the east. Assuming one is willing to work through a fair bit of steep and loose slip-sliding rock here and there, this is a fine mountain with awesome views of Hoover Dam, the Colorado River, and Lake Mead. The peak is most easily approached by driving/walking a mostly good dirt road (4WD required in one nasty spot) to its end due west of the peak. There, work down through some dirty cliffs for less than 100 feet (class 2 can be found) and then traverse south to the crest (which is then followed east toward the peak). From the summit, note a narrow notch/slot in the cliffs to the west-southwest. For the descent, work down into the wash leading to the notch. The wash sports several fun climbing problems, including a handful of (bypassable) semi-keeper potholes, which were full of clean(ish) water when I was there one November. Continuing up the canyon to the notch, you'll find that the notch is easily worked through (despite some acacia). A short hike/scramble from the top of the notch leads back to the road. This is rugged country, so be careful. But enjoy!

-WGS84 Lat: 35.9893 deg N Lon: -114.7566 deg W
-II, Class 2 via West Slope ***

"Goldstrike Pass Peak" (2,710)

The east ridge is a pleasant, meandering hike from Goldstrike Pass, just west of Pass Benchmark. Although less pleasant, for the return one can drop straight down the southeast slope then follow a Jeep road back to the powerline road, where you'll turn left and walk back up to your vehicle at the pass.

-WGS84 Lat: 35.9940 deg N Lon: -114.8042 deg W
-II, Class 1-2 via Southeast Slope *
-II, Class 2 via East Ridge **

Pass Benchmark (2,695)

Nice views can be had from the summit of this easy peak near Hoover Dam. A decent dirt road approaches the peak from the north and runs within 0.3 mile of the summit. From there, ten minutes of hiking takes one to the top. Can you pass the test?!?

-WGS84 Lat: 35.9965 deg N Lon: -114.7823 deg W
-I, Class 1 via West Ridge *
-I, Class 1-2 via Northeast Slope *

"Hoover Peak" (1,940)

Hoover Peak forms the north wall of the rugged canyon which contains Goldstrike Hot Springs. Leave the main canyon southwest of the summit and follow game trails up a lesser wash to the saddle west of the peak. From there, it's a pleasant scramble to the top.

-WGS84 Lat: 36.0059 deg N Lon: -114.7508 deg W
-II, Class 2 via West Face **

The brand new bridge (and Hoover Dam) from the summit of Gold Strike Mountain. The view looks northeast.

Northwest of Boulder City

The peaks in this subsection are located northwest of Boulder City, and north of the US-95/US-93 junction. They are arranged here south-to-north.

"Easter Island Peak" (3,220+)

There are funky, Easter Island-like cairns on the summit. Park along the highway north of Railroad Pass to grab this little guy.

-WGS84 Lat: 35.9777 deg N Lon: -114.9064 deg W
*-I, Class 2 via West Face **
*-I, Class 2 via Northeast Slope **

"Leaning Arch Peak" (3,262)

There's a large arch on the peak's west face that can be clearly seen from the south along the highway between Railroad Pass and Boulder City. From the same vantage point, check out the ridiculous and cheesy fake cascade on the hillside.

Approach this peak by climbing up and over Easter Island Peak.
-WGS84 Lat: 35.9803 deg N Lon: -114.9023 deg W
*-I, Class 2 via Southwest Slope **
*-I, Class 2 via Northwest Slope **

"Bootleg Mountain" (3,565)

Bootleg is a nice peak that lies amidst a world-class network of mountain biking trails.

-WGS84 Lat: 35.9935 deg N Lon: -114.8791 deg W

-I, Class 2 via Northeast Face **

Urban Las Vegas

The urban peaks in this section lie along the edge of the Las Vegas Valley. They are arranged here in a clockwise fashion around the Valley, starting in the northwest.

"Cheyenne Mountain" (3,833)

Cheyenne Mountain is the small mountain sitting at the western end of Cheyenne Avenue, just west of CC-215, in northwestern Las Vegas. A number of interesting routes and variations have been established on its slopes and faces.

To climb the mountain via the North Ridge: Park at either the equestrian park (makes less sense) or the small city park (makes more sense) at the western dead end of Alexander (west of Cliff Shadows Parkway). Hike to the toe of the north ridge. The ridge can be followed with relative ease, though it does feature one short, craggy section about halfway up.

To climb the mountain via the East Face: From the equestrian park lot, hike the paved road (Cliff Shadows Parkway) a couple hundred yards north to the base of the mountain's east face. The face faces Cliff Shadows Parkway and is immediately north of an office building near its base. Work your way up the concave face (something of a shallow bowl) for a few hundred feet until you reach a band of cliffs preventing further easy progress. Although a number of weaknesses in the cliff band can be found, look for a 3rd class weakness (appearing as a steep ledge system) near the right (north) edge of the face. Working through the weakness, find yourself on gentler terrain above. Once there, traverse up and left a short bit until you come to another cliff band. You should note a prominent drainage heading down to your right. Cross to the head of the drainage and then scramble up and right (class 2+) to gain the top of the low band of rock there. Continue up left for a couple hundred feet, before angling right and following class 1-2 terrain to the summit a few hundred feet above. Roundtrip numbers are around a mile, with less than 1,000 feet of gain.

To climb the mountain via the West Face: From the equestrian park lot, hike a horse trail around the base of the south ridge and then continue cross-country through open desert or on one of the mountain bike trails to the base of the west face. Any line to the summit will work, with varying degrees of difficulty. Some steeper sections should be anticipated near the summit.

To climb the mountain via the South Ridge: From the equestrian park lot, hike a horse trail a couple hundred yards to the base of the semi-rugged south ridge of the mountain. Start working up, staying on or near the crest (where the most fun is found!). Difficulties along the way include a short knife-edge immediately followed by a 25-foot cliff band requiring some loose 5.0 face climbing (immediately right of the crest; but can be bypassed 100 yards left of the crest) about halfway up the mountain, as well as a beautiful 50-foot or more section of exposed (but mostly solid) 5.0 climbing along the crest of the upper ridge. This last bit of 5th class climbing can be bypassed on its left via a short bit (perhaps 30-40 feet) of 4th class climbing, followed by class 2 terrain leading to the top.

-WGS84 Lat: 36.2241 deg N Lon: -115.3388 deg W
-I, Class 2-3 via North Ridge **
-I, Class 3 via East Face **
-I, Class 3-4 via West Face **
-I, YDS 5.0 via South Ridge ***

Some fool just above the knife edge
portion of Cheyenne Mountain's south ridge.

Lone Mountain (3,342)

Lone Mountain is not a classic. It is not the sentinel of the Las Vegas area. It's not a climber's paradise (though Urban Crag, a feature of the mountain, does host a number of moderate-to-difficult sport routes). You're not going to find solitude or breathtaking wilderness views. But this prominent little mountain, stuck all by itself out in the middle of the northwest portion of the Las Vegas valley, makes a fine mid-week conditioner and has more semi-interesting routes on it than meet the eye.

Lone Mountain is a local's mountain.

On a typical evening in the desert, you'll find folks with dogs, spouses, and kids hiking the half-mile use trail to the top of the peak. For those easily winded, there's even a concrete bench about halfway up to rest on and take in the city scenes below. The graffiti on the summit contributes nicely to the urban feel of the peak, and those enthralled by the blinding neon of this impulsive city will be enamored of the view.

From US-95 in downtown Las Vegas, head north. Get off at the Cheyenne Avenue (SR-574) exit (exit 83) and head west. Continue 1.8 miles to the intersection of Cheyenne Avenue and N. Durango Drive then turn right onto Durango. Follow Durango for about a mile to W. Alexander Road. As you turn left onto Alexander and proceed toward the semi-impressive desert peaks in the distance, you'll note the much smaller Lone Mountain in the foreground. Follow Alexander for two miles to the base of the mountain and then use surface streets (Alexander, N. Jensen Street to Lone Mountain Park, or Vegas Vista Trail) appropriate to whichever access point you're looking for. Navigation from this point is not problematic.

To climb the mountain via the trail: This route is accessed by a residential road (N. Vegas Vista Trail) running north from Alexander on the southwest side of the peak. Follow Vegas Vista Trail (paved) north from Alexander for about 0.5 to its end at a dirt parking area. A few hundred yards north, a well-worn use trail comes down from a gully on the west side of the mountain's north ridge. Take the at-times-primitive trail to the summit. The effort requires a roundtrip of less than a mile, with about 600 feet of gain.

To climb the mountain via the North Ridge: From either the access point mentioned for the trail or from the city park on Lone Mountain Road (just off CC-215) make your way to the toe of the north ridge and follow it to the summit.

To climb the mountain via the East Ridge Direct: From the south parking lot of the city park on N. Jensen Street, gain the ridge at its toe and head up any line you deem suitable. This is a pleasant scrambling route that leads directly to the top.

To climb the mountain via the West Ridge: This short and stubby ridge is accessed directly from N. Vegas Vista Trail.

To climb the mountain via the South Ridge: Park in the lot of the softball complex (Majestic Park) across the street from the toe of the ridge. Sticking to the crest of the ridge, the going is mostly in the class 2 range, with occasional short class 3-4 sections. (There is an interesting keyhole-like feature about halfway along the ridge. Looking carefully, you may notice the fairly large limestone arch on the west side of the ridge.)

To climb the mountain via the East Ridge Indirect: From the south side of the city park on N. Jensen Street, work your way to the base of the east ridge. From there, stay low and skirt along the south side of the ridge until you reach the base of a dry waterfall (about 50 feet high). Climb class 3-4 terrain straight up the waterfall, traversing to the left at the top, and then work your way up the route of least resistance to the crest of the east ridge above. Once there, you will find that you are about halfway to the summit already. Scurry the last few minutes to the top.

To climb the mountain via the South Ridge (Bandanna Variation): This is a more beefy variation of the south ridge route talked already mentioned. About 2/3 way up the route, at a level section of ridge just below the upper headwall, notice a 15-foot, deep vertical gash in the wall to the right, immediately below a small (but obvious) cave. Gaining a groove just right of the vertical gash, cruise up 100+ feet of sustained (broken only by a single wide ledge halfway up) and steep class 4 with (mostly) good, frictional rock. At the top of the groove/face, angle left on easier rock to regain the crest of the ridge.

To climb the mountain via the West Face Indirect: This route heads up the west face of the peak, as approached from the bowl between the west and south ridges, and contains about 200 feet of class 4 and 5 climbing. The face, if climbed directly, tops out at the summit and is steep and exposed (YDS) 5.7. The indirect route follows the west face, but veers slightly to the right as the steepness gets severe about halfway up, ultimately bringing you out on the south ridge about 30 feet below the summit. Any line will go, with varying degrees of difficulty.

-WGS84 Lat: 36.2382 deg N Lon: -115.3152 deg W
*-I, Class 2 via trail **
*-I, Class 2 via North Ridge **
*-I, Class 2-3 via East Ridge Direct ****
*-I, Class 2-3 via West Ridge **
*-I, Class 3-4 via South Ridge ****
*-I, Class 4 via East Ridge Indirect **
*-I, Class 4 via South Ridge (Bandanna Variation) ****
*-I, YDS 5.2 via West Face Indirect **

Peak 2,980 (2,980)
This minor peak, sporting the same elevation as the unofficially named Division Peak just to the east, is closely southwest of Sunrise Mountain.

The southeast gully route terminates at the saddle northeast of the summit, where you head southwest and hike easily to the top. The southeast ridge is loose and not entirely pleasant.

-WGS84 Lat: 36.2194 deg N Lon: -114.9919 deg W
*-II, Class 2 via Southeast Ridge ***
*-II, Class 2 via Southeast Gully ***

Sunrise Mountain (3,364)
This is the real Sunrise Mountain, not the one most Vegas locals think is Sunrise. Approach from the area of the pass along NV-147, north of Frenchman Mountain.

-WGS84 Lat: 36.2244 deg N Lon: -114.9769 deg W

-I, Class 2 via Southwest Ridge **
-I, Class 3 via South Face **

Approximate line of the Bandanna Variation on Lone Mountain.
The deep, vertical gash (and small cave above it) can be seen at left.

"NW Frenchman Peak" (3,952)
The prominent northwest summit of Frenchman Mountain. Approached as per Frenchman Mountain.

-WGS84 Lat: 36.1881 deg N Lon: -114.9981 deg W
-I, Class 2 via service road *

"NE Frenchman Peak" (3,858)

As per Frenchman Mountain, gain the service road (at your own risk, of course) from the north.

-WGS84 Lat: 36.1886 deg N Lon: -114.9934 deg W

*-I, Class 2 via service road **

Frenchman Mountain (4,052)

Careful 'round here, as there's a history of stolen and vandalized vehicles left at/near the trailhead along NV-147.

I remember hiking up here once in August; I was certain I was going to die of heat stroke. Somehow, I didn't.

-WGS84 Lat: 36.1791 deg N Lon: -114.9977 deg W

*-II, Class 2 via service road ***

"Mount Turtle Island" (3,332)

This peak isn't particularly urban (for now), though its position is such that it seems to belong in this section.

The name is as much a nod to poet Gary Snyder as it is to the desert tortoise conservation center at the mountain's base. A powerline road north of the peak can be driven to within less than a mile of the mountain. From there, a pleasant cross-country stroll leads to the rocky top.

-WGS84 Lat: 35.9574 deg N Lon: -115.2420 deg W

*-I, Class 2 via Northwest Ridge ***

Pipe Benchmark (2,847)

Since development has crowded out this small mountain on the outskirts of Las Vegas, the locals have come to call it *Exploration Peak*. Who knows why. I guess that sounds cooler than *Pipe* Benchmark.

There are several maintained trails that lead to the summit.

-WGS84 Lat: 36.0173 deg N Lon: -115.2587 deg W

*-I, Class 1 via trails **

"Mesa Mesa" (3,405)

Once approached quickly and easily from the park east-northeast of the summit, access issues might soon require a longer approach from the west or southwest sides.

-WGS84 Lat: 36.0833 deg N Lon: -115.3342 deg W

*-I, Class 2 via North Ridge **

North of Las Vegas

Apex

All of the southernmost peaks in this subsection (except Tracked Peak) are located west of the junction of US-93/I-15, northeast of the Las Vegas Valley. The northernmost peaks are located east of I-15, in the Dry Lake Range. Access is varied, and occasionally complicated by private property. The peaks are arranged here from south-to-north.

"Tracked Peak" (2,860)
Easily approached from the ATV-area at the northern end of Las Vegas Boulevard.

-WGS84 Lat: 36.3131 deg N Lon: -114.9123 deg W
*-I, Class 2 via West Slopes **

Game Benchmark (3,540)
Nellis Air Force Base calls this small mountain Apex Peak. A service road from the northeast goes nearly to the summit. There is a 'No Trespassing' sign at a gate near the bottom of the service road. The final 100-foot summit cliffbands can be climbed class 4 from the northwest.

-WGS84 Lat: 36.3337 deg N Lon: -114.9748 deg W
*-I, Class 4 via East Slopes ***

"Hidden Arch Mountain" (3,403)
A cool, little peak. Approach from one of the many dirt roads in the area.

-WGS84 Lat: 36.3460 deg N Lon: -114.9532 deg W
*-I, Class 2-3 via Southeast Slope ***

"Mount Formidable" (3,083)
This surprisingly rugged little mountain is well-protected by rings of cliffs around its entire perimeter. Fortunately, weaknesses on the southwest face allow class 2 access (with one short class 3 spot) in the upper bands.

-WGS84 Lat: 36.3639 deg N Lon: -114.9397 deg W
*-I, Class 2-3 via Southwest Face **

Bark Benchmark (3,388)
Fun scrambling through several cliff bands.

-WGS84 Lat: 36.3700 deg N Lon: -114.9575 deg W
*-I, Class 3-4 via Northwest Face ***

"Divided Peak" (3,107)

The junction of the north ridge and the head of the peak's northeast wash is an interesting place to visit. Unfortunately, private property issues in the area could complicate access.

The peak is located just south of US-93, a short distance west of I-15.

-WGS84 Lat: 36.4007 deg N Lon: -114.9510 deg W

*-I, Class 2 via North Ridge ***

*-I, Class 2 via Northeast Wash **

Peak 3,235 (3,235)

Exit I-15 at the Great Basin Highway and take the frontage road past the landfill on the east side of the interstate. As the frontage road bends to the east, it turns to dirt and soon parallels railroad tracks. Park at a point slightly southwest of the summit, cross the tracks, and then follow the drainage to the saddle above. From there, angle left and work through a couple short cliff bands to reach the highpoint.

-WGS84 Lat: 36.4143 deg N Lon: -114.8397 deg W

*-II, Class 2 via West Slopes ***

"Blissful Peak" (3,303)

Approach as per Peak 3,235 but park along the east-west stretch of dirt road where a tunnel leads under the railroad tracks. Go under the tunnel then walk east across the desert to reach the base of the peak's steep west slope.

-WGS84 Lat: 36.3942 deg N Lon: -114.8397 deg W

*-II, Class 2 via West Slope ***

*-II, Class 2 via South Slope **

"Friendship Peak" (3,228)

Friendship and Blissful can be combined for a decent half-day out by the landfill. Ugh.

-WGS84 Lat: 36.3777 deg N Lon: -114.8462 deg W

*-II, Class 2 via North Slope **

*-II, Class 2 via West Slope **

"Sneaky Peak" (3,058)

Approach as per Friendship Peak and cross through the tunnel then head southwest toward the peak, walking up the disgusting (lots of trash blown over from the nearby landfill) canyon splitting the peak's twin northern ridges. As you near the head of the canyon, angle left to scramble to the summit.

-WGS84 Lat: 36.3760 deg N Lon: -114.8701 deg W

*-II, Class 2 via North Canyon **

Tony Benchmark (2,828)

Tony Benchmark is the northernmost peak in the Dry Lake Range. Access as per Peak 3,235 and continue along the dirt road to a point southwest of the summit. From there, any number of lines up the southwest slope leads to the south ridge and the top, where a register sits in a cairn.

-WGS84 Lat: 36.4477 deg N Lon: -114.8330 deg W

-II, Class 2 via South Ridge **

Muddy Mountains

Most of the peaks in this subsection are accessed from the Buffington Pockets area, which has a decent dirt road leading to it from NV-169 to the north. South of Buffington Pockets, the road deteriorates quickly and becomes 4WD as it heads toward Hidden Valley. The peaks are arranged here generally south-to-north.

Muddy Mountains Highpoint (5,432)

I'd always envisioned this peak as a lame slog (especially compared to its classic neighbor, Muddy Peak), but was pleasantly surprised by what I found. It's a nice peak.

Initially approached as per Muddy Peak via Hidden Valley.

-WGS84 Lat: 36.2986 deg N Lon: -114.7142 deg W

-III, Class 2-3 from the North ***

"Muddy Peak" (5,363)

Another desert classic. Although the dirt road sucks on the drive in toward Hidden Valley on the standard approach, the valley itself is charming.

-WGS84 Lat: 36.2984 deg N Lon: -114.6933 deg W

-III, Class 3 via Northwest Ridge ****

"Colorock Summit" (4,239)

A nice peak above Hidden Valley in the neighborhood of Muddy Peak and Muddy Mountains Highpoint. Approach as if you're going to Muddy Peak, leaving for this summit once in Hidden Valley.

-WGS84 Lat: 36.3474 deg N Lon: -114.7255 deg W

-II, Class 2-3 via South Ridge ***

"White Basin Overlook" (4,446)

This interesting peak in the northern Muddy Mountains has nice views and more than 1200' of prominence. According to the summit register, it is seldom climbed. It was named by Vegas local Ed Forkos.

-WGS84 Lat: 36.3627 deg N Lon: -114.6641 deg W

-II, Class 2-3 via West Face ***

Muddy Peak, to the east, from Muddy Mountains Highpoint.

"Buffington Peak" (4,423)

A decent peak with good views looking out and down onto the Buffington Pockets area. The peak is just north of White Basin Overlook.

-WGS84 Lat: 36.3745 deg N Lon: -114.6632 deg W
*-II, Class 2-3 via West Face ***

"Surprise Peak" (3,330)

This small peak affords nice views of the Buffington Pockets area.

-WGS84 Lat: 36.3804 deg N Lon: -114.7004 deg W
*-I, Class 1-2 via East Slope **

"Midridge Peak" (4,252)

A very nice peak with an isolated, "big peak" feel. A Howard Booth register from 2002 referred to the peak as Midridge Peak.

-WGS84 Lat: 36.3967 deg N Lon: -114.6402 deg W
*-II, Class 2-3 via Northeast Aspect ****

The view east from the top of Colorock Summit

White Benchmark (4,117)

Like nearby Piute Point, White Benchmark (a part of the Muddy Mountains) lies outside of Valley of Fire State Park but is close enough to be lumped in with this funky group.

Although a number of routes up this puppy are feasible, expect an interesting day with lots of steep, loose scrambling, and plenty of route-finding challenges. While I found an exploratory canyon/ridge route I climbed up the northwest bowl to be stimulating, one must be prepared for some spicy scrambling up to 5.0 or so, on loose rock. The west ridge, while still steep and loose in places, was more relaxed.

This is yet another seldom-visited southern Nevada summit – the register hadn't seen a sign-in in more than 8 years.

-WGS84 Lat: 36.4126 deg N Lon: -114.6473 deg W

*-II, Class 3-4 via West Ridge ***

*-III, Class 4-5 via Northwest Bowl ***

Piute Point Highpoint (3,002)

This is the unnamed highpoint of the Piute Point massif. It can be readily combined with the named Piute Point in a 2-hour roundtrip effort.

-WGS84 Lat: 36.4347 deg N Lon: -114.6549 deg W

*-I, Class 2 via North Ridge **

Piute Point (2,771)

This is a minor, named summit midway between I-15 and the entrance to Valley of Fire State Park. An unnamed higher summit, the highpoint of the Piute Point massif, lies just a bit to the southeast on the same massif.

-WGS84 Lat: 36.4388 deg N Lon: -114.6588 deg W

*-I, Class 2 via Northeast Face **

Beginning the descent of White Benchmark's west ridge

Ute

The peaks in this subsection are accessed from the Ute exit off I-15, between the Valley of Fire and Glendale/Moapa exits.

Peak 2,963 (2,963)

A short outing near the obscure northwest boundary of Valley of Fire. Although a bit contrived, one can follow some fun class 2 steep rock slabs for much of the lower route, turning this into something resembling a bit of fun.

Approach this peak via the Ute exit off of I-15.

-WGS84 Lat: 36.5396 deg N Lon: -114.5863 deg W

*-I, Class 2 via Southeast Ridge ***

Peak 3,001 (3,001)

This is a semi-interesting peak, once you get on the narrow crest. Take the Ute exit and park along the pavement northwest of the summit (as the road bends to the east) then hike south along a short dirt road until you can cut east through a gap. Then, follow a shallow wash south until a short canyon appears on the left. The direct route to the summit via the west face can be taken from here, or an easier variation aims for the ridge south of the summit then works north along the crest to the highpoint.

-WGS84 Lat: 36.5363 deg N Lon: -114.6195 deg W
*-II, Class 3 via South Ridge ***
*-II, Class 3-4 via West Face Direct ***

Ute Benchmark (3,281)

Ute Benchmark and Peak 3284 should be combined for a pleasant half-day hike. Take the Ute exit and park along the pavement a few miles north of the peak. An old dirt road (hard to find at first) can be followed to the northern base of the peak. Angle onto the northeast slope by avoiding cliff bands guarding the northern aspect. Follow the mellow northeast slope and then wander to the highpoint. A bit of minor scrambling and route-finding will be encountered just before the top.

-WGS84 Lat: 36.5002 deg N Lon: -114.6159 deg W
*-II, Class 2 via Northeast Slopes ***

Peak 3,284 (3,284)

This unnamed peak is actually higher than nearby Ute Benchmark, to the northwest. The two can be easily combined.

-WGS84 Lat: 36.4965 deg N Lon: -114.6104 deg W
*-I, Class 2 via North Slope ***

Virgin Mountains

The peaks in this subsection are accessed as if one was headed to Gold Butte (see Jumbo Peak, etc.). The peaks are arranged here generally south-to-north.

Billy Goat Peak (5,735)

An enjoyable, easy scramble near Virgin Peak.

-WGS84 Lat: 36.5123 deg N Lon: -114.0645 deg W
*-I, Class 2 via North Face ****

"Whitney Pocket Point" (3,329)

This minor but aesthetic sandstone peak sits immediately east of where the paved Gold Butte road turns to dirt at Whitney Pocket. Practice solid route-finding, or expect the scrambling to get stiff and scary in spots.

-WGS84 Lat: 36.5248 deg N Lon: -114.1366 deg W
*-I, Class 3 via West Ridge ****
*-I, Class 4 via South Face *****

Quail Point (4,075)
Quail Point is south of Virgin Peak and northwest of Billy Goat Peak near Gold Butte, Nevada. This is another one of those peaks that you'll do and then ask yourself, "*Why?*"

-WGS84 Lat: 36.5298 deg N Lon: -114.0997 deg W
*-I, Class 2 via Northwest Ridge **

Little Virgin Peak (3,514)
I somehow ended up hiking this thing in my underwear once. Don't ask.

-WGS84 Lat: 36.6030 deg N Lon: -114.2239 deg W
*-I, Class 2 via Northeast Slope **

Virgin Peak (8,125)
A landmark above Mesquite, Nevada.

-WGS84 Lat: 36.6028 deg N Lon: -114.1123 deg W
*-II, Class 2 via Southeast Ridge ****

Virgin Benchmark (8,085)
Hit this one by accident once while trying to climb Virgin Peak. To our surprise, we found a register on top.

-WGS84 Lat: 36.6141 deg N Lon: -114.0855 deg W
*-III, Class 2 via West Ridge **

Juanita Benchmark (3,494)
This is a short, easy hike from the pavement.

-WGS84 Lat: 36.6269 deg N Lon: -114.2217 deg W
*-II, Class 2 via South Ridge ***

I-15 Corridor Between Glendale & Mesquite

The peaks in this subsection are spaced out widely along I-15 between Glendale and Mesquite, Nevada, with the exception of and Tabeau Peak. Tabeau, the only peak in this book which is located in Utah, is *northeast* of Mesquite but of enough interest that I simply *had* to include it in this book. I also included Mormon Peak and Sharks Tooth, both of which are well off I-15 but approached from the Glendale area. The peaks are arranged here generally south-to-north.

California Ridge (3,123)
This outing near Glendale is a decent hike to a very nice viewpoint of the area. California Ridge has 646' of prominence.

-WGS84 Lat: 36.5781 deg N Lon: -114.6036 deg W
*-II, Class 2 via North Ridge ***

Glen Benchmark (2,981)

Not far from Glendale, Nevada. A good dirt road off (and east of) I-15 puts you within easy striking distance of the top.

-WGS84 Lat: 36.6051 deg N Lon: -114.5812 deg W

*-I, Class 2-3 via Southwest Ridge **

"Glendale Point" (1,932)

Glendale Point is due west of Peak 2,050 and accessed via the dirt road mentioned for the latter peak. Powerline and subsidiary roads lead to the base of the north slope.

-WGS84 Lat: 36.6599 deg N Lon: -114.5366 deg W

*-I, Class 2 via North Slope **

Peak 2,050 (2,050)

This peak, located just southwest of the I-15 interchange with NV-169 (near Glendale and Logandale), is a quick hike, especially if one drives the good dirt road to the saddle north of the peak. The dirt road is accessed from NV-169, just south of I-15.

-WGS84 Lat: 36.6611 deg N Lon: -114.5243 deg W

*-I, Class 2 via North Ridge **

Huntsman Hill (1,500)

This is an indiscernible bump on the eastern ramparts of Mormon Mesa. A good dirt road runs within feet of the "summit."

-WGS84 Lat: 36.5955 deg N Lon: -114.3500 deg W

*-I, Class 1 via West Slope **

Mormon Mesa (2,234)

This mega-lame named summit is just southeast of the I-15/Carp-Elgin Interchange, northeast of Glendale.

-WGS84 Lat: 36.7244 deg N Lon: -114.4125 deg W

*-I, Class 1 from any direction **

Peak 2,335 (2,335)

This lame but obvious peak close to I-15 near the Overton exit requires only a short walk up a service road. One can drive a passenger car to the gate, perhaps 100' below the top.

-WGS84 Lat: 36.6852 deg N Lon: -114.5201 deg W

*-I, Class 1 via service road **

Candy Benchmark (3,438)

Fancifully named Candy Benchmark is a couple miles northwest of I-15 at exit 100. A network of decent dirt roads allows one to drive quite close to the peak. In the canyon on the north side of the long and pleasant east ridge is an interesting cave with a hole in the ceiling.

Candy Benchmark has 898' of prominence.

-WGS84 Lat: 36.7662 deg N Lon: -114.4928 deg W

-II, Class 2 via East Ridge **

-II, Class 2 via East Canyon *

"Sheep Canyon Peak" (3,875)

Sheep Canyon Peak lies west of I-15, between Candy Benchmark (to the southwest) and Moapa Peak (to the northeast). A decent dirt road leaves I-15 at exit 100 and heads to Sheep Canyon Reservoir, south of the peak. A nice hike past the old dam in Sheep Canyon soon angles north then picks up the southwest ridge leading to the summit.

-WGS84 Lat: 36.8238 deg N Lon: -114.4666 deg W

-II, Class 2 via Southwest Ridge **

Moapa Peak (6,471)

One of the most classic peaks of the Mojave Desert, it is renowned for its dramatic summit knife edge ridge. The peak is accessed via a dirt road network north of I-15 at exit 100.

-WGS84 Lat: 36.8585 deg N Lon: -114.4516 deg W

-III, Class 3 via Southwest Slope ****

"Beacon Peak" (3,393)

-WGS84 Lat: 36.8564 deg N Lon: -114.3000 deg W

-I, Class 2 via service road *

Davidson Peak (5,324)

A traverse of the longish north ridge is a fun half-day out. Yowser, though—there were dozens of ticks crawling on the summit rocks! Approach via decent dirt roads gained from exit 100 off I-15.

-WGS84 Lat: 36.8963 deg N Lon: -114.3246 deg W

-II, Class 2 via East Ridge **

-II, Class 4 via North Ridge ***

"Little Davidson Peak" (3,849)

Approach as if heading to Davidson Peak.

-WGS84 Lat: 36.8987 deg N Lon: -114.2886 deg W

-I, Class 2-3 via North Slope *

"Sharks Tooth" (7,249)

Sharks Tooth is an aesthetic peak just east of Mormon Peak. A steep class 3 scramble gains the interesting upper southeast ridge from the south face. The summit is tiny, and the rock is very loose and exposed.

-WGS84 Lat: 36.9734 deg N Lon: -114.4921 deg W

*-III, Class 3 via South Face ****

Mormon Peak (7,414)

Mormon Peak, boasting 4034' of prominence, is a wonderfully isolated mountain that requires about 25 miles of dirt roads to approach. Most of the drive, which leaves NV-168 near Moapa and generally follows the railroad tracks before turning away and heading roughly northeast toward the peak, is on decent dirt; however, the final couple of miles, where the road enters the wide canyon south of the peak, is very rough and suitable only for 4WD vehicles. For Mormon Peak, park near the wash confluence south of the mountain, marked with 'ruins' on the map.

The standard route (southwest face) meanders a bit but generally heads up the left fork from the confluence then breaches cliffs midway up the mountain before angling off for the final slog to the top. The route is unpleasant due to loose gravel much of the way.

The route up the northeast face, which we approached from the saddle between Mormon Peak and Sharks Tooth, cannot be recommended. While interesting and adventurous, the route is sketchy, improbable and relatively committing.

-WGS84 Lat: 36.9741 deg N Lon: -114.5005 deg W

*-III, Class 2-3 via Southwest Face ***

*-III, Class 4-5 via Northeast Face ***

Tabeau Peak (4,500)

Technically inside of Utah, Tabeau Peak sits near the Arizona-Utah-Nevada tri-border just outside of Mesquite, Nevada. Though some maps show the west summit as being higher, the east summit (where the summit register resides) appears to be a touch more prominent. The hike up the north ridge from the good dirt road at its base, while a bit of a slog most of the way, culminates in a fantastically aesthetic, steep class 4 scramble up the final face before the summit. The views from the top are immense.

From I-15 in far northwestern Arizona, leave the interstate at exit 8 (Littlefield/Beaver Dam) and head north for 9.7 miles. There, turn right onto a good dirt road (signed 'Woodbury Desert Study Area') that will take you to the base of the peak's north ridge.

-WGS84 Lat: 37.0123 deg N Lon: -113.8726 deg W

*-II, Class 4 via North Ridge ****

Coyote Springs & Alamo

The peaks in this subsection are spaced out widely along highway 93 from south of Coyote Springs (and west of the Arrow Canyon Range) to north of Alamo (and west of Hiko along highway 318). The peaks are arranged here generally south-to-north.

Juniper Benchmark (5,850)

This obscure peak offers a commanding view toward the Arrow Canyon Range. Although the route is primarily just a longish desert slog (about 10 miles roundtrip, with 3,000 feet of elevation gain, all off-trail), lots of talus and gravel, as well as four distinct class 4 rock bands that need to be surmounted on the upper southeast ridge, make this a peak best left for truly inspired desert rats.

-WGS84 Lat: 36.5817 deg N Lon: -115.0176 deg W
-III, Class 4 via Southeast Gully and Ridge **

The Arrow Canyon Range, from the summit of Juniper Benchmark, stretches across the picture. This view looks northeast.

"Hand Peak" (3,660)

While lacking the dramatic position of Moapa Peak, Hand Peak's south ridge has a gnarly and exposed knife edge that makes Moapa Peak's classic knife edge ridge look like a sidewalk. Unfortunately, the knife edge can be bypassed via class 2-3 terrain to the east. The south ridge is approached via a 5-minute walk from US-93.

-WGS84 Lat: 36.5932 deg N Lon: -114.9339 deg W
-I, Class 2-3 via South Ridge ***

*-I, Class 2-3 via North Ridge ***

"The Pincher" (3,608)

This ultra-obscure peak showed no signs of visitation when I arrived on its summit in February 2010. The southeast ridge appears to be the easiest route up the peak. A descent of the west fork of the slot canyon that drains southeast from the summit area is an enjoyable technical endeavor – expect the east fork to be technical as well. For the west fork, be prepared to construct natural anchors and do rappels up to 50 feet.

Approach this peak directly from the shoulder of US-93, as per Hand Peak.

-WGS84 Lat: 36.5948 deg N Lon: -114.9499 deg W
*-II, Class 2-3 via Southeast Ridge ***

"Fleur de Lis Peak" (4,484)

A wonderful and interesting mountain. Unfortunately, a direct traverse from it to the Elbow Range Highpoint is sketchy and not recommended. It *might* be somewhat more feasible from the other direction. Squiggly Ridge is the long and meandering ridge whose toe lies northeast of the mountain and ultimately meets the exposed summit from the southeast. It is an enjoyable scramble. One can also descend the northeast ridge directly from the summit, dropping into the east bowl via short class 3 terrain midway down. Descending the canyon the bowl drains into is wonderful, though a few dryfalls must be bypassed (unless one is prepared to build anchors and do rappels) on the right via class 3 terrain.

As of fall 2009, signage declaring 'Unauthorized Entry Prohibited' has been placed along the eastern base of The Tri-Lambs, Marble 2 Benchmark, Fleur de Lis Peak and Elbow Range Highpoint. Per folks at the BLM, *hiking* into these areas is still permitted.

-WGS84 Lat: 36.6365 deg N Lon: -114.9490 deg W
*-III, Class 2-3 via Squiggly Ridge *****

Elbow Range Highpoint (4,650)

The Elbow Range is a small group of mountains across highway 93 from the north-central Arrow Canyon Range. The highpoint of the range is a very steep and imposing mountain – one of the most aesthetic mountains in southern Nevada, actually. Of potential interest to some, certain maps show this mountain as part of the Las Vegas Range, while others show it as the Elbow Range.

-WGS84 Lat: 36.6387 deg N Lon: -114.9531 deg W
*-II, Class 2-3 via North Ridge ***
*-III, Class 3-4 via Southeast Col from the north *****

"Elbow Butte" (3,488)

A short objective that makes for an enjoyable bonus peak on the way back from Fleur de Lis Peak or the Elbow Range Highpoint.

-WGS84 Lat: 36.6537 deg N Lon: -114.9370 deg W
*-I, Class 2 via South Face (with harder variations possible) ***
*-I, Class 3 via East Face ***

Center Benchmark (4,230)

Center Benchmark, a part of the Elbow Range, is a pleasant hike with good views. It's reasonable to link up multiple peaks in this area. This peak has 770' of prominence.

-WGS84 Lat: 36.6814 deg N Lon: -114.9712 deg W
*-II, Class 1-2 via Northeast Ridge ***
*-II, Class 1-2 via Northwest Slope **

"Perkins Peak" (3,935)

Perkins Peak, just north of Center Benchmark, can be easily combined with the latter peak for a pleasant half-day hike.

-WGS84 Lat: 36.6900 deg N Lon: -114.9746 deg W
*-II, Class 1-2 via South Slope via East Canyon ***

"Toy Train Peak" (4,066)

This, the next peak north of Perkins Peak, can be approached via an interesting canyon system on the east side of the peak. While descending the north ridge, I once encountered a small, metal toy train inscribed with family names and a date. The train was tucked under a rock.

Toy Train Peak has 631' of prominence.

-WGS84 Lat: 36.7015 deg N Lon: -114.9789 deg W
*-II, Class 2 via East Canyon ****
*-II, Class 2 via North Ridge ***

"Dinosaur Fins" (3,855)

Dinosaur Fins is north of Toy Train Peak. The peak has a very interesting appearance, with striking fin-like rock features covering its south face. There's also a curious "eye" pocket feature near the southwest side of the peak.

-WGS84 Lat: 36.7235 deg N Lon: -114.9798 deg W
*-II, Class 2 via Southwest Aspect ****
*-II, Class 2 via Northeast Slope ***

"Secret Point" (3,324)

This minor peak is slightly northeast of Dinosaur Fins.

-WGS84 Lat: 36.7258 deg N Lon: -114.9710 deg W

*-II, Class 1-2 via West Slope **

*-I, Class 2 via East Face ***

Meadow Valley Mountains Highpoint (5,772)

Sometimes referred to as Cathedral Peak, one might stumble across the sprawling debris field of an F-4 wreck on the west side of the mountain. The upper mountain is well-protected by cliff bands and one must look around to find a reasonable (and safe) way to the summit.

To approach, take highway 93 north of Las Vegas to its junction with NV-168. Continue north to a good dirt road branching off to the right and heading northeast in parallel to the Meadow Valley Mountains. Follow the dirt road to a point west of the mountain and park.

-WGS84 Lat: 37.0311 deg N Lon: -114.7928 deg W

*-III, Class 3 via loose North Arete (from West) *****

*-III, Class 3 via Southwest Chimney (from West) ****

Below the rugged Meadow Valley Mountains highpoint.
The view is east.

Tikaboo Benchmark (7,913)

Tikaboo Benchmark (also known as Tikaboo Peak) has the distinction of being the only *legal* summit viewpoint into Groom Lake. Groom Lake is better known by its other, more famous name—Area 51. Being 26 miles distant from the site, on clear days and at night, you can check out some of the activities going on at the once-super-secret military site. Binoculars or a telescope are helpful.

From Las Vegas, Nevada, head north on I-15 to the US-93 (Great Basin Highway) exit (exit 64). Once on the Great Basin Highway, continue for 58.2 miles to the boundary of Pahranagat National Wildlife Refuge near

Lower Pahranagat Lake. The lake is signed, and if you reach a town called Alamo, you've gone too far.

About 0.25 mile past mile post 32, you'll come to a gated dirt road on the left. The gate should not be locked; it is lawful to enter, as it is Bureau of Land Management land.

Ignoring the occasional side road, follow the main dirt road for 8.5 miles until it makes a sharp right turn. Make the turn and continue along the main dirt road for another 10 miles. At 18.7 miles from the pavement, the main road turns to the right, while a minor dirt road continues straight ahead. Take the minor road. Three and a half miles after getting onto the minor dirt road, you will come to Badger Spring. You should note a cattle trough there. Continue on as far as you feel comfortable past the spring and look for a good place to park. Ensure you park at least 100 yards away from the trough.

Although high clearance vehicles are fine up to the area of the spring, 4WD vehicles can continue for another 0.5 mile, going left at a fork. The road eventually reaches a saddle, which is generally considered to be the trailhead. People commonly camp here.

From the saddle, hike a use trail up the ridge to your left. Although you may eventually lose the trail, keep striving for the highest point in the area. A little trial and error should get you there. At the top of the ridge, drop a bit to the right to a minor saddle then work up to the next ridge. You'll soon come to the summit. Gaze westward toward some distant buildings and a landing strip. That's what all the hype's about.

Expect a roundtrip of a couple miles, with perhaps 1,000 feet of gain.

-WGS84 Lat: 37.3443 deg N Lon: -115.3590 deg W

-II, Class 2 via trail **

South Pahroc Range Highpoint (7,950)

Also known as Hyko Benchmark, the highpoint of this rugged and bouldery range has 2995' of prominence. What I presume to ordinarily be a casual hike and easy scramble felt rather epic when I did it during a blizzard in May.

-WGS84 Lat: 37.4834 deg N Lon: -115.0304 deg W

-II, Class 3 from the west ***

"Pahroc Summit Peak" (5,513)

This little peak is situated just north of US-93 at Pahroc Summit Pass, between Caliente and Alamo. In addition to the fun, short scramble to the summit via the east face, there's a short, 5.5 boulder problem at the base of the face that's worth a try. I built a small cairn on the summit of the boulder.

-WGS84 Lat: 37.6246 deg N Lon: -114.9965 deg W

-I, Class 3 via East Face **

"Oak Spring Peak" (6,716)

This forgettable peak in the Delamar Mountains is easily accessed from highway 93 at Oak Spring Summit (west of Caliente, Nevada). There are nice views from the summit.

-WGS84 Lat: 37.6054 deg N Lon: -114.6861 deg W
-I, Class 1 via South Slope *

A hiker (look closely) approaches the summit of Mount Irish.
Open desert and lonely mountain stretch out to the southeast below and beyond.

Mount Irish (8,743)

With outstanding views from its summit, an upper mountain studded with ponderosa pine and fir trees, interesting coloration on its mid-level cliffs, 2,563 feet of prominence (putting it among the 100 most prominent peaks in Nevada), and a large collection of petroglyphs on the rocks at its southeastern base, Mount Irish is an excellent, classic and highly underrated, obscure desert peak. During an August 2010 hike up to its high summit, I was doubly inspired by the awesome wildflower displays on the upper mountain. The peak is easily scrambled from Logan Pass, which is reached via several miles of good dirt road (Logan Canyon Road) from Hiko, Nevada.

-WGS84 Lat: 37.6447 deg N Lon: -115.4014 deg W
-II, Class 2-3 (dependent upon variation) via South Ridge ****

Sanderson Mountain (8,607)

Though just a touch lower than its impressive neighbor to the south (Mount Irish), Sanderson Mountain is an equally impressive mountain with outstanding views from its seldom-visited summit. By following the Logan Pass Road to its unmarked junction with the Silver Canyon Road, one can easily take a passenger car several miles up Silver Canyon Road (right) to a rougher dirt road heading left (west) immediately east of the saddle between

Sanderson Mountain and Mount Irish. From here, mellow pinyon-juniper ridges can be picked up and followed toward the southeast face of the mountain. As one nears the imposing limestone cliffs of the mountain, a formidable obstacle (a very steep, 40-foot class 4 face) stops what has been very easy hiking up to this point. One can either tackle the class 4 directly (everything else in the immediate vicinity is much harder) and then hike to the summit, or work 100 yards north from the class 4 break to what appears to be a class 2-3 weakness allowing access to the upper mountain. Alternatively, one can make a rough and uneven traverse for 0.4 miles counterclockwise to a class 2 break that allows access to the top.

-WGS84 Lat: 37.6544 deg N Lon: -115.3911 deg W
*-II, Class 4 via the direct Southeast Face ****

Looking south to Mount Irish from the summit of Sanderson Mountain.

Pahrump & Crystal

The peaks in this section are spaced out widely around the greater Pahrump metropolis. They are arranged here south-to-north.

Black Butte (3,585)

This is an isolated, small mountain out in Sandy Valley. Get here from either Goodsprings or from NV-160, southeast of Pahrump.

-WGS84 Lat: 35.8829 deg N Lon: -115.7215 deg W
*-I, Class 2 via East Ridge from mining road **

High Peak (4,006)

The locals really like this one; one of them has signed the register about a dozen times. I hiked it directly from Ash Meadows Road.

-WGS84 Lat: 36.2511 deg N Lon: -116.1343 deg W
-II, Class 2 via North Ridge ***
-II, Class 2-3 via North Wash & Slope ***

"Skull Peak" (3,550)

The diminutive easternmost mountain in the Last Chance Range near Pahrump, Nevada, Skull Peak is a steep, enjoyable scramble via its east face. The route, which initially follows the stubby east ridge, gains about 650 feet of elevation in 0.3 mile. It is approached from NV-160, north of Ash Meadows Road.

-WGS84 Lat: 36.3346 deg N Lon: -116.0521 deg W
-I, Class 2-3 via East Face **

"North Chance Peak" (4,610)

A good dirt road can be followed for 0.5 mile from the pavement to the toe of the north ridge. The north ridge is a nice route. It features a steep, 100-foot section of class 2-3 scrambling.

-WGS84 Lat: 36.3484 deg N Lon: -116.0765 deg W
-II, Class 2-3 via North Ridge ***

Mount Montgomery (4,268)

This is a mostly uninteresting peak, though there are fun scrambling options on the south face. Approach via decent (high clearance) dirt roads heading west from NV-160, north of Pahrump.

-WGS84 Lat: 36.4135 deg N Lon: -116.0937 deg W
-I, Class 2 via Northwest Ridge from Southeast Face *

Mount Schader (3,998)

Mount Schader lies east of Crystal, Nevada, and east of NV-160. A good service road can be walked or driven to the summit from the highway. Nice views from the top.

-WGS84 Lat: 36.4621 deg N Lon: -116.0580 deg W
-I-II, Class 1 via service road **

"Crystal Mountain" (2,862)

A short hike from the pavement on the drive to Crystal, Nevada (off of NV-160, south of US-95).

-WGS84 Lat: 36.4839 deg N Lon: -116.1424 deg W
-I, Class 2 via North Ridge *

On the high summit of North Chance Peak.
Far to the west, at distant-left, the high peaks of the Panamint Range can be seen.

Great Basin National Park

Established in 1986, this out-in-the-middle-of-nowhere National Park is a treasure waiting to be discovered. With dozens of caves (Lehman Caves offers tours into its highly decorated, stunning depths), bristlecone pines (the oldest known living organisms, one specimen of which, called "Prometheus," was chopped down in 1964, at which time it was learned to be 4950 *years* old), and the many peaks of the high Snake Range, this park will inspire anyone with a love for the outdoors.

Mostly buried under a huge pile of rock debris at the base of the cirque between Jeff Davis Peak and Wheeler Peak is Nevada's only glacier. While some argue that Wheeler Glacier, which rarely displays crevasses, is merely a permanent snowfield covered by fallen rock, in early season it makes a nice spot to practice glacier travel, glissading, and whatnot on the gentle slopes of the ice.

Though not known as a destination for technical climbing (or even stiff scrambling) routes, the park is a hiker's paradise. With about a dozen named peaks in the Snake Range (including Wheeler Peak, Nevada's second highest mountain), miles of timberline country await the enthusiastic explorer. Lakes and creeks can be found throughout the park. There are thick forests, deer, funky art work along the road from Baker, several beautiful campgrounds with clean bathroom facilities, and running brooks too.

The high mountains of Great Basin NP are most easily climbed from June-September when the roads are plowed and/or free of snow. During the snow months of fall, winter, and spring, the roads are not plowed and climbers will need to start their climbs much lower (and farther away). Beware of afternoon thunderstorms in summer. They are common, and lightning is dangerous.

The peaks in this section are arranged south-to-north.

Some comments from Great Basin NP staff regarding routes passing through the bristlecone groves at the base of Wheeler Peak and Jeff Davis Peak:

"Unless it is winter and there is snow covering the ground, people need to stay on trail in the Bristlecone grove at the base of Wheeler Peak/Jeff Davis Peak.

This is an issue between Memorial Day and the end of September because of several reasons:

1. We tell people they need to stay on trail in the Bristlecone area because the high visitation is causing soil erosion.

2. Soil erosion kills the Bristlecone trees by exposing their roots.

3. One person seen leaving the trail encourages others to do the same thing.

4. Photo monitoring has documented considerable changes and some of the old trees are dead due to exposure of their roots caused by people leaving the trail."

Please help preserve these noble, ancient trees by heeding the park's recommendation and only using these approaches when there is complete snow coverage in the area.

Great Basin National Park is located 69 miles from Ely, Nevada, five miles west of scrawny Baker, Nevada, and not far from US-50/6 and the Utah border in east central Nevada.

From the US-50/6 and SR-487 junction north of Baker, follow SR-487 five miles south to Baker. Once in Baker turn left on SR-488 and follow it five miles to the park entrance.

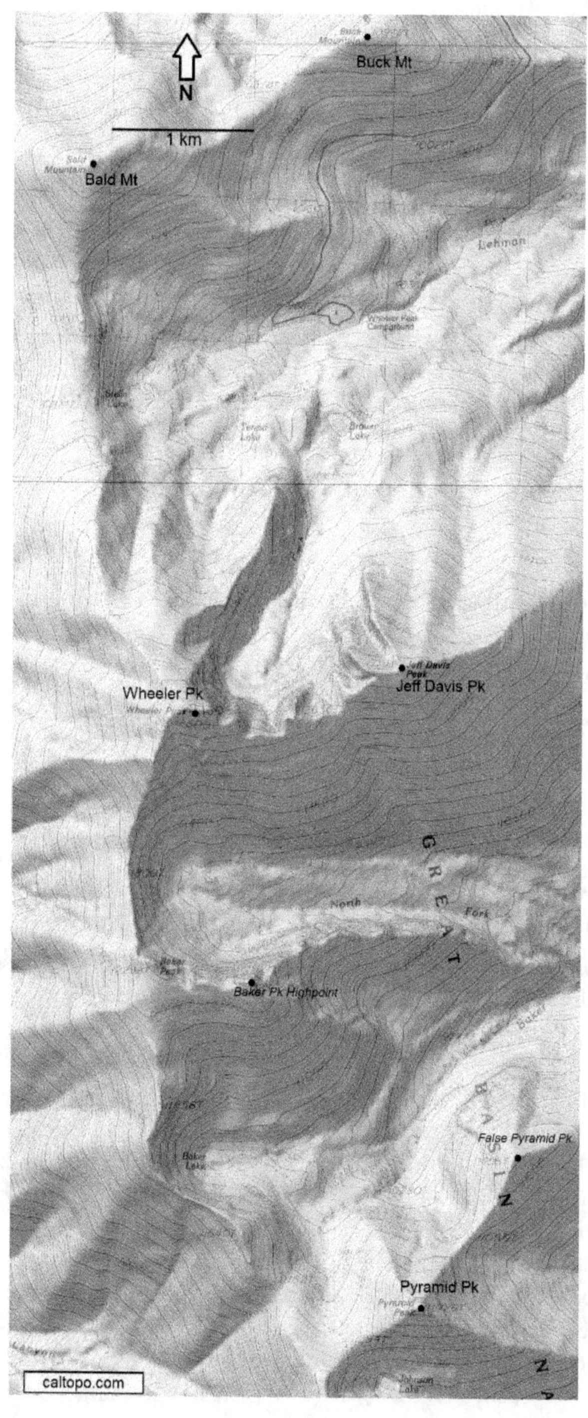
N
1 km
Buck Mt
Bald Mt
Lehman
Wheeler Pk
Jeff Davis Pk
GREAT
North Fork
Baker Pk Highpoint
BASIN
False Pyramid Pk
Pyramid Pk
caltopo.com

Pyramid Peak (11,926)

A nice, high peak that doesn't get as much love as it deserves. This is one of the highest peaks in the entire state!

Start hiking from the trailhead at the end of the graded dirt Baker Creek Road, at about 8,000 feet.

-WGS84 Lat: 38.9486 deg N Lon: -114.2953 deg W

-III, Class 2 via East Ridge ****

-III, Class 2 via Northeast Ridge from False Pyramid Peak ***

"False Pyramid Peak" (11,456)

This is a worthwhile bonus just northeast of Pyramid Peak. The two can be combined for a highly enjoyable loop hike. Start hiking from the trailhead at the end of the graded dirt Baker Creek Road, at about 8,000 feet.

-WGS84 Lat: 38.9579 deg N Lon: -114.2873 deg W

-III, Class 2 via Southwest Ridge from Pyramid Peak ***

-III, Class 2 via Northeast Ridge **

Baker Peak (12,305)

Baker Peak is the 4th highest mountain in Nevada. The mountain, part of the Snake Range, a spectacular range of beautifully forested canyons, rugged glacial cirques and high desert peaks, lies about a mile south of the much more famous Wheeler Peak. Although Baker's west summit (12,298 feet) lies directly along the north-south trending crest of the range, the mountain's higher east peak lies a 0.5 mile or so east of the crest.

As is typical with any of the high peaks of the Great Basin desert, the summit views are enormous and pleasing. Additionally, from Baker Peak's summit you get an interesting and seldom seen view of both Wheeler Peak and Jeff Davis Peak to the north.

Although a number of possible summit routes exist, a common one (and arguably, the easiest) is from Wheeler Peak itself. To use that route, follow the directions given for Wheeler Peak to the summit of that peak via the Wheeler Peak Trail. From the summit of Wheeler Peak, Baker Peak is directly south.

Walk westward a short distance along the summit ridge, then drop onto the south ridge of Wheeler Peak, aiming for the Wheeler-Baker saddle at about 12,000 feet. While descending to the saddle, although it at times involves many ups and downs, staying near the crest of the ridge is more pleasant than dropping onto seemingly easier terrain (stable but tedious talus) on the west side of the ridge. If uncomfortable with the occasional class 3 terrain encountered along the ridge crest, drop slightly to the west, trying to stay near the crest, and look for easier terrain.

Once at the saddle, continue working your way over class 2 (and occasional, but easily avoided, class 3) terrain, looking for paths of least resistance as you head up toward Baker's lower west peak. While traversing along the ridge, be sure to look down into the many ice couloirs you will be passing.

Once you reach the base of the west peak, either scramble up the remaining 100 feet or so to the summit, or traverse in a counter-clockwise fashion and head straight toward the saddle separating the west peak from the east peak. The last 0.5 mile or so from the west to east peak is straightforward but tedious class 2 talus.

For this route, expect about 12 miles (roundtrip) and 4,500 feet of gain.

-WGS84 Lat: 38.9687 deg N Lon: -114.3092 deg W

-III, Class 2 via North Ridge & West Ridge from Wheeler Peak ****

Wheeler Peak in early summer

Wheeler Peak (13,063)

Wheeler Peak is the showpiece of Great Basin National Park. Rising 8,000 feet above the valleys below as the second highest peak in the state, Wheeler Peak is far more aesthetic, awe-inspiring, prominent, and majestic than the state's highest mountain, Boundary Peak (13,140 feet), over there on the other side of the state.

To get to the mountain: Immediately upon entering the park, turn right onto the Wheeler Peak Scenic Drive, where good signage leads visitors past the Lower and Upper Lehman Creek Campgrounds, and ultimately, to the 10,000 foot Wheeler Peak Campground. The road ends after 12 miles at the parking lot immediately before the entrance to Wheeler Peak Campground. Park here.

Across the road from the parking lot is one starting location for summiting Wheeler Peak—the Bristlecone Trailhead. You can also access the glacier, the ancient Bristlecone pine stands, and the alpine lakes from this parking area.

A Wheeler Peak summit hike can also begin from the nearby Summit Trailhead, though I prefer the Bristlecone Trailhead approach mentioned here.

To get to the mountain via the Wheeler Peak Trail: From the Bristlecone Trailhead, follow the well-traveled route toward Stella Lake. The summit trail forks off just before you arrive at the lake. (You can take a beautiful 5-minute detour off of the main trail to see the lake.) Continuing along on the main trail, meander your way up to the summit high above. Deer are frequently seen along the trail. The views above tree-line are incredible.

The roundtrip involves 8.2 miles, with just under 3,000 feet of gain.

To climb the mountain via the East Ridge & Slope from Jeff Davis Peak, follow the directions (reversed, of course) for Jeff Davis Peak's traverse between the two peaks. Doing this as a loop involves a roundtrip of about 9 miles, with roughly 3,500 feet of gain.

-WGS84 Lat: 38.9857 deg N Lon: -114.3140 deg W

-III, Class 1 via Wheeler Peak Trail ****

-III, Class 2-3 via East Ridge & Slope from Jeff Davis Peak (snow route only) ****

Jeff Davis Peak (12,771)

Jeff Davis Peak is the third highest peak in Nevada. Overshadowed by its neighbor, the slightly higher Wheeler Peak, which, unlike Jeff Davis Peak, has a class 1 trail to the summit, the mountain is seldom climbed.

There are several routes of varying degrees of difficulty to climb Jeff Davis Peak. The routes range from class 1-3 scrambles on the north, east and south sides of the mountain to technical climbs in the loose and generally icy couloirs or on the rock faces of the cirque that connects the mountain with Wheeler Peak to the west.

Although a couple of summit options are provided herein, between May and September it is encouraged that you summit Jeff Davis Peak by first summiting Wheeler Peak via either the Bristlecone Trail or the Summit Trail, and then completing the traverse over to Jeff Davis Peak (described here) and backtracking to the trailhead.

To approach the peak, follow the directions given for Wheeler Peak.

To climb the peak via the North Slope under full snow conditions (see comments in section introduction): From the Bristlecone Trailhead, follow signs leading one to the glacier. Before reaching the toe of the glacier, you will pass through a grove of bristlecone pines with many interpretive signs—a pretty special spot. Take a few minutes, enjoy the grove, and learn about the ancient trees. Once past the end of the grove, rather than take the looping trail back toward where you came, continue on the left fork of the trail toward the glacier. Perhaps 50 yards later, leave the trail and start hiking cross-country toward the Jeff Davis' north slope, which is obvious across the moraine to the east. Once you gain the north slope work your way up the fairly stable talus and occasional loose and crappy scree to the upper reaches of the mountain. Generally speaking, you will find more class 3 terrain as you approach the ridgeline above the cirque and more class 2 if you stick to the north slope itself. Before you know it, you'll be standing on the summit.

Expect about 7 miles roundtrip with roughly 2,700 feet of gain.

To climb the peak via the Southwest Ridge and Slope from Wheeler Peak: Follow the Wheeler Peak directions to the summit of that peak. From the summit of Wheeler Peak, drop down the south side of the mountain, gradually working over class 2 talus eastward toward the saddle between Wheeler and Jeff Davis. From the east side of the saddle, take class 2 talus to the summit of Jeff Davis Peak.

Expect about 9 miles roundtrip with roughly 3,500 feet of elevation gain.

-WGS84 Lat: 38.9886 deg N Lon: -114.2972 deg W
-III, Class 2-3 via North Slope (snow route only) ***
-III, Class 2-3 via Southwest Ridge & Slope from Wheeler Peak ****

Bald Mountain (11,562)

Bald Mountain is a fine peak that offers an outstanding (and probably the best) view of Wheeler Peak. The peak is an enjoyable and straightforward alternative for those chickening out on the more physically-demanding Wheeler Peak, which lies directly to the south. Bald Mountain, only two miles from Wheeler Peak, is readily accessed from the saddle connecting the two mountains.

Follow the directions given for the Wheeler Peak trailhead. From there, follow the well-signed Bristlecone Trail to the summit trail leading to the obvious saddle (approx. 11,000 ft) due north of Wheeler. Bald Mountain will be to the north. Keep your eyes open for the scattered bristlecone pines growing at the saddle, and the large number of deer that seem to live in their thickets.

From the saddle, leave the trail and head cross-country north toward Bald Mountain. The grade is gentle, the terrain is never more than class 2, and it's only a mile or so to the summit. The summit is marked by a small structure and a large windbreak built from rocks and boulders.

Roundtrip is about 6 miles, with around 1,600 ft of gain.

-WGS84 Lat: 39.0200 deg N Lon: -114.3227 deg W
*-II, Class 2 via South Slope ****

Buck Mountain (10,972)

This oft-overlooked peak offers an astounding summit view of Wheeler Peak, Jeff Davis Peak, and Nevada's only glacier, in the impressive cirque connecting the two peaks.

The various cross-country routes up to the top of Buck Mountain, none of them exceeding 2nd class, make a fine half-day out with plenty of solitude. From the sporadically-treed summit, one can clearly see Mount Moriah, Nevada's 5th highest peak, as well as the ultra-cool Notch Peak, over the border in Utah.

The route up Buck Mountain starts at the signed Wheeler Peak Summit Trail (10,100 feet), 11 miles up the Wheeler Peak Scenic Drive. From the trailhead, walk down the road 0.25 mile to the base of a drainage heading directly up toward the saddle between Buck Mountain and Bald Mountain, the slightly higher mountain just to the west/southwest of Buck Mountain. Hike up the drainage for 500-600 feet to the saddle. The going is mellow, there's hardly any brush, and in the fall the aspen trees are brilliant. Once at the saddle hang a right and head up the final 300 feet to the summit.

Expect a roundtrip of about 900 feet and two miles.
-WGS84 Lat: 39.0280 deg N Lon: -114.3002 deg W
*-II, Class 2 via Southwest Slope ***

Mount Moriah (12,067)

Mount Moriah lies north of US-6 (whereas Great Basin National Park lies *south* of US-6). Although the mountain is not a part of Nevada's only national park, it's very close to the park, and being the state's 5th highest peak, it would seem inappropriate to exclude it.

This is a classic peak in the Great Basin area. A network of decent dirt roads can be followed close enough to the mountain to make the northwest ridge route a pleasant half-day. Pick up the initial dirt road by leaving US-6 near the apex in the big road bend a few miles west of Sacramento Pass.

-WGS84 Lat: 39.2731 deg N Lon: -114.1988 deg W
*-II, Class 2 via Northwest Ridge *****

Scattered

The peaks in this section have been selected from random (but noteworthy) spots around Nevada.

Quinn Canyon Range

This lonely range is north of Rachel, Nevada and Area 51, and accessed via a network of mostly really-good dirt roads. The peaks in this subsection are arranged south-to-north.

"Steep Mountain" (9,644)

Steep Mountain is due east of Sage Mountain. Follow the approach for Quinn Canyon Range Highpoint to a point near the base of that peak's south ridge. Prior to reaching that point, gain Steep Mountain's steep northeast ridge and slog up. There are no major difficulties.

-WGS84 Lat: 38.0786 deg N Lon: -115.7215 deg W

*-II, Class 2 via Northeast Ridge ***

"Sage Mountain" (10,076)

This high viewpoint lies southwest of the range highpoint.

-WGS84 Lat: 38.0793 deg N Lon: -115.7389 deg W

*-II, Class 1-2 via East Ridge from Steep Mountain ***

*-II, Class 2 via North Ridge from Sage Mountain – North ***

"Sage Mountain – North" (9,962)

This sub-peak of Sage Mountain is most easily approached from the east then by heading up a beautiful valley to the saddle between it and Staircase Mountain, to the north.

-WGS84 Lat: 38.0849 deg N Lon: -115.7388 deg W

*-II, Class 1-2 via North Ridge ***

*-II, Class 2 via South Ridge from Sage Mountain ***

Quinn Canyon Range Highpoint (10,185)

This is a beautiful area easily accessed via 37 miles of mostly excellent dirt road heading north from the pavement just east of Rachel, Nevada.

The range highpoint has 2587' of prominence.

-WGS84 Lat: 38.1223 deg N Lon: -115.7085 deg W

*-II, Class 1-2 via South Ridge ****

Pioche Area

The peaks in this area are located near highway 93 in the Pioche/Caliente area.

Connor Peak (9,050)

This minor peak on the high eastern shoulder of Highland Peak is an easy bonus after bagging Highland.

-WGS84 Lat: 37.8967 deg N Lon: -114.5692 deg W

*-II, Class 1-2 via West Ridge **

Comet Peak (9,350)

Shameless peakbaggers like me won't pass up the opportunity to snag this bonus peak on the way to/from Highland Peak. It is a short walk from the summit of Highland.

-WGS84 Lat: 37.8983 deg N Lon: -114.5855 deg W

*-I, Class 1 via East Slope **

Highland Peak (9,395)

This dominant peak (3285' of prominence) near Pioche, Nevada, provides a nice viewpoint of the area. The summit is reached via an easy walk up a service road.

-WGS84 Lat: 37.8939 deg N Lon: -114.5788 deg W

*-II, Class 1 via service road ***

Lida Summit Area

A handful of worthwhile peaks reside in this obscure patch of Nevada, the highways of which are most commonly used by Las Vegans headed to the nearby glorious Sierra Nevada.

Blue Dick Benchmark (9,286)

This high peak in the Palmetto Mountains is an outstanding viewpoint of the region. Much of that can be attributed to its 2425' of prominence. And, an excellent dirt road leaves the pavement west of Lida Summit and meanders north-ish all the way to the top of the mountain.

-WGS84 Lat: 37.5062 deg N Lon: -117.5911 deg W

*-I, Class 1 via service road ****

Magruder Mountain (9,046)

Magruder Mountain hovers on the south side of NV-266 near Lida Summit. It is easily approached by hiking south from the highway, from a point east of Lida Summit.

Magruder Mountain has 1624' of prominence.

-WGS84 Lat: 37.4104 deg N Lon: -117.5474 deg W

*-II, Class 1 via North Slopes ***

Palmetto Mountain (8,935)

Palmetto Mountain, with 1000' of prominence, is a large, sprawling, mellow mountain easily accessed via a good dirt road heading north from NV-266, a few miles west of Lida Summit.

-WGS84 Lat: 37.4622 deg N Lon: -117.5740 deg W

*-II, Class 1 via West Slope ***

Schell Creek Range

The Schell Creek Range is one of the highest ranges in the state. Located close to Ely, Nevada, a decent dirt road leads into upper Timber Creek, where a primitive campground can be found. The peaks in this subsection are arranged south-to-north.

"Uinta Peak" (11,545)

Uinta Peak is the second peak south along the spine of the Schell Creek Range from the highpoint, North Schell Peak. The peak is northwest of Taft Peak. We once encountered 80mph winds along the crest, forcing us to abort plans to continue our traverse south toward Taft Peak.

Although the talus slog of the northwest face is unpleasant, the upper reaches of the south fork of Timber Creek at its foot are lovely.

-WGS84 Lat: 39.3621 deg N Lon: -114.6013 deg W
*-III, Class 1 via North Ridge ***
*-III, Class 2 via Northwest Face ***

"Ptarmigan Peak" (11,085)

Approached from road's end in upper Timber Creek, the north ridge is an aesthetic way to climb this anonymous but pleasant peak.

-WGS84 Lat: 39.3812 deg N Lon: -114.6195 deg W
*-II, Class 2 via North Ridge ****

"Middle Schell Peak" (11,794)

While hardly an objective of its own (unless one is determined to climb each of the nearly 60 Nevada summits over 11,000 feet with at least 300 feet of prominence), Middle Schell Peak is a logical (and practically necessary) bonus peak while traversing the delightful high ridge south from North Schell Peak.

Middle Schell Peak has 689' of prominence.

-WGS84 Lat: 39.3902 deg N Lon: -114.5952 deg W
*-III, Class 1 via North Ridge from North Schell Peak ****
*-III, Class 1 via South Ridge ***

North Schell Peak (11,883)

Though just a large mellow mound, North Schell Peak is an inspiringly prominent peak, boasting 5413' of prominence. From road's end in upper Timber Creek, one can follow an old trail high into the north fork of Timber Creek, where a lesser use trail works right and approaches the summit from the northwest.

-WGS84 Lat: 39.4132 deg N Lon: -114.5997 deg W
*-II, Class 1 from Timber Creek road ****
*-III, Class 1 via South Ridge from Middle Schell Peak ****

Traversing to Middle Schell Peak

Ruby Mountains

The Ruby Mountains, lying close to Elko, Nevada, are undeniably the closest Nevada has to an alpine mountain range. As such, one is inclined to wonder why I've included it in a book on desert peaks. Further, one may ponder why I've also included Greys Peak, which is technically part of the East Humboldt Range. In any case, this is a fine, under-represented area.

The peaks in this subsection are arranged south-to-north.

Wines Peak (10,940)

Wines Peak, which has 800' of prominence, is a high and obscure summit on the southern edge of the best-of-the-Rubies. The Ruby Crest Trail passes within a couple hundred yards of the summit as it slowly meanders south from Liberty Pass and road's end in upper Lamoille Canyon. I once snagged this peak during a wonderfully satisfying 20-mile, multi-peak outing deep in the Ruby backcountry.

Oh yeah—I saw my very first Nevada mountain goat just below the summit!

-WGS84 Lat: 40.5500 deg N Lon: -115.4078 deg W

*-III, Class 1 via Ruby Crest Trail ****

Lake Peak (left) and Wines Peak (distant; left of upper-center) from near the summit of Tri-Lake Peak.

Lake Peak (10,922)
Lake Peak, which has 702' of prominence, has excellent views from its summit. The west ridge is probably the shorter route to the summit from the pass to the west (which the Ruby Crest Trail passes over), though it requires one to traverse on the south side of the crest (but avoids some of the elevation loss/gain required for the southwest slope route).

-WGS84 Lat: 40.5636 deg N Lon: -115.3950 deg W
*-III, Class 1-2 via Southwest Slope ****
*-III, Class 1-2 via West Ridge ***

Peak 10,500 (10,500)
This minor peak, situated near the Ruby Crest Trail northwest of Lake Peak, is a very pleasant, scrambly objective from the pass to the southeast.

-WGS84 Lat: 40.5695 deg N Lon: -115.4186 deg W
*-III, Class 2-3 via Southeast Ridge ****

"Tri-Lake Peak" (10,865)
Named for the stunning lake views from its summit, Tri-Lake Peak is east of Liberty Pass. It's a logical bonus peak when traveling from the pass to Favre Benchmark.

-WGS84 Lat: 40.5849 deg N Lon: -115.3885 deg W

*-II, Class 2 from Liberty Pass ****

Favre Benchmark (10,879)

Favre Benchmark is due east of Tri-Lake Peak. It is a rugged and aesthetic mountain, with a complicated northwest face viewable from upper Lamoille Canyon. Although it's probably easiest to approach the peak from Liberty Pass (via Tri-Lake Peak), the ridge crest cannot be followed the entire way and one is forced below the south side of the crest near the saddle connecting the two peaks. Alternatively, at least one of the couloirs on the northwest face provides a relatively safe method to reach the summit. Finding the suitable route is best accomplished during the ascent.

-WGS84 Lat: 40.5852 deg N Lon: -115.3762 deg W
*-III, Class 2 via West Ridge ****
*-III, Class 2 via Northwest Couloir ****

"Liberty Peak" (11,036)

Liberty Peak, with 772' of prominence, is a great introduction to peaks in the Ruby Mountains. Approached from the paved road's end in Lamoille Canyon, three miles of beautiful groomed trail are followed to Liberty Pass, where a few hundred feet of mellow cross-country travel west leads to the top.

-WGS84 Lat: 40.5865 deg N Lon: -115.4001 deg W
*-II, Class 2 via East Slopes ****

Peak 10,545 (10,545)

This unassuming peak is just below road's end in Lamoille Canyon, opposite (and east across the canyon from) Thomas Peak. Climbing the peak is a steep affair, as the west face gains a bit more than 2,000 feet of elevation in about 0.5 mile. Speedy types can roundtrip this baby in a hair over an hour.

-WGS84 Lat: 40.6170 deg N Lon: -115.3569 deg W
*-II, Class 2 via West Face ****

Greys Peak (10,674)

Greys Peak is at the north end of the East Humboldt Range, west of the paved road's end at Angel Lake. The east ridge route, which is at times sloggy and at other times sort of interesting, terminates just south of the summit, a short hike away.

Greys Peak has 734' of prominence.

-WGS84 Lat: 41.0237 deg N Lon: -115.1049 deg W
*-II, Class 2-3 via East Ridge ****

Angel Lake (and the trailhead) from the summit of Greys Peak

White Pine Range

The White Pine Range is a wonderful range of high, obscure peaks about an hour southwest of Ely, Nevada. Although Troy Peak is not part of the White Pine Range, it is the homeless highpoint of the high range to the south and is thus included as an outlying cousin.

The peaks in this subsection are arranged south-to-north.

Troy Peak (11,298)

Troy Peak is one of the classic peaks of the Great Basin. John Muir once declared it his favorite peak in the region. The southeast ridge route from Schofield Canyon is a pretty, casual route. Unfortunately, the condition of the road in Schofield Canyon is highly variable, and it is sometimes impassable.

Troy Peak has 4790' of prominence.

-WGS84 Lat: 38.3194 deg N Lon: -115.5018 deg W

-III, Class 2 via Southeast Ridge ****

"Eagle Feather Peak" (11,315)

Eagle Feather Peak is the next summit south of Currant Mountain.

-WGS84 Lat: 38.8975 deg N Lon: -115.4209 deg W

-III, Class 2 via Northeast Gully ***

Gaining the ridge between Eagle Feather Peak and Currant Mountain

Currant Mountain (11,513)

Currant Mountain is the highpoint of the beautiful White Pine Range, which forms the eastern border of the wide, pleasant valley that is home to Duckwater Shoshone Indian Reservation.

Currant Mountain has 4575' of prominence.

-WGS84 Lat: 38.9097 deg N Lon: -115.4247 deg W

*-III, Class 2 via South Ridge from the east ****

Duckwater Peak (11,175)

From the dirt road that runs south-to-north along the east base of Duckwater Peak, the east slopes are easily accessible, making for a very short hike to the summit.

-WGS84 Lat: 38.9368 deg N Lon: -115.4297 deg W

*-II, Class 1-2 via East Slope ****

☯ Arizona ☯

The author and his wife atop Morning Glory Spire, Sedona. Photo by Walt Hutton.

Northwest Region

Northwestern Arizona is an interesting part of an interesting state. From the surprising lushness of the Hualapai Mountains outside of Kingman, to the arid desolation and unexplored wonderland of spires, needles and knobs of the Black Mountains near Bullhead City, to the Cerbat Montains, where Mount Tipton rises to its Ponderosa Pine-covered top from the desert above Dolan Springs, this part of the state is a necessary destination for the mountain explorer.

Hualapai Mountains

The Hualapai Mountains is a surprisingly beautiful area, lush and green, considering its desert environment. With thick pine forests across much of the range, it's a far cry from the hair-dryer blowing heat of summer and sand down in Kingman. The range's craggy peaks are also noteworthy for hosting far more scrambling opportunities than meet the eye.

The Hualapai Mountains are located south (and east) of I-40, and southeast of Kingman, Arizona. The peaks in this subsection are arranged south-to-north.

Hualapai Peak (8,417)

Driving through Kingman, Arizona, one can't help but notice the Hualapai Mountains to the south. Though they are topped by Hualapai Peak, from the highways the more obscure peaks of the range, such as Hayden Peak and Dean Peak, are more prominent. Don't let that fool you, though—Hualapai Peak is a fine peak, well worth visiting. The peak is a trail hike (with some fun scrambling at the end).

From Kingman, using either the Beale/Route 66, Andy Devine or Stockton Hill exits off of I-40 (your choice), follow prominent signage about 10 miles to Hualapai Mountain Road and the park entrance station. All three exit roads converge on Hualapai Mountain Road. At the entrance station, pay the entrance fee and receive a brochure with directions to the trailhead. If not, follow signs to the Aspen–Potato Patch trailhead, a mile up the road and not hard to find. You'll past a couple of nice campgrounds and picnic areas along the way.

From the area of the trailhead (6,750 feet), note the impressive crags and cliffs above. They are part of Aspen Peak's north and northeast faces. Hualapai Peak, not visible, is behind Aspen Peak. Heading either left (scenic trail underneath Aspen's cliffs) or right (service road), start hiking steeply up. You'll eventually come to a trail junction (Potato Patch Loop junction) near Aspen Peak's southwest side. From there, with Hualapai Peak visible about a mile to the south (don't confuse it with the closer Hayden Peak), get onto the signed trail heading toward the peak. I encountered some difficulties finding the quickest, most efficient way of getting to the peak from here, but rest assured a little common sense can get the job done without too much trouble. Somehow I lost the trail and ended up in a forest, crossing a dry creek bed. Eventually, though, I stumbled back across the trail (an old road, mostly) and wandered my way to the top.

The approach to the peak is class 1; however, as you near the top on the old road, you'll encounter the craggy summit area. As the road passes directly below the summit crags on its south side, you can climb straight up to the top (class 4, and fun), or backtrack a touch and work counter-clockwise around, following weaknesses (class 2-3) to the highest of the summit rocks. Gaining the actual highpoint requires an enjoyable, funky class 3 move.

The roundtrip involves about 6 miles, with roughly 2,000 feet of gain.

-WGS84 Lat: 35.0751 deg N Lon: -113.8978 deg W

-II, Class 4 via Aspen-Potato Patch trail system ***

"Aspen Peak" (8,167)

Another of the more prominent peaks of the Hualapai Mountains is the locally-named Aspen Peak. Though Aspen Peak has not found a name on the official map, the mountain is named on the Hualapai Mountain Park literature you get at the fee booth, and also has been honored with the naming of the Aspen–Potato Patch trail system within the park.

Although I'm confident the craggy Aspen Peak sees very little climbing traffic, the mountain holds potential for routes on the so-so-to-decent rock on the mountain's north and northeast faces. For the less ambitious, there's an interesting trail that can be followed to the top.

Aspen Peak sits a mile north of Hualapai Peak, and about a mile northeast of Hayden Peak.

Follow the directions given for Hualapai Peak to the trailhead. From the area of the trailhead (6,750 feet), note the impressive crags and cliffs above you. They are part of Aspen Peak's north and northeast faces. Heading either left (scenic trail underneath Aspen's cliffs) or right (service road), start hiking steeply up. After some scenic and enjoyable hiking, you'll eventually come to a trail junction (Potato Patch Loop junction) near Aspen's southwest side. From there, catch a signed trail that heads directly for Aspen Peak, initially traversing around the peaks' south and southeast sides. The trail is scenic, interesting, and enjoyable. There are a couple of spots where you *might* lose the trail briefly, but it's not hard to re-find. The trail ends amongst the summit crags. The highest crag is apparent, and a couple class 3 moves will put you on top of it.

Roundtrip numbers are perhaps 4 or 5 miles and 1,500 feet of gain.

-WGS84 Lat: 35.0906 deg N Lon: -113.8974 deg W

-II, Class 3 via Aspen-Potato Patch trail system **

Peak 7,745 (7,745)
This and Peak 7,680 are located closely southwest of Dean Peak (and northeast of Hualapai Mountain and Aspen Peak). The trio of this, Peak 7,680 and Dean Peak can easily be done together in a day.

-WGS84 Lat: 35.1079 deg N Lon: -113.8784 deg W
-I, Class 2 via Northwest Ridge **

Peak 7,680 (7,680)
Only the summit rocks require any scrambling. An easy bonus while heading to/from Dean Peak.

-WGS84 Lat: 35.1133 deg N Lon: -113.8845 deg W
-I, Class 2-3 via service road **

Dean Peak (8,013)
Spectacular when viewed from points along Interstate 40 near Kingman, Arizona. The peak's got a nice backcountry feel. The crux is found just below the summit.

-WGS84 Lat: 35.1176 deg N Lon: -113.8681 deg W
-III, Class 4 via Northeast Face ***

Bullhead City & Oatman

The peaks in this subsection are located east of Bullhead City (and the Colorado River) and west of Kingman. They are scattered around AZ-68 and the tiny hamlet of Oatman. Pet a burro!

The peaks are arranged here south-to-north.

Boundary Cone (3,430)
The Black Mountains of northwestern Arizona, roughly bordered by Kingman (AZ) on the east, Laughlin/Bullhead City (NV/AZ) on the west, Boulder City (NV) on the north, and Needles (CA) on the south, is an impressive range consisting of rugged and seldom-visited peaks, jagged spires, unbelievable pillars, presumably unclimbed pinnacles, cactus-covered crags...and Boundary Cone.

Lying near the southern end of the range, Boundary Cone is striking enough to have a road named after it. Rather reminiscent of Mopah Point near Needles, California, this impressive mountain, despite being right next to a paved highway, does not yield its summit readily. An enjoyable exercise in route-finding, the only apparent non-technical route to its top is found on its west side. The other faces of the mountain present themselves as imposing 1,000+ foot cliffs. With a little effort in the way of a mile and a half roundtrip, 1,500 feet of gain, and some steep scrambling up the west ridge, the impressive views from the summit can be yours.

To get to the mountain: From the Davis Dam Road connecting Laughlin, NV and Bullhead City, AZ, get on AZ-95 (just east of the Colorado River) and head south through Bullhead City. Just a few miles down the road, between mile markers 246 and 247, look for Silver Creek Road (CR-155). Hang a left there. As you head out of Bullhead City on Silver Creek Road, the views from this extremely good dirt road (at first paved, then dirt once it crosses Bullhead Parkway) open up and the funky spires and rugged peaks and jaw-dropping pillars you saw from a distance on the way in come closer into the foreground.

After 10.6 miles, Silver Creek Road ends at its junction with the paved Route 66. If you hang a left, Route 66 will eventually take you to Kingman. If you hang a right, you're headed toward Oatman and Boundary Cone. Turning right onto Route 66 (aka The Oatman Highway), follow it south for 1.25 miles to Oatman (a ghost town sort of place with some stores and restaurants—touristy) and continue on. About 2.5 miles outside of town, you'll reach a fork. The right fork is the paved Boundary Cone Road. This road will take you back to AZ-95, a few (about 15) miles south of Bullhead City. Take the left fork and continue south for a mile on the paved highway toward the very obvious and impressive Boundary Cone directly in front of you. There's a dirt pull-out just before you reach the base of the mountain's west ridge. Park here.

Hike toward the low end of the west ridge. Although the ridge can be readily gained at its toe, there are some nice breaks (class 3) mid-way up that work nicely. Either way, gain the ridge and start heading up. Travel on the lower half of the ridge is relatively laidback and reasonably enjoyable. As you ascend, follow the easiest line you find until you hit a cliff band that stops further easy progress. You can scramble up any number of sweet spots (class 4 and higher) along the cliff band, but a class 3 weakness can also be found at the far left side of the band, just before the cliffs become significantly larger and quite vertical (you should know it when you see it). Above the class 3 weakness in the cliffs, continue up class 1-2 terrain (a wide, shallow gully) until you reach some more cliffs just below the summit. From here, work around a bit toward the north face until you see class 2-3 terrain allowing you up. Once above this next bit of cliffs, the summit is just a short walk away over mellow terrain.

Although this route was hard to describe in any detail, the route-finding is not particularly difficult. When difficulties present themselves, they are obvious; correspondingly, the weaknesses are obvious as well. If you're faced with something harder than 3rd class (and you're uncomfortable with it) you need only look a little harder, because the 3rd class is there (unless you're grossly off-route). For those comfortable with stiffer terrain, consider picking a tasty line of your own and giving it a shot. The rock is of reasonable quality. The harder sections are frequent and typically short.

-WGS84 Lat: 34.9837 deg N Lon: -114.4157 deg W
-II, Class 3 via West Ridge ****

Negrohead (3,024)
Negrohead is located southwest of Battleship Mountain and north of Oatman. It is a short hike from the main road.

-WGS84 Lat: 35.0538 deg N Lon: -114.4076 deg W
-I, Class 2-3 via East Slope *

On the summit of Negrohead in the Black Mountains, looking northeast to Battleship Mountain (far right).

Battleship Mountain (4,165)
Indeed looking quite a bit like a decrepit and wasting battleship in the rugged desert, Battleship Mountain is a large and surprisingly inhospitable, well-guarded mountain recognizable by a large notch separating the southern portion of its summit mesa from the north portion (and the true summit).

Of the few scant bits of beta one can find about Battleship Mountain on the internet, it seems the only routes traveled are limited to a class 3 route up the east face of the northern summit mesa via the mountain's southeast gully and a vague reportedly class 4 route up from the southern end of the summit mesa.

With a good bit of route-finding, we were able to clarify this vague route up from the southern end of the mesa, and also found a class 4 route up the west face of the mountain.

The west face route gains about 1,800 feet over a roundtrip of roughly 4.5 miles. No matter which route you try, be prepared for loose rock.

To get to the mountain: Follow the directions given for Boundary Cone toward the Silver Creek Road/Route 66 junction. At 1.5 miles before reaching the aforementioned junction (and 9.1 miles from the AZ-95 junction), pull off at a point where the road bends slightly near the toe of a prominent wash on the east side of the road. Park here (at a point west or slightly southwest of Battleship Mountain, the prominent peak a couple miles away).

Hike east into the wash toward the obvious objective in the distance. As you approach, you'll notice the heavily-guarded nature of Battleship Mountain, with its many bands of cliffs surrounding it. After a mile or so in the wash, start looking for a break at the western end of the lowest cliff band on the mountain. This break is quite easy to find, as it is the very first point where you can easily get past vertical cliffs on the southwest side of the mountain. There's also a very prominent rock outcropping immediately west of the break. Class 2 hiking will get the job done.

You're now atop the western ridge, if you wanna call it that. Looking up at the rest of the mountain above you, you'll notice that all but the highest cliff band above you will be worked around with minimal difficulties. The highest one is where the greatest difficulties are found. A couple key areas to make note of are the notch (very obvious) separating the northern end of the summit mesa from the southern end, and the white or yellowish coloration on a high portion of the uppermost cliff band just south of the notch. These are landmarks you'll use later.

As you work your way up, you may be tempted to head directly toward the notch. Although the going is steep and cliffy, it appears that it's passable. If you're willing to trust the bad rock, and climb rather well, you won't have a problem; otherwise, don't expect easy passage. We spent well over an hour trying to find easy passage directly to the notch—it's not to be found. Instead, look for one of two breaks in the cliff band below the uppermost band, ultimately aiming for the white/yellow cliffs mentioned above. One break consists of class 2-3 terrain below and just north of the colored cliffs, while the other consists of class 2 terrain below and just to the south of them. Once the base of the white/yellow cliffs is gained, work south to the very first point where the cliffs are steep, but not quite vertical. This is your ticket to passage.

Head up a shallow chute on loose scree and talus and look for a ledge leading south about 30 feet below the top of the face. Follow the ledge south until you feel like you can't safely go any further (further passage would require awkwardly stepping over desert plant-life onto the narrowing ledge, which is covered with loose rock and becomes progressively more exposed). Looking up at the last 20 feet or so of face, start climbing. The climbing is not terribly hard (though class 4), but it is steep and the rock is poor. The exposure, while not bad, is enough to get your attention. Once the summit mesa above is gained, follow varying class 1-3 terrain to the north until you come to an obvious deep notch. You can head straight down via a steep, knife-edge-like rock fin (class 3-4) to the bottom of the notch, or angle westward a bit and look for class 2-3 scrambling that will take you down. From the bottom of the notch, hike up moderate terrain on the other side a couple hundred feet to the summit.

A variation, described as if one was ascending: As mentioned above, there are two breaks in the cliff band below the uppermost cliff band. One of these breaks lies below and just south of the white/yellow cliffs mentioned earlier. Take this break to the wide ledge-like area below the uppermost cliff band and work your way south to the southern end of the summit mesa. Class 3 scrambling can get you onto the summit mesa via this southern end. From there, follow the directions already provided to the summit. This variation brings this route down to an enjoyable class 3 scramble, assuming one downclimbs the notch via the easier of the two options mentioned.

-WGS84 Lat: 35.0737 deg N Lon: -114.3820 deg W
*-II, Class 4 via West Face ****

Sugarloaf Mountain (3,205)
Not one, but *two* summit registers on this small, largely uninteresting mountain. The peak is a mere 0.5 mile north of highway 68. Approach directly from the highway or from the good dirt road that brings you even closer.

-WGS84 Lat: 35.2030 deg N Lon: -114.4362 deg W
*-I, Class 2 from any direction **

"Sugarloaf Peak" (4,640+)
Sugarloaf Peak is the eye-catching peak just barely north of northwestern Arizona's highway 68 between Laughlin/Bullhead City and US-93 north of Kingman. Like the many other obscure peaks in the Black Mountains, Sugarloaf Peak, well protected on all sides by high cliffs, does not readily give up its summit. It is a fine objective.

From the US-93/I-40 junction in Kingman, Arizona, head north on US-93 for 3.3 miles to the signed AZ-68 exit. AZ-68 will take you to Bullhead City, AZ and Laughlin, NV. Get on AZ-68 and head west 18 miles to Union Pass. This Sugarloaf, not to be confused with its officially-named neighbor, Sugarloaf Mountain (a mere three miles to the southwest) is the obvious, blocky summit a mile northwest of the pass. Cross Union Pass and continue west for a four miles to a paved dirt road heading off to the north. It's the only one of its kind and lies just south of the official Sugarloaf Mountain.

Turn north onto the paved road and follow it northeast about 2.25 miles to its end immediately south of our objective. Although the road is paved, it is not maintained and is in rather poor condition. Still, passenger cars should have no problem making it to the end of the road.

Get onto a rough dirt road that heads off north from the end of the paved road, and following it for 0.25 mile or so you'll soon need to leave the road and head cross-country into the wash running north toward the mountain. As you near the base of the mountain, follow the left fork of the wash as it heads to a saddle on the west side of the mountain. Gain the saddle and look up at the mountain's impressive, cliffy, and very complex west face—you now need to find a steep chute near the northern edge of the west face; the chute faces north/slightly northwest.

Heading east up from the saddle, begin traversing north a bit, looking for the chute in question. The bottom of the chute is at the base of the cliffs of the west face. Although it becomes brushy and treed as you ascend, the bottom is essentially brush-free and rocky. With a little trial and error, you should be able to find the chute in question. If what you're trying out involves anything harder than class 3, you're probably in the wrong place. Having climbed all over this mountain and its various faces, and explored every weakness I could locate, the chute I'm describing appears to offer the *only* reasonable way up.

Once the magical chute is found, head up it to a notch at its head. From there, either step left and squirm up a short chimney, or traverse south for 30-40 feet until you can scramble (class 2-3) up the short cliff above and to the left. Atop this short band of rocks above the notch, head up and generally east, following the occasional use trail, as well as the easiest line of ascent, to the upper mountain. A couple short sections of class 3 should be expected. Wandering around a bit (rather fun, actually) you'll soon find yourself at the summit.

The roundtrip is about 2 miles, with perhaps a bit over 1,000 feet of gain.

-WGS84 Lat: 35.2266 deg N Lon: -114.4076 deg W
*-II, Class 3 via West Face Chute ****

Dolan Springs Area

The peaks in this subsection are arranged generally south-to-north.

Mount Tipton (7,148)

Mount Tipton, the highpoint of the Cerbat Mountains, is the high mountain one sees on the east side of US-93 when traveling between Las Vegas, Nevada and Kingman, Arizona. With beautiful scenery, surprising lush forest, enjoyable rock scrambling options, and views of the nearby Tipton Needles, Mount Tipton is something of a desert classic.

From either Las Vegas, NV or Kingman, AZ, follow US-93 to the signed and paved Dolan Springs Road (aka Pierce Ferry Road; mile post 42), in the bustling (*kidding*) town of Dolan Springs, Arizona. Turn onto the road and follow it for 1.2 miles to its intersection with 5th Street (dirt). Hang a right on 5th Street and continue east for 4.4 miles to an intersection with a minor road near a fence line on the left. Turn onto this minor road and follow it for 0.25 mile to a gate. There will be a water tank nearby. Going through the unlocked gate, continue as far as you feel comfortable on the rough road. After about 1.5 miles, the road ends at a locked gate at the Mount Tipton Wilderness boundary. A high clearance vehicle should get you to the locked gate. Primitive camping is available here, if one needs it.

From the locked gate, continue on foot on the dirt road. Although you may lose the road near a cluster of old corrals a half mile away, try to keep on the road until it ascends a prominent hill in the desert Dropping down on the road from the top of the hill (about a mile from the gate), Mount Tipton will be visible in the distance to the southeast. Near the bottom of the hill, leave the road and continue cross-country across the desert toward the mountain. There will be a prominent drainage in the distance. Gaining the drainage, follow it to a saddle between Mount Tipton and a minor peak to its west. From the saddle, head up and left until you reach Mount Tipton's west ridge. Hang a left and follow the west ridge upward. Although brushy in places, and surprisingly rugged at times, the west ridge is an enjoyable ascent. At the top of the ridge, angling to the right a bit, you'll come to a false summit. The true summit will be visible just beyond it, a short hike away. The summit views are immense.

The roundtrip involves about 8 miles and 3,400 feet of gain.

-WGS84 Lat: 35.5389 deg N Lon: -114.1926 deg W

-III, Class 2-3 via West Ridge ***

Mount Perkins (5,456)

The peak is located west of Dolan Springs, and slightly northwest of the junction of US-93 and Pierce Ferry Road. A nice diversion on the tedious drive between Las Vegas and Kingman, a high clearance vehicle can take one quite close to the peak on decent dirt roads. From road's end, fit hikers can do the roundtrip in less than an hour.

Leave US-93 and head west on a good dirt road roughly halfway between the Dolan Springs turn-off and Temple Bar Road.

-WGS84 Lat: 35.5695 deg N Lon: -114.5080 deg W

-I, Class 1-2 via Northwest Ridge *

"Housholder Peak" (2,794)
This peak is just north of Housholder Pass, just off highway 93 between Dolan Springs, Arizona and Hoover Dam. There's an antenna installation not far from the highpoint.

-WGS84 Lat: 35.8552 deg N Lon: -114.5869 deg W
*-I, Class 1-2 via South Slopes **

Colorado River

The peaks in this subsection are accessed via a variety of points. They are arranged here generally south-to-north.

"Gold Bug Peak" (2,137)
This peak can be readily combined with Fire Mountain for a pleasant half-day hike. There is some loose and unpleasant rock in the area, unfortunately. If one parks near where the Jeep road meets the wash draining southeast from the peak, Gold Bug Peak can be grabbed as a very fast, short and pleasant outing.

The peak is named for the nearby Gold Bug Mine.
-WGS84 Lat: 35.6654 deg N Lon: -114.6409 deg W
*-II, Class 2 via Southeast Wash ***
*-II, Class 2-3 from Fire Mountain ***

Approaching the summit of Fire Mountain

Fire Mountain (2,531)
A network of Jeep roads from highway 93 near Dolan Springs leads one miles west toward Fire Mountain and the river. The mountain is surprisingly rugged

and interesting near the top. Exposure and loose rock is found in the summit area.

-WGS84 Lat: 35.6828 deg N Lon: -114.6464 deg W
*-II, Class 2-3 from the east ****
*-II, Class 2-3 via South Ridge (via Gold Bug Peak) ***

"Mohave Mine Peak" (3,542)

Jeep roads coming in from the southeast allow easy access to the summit of this minor peak.

-WGS84 Lat: 35.6884 deg N Lon: -114.5435 deg W
*-I, Class 1 via East Saddle **

"Sheep Tank Peak" (2,740)

Named for nearby Sheep Tank, this minor peak is a quick, 1-hour bonus from the dirt road to the southeast.

-WGS84 Lat: 35.6947 deg N Lon: -114.6076 deg W
*-I, Class 1-2 from the southeast **

Malpais Flattop Mesa (2,771)

A number of different canyons and/or ridges could be used to reach the top of this sprawling mesa. A good dirt road from Willow Beach leads south to the east side of the mesa, allowing for short access from a variety of points.

Nice views from the top.

-WGS84 Lat: 35.7930 deg N Lon: -114.6749 deg W
*-II, Class 2 from the east ***

Peak 1,712 (1,712)

This peak is just west of Willow Beach Peak. From the summit of Willow Beach Peak, drop to the south over steep and loose terrain to the saddle connecting the two peaks then walk northwest to the summit. Alternatively, one could utilize a cross-country route from the service road to the south.

From Peak 1712, I ventured down to Monkey Rock, a chossy tower right on the river. It looked too dangerous to climb safely.

-WGS84 Lat: 35.8482 deg N Lon: -114.6898 deg W
*-II, Class 1-2 via Southeast Ridge **

"Kenny Peak" (2,191)

Named for the young son of a Las Vegas local, Kenny Peak is southeast of Willow Beach Peak and southwest of Sarada Devi. It is an easy bonus peak while following the ridge connecting the two.

-WGS84 Lat: 35.8478 deg N Lon: -114.6743 deg W
*-II, Class 2 via Northeast Ridge ***

*-II, Class 2 via Northwest Face **

"Willow Beach Peak" (2,321)

Willow Beach Peak, with just over 1000' of prominence, dominates the immediate Willow Beach area. Unfortunately, it's not that great of a peak, though the summit views are nice.

With easy access via a network of (mostly) good dirt roads from Willow Beach, one can get quite close to the southeastern base of the peak and then make a dash for the top. I reached the summit in 1h:10m via Saradi Devi and Kenny Peak. Any number of routes should take you to the top—beware of loose rock, though.

-WGS84 Lat: 35.8515 deg N Lon: -114.6770 deg W

*-II, Class 2 from Service Road to the southeast ***

"Sarada Devi" (2,122)

Sarada Devi is the highpoint of the rough ridge extending east from Willow Beach Peak. From the service road to the south of Sarada Devi, it's a simple affair of gaining the peak's south ridge at a point that seems logical and then following it up, bending right to aim for the highpoint near the top. From Sarada Devi, one can mosey on along toward Willow Beach Peak to the west, snagging Kenny Peak along the way.

-WGS84 Lat: 35.8526 deg N Lon: -114.6672 deg W

*-II, Class 2 via South Ridge ***

"Peanut Peak" (2,503)

Parking on the shoulder of highway 93 south of Hoover Dam, it's easy to gain the peak's northeast ridge and follow it over a few easy bumps to the highpoint. The views from the top are nice.

-WGS84 Lat: 35.9481 deg N Lon: -114.6845 deg W

*-I, Class 1 via Northeast Ridge ***

Peak 2,060 (2,060)

Although just a large mesa, the view from the top is outstanding. The route up the northeast face is relatively straightforward, though one may need to weave around in a place or two to work around some cliffs. We descended to the west, finding a steep and loose class 3 break in a significant cliff band then worked north to gain the wash that heads back up toward the saddle southeast of Fortress Peak.

-WGS84 Lat: 35.9497 deg N Lon: -114.7150 deg W

*-II, Class 2 via Northeast Face ***

*-II, Class 3 via West Face ***

"Fortress Peak" (1,884)
This is a short, fun-ish scramble to a nice viewpoint. The somewhat meandering northeast face route, likely the only reasonable route up this well-guarded peak, is readily followed by keeping eyes open for cairns, signs of prior use (this route gets a fair bit of use) and the application of common sense.

-WGS84 Lat: 35.9596 deg N Lon: -114.7124 deg W
*-II, Class 2-3 via Northeast Face ***

"Liberty Bell Arch Peak" (1,730)
This fun, short hike just north of Arizona Hot Springs is easily accessed from the highway to the east. A good use trail leads to the top. The stunning Liberty Bell Arch is a short diversion from the hike to the summit.

-WGS84 Lat: 35.9733 deg N Lon: -114.7248 deg W
*-II, Class 1-2 via East Slopes **

Sugarloaf Mountain (1,954)
This rounded mound is immediately south of Hoover Dam. It's a logical objective for anyone passing through the area with an hour or so to use up.

-WGS84 Lat: 36.0087 deg N Lon: -114.7372 deg W
*-I, Class 2 via East Slope ***

Flagstaff & Williams

Flagstaff—that sparkling green jewel nestled at 7,000 feet in the middle of all that desert. It is a wonderful little college town hosting the highest mountain in the state of Arizona—Humphreys Peak.

Lying along I-40 just south of Grand Canyon National Park, the Flagstaff area is a volcanic region hosting a number of interesting peaks and funky features, like lava tubes, lava fields and craters. The thickly forested region is the only one in this book that is home to bears, though it is unlikely you'll see one.

Just south of Flagstaff, off highway 89, there lies the beautiful, sandstone, artsy New Age community of Sedona. With generally poor rock, the monoliths and buttes of Sedona will intrigue and draw the intrepid explorer. The area brings many to its vortices for enlightenment. One of the vortices, Bell Rock, is attempted and failed on by many, for its summit is heftily exposed 5th class.

The old fire lookout on the summit of Red Butte.
The view looks north toward the Grand Canyon, the north rim of which can just barely be discerned.

Williams Area

The peaks in this subsection are arranged here generally south-to-north, though Squaw Peak is well west of Williams.

Summit Mountain (7,797)
Outside of Williams. Leave I-40 at exit 163 and head south to a point west of the mountain. Here, pick up the service road that leads to the top.

-WGS84 Lat: 35.1313 deg N Lon: -112.1328 deg W
*-I, Class 1 via service road **

Bill Williams Mountain (9,356)
This prominent mountain is located just south of Williams, Arizona. A fine trail system can be followed to the top, or you can simply drive the service road to the jungle of antennae and other manmade paraphernalia crowding the highest point. To get to the service road, leave I-40 at exit 163 and head south, looking for the graded dirt service road on the west, just east of the mountain.

-WGS84 Lat: 35.2000 deg N Lon: -112.2047 deg W
*-II, Class 1 via service road ***

Squaw Peak (6,610)

Take Anvil Rock Road (I-40; exit 109; about 20 minutes west of Seligman) south until you intersect the minor service road that leads west toward the summit. A high clearance 2WD vehicle should have no problem driving to the top, assuming you're too effin lazy to walk.

-WGS84 Lat: 35.2155 deg N Lon: -113.1020 deg W

*-II, Class 1 via service road ***

Boxcar Hill (7,418)

Although the forest walk is pleasant, this is an uninteresting hike to a wooded summit with no views. We did see a couple dozen elk near the summit one November morning though.

-WGS84 Lat: 35.2541 deg N Lon: -112.1035 deg W

*-I, Class 1 via South Slopes **

Moore Benchmark (7,382)

From Kaibab Lake on the eastern outskirts of Williams, follow the trail across the dam then walk east along the north lake shore. Any line up the south slopes will take one easily to the summit.

-WGS84 Lat: 35.2913 deg N Lon: -112.1602 deg W

*-I, Class 1 via South Slopes ***

Sunset Crater National Monument

Although all of the peaks in this subsection are technically outside of the Monument boundary, each is accessed from the paved park entrance road shortly before the fee booth. They are arranged here randomly.

Crater 7,480

The peak's summit crater makes for a lovely nap spot on a warm spring day. To get here, take highway 89 north from Flagstaff to the turn-off to Sunset Crater National Monument.

-WGS84 Lat: 35.3911 deg N Lon: -111.5674 deg W

*-I, Class 1 via Southeast Slope ***

Crater 7,682

When I was here, one of the summit register entries was a rant against the Sierra Club. Made for an interesting read. I found an Indian relic not far below the top.

Follow the approach directions given for Crater 7,480.

-WGS84 Lat: 35.3782 deg N Lon: -111.5678 deg W

*-I, Class 1 via East Slope ***

*-I, Class 1 via West Ridge ***

Robinson Mountain (7,911)

This is a short hike in the O'Leary Peak and Sunset Crater area. On the summit we found a register placed three weeks earlier by Barbara Lilley.

-WGS84 Lat: 35.3860 deg N Lon: -111.5446 deg W

*-I, Class 1 via Northeast Slope **

Darton Dome (8,408)

From the service road leading to the summit of O'Leary Peak, gain the northwest face at the saddle connecting the two peaks and hike to the highpoint. A small cairns sits on a boulder amongst the trees.

-WGS84 Lat: 35.3942 deg N Lon: -111.5196 deg W

*-II, Class 2 via Northwest Face ***

"O'Leary Peak – West" (8,938)

This is the unnamed highpoint of the O'Leary Peak massif. It is an easy snag on the way to the O'Leary Peak lookout if one leaves the service road at the base of the highpoint's east face, shortly before reaching the lookout.

This higher west summit of O'Leary has 1788' of prominence.

-WGS84 Lat: 35.4021 deg N Lon: -111.5325 deg W

*-II, Class 1 via East Slope ***

Relaxing on the summit of O'Leary Peak

O'Leary Peak (8,916)

A quarter mile before reaching the Sunset Crater National Monument fee booth northeast of Flagstaff, turn onto the paved O'Leary Group Campground spur road and follow it 0.25 mile to the signed O'Leary Lookout trailhead. From there, hike five miles (and about 2000' of gain) up the service road to the lookout tower on the summit. O'Leary Peak – West and Darton Dome are logical, easy bonus peaks along the way.

-WGS84 Lat: 35.4013 deg N Lon: -111.5264 deg W
*-II, Class 1 via service road ****

Flagstaff Area

The peaks in this subsection are arranged generally south-to-north. Included are some peaks that are well north of Flagstaff but fit into the general scheme of things around there.

Woody Mountain (8,045)

Although the graded Woody Mountain Road runs toward the mountain from the south side of Flagstaff, the spur service road that leads to the summit lookout is closed due to private property. We opted to take a lesser (but still good) dirt road to the northeast side of the peak, where we hiked easily cross-country to gain and follow the northeast ridge to the top.

-WGS84 Lat: 35.1422 deg N Lon: -111.7517 deg W
*-II, Class 1 via Northeast Ridge **

Mars Hill (7,246)

Lowell Observatory sits on the summit of Mars Hill. The observatory can be driven to from downtown Flagstaff.

-WGS84 Lat: 35.2022 deg N Lon: -111.6639 deg W
*-I, Class 1 via Lowell Observatory **

Elden Mountain (9,299)

A fine mountain with a variety of ascent routes. Over the years there have been more than a few reports of interesting animal encounters, including attacks from mountain lions and rabid foxes.

Gain the service road by leaving highway 180 north of Flagstaff and turning east onto the signed Elden Lookout Road. Whether by foot or tire, follow the graded dirt road all the way to the top.

-WGS84 Lat: 35.2411 deg N Lon: -111.5977 deg W
*-II, Class 1 via service road ***

Doyle Peak (11,460)

Doyle Peak via Weatherford Trail (13 miles RT, 3400' gain) is a beautiful hike to a tranquil summit with nice views into the crater. The highpoint is on the east end of the wooded summit ridge.

-WGS84 Lat: 35.3302 deg N Lon: -111.6459 deg W
*-III, Class 1 via Weatherford Trail ****

Humphreys Peak (12,633)

Humphreys Peak is the highest peak in Arizona. With a number of established hiking routes up the high mountain, a maintained trail through beautiful forest from a nearby ski resort is the common approach. The summits views, which include the north rim of Grand Canyon and nearby Painted Desert, are awesome. Humphreys Peak is an indisputable classic.

Humphrey's neighbor, Agassiz Peak, often mistaken for Humphreys Peak when viewed from downtown Flagstaff, is another 12,000-foot peak worth hiking up. Due to a timberline plant (senecio franciscanus) found on its slopes and nowhere else, Agassiz Peak is only legally climbable when there is complete snow cover.

From Flagstaff, Arizona, get on US-180 and follow it north toward Grand Canyon. Seven miles outside of town, you'll come to Snow Bowl Road on your right. Turn onto the paved Snow Bowl Road and follow it seven miles to its end at the Arizona Snow Bowl ski resort. Pull into the dirt parking area below the resort. The trailhead is at the end of the parking area.

From the trailhead, cross the open meadow (a ski run, in winter) and head for the forest on the other side. Once there, head up the mountain on a good trail. Above timberline, at the saddle between Humphreys Peak (on the left) and Agassiz Peak (on the right), hang a left and continue along the trail toward Humphreys Peak. As you approach the summit over a few false peaks, the views become greater and greater.

The roundtrip involves about 8 miles, and roughly 3,300 feet of gain.

-WGS84 Lat: 35.3464 deg N Lon: -111.6779 deg W

-III, Class 1 via Humphreys Peak Trail ****

Kendrick Peak (10,418)

Kendrick Peak is a beautiful heavily forested lava dome that sits about 12 miles northwest of Humphreys Peak. With a few maintained trails leading to the fire lookout tower on the summit, the mountain can be approached from different directions. The approach via the pleasant and scenic Kendrick Trail is described here.

In a beautiful meadow near the top, be sure to check out an old cabin. Built in 1911-12, the cabin served as a residence for the mountain's first lookout worker. With fantastic forests of pine, aspen and fir, the mountain hosts elk, bear and porcupines. On summer evenings, one can sometimes sit on the summit and hear the elk calling each other in the trees below. Oh yeah, the north rim of the Grand Canyon can also be seen from the summit tower.

I spent three summers working as a volunteer fire lookout on the summit of this mountain. It holds special significance to me.

To get to the mountain: Travel north from Flagstaff, Arizona on US-180 and turn left at 18 miles onto Forest Road 193 (just past the Nordic

Center). Stay on FR-193 until you reach the junction with FR-171 (3 miles). Turn right onto FR-171 and continue two miles to FR-190. FR-190 is signed for the Kendrick Trail. Turn right (north) onto FR-190 and drive a mile to the Kendrick Trailhead, which is signed, has a bathroom, trash receptacles, a recycle bin (sweet!), and ample parking. Passenger cars should have little or no difficulty on this approach.

From the parking area, follow the well-marked trail 4.4 miles to the summit. The trail gains about 2,400 feet over the course of the route. Shortly after reaching a level meadowy area at about 10,200 feet, you will come to an old cabin with a wooden sign in front of it. At the sign, a trail (Bull Basin Trail) heads off to the right and the Kendrick trail continues to the left. Go left and take the Kendrick Trail the remaining 0.25 mile up multiple switchbacks to the summit and the lookout.

The cabin in the meadow area once served as the sleeping quarters for the original fire lookout. Sometime after that, a lookout structure was built at the top of the mountain. A concrete foundation is all that remains of the original lookout, as the current lookout was constructed slightly east of the original one in 1964.

-WGS84 Lat: 35.4080 deg N Lon: -111.8511 deg W

-III, Class 1 via Kendrick Trail ****

Slate Mountain (8,192)

The Slate Mountain Trail is 4.4 miles roundtrip with 900 feet of elevation gain. I car-to-car'd it in 45 minutes.

The trailhead is found off a dirt road just west of highway 180.

-WGS84 Lat: 35.4943 deg N Lon: -111.8426 deg W

-I, Class 1 via maintained trail **

Red Butte (7,254)

In the early 70s, a murder occurred inside the forest service lookout on the mountain's summit. Creepy, eh?

Leave highway 64 south of Tusayan (and west-southwest of Red Butte) and look for a graded dirt road heading east. This dirt road leads to another dirt road leading to the trailhead. The initial dirt road is generally gated and locked just off the highway during winter and spring.

-WGS84 Lat: 35.8204 deg N Lon: -112.0907 deg W

-II, Class 1 via maintained trail **

Sedona

East & Southeast of Sedona

The peaks in this subsection are accessed from a variety of points. The peaks are arranged here south-to-north.

"West Twin Butte" (5,335)

Largely a trivial ascent, the class 3 crux does require some care.

-WGS84 Lat: 34.8355 deg N Lon: -111.7661 deg W

*-II, Class 3 via Southeast Ridge ***

"Battlement Mesa" (4,780+)

An awesome narrow summit ridge leading to a tiny, exposed summit. A fun, short hike/scramble. The peak is located east of highway 179, south of downtown Sedona.

-WGS84 Lat: 34.8403 deg N Lon: -111.7600 deg W

-I, *Class 3 via North Ridge (from the east/northeast)* ***

Northwest of Sedona

The peaks in this subsection are accessed from a variety of points. The peaks are arranged here south-to-north.

The Cockscomb (5,009)

We found some Indian ruins just below the top, though a Sedona-savvy buddy of mine thinks they're fake. The trail to the top is class 2, with a class 3 move or two near the summit.

-WGS84 Lat: 34.8753 deg N Lon: -111.8585 deg W

*-I, Class 3 via trail ***

"Little Sugarloaf" (4,872)

I once encountered a homeless man sleeping on the summit.

-WGS84 Lat: 34.8729 deg N Lon: -111.8159 deg W

*-I, Class 2-3 via East Face **

"Sugarloaf Mountain" (4,911)

A quick scramble from the car. Start from the Sugarloaf Loop trailhead near the small mountain's southwest side.

-WGS84 Lat: 34.8762 deg N Lon: -111.7941 deg W

*-I, Class 2 via Northwest Slope **

On the small, exposed summit of Battlement Mesa

Capitol Butte (6,355)

One of the more striking mountain features in Sedona. I car-to-car'd this puppy in 1 hour, 53 minutes.

Supposedly Walt Disney, who lived in Sedona, designed his Thunder Mountain Railroad ride to resemble Capitol Butte.

-WGS84 Lat: 34.8859 deg N Lon: -111.8069 deg W

-II, Class 4 via South Face ****

Doe Mountain (5,267)

A nice Sedona trail hike to a flat summit with rewarding views. Speedy-types can roundtrip this bad-boy in 12 minutes, dodging and weaving around slow-moving tourists in both directions!

-WGS84 Lat: 34.8902 deg N Lon: -111.8609 deg W

-I, Class 1 via Doe Mountain Trail **

At Sedona's Amitabha Stupa, on the south side of Capitol Butte

Mescal Mountain (5,097)
It is said that in years past, Mescal Mountain's ambiance was found to be ideal for the magic mushroom experience.

-WGS84 Lat: 34.9095 deg N Lon: -111.8391 deg W
-I, Class 4 via Southwest Face ***

Grassy Knolls (4,869)
Largely, er, *completely* uninteresting.

-WGS84 Lat: 34.9109 deg N Lon: -111.8218 deg W
-I, Class 1-2 via (lame and brushy) Southwest Slope *

Bear Mountain (6,506)
A wonderful trail hike down in Sedona, the slightly higher true summit is an agonizing bushwhack a mile (or more) beyond trail's end.

-WGS84 Lat: 34.9189 deg N Lon: -111.8841 deg W
-II, Class 2 via Bear Mountain Trail ***

Three Sisters (5,500+)
There are fantastic views from the top. You're gonna have to snoop around to find your way up this – it's half the battle, and half the fun!

-WGS84 Lat: 34.9289 deg N Lon: -111.8285 deg W
-II, Class 3-4 (depending on variation of easiest route) ***

Approaching the summit of Three Sisters, looking west

Loy Butte (5,700)

An enjoyable scramble. My partners and I dubbed the route we climbed the "Lib Route." Regular people might simply call it the *East Face.*

-WGS84 Lat: 34.9432 deg N Lon: -111.9314 deg W

-II, Class 3 via East Face ****

North of Sedona

The peaks in this subsection are accessed from a variety of points. The peaks are arranged here south-to-north.

"Morning Glory Spire" (5,282)

Morning Glory Spire is a classic desert spire that doesn't require superhero status to surmount.

-WGS84 Lat: 34.8897 deg N Lon: -111.7811 deg W

-II, Class 4 via Northwest Ridge ****

"The Fin" (5,667)

Stunning, especially while walking along the summit ridge (or when viewed from the north saddle of The Acropolis). The west arête is the easiest route up the mountain. Most parties will want to rope up for two pitches on the arete; some might also want to do an initial pitch up the ramp leading to the base of the arete.

-WGS84 Lat: 34.8947 deg N Lon: -111.7644 deg W

-II, 5.7 via West Arete ****

Walt H. on the summit of Morning Glory Spire.
The view looks west toward Capitol Butte (left).

"Brins Butte" (5,502)

An enjoyable hike/easy scramble behind Morning Glory Spire.

-WGS84 Lat: 34.8969 deg N Lon: -111.7811 deg W

-I, Class 2-3 via North Face **

Wilson Mountain (7,122)

The common trailhead's at Midgley Bridge, on Alt-89 just north of Sedona. The small, exposed summit block is a bit beyond trail's end.

-WGS84 Lat: 34.9179 deg N Lon: -111.7508 deg W

-II, Class 1-2 via trail (with class 2-3 summit crag) ***

Our boy Walt on the awesome summit of The Fin. The Acropolis (to the east) is behind him.

West & Southwest of Sedona

The peaks in this subsection are accessed from a variety of points. The peaks are arranged here generally south-to-north.

Woodchute Mountain (7,860)

Take the paved spur road opposite the signed and paved Mingus Lake spur road at the highpoint of Alt 89 (about 7,000'), outside of the funky town of Jerome. The spur road soon turns to dirt and becomes a little rutted out. In about a mile you will reach the signed trailhead for Woodchute Trail #102. Hike the trail for a couple miles until you reach a point due east of the summit. An easy off-trail hike through the trees leads to the highpoint. No views, sorry.

Woodchute Mountain boasts 2930' of prominence.

By the way, Jerome is worth visiting after you're done with the peak. It has a strange charm, a few good restaurants, curious history, and plenty of interesting characters. I once sat next to Tool and A Perfect Circle singer Maynard James Keenan in one of the town's restaurants.

-WGS84 Lat: 34.7498 deg N Lon: -112.1753 deg W

*-II, Class 1 via Woodchute Trail #102 ***

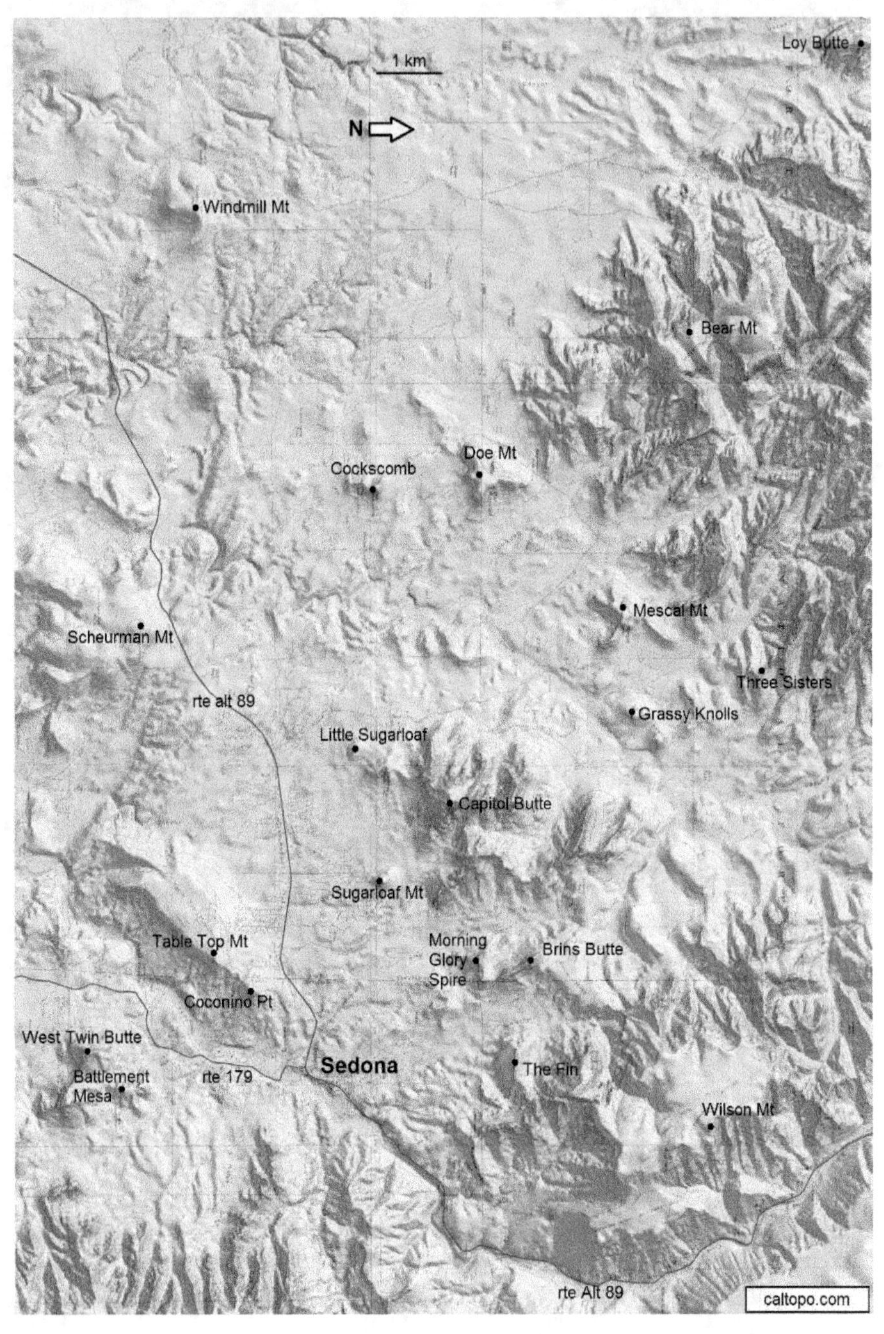
1 km
N
Loy Butte
Windmill Mt
Bear Mt
Doe Mt
Cockscomb
Mescal Mt
Scheurman Mt
Three Sisters
rte alt 89
Grassy Knolls
Little Sugarloaf
Capitol Butte
Sugarloaf Mt
Table Top Mt
Morning Glory Spire
Brins Butte
Coconino Pt
West Twin Butte
Sedona
Battlement Mesa
rte 179
The Fin
Wilson Mt
rte Alt 89
caltopo.com

Scheurman Mountain (4,899)

A short trail hike leads to the flattish summit of this sprawling mountain. With an indistinct highpoint, we bagged a couple protrusions just to be sure. The trailhead is near the high school, on the south side of Alt-89, west of Sedona.

-WGS84 Lat: 34.8431 deg N Lon: -111.8360 deg W

-I, Class 2 via maintained trail **

Windmill Mountain (4,641)

Park along the short dirt road just off Alt-89 southeast of the peak then follow the gentle wash up to a point where the southeast ridge can be gained and followed to the summit through awesome stands of cacti. A Lilley-MacLeod register was found in the summit cairn.

-WGS84 Lat: 34.8506 deg N Lon: -111.9046 deg W

-II, Class 1-2 via Southeast Ridge *

Table Top Mountain (4,830)

This is where the Sedona airport is. Talk about an *un*inspiring summit! Get to it by following the paved airport road south from Alt-89, just west of the junction of Alt-89 and SR-179.

-WGS84 Lat: 34.8532 deg N Lon: -111.7821 deg W

-I, Class 1 via paved road *

"Coconino Point" (4,874)

Approach this small mountain from the trailhead at the saddle between it and Table Top Mountain. Follow the Coconino Loop Trail to a point below the southwest face. Pick a line and follow a number of use trails to the top.

-WGS84 Lat: 34.8583 deg N Lon: -111.7760 deg W

-I, Class 2 via Southwest Face *

Grand Canyon National Park

How could I possibly babble on about northern Arizona and let Grand Canyon National Park go without any representation? I *couldn't*! This world famous gorge, whether viewed from its south rim, its north rim, from the Colorado River flowing at its bottom, or from points in between, is a sight to behold. Spanning some ten miles wide in places and over a hundred miles in length, Grand Canyon National Park boasts some of the most intense and inspiring scenery to be found anywhere in the world.

Gazing at a map of the park, the mountain explorer will be drawn by the names of the various features of the park—Buddha Temple, Shiva Temple, Tower of Set…the list goes on. For the hiker/scrambler/climber, do some of these obscure features have routes to their summits? You bet.

Lodging is (sometimes) available (and typically expensive) on both rims of the canyon, and other options are available in nearby Tusayan or Williams. Developed and backcountry camping is also available both high and low, though reservations (and/or permits) are strongly encouraged. Reserve way early.

The south rim, from which every route described herein approaches, is open year-round. The peaks are arranged here west-to-east.

These are some of the sweetest and most awe-inspiring peaks in the book.

Andy M. in Grand Canyon (near the summit of O'Neill Butte).
The views looks to the northeast.

Whites Butte (4,860)

Whites Butte is a long, mellow hike (with just a touch of scrambling) that ventures into remote, seldom-visited classic Grand Canyon country. From Hermit's Rest, take the Hermits Trail to the Dripping Springs Trail. Follow the Dripping Springs Trail to the Boucher Trail then follow the Boucher Trail many miles to the flat area immediately south of Whites Butte. From there, work your way through a few easy cliffbands (the two hardest each involved two or three class 3-4 moves, though I suspect an easier way could be found) to gain the summit and its Colorado River views.

Expect a roundtrip of 16 miles. Be sure and bring plenty of water into this dry country. In March, I brought along a gallon and used all of it, since nearly all the route receives full sun.

-WGS84 Lat: 36.0976 deg N Lon: -112.2313 deg W

-III, Class 3-4 via South Slopes from Boucher Trail ***

The Battleship (5,850)

Approach from Bright Angel Trail. There's supposedly an easier route north of my route on the east face. On my route, I happened upon some relics of early exploration.

-WGS84 Lat: 36.0759 deg N Lon: -112.1384 deg W

-II, YDS 5.6 via East Face ****

Cheops Pyramid (5,401)

Cheops Pyramid. Great name, though some sources refer to it as Cheops *Plateau* (a somewhat less-cool name). This named feature lies just to the southeast of the awe-inspiring Isis Temple on the north side of the Colorado River roughly opposite Grandeur Point between Yavapai Point and the Bright Angel trailhead on the south rim of the canyon. Though overshadowed by its higher and more striking neighbor to the northwest, Cheops is a fine endeavor. The two peaks are connected by a saddle, but don't expect to be able to bag Isis while you're there for this one – the high, red vertical cliffs rising toward Isis above the connecting saddle shall most likely stop you.

With a roundtrip of about 21 or 22 miles and roughly 8,000 feet of gain, Cheops Pyramid is an excellent dayhike for the fit and prepared. And you will never forget the views.

Enjoying ourselves just off the Boucher Trail

Take the South Kaibab Trail to the cabins along the river. From there, head north along the trail to Phantom Ranch then get onto a well-worn use trail heading north from the west side of the footbridge just before the ranch. The trail will take you to a notch in the cliffs above then into a shallow canyon running northwest. From here, hike cross-country to the northwest (Cheops is now visible before you), working counter-clockwise to the base of the peak's northwest ridge. The ridge is largely class 2-3, with one short (6-foot) section of class 4.

-WGS84 Lat: 36.1204 deg N Lon: -112.1200 deg W

-IV, Class 3-4 via Northwest Ridge ****

The awkward dihedral immediately below the very awkward squeeze chimney on the north face of O'Neill Butte.

O'Neill Butte (5,822)

This is a fun climb with an interesting squeeze chimney. Some route-finding will be required to keep it "easy," as the most obvious line involves a YDS 5.8 roof. Approach from the South Kaibab Trail (off highway 64 below Yaki Point), leaving the trail when it passes along the south side of the butte. Work around the east side of the butte to the edge of the north face. Near the northeast corner, scramble up an 8-foot class 3 slab then work west on a ledge until you encounter a steep, 40-foot class 4 crack/ramp leading to another ledge. Take that ledge west to an awkward YDS 5.4 dihedral (10 feet) immediately below a *very* awkward 15-foot class 5 squeeze chimney. Above the chimney, continue directly up into a wider chimney (stemming; 20 feet) until you find a very exposed, scary slither-around move leading to class 2 terrain just below the summit.

-WGS84 Lat: 36.0707 deg N Lon: -112.0904 deg W
-II, YDS 5.4 via North Face ****

"Unnamed Butte" (6,633)
This unnamed butte sits just off the Grandview Trail, immediately north of Grandview Point itself. Follow the good trail down until you reach a lesser use trail leading 75 feet out onto a flat (unofficial) overlook area on the ridge that directly connects with Unnamed Butte. The use trail fades shortly after the overlook area and one must route-find along the ridge north, scrambling into a notch (class 3; loose) and back out to continue along the ridge toward the butte. Eventually, the ridge narrows and you run out of "easy" options. Here, look for a steep, class 3 chimney (40 feet) allowing escape off the east side of the ridge. Once down, regain the narrow ridge by walking and scrambling 50 feet north and then downclimb into an 8-foot slot (*careful route-finding required here*) to the east, step around an exposed corner, and then downclimb a class 3-4 crack (15 feet). From there, follow a class 2 ramp to gentle terrain at the base of the ridge's eastern cliffs. Follow the base of the cliffs north all the way around to the southwest corner of Unnamed Butte (*that's right, you are going to do a nearly complete circle around the peak*) until you can gain loose and steep, class 2 terrain that leads up to the class 2 summit ridge. A cairn rests upon the second-highest summit boulder.

-WGS84 Lat: 36.0108 deg N Lon: -111.9883 deg W
-III, Class 3-4 via Grandview Trail ***

Sinking Ship (7,344)
Fun, and only a short scramble from the pavement. From highway 64 directly south of Sinking Ship, walk through gentle forest to gain the apex of the rim immediately south of the objective butte. Scramble easily (class 2) down to the saddle and then work north along the east side of the butte to gain the north face of the south (main) butte. Head up class 2-3 terrain to an 8-foot class 4 rock step just below a 20-foot, vertical YDS 5.3 chimney. Once above the chimney, exit east then climb up and through a short (5-foot) class 4 band to gain easier (albeit still loose and exposed) ground. Work around a corner at the top of the loose talus/gravel then climb an 8-foot class 3-4 face. From there, bounce on over to the highpoint.

We once climbed this in heavy spring snow conditions—quite the desert alpine experience!

-WGS84 Lat: 35.9907 deg N Lon: -111.9588 deg W
-II, YDS 5.3 via North Face ****

Can you spot Hugh de Q trying to find the elusive escape
from the ridge leading out to Unnamed Butte?
Hint: he's gone just a bit too far.
The crucial "8-foot slot" is halfway between Hugh and the bottom of the photo.
This view looks north.

Sinking Ship from the east along the south rim of the Canyon.
The final route to the top somewhat follows the right skyline of the left summit.
The approach follows the wooded, left skyline.

Grandview Benchmark (7,530)

Follow a service road (RD E10) for a mile south from highway 64 (a bit east of the Grandview turn-off) to the lookout tower, restrooms and a trailhead or two. The benchmark is about 50 feet from the toilet. While nothing dramatic, it's a pleasant walk from the pavement of highway 64.

-WGS84 Lat: 35.9576 deg N Lon: -111.9548 deg W

-I, Class 1 via service road *

Coronado Butte (7,108)

This is my favorite climb in Grand Canyon. The final bit of route-finding to the summit is great fun.

Approach the peak via New Hance Trail, whose trailhead is right off highway 64, southeast of the mountain. Follow the rough trail to a point east of the saddle that is south of the mountain. There, leave the trail, gain the saddle, and work your way up the south ridge to a point near the base of the final summit crag. Work around to the 4th chute north on the east face of the mountain. Heading up the chute (class 3-4), one will encounter interesting route-finding, including a squeeze through a hole, a tree climb, a chimney climb, and several ledges to work around in order to gain the top.

-WGS84 Lat: 36.0044 deg N Lon: -111.9443 deg W

-III, Class 3-4 via South Ridge & East Face ****

Looking northwest to Coronado Butte from New Hance Trail.

Escalante Butte (6,529)

Approach via Tanner Trail from Lipan Point. After a class 2-3 approach, the final step-over move (exposed class 4) to the highpoint (via its northwest corner) is unforgettable.

-WGS84 Lat: 36.0493 deg N Lon: -111.8499 deg W

-III, Class 4 via South Slope or East Slope ****

Cardenas Butte (6,269)

Approach via Tanner Trail (from Lipan Point), a short distance west of the park's east entrance station on highway 64. At a point below the butte, head up the easiest line (class 2-3), weaving around the occasion obstacle encountered. Just below the top, the crux is encountered. It involves two class 4-5 moves in a dihedral.

-WGS84 Lat: 36.0593 deg N Lon: -111.8427 deg W

-III, Class 4-5 via South Slope ****

Desert View Point (7,498)

This flattish point offers great views of Cardenas Butte, Escalante Butte and the Colorado River near its confluence with the Little Colorado River, as well as an opportunity to visit the historical lookout tower on the rim. The Point also has 478' of prominence. Desert View Point is adjacent to the park's east entrance station on highway 64.

-WGS84 Lat: 36.0408 deg N Lon: -111.8300 deg W

*-I, Class 1 from parking lot **

Cardenas Butte from the vicinity of Escalante Boulder camp to the southwest.

Cedar Mountain (7,061)

Approached from the Grand Canyon National Park sign (and park boundary) a mile or so east of the park's east entrance station on highway 64, the route follows an old road (RD E15) north into and through a lovely canyon before heading up a low ridge to gain an east-west road that leads right to the southwest corner of the mountain. Expect a roundtrip of about 10 miles and 1,200 feet of gain from highway-64.

-WGS84 Lat: 36.0530 deg N Lon: -111.7732 deg W

*-III, Class 2 via Southwest Slopes ***

Grand Canyon-Parashant National Monument

This lonely patch of wonderfulness, also sometimes referred to as the Arizona Strip, snuggles the northwest edge of Grand Canyon National Park. The National Monument, which is crisscrossed by hundreds of miles of dirt roads, is most easily accessed from St. George, Utah. While in this area, one should make a point to visit perhaps the finest overlook of Grand Canyon, a place called Toroweap. Doing so requires many miles of dirt road driving, some of it rather rough.

Some of the peaks in this subsection are not technically within the National Monument but are included due to their proximity.

The peaks in this subsection are arranged from roughly most-remote to least-remote.

Mount Dellenbaugh (7,072)
Mount Dellenbaugh is likely the most remote peak in this book. It is deep in the solemn and lonely Grand Canyon-Parashant National Monument. The peak has 1762' of prominence, though the views, while nice, are not outstanding.

Take River Road in St. George, Utah, into Arizona, where the pavement will soon turn to dirt. Stay on the main (and mostly excellent) dirt road and follow good signage for Mount Dellenbaugh for 85 miles to a signed trailhead on the right side of the road. A roundtrip hike of 5 miles (and about 900 feet of gain) is all that's required from there.

-WGS84 Lat: 36.1087 deg N Lon: -113.5406 deg W
*-II, Class 1 via trail from the northeast ***

Hudson Point (6,688)
This awesome overlook of the Grand Wash Cliffs area sits 1.3 miles northwest of Last Chance Knoll. The same road that leads to the knoll ends at a structure and antenna 0.25 mile from Hudson Point. From road's end, simply drop down a bit and walk out to the overlook.

-WGS84 Lat: 36.4085 deg N Lon: -113.7367 deg W
*-I, Class 1 via road's end ***

Last Chance Knoll (6,758)
Last Chance Knoll is a tree'd, viewless minor summit atop Grand Wash Cliffs. A bumpy dirt road passes within 100 yards of the summit. The lump somehow has 953' of prominence.

-WGS84 Lat: 36.3992 deg N Lon: -113.7144 deg W
*-I, Class 1 via dirt road **

Mount Trumbull (8,029)
Mount Trumbull, a high (but not overly impressive) peak with 2974' of prominence, requires driving 70 miles of dirt road from St. George, Utah to hike. Although most of the roads are quite good, some of the latter miles are a bit bumpy and narrow.

Take River Road in St. George, Utah, into Arizona, where the pavement will soon turn to dirt. Stay on the main dirt road and follow good signage for Mount Trumbull to the Nixon Spring Trailhead on the left side of the road on the southwest side of the peak. A roundtrip hike of 6 miles (and less than 2000' of gain) is required.

-WGS84 Lat: 36.4100 deg N Lon: -113.1385 deg W

*-II, Class 1 via Nixon Spring Trailhead ***

Mount Logan (7,866)
A short hike from the end of a dirt road, Mount Logan's finale is a pleasant, woodsy hike to an excellent viewpoint. The peak has 1246' of prominence.

-WGS84 Lat: 36.3602 deg N Lon: -113.2131 deg W
*-I, Class 1 via East Slope ***

Cinder Knoll (5,331)
This shamefully lame summit lies a mile or two west of the road to Mount Trumbull, a few miles south of Diamond Butte.

-WGS84 Lat: 36.4970 deg N Lon: -113.3921 deg W
*-I, Class 1 via Northeast Slope **

Diamond Butte (6,345)
This eye-catching peak dominates the view for much of the long drive to Mount Trumbull or Mount Dellenbaugh. It sits near the road-split where one heads left to Trumbull or right to Dellenbaugh.

Despite Diamond Butte's mighty stature, speedy types can easily roundtrip it in under an hour.

-WGS84 Lat: 36.5711 deg N Lon: -113.3738 deg W
*-I, Class 2 via Northwest Face ****

Black Knolls (4,992)
Black Knolls is not a destination peak. It is a lame and unremarkable bump in the Arizona Strip, not far from the scene in Colorado City. You can drive to within a 20 second walk to the highpoint. A benchmark sits on the summit.

-WGS84 Lat: 36.8523 deg N Lon: -113.0729 deg W
*-I, Class 1 from any direction **

Point of Rock (5,210)
One can drive to within 150 yards of the highpoint. The feature's southern cliffs are somewhat dramatic and quite pretty.

-WGS84 Lat: 36.8841 deg N Lon: -113.0090 deg W
*-I, Class 1 from the north **

Seegmiller Mountain (6,220)
Initially approached as per Mount Trumbull or Mount Dellenbaugh, this sprawling mountain is a short drive from St. George, Utah. A signed service road on the southwest side of the peak leads all the way to the summit. The views from atop are outstanding.

-WGS84 Lat: 36.8470 deg N Lon: -113.4921 deg W
*-I, Class 1 via service road ****

Little Black Mountain (3,504)
A decent dirt road closely outside of St. George leads to a parking area on the southeast side of the peak. Easier routes than those described probably exist.

-WGS84 Lat: 36.9951 deg N Lon: -113.4996 deg W
-II, Class 2 via East Cliffs
*-II, Class 3-4 via South Cliffs ***

Scattered

The peaks in this section have been selected from random (but noteworthy) spots around Arizona.

Lake Havasu City Area

This odd but interesting oasis, home of London Bridge, is accessed from AZ-95 between I-40 (to the north) and I-10 (to the south).

"Little Haystack" (1,380)
With a very short approach from highway 95 north of Lake Havasu City, Arizona, this small peak offers outstanding scrambling from base to summit.

-WGS84 Lat: 34.6082 deg N Lon: -114.3536 deg W
*-I, Class 3-4 via South Face ****

"Shangri La Butte" (1,540)
Shangri La Butte is just off highway 95 north of Lake Havasu City. Reaching the summit requires some very interesting and enjoyable (though steep and loose) scrambling, starting in a steep gully on the northeast aspect then zig-zagging up the north arete to the summit. The crux is probably no harder than easy class 4 but this is a dangerous peak.

-WGS84 Lat: 34.6120 deg N Lon: -114.3447 deg W
*-II, Class 4 via Northern Aspect *****

Goat Hill (1,300)
Goat Hill is just west of highway 95, southwest of Shangri La Butte and north of Lake Havasu City. It is an easy hike via a service road.

-WGS84 Lat: 34.6024 deg N Lon: -114.3710 deg W
*-II, Class 1 via service road **
*-II, Class 2 via South Ridge **

Kofa National Wildlife Refuge

Located south of I-10 and east of highway 95, this sprawling and obscure desert wonderland near Quartzsite, Arizona, hosts some of the sweetest and most-difficult-to-climb peaks in the region. The peaks included in this subsection are a mere sampling of what the Refuge offers. The peaks are loosely clustered here by proximity to one another.

Two of the peaks in this subsection, Ibex Peak and Haystack Peak, are not technically part of Kofa but included here due to their proximity.

Castle Dome Peak (3,788)

This eye-catching, blocky peak is one of the most impressive in the region. It has 2098' of prominence.

From highway 95 at mile marker 55, turn onto Castle Dome Mine Road (good dirt) and follow it 9 miles to the museum. Continue straight for an additional 4.5 miles (4WD) to a pullout at the mouth of a wide wash. Hike up the main wash (angling left) to a large rock arrow in the watercourse. Leave the wash at the arrow and follow a good use trail toward the notch on the south side of a prominent pillar on the left skyline of Castle Dome Peak. Twenty feet below the notch, scramble up a groove then follow cairns and signs of use to the summit.

For a variation of the standard route: While making the final scramble up the mountain, cut right through a prominent arch along the route and follow signs of use up and around a variety of obstacles. There is some loose talus, and this route is not as pleasant as the standard route.

-WGS84 Lat: 33.0848 deg N Lon: -114.1434 deg W
-II, Class 3 via Northwest Wash ****
-II, Class 4 via Northwest Wash Variation ***

"Spaghetti Peak" (3,820)

This minor peak is closely southeast of Squaw Peak. It makes for a reasonable bonus peak on the way to Old Smokey Mountain. The peak is a dirty choss pile with some interesting features to it.

-WGS84 Lat: 33.3305 deg N Lon: -114.0295 deg W
-II, Class 2-3 via North Face **

Old Smokey Mountain (4,373)

Located west of Squaw Peak, which is arguably the most aesthetic peak in the entire desert southwest, Old Smokey Mountain is an interesting mountain with a very interesting finish along an exposed, narrow, and chossy ridge to a tiny summit with great views. The peak is probably best approached from the southeast of Squaw Peak, near the end of the road at the mouth of Big Dick Canyon. Many may wish to make a short (20-foot) rappel from the summit.

-WGS84 Lat: 33.3413 deg N Lon: -114.0470 deg W

*-III, Class 3-4 via Northeast Face ****

Beginning our descent from the summit of Castle Dome Peak

Polaris Mountain (3,624)

This is a fantastically beautiful area, though old hiking reports suggest one may want to stay away from this peak due to absurd amounts of cacti. To the contrary, it's not all that bad. The peak makes a fine hike from a camp near the end of the road at the mouth of Big Dick Canyon.

-WGS84 Lat: 33.3080 deg N Lon: -113.9812 deg W

*-II, Class 2 via Southwest Slope ***

Kofa Butte (3,247)

This large mesa is easily climbed via an interesting class 2 chute on the north-northeast side. There are nice views from the summit looking straight down the steep cliffs overlooking broad King Valley.

The peak has 947' of prominence.

-WGS84 Lat: 33.2771 deg N Lon: -113.9298 deg W

*-II, Class 2 via North Face ***

Peak 2,550 (2,550)

This peak is close to highway 95, near Stone Cabin.

From mile marker 77 (just north of King Road) on highway 95, head slightly northeast across the desert to the mouth of the canyon separating High Peak (the first major peak to the north) from this peak. Enter the canyon then take the first right fork (brushy). Head up this fork and again take the first right fork, which leads to the crest of the peak's north ridge. Stay on or near the crest (nice, solid class 3 in one stretch near the top) up to the summit.

For an alternative approach, head east across the desert to the first canyon south of the major canyon separating High Peak from this peak. An old rusted car is in the desert 100 yards left of the mouth of the canyon. The canyon is mostly pleasant, with a couple of dry falls near the mouth, both bypassed on the left (the first via exposed class 3 scrambling). At the head of the canyon, angle south toward the crest of the north ridge.

-WGS84 Lat: 33.2606 deg N Lon: -114.2067 deg W
-II, Class 3 via North Ridge ***

High Peak (2,716)

Despite 1006' of prominence, this otherwise unassuming mountain is remarkably interesting. An ascent of the upper west face coupled with a descent of the southeast ridge is an outstanding and adventurous desert mega-classic.

Follow the directions given for Peak 2,550 to the mouth of the canyon separating the two peaks. From the mouth, continue up the canyon for a couple hundred yards then head up the first canyon on the left. Proceed to a prominent notch in the right fork of this canyon. From the notch, scramble up and around a variety of obstacles (tricky route-finding; class 4), generally working directly up the west face, arriving on gentle terrain just north of the summit. Bring two 30m ropes and several long slings for the route.

For the southeast ridge descent, stay on the crest virtually all the way to the final huge drop-off at its toe then cut right into a gully, where two 100' rappels down the watercourse put you on the ground.

-WGS84 Lat: 33.2735 deg N Lon: -114.2022 deg W
-II, Class 3 via Southeast Ridge (as a descent route) ****
-II, Class 4 via Upper West Face ****

"La Cholla Peak" (2,470)

This is a nice hike near the King Valley entrance to Kofa off highway 95 at Stone Cabin. The north gully is a short and pleasant route, assuming one enjoys dodging cacti and weaving around low brush.

-WGS84 Lat: 33.2342 deg N Lon: -114.2217 deg W
-II, Class 2 via North Gully **

Double A and Tracy F. doing some exposed scrambling on the upper west face of High Peak.

"Little Cholla Peak" (2,171)

This and La Cholla Peak (to the south) are easily accessed from King Road, not far off highway 95 at Stone Cabin, south of Quartzsite, Arizona.

-WGS84 Lat: 33.2420 deg N Lon: -114.2237 deg W

*-II, Class 2 via Southeast Face ***

*-II, Class 2-3 via Northeast Ridge ***

"Yellowfin" (1,951)

Yellowfin is a few miles east of La Cholla Peak, on the north side of King Road. From the road, the peak looks like it might be tricky but it's easy enough to work to the saddle to the right of the summit and then sneak up the backside to the summit, where a register was found.

-WGS84 Lat: 33.2446 deg N Lon: -114.1531 deg W

*-I, Class 3 from the southeast ***

Signal Peak (4,877)

Signal Peak is the highpoint of the Kofa Range and Yuma County. It has 3482' of prominence.

The dashed line is where the route is in view, while the dotted line is where the route goes out of view behind rocks. Note the GPS track on the map.

Travel highway 95 south from Quartzsite, Arizona for 18.5 miles to Palm Canyon Road. Head east on Palm Canyon Road (2WD dirt) to its end at the mouth of Palm Canyon.

Hike up the canyon to its head, where it opens and you can hike up the loose slope on the right to the rib above. Drop down the backside of the rib and scramble up the next canyon to its headwall, where two roped pitches (20' and 100'; YDS 5.4) protected by fixed pins (bring two quick draws for the route) with fixed belays leads to easier scrambling. Scramble up the canyon until it opens and three brushy gullies present themselves. Take the middle gully to its head then drop slightly into the gully on its backside and angle left toward the summit 0.25 mile to the northeast.

The descent of this route can be done in two rappels with a single 60m rope.

-WGS84 Lat: 33.3592 deg N Lon: -114.0827 deg W

*-III, YDS 5.4 via Rusty Bailie (West Canyon) Route ****

Ibex Peak (2,822)

With 1082' of prominence, Ibex Peak is a dominant peak northeast of Quartzsite, Arizona. The peak's huge northwest face is dramatic.

Follow highway 95 north from Quartzsite for 5.7 miles then turn right and follow the paved road just over 8 miles to a dirt road on the right. Follow the main dirt road (trending left; 4WD) about 4 miles, then turn right onto a lesser dirt road that ends at an old mine 0.5 mile northwest of the peak.

Hike to the base of the great northwest wall of the peak then follow up along the base to its terminus (class 2-3 near the end), where you'll turn lerft and hike the gentle slope to the summit.

-WGS84 Lat: 33.7684 deg N Lon: -114.0334 deg W

*-II, Class 2-3 from the northwest ****

Haystack Peak (2,783)

Haystack Peak is an outstanding, alpine-like desert peak. The full west ridge is easily one of the finest desert scrambles I've done. The peak, which sits just to the northeast of Ibex Peak, has 923' of prominence.

Follow the directions given for Ibex Peak to the parking area near the old mine. From there, hike to the Haystack-Ibex saddle. At the base of Haystack Peak's west ridge, cut right for a couple hundred yards until you can scramble up and left (class 3) to gain the ridge. Follow the ridge up and over the west summit (nice knife-edge) to the saddle between the west summit and the main summit. With careful route-finding, scrambling over and around a variety of obstacles (class 3) then scramble to the summit from its southeast side.

A somewhat easier but less interesting approach is to follow the gentle (albeit full of talus) north slope (a class 2-3 rock band just below the saddle) to the saddle between the west and main summits. There are other roads in the area that will put you closer to the base of the north slope.

-WGS84 Lat: 33.7738 deg N Lon: -114.0207 deg W
*-II, Class 3 via North Slope to Upper West Ridge ****
*-II, Class 3 via West Ridge ****

Double A on the descent from Haystack Peak. The summit is above him.

Superstition Mountains

The Superstition Mountains are a delightfully aesthetic range just east of the fifth largest city in the country, the shamelessly sprawling Phoenix. Though the information here only touches the tip of the iceberg, there is a tremendous amount of cool stuff here worthy of further exploration.

Superstition Peak (5,057)

Superstition Peak is the highpoint of the Superstition Mountains. It is a classic desert peak. The Carney Spring route, whose trailhead is southeast of the summit, is a wonderful and constantly interesting trail hike. The summit spires are other-worldly. Superstition Peak has 1837' of prominence.

-WGS84 Lat: 33.4110 deg N Lon: -111.4008 deg W
*-III, Class 2 via Carney Spring Trail ****

Weavers Needle (distant center)
from near the summit of Fremont Peak

"Fremont Peak" (4,180)

Fremont Peak is closely southwest of Fremont Saddle and south of Weavers Needle. It is a quick bag from Fremont Saddle, which Peralta Canyon Trail passes over. The route from Carney Spring is much more aesthetic and interesting. The summit is not easy to identify, due to numerous, craggy outcroppings of approximately the same height clustered closely together.

-WGS84 Lat: 33.4143 deg N Lon: -111.3671 deg W

*-II, Class 2-3 via Southwest Aspect from Carney Spring trailhead ****

*-II, Class 2-3 via Northeast Face from Fremont Saddle ***

Weavers Needle (4,553)

Weavers Needle is one of the finest peaks in the desert southwest. Although many trip reports proclaim it a fairly significant 10-12-hour outing, with an easy trail approach from the Peralta Trailhead, taking the right fork up Barks Canyon then hiking over Bluff Saddle to approach the east gully from the southeast, our party of three casually made the roundtrip in less than 7 hours.

The route's crux is near the bottom, where a 40-foot face on the right side of the gully is climbed. Although the route is easier above, anticipate a few rappels on the descent.

Weavers Needle has 1013' of prominence.

-WGS84 Lat: 33.4330 deg N Lon: -111.3708 deg W

-III, YDS 5.0 via East Gully ****

Tucson Area

Although the cool funkiness of Tucson is inadequately addressed in this book, the book itself would be inadequate if it did not contain one of the most awesome peaks in the entire desert southwest—Baboquivari Peak.

Baboquivari Peak (7,780)

Baboquivari Peak is located on Tohono O'odham Nation land about 1.5 hours southwest of Tucson. With a beautiful trail approach from the western base of the mountain to the base of the summit monolith, the Forbes Route is a wonderful scramble with a couple short stretches of stiffer scrambling (or easy climbing). Route-finding is straightforward. A permit to hike on the reservation is required. There's good camping at the trailhead.

Baboquivari Peak has 4204' of prominence.

-WGS84 Lat: 31.7710 deg N Lon: -111.5959 deg W

-III, YDS 5.3 via Forbes Route ****

Kitt Peak (6,680)

Kitt Peak, a respectable mountain with 2092' of prominence, is a logical bonus peak for those in the Tucson area for the nearby iconic Baboquivari Peak. A paved road off highway 86 leads all the way to the summit.

-WGS84 Lat: 31.9649 deg N Lon: -111.5994 deg W

-II, Class 1 via observatory road ***

Ragged Top (3,907)

Ragged Top, which sports 1357' of prominence, is close to I-10, 25 miles northwest of Tucson. Leave I-10 at exit 236 and make your way to Silverbell Road which eventually turns to dirt and proceeds along the north side of the peak. Park in a designated parking area 1.5 miles due north of the peak. The north gully, which is visible from the parking area, leads to a wide notch immediately right (west) of the summit mass, a couple hundred feet below the summit. At the top of the north gully, head left from the notch and scramble 200 feet to the top.

-WGS84 Lat: 32.4497 deg N Lon: -111.4898 deg W

-II, Class 2-3 via North Gully ***

Ragged Top, from Silverbell Road

Picacho Peak (3,370)

Picacho Peak is the Angels Landing of Tucson. It has 1573' of prominence.

The peak (and trailhead) are in Picacho Peak State Park, northwest of Tucson.

-WGS84 Lat: 32.6352 deg N Lon: -111.4007 deg W

*-II, Class 3 via Hunter Trail *****

"Razorback Ridge" (3,161)

Razorback Ridge is 0.5 mile northwest of Picacho Peak.

Approach as per Picacho Peak via the Hunter Trail. At the saddle Razorback Ridge shares with Picacho Peak, leave the trail and follow a use trail along the southeast ridge to the summit. Anticipate a delightful 75-foot long knife-edge ridge just before the summit.

-WGS84 Lat: 32.6394 deg N Lon: -111.4074 deg W

*-II, Class 3 via Southeast Ridge *****

Peak 2,540 (2,540)

This minor peak is 0.3 mile north-northeast of Picacho Peak. From the Hunter Peak trailhead, follow the Callaway Trail to the saddle the peak shares with Picacho Peak. Angle left at the saddle for 200 yards through a nasty cholla field to the base of the south face of the peak's east arête. Looking around should reveal that the only reasonable line to the crest of the arête is a steep 40-foot class 3-4 groove in the wall. Once on the crest, follow along its north side to the summit.

Picacho Peak, from near the summit of Razorback Ridge.

As an alternative route, the northwest face possesses none of the troublesome cholla but makes up for it by being loose and unpleasant.

-WGS84 Lat: 32.6406 deg N Lon: -111.3989 deg W

*-I, Class 2 via Northwest Face **

*-I, Class 3-4 via South Face of East Arete ***

☯ California ☯

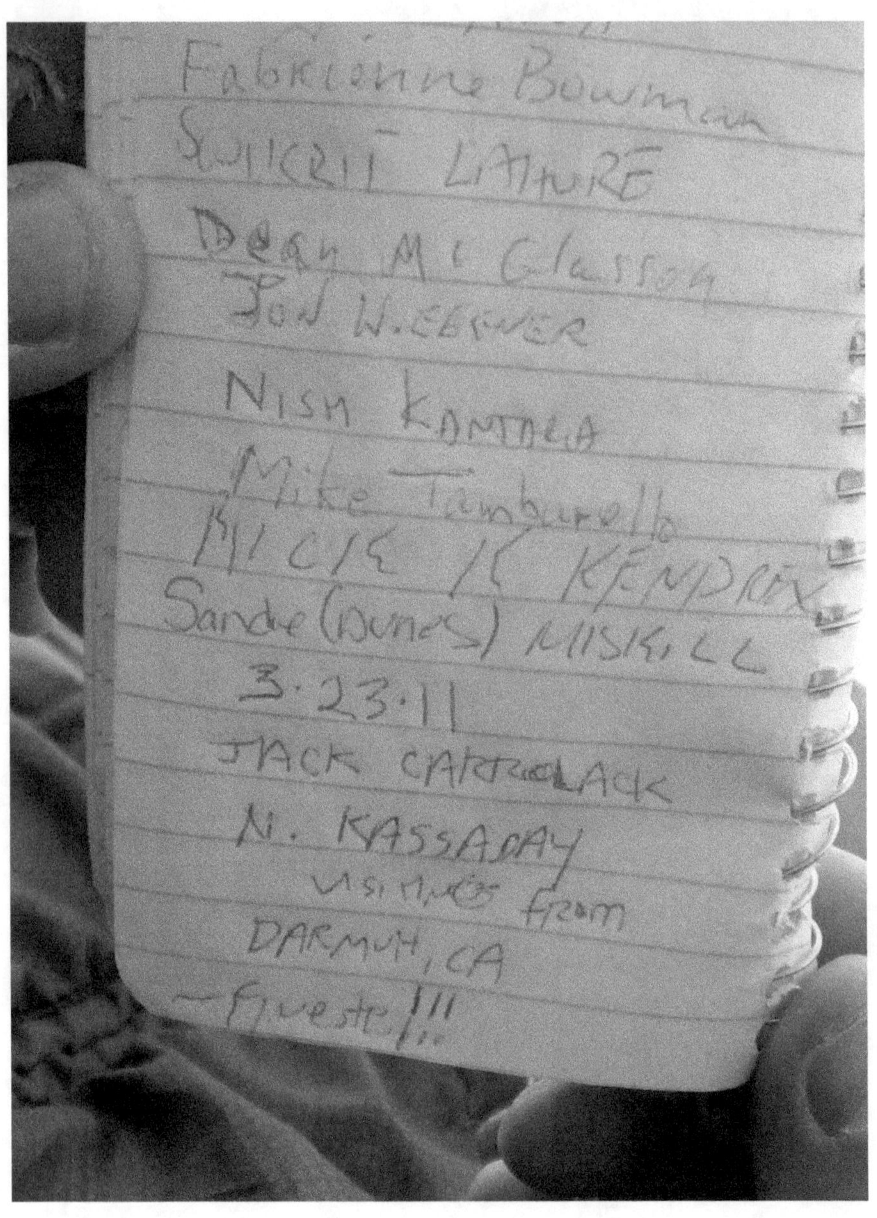
Mike Tamburello
3·23·11
N. KASSADAY
visiting from

Mojave National Preserve

This vast and special park sits near the California/Nevada border and sprawls along the outskirts of towns as weird and varied as Primm, Barstow and Needles. Its peaks are both fabulous and obscure. This lonely but lovely part of the Mojave Desert is, as they say, "in the middle of nowhere." Primitive camping is available and highly aesthetic. Much of the area is managed by the National Park Service.

This section features some peaks that are not technically part of the Preserve, though they are close enough (and possess enough of the Preserve's spirit) to be included. The region is hot, and the vast majority of the peaks here are best hiked during the cold months.

The northern part of the Preserve hosts one of the largest and most dense Joshua Tree forests in the world. It is fabulous. It also contains Clark Mountain, whose summit offers outstanding views of the surrounding area.

Near the Preserve's eastern border are the New York Mountains, an impressive granite range of rugged peaks. Just to the north of the main New York Mountains cluster, one will find Castle Peaks, a group of crags readily visible from I-15 between Mountain Pass and Primm, Nevada, which offers interesting technical climbing opportunities. Further south in the Preserve can be found some good caving (some commercialized, some wild) in the Providence Mountains, including Mitchell Caverns, where scenes from the Oliver Stone film "The Doors" were shot.

Kelso Dunes, contained within an area called the Devil's Playground, is a vast expanse of sand dunes located in the southern portion of the Preserve. Kelso Dunes are the highest dunes in California. Also located in this vicinity are a few lava tubes. Cool stuff.

Additionally, the area has a rich mining history, as evidenced by a huge number of abandoned mines (stay out!) and some historical buildings (including an old train station, which has since been converted into a visitor center).

In the central part of the preserve lies the sprawling mass of Cima Dome. While others disagree, some geologists say that Cima Dome is all that remains of an ancient mountain range in its last stages of decay and erosion. The huge rounded hump of Cima Dome can be clearly viewed while traveling on I-15 between Baker, California and Mountain Pass.

Northern Kelbaker Road

This section of Kelbaker Road starts in Baker, California and runs generally southeast to Kelso, where you'll find the park's visitor center in a quaint old train station. The peaks in this subsection are arranged roughly west-to-east.

"Cairned Ridge Peak" (1,791)
This minor peak lies close to CA-127 north of Baker, California. The peak has a neat summit ridge with cool, craggy views.

-WGS84 Lat: 35.3800 deg N Lon: -116.0825 deg W
*-II, Class 2 via Northern Aspect ***

Otto Mountain (1,715)
This small mountain sits just northwest of Baker, California. The northeast slope makes for a pleasant hike to a neat viewpoint.

-WGS84 Lat: 35.2775 deg N Lon: -116.0984 deg W
*-I, Class 2 via Northeast Slope ***

Nickel Mountain (1,393)
Near the bottom of the east ridge, look for several funky Explorer Troop plaques that have been placed on the mountain. The ridge, by the way, has surprisingly nice rock for an otherwise rather rubble-covered mountain.

The peak sits on the western edge of Baker, right next to I-15. Park on the shoulder of the paved roadway (not I-15!) and head up.

-WGS84 Lat: 35.2614 deg N Lon: -116.0911 deg W
*-I, Class 2 via East Ridge **

Squat Hill (1,138)
Super lame. Initially approached as per Cowhole Mountain, or approached as Hanks Mountain. Either way, the small peak is a couple miles south of Baker, and readily gained from Kelbaker Road.

-WGS84 Lat: 35.2415 deg N Lon: -116.0697 deg W
*-I, Class 2 from any direction **

Hanks Mountain (1,522)
Desert rat Andy Smatko once dubbed this peak Lost Thing Mountain. The southeast ridge was mostly solid and surprisingly fun, despite its brevity. Initially approached as per Cowhole Mountain (or directly from Kelbaker Road).

-WGS84 Lat: 35.2401 deg N Lon: -116.0415 deg W
*-I, Class 2-3 via Southeast Ridge ***

Little Cowhole Mountain (1,699)
Cowhole Mountain is a better mountain than *Little* Cowhole Mountain. They can be done together in a half-day. Approach via the same network of dirt roads as Cowhole Mountain.

-WGS84 Lat: 35.1772 deg N Lon: -116.0086 deg W
*-I, Class 2 via North Slope ***

Cowhole Mountain (2,250)
The peak is situated to the southeast of Baker, California, south of Kelbaker Road. Take Kelbaker Road for less than 0.5 mile to a dirt road on the right. From here, a network of decent dirt roads takes you close to the peak.

-WGS84 Lat: 35.1353 deg N Lon: -115.9941 deg W
*-II, Class 2-3 via Northwest Ridge ***
*-II, Class 3 via North Face ***

Old Dad Mountain (4,120)
The south ridge offers a more stimulating summit route than the meager east face gully described here. Unfortunately, I haven't yet done the south ridge.

-WGS84 Lat: 35.1013 deg N Lon: -115.8611 deg W
*-II, Class 2-3 via East Face Gully ****

Crater 3,152
A good (albeit sandy) dirt road leads to the southern base of the crater off Kelbaker Road, roughly halfway between Baker and Kelso. Outstanding camping (in dry conditions) can also be found here.

-WGS84 Lat: 35.1877 deg N Lon: -115.8278 deg W
*-I, Class 1 via North Slope **
*-I, Class 2 via South Face **

Crater 3,221

This peak is approached as per Crater 3,152. There's an awesome lava flow from the blown-out crater. This and Crater 3,152 lie to the north of Kelbaker Road.

-WGS84 Lat: 35.1805 deg N Lon: -115.8170 deg W
-I, Class 1 via North Ridge **
-I, Class 1 via Crater Breach **

Kelso Peak (4,746)

Kelso Peak is a fine little peak that offers stunning views of the bulk of Mojave National Preserve. On clear days the views extend on to Charleston Peak (outside of Las Vegas), Telescope Peak (in Death Valley), Mount San Gorgonio (in southern California), and to points in between, like Kingston Peak and the Avawatz Mountains. Along the route to this peak, the desert visitor might expect to stumble across a beautiful granite arch. Worth seeing!

From Baker, California, cross over I-15 and head south for 23.2 miles on Kelbaker Road. As Kelbaker passes underneath a set of power lines, pull off the road at a large, dirt pull-out on the right. From the dirt pull-out an old jeep track heads off roughly southeast. A hundred yards from the pull-out, the track is blocked by some wilderness boundary signs. From the wilderness boundary signs, Kelso Peak is the obvious high peak to the south.

Hiking the dirt track for about 3 miles, it will land (and probably lose) you in a wash near the base of the foothills north of the peak. Although any number of possible paths will put you where you eventually need to be, hike south to a prominent canyon that cuts southwest between the northernmost foothill north of Kelso and the prominent foothill immediately north of Kelso. Getting into the canyon, follow it initially southwest (passing the John Doll big game guzzler) and then more southerly, climbing up over a short man-made wall, toward the peak, which will soon come into view. (Oh yeah, 0.25 mile or less south of the guzzler, keep your eyes peeled for the awesome arch mentioned before. It's on the right side of the wash as you head up-canyon.)

Shortly after the guzzler, wall and arch, Kelso Peak will again come into view behind the foothills you've been passing under. A large bowl on the peak's northwest face will be presented. As you approach the base of the peak, the wash splinters off a bit. Make your way to the base of Kelso's northwest face. Once there, either head directly up the bowl (class 2) or up the ridges (class 2) on either side. Once atop the ridges, scramble the last few feet to the summit. The far-reaching views are unforgettable.

The roundtrip is about seven miles, with a touch over 1,000 feet of gain.

-WGS84 Lat: 35.1048 deg N Lon: -115.7247 deg W
-II, Class 2 via North Slopes **

Southern Kelbaker Road

This section of Kelbaker Road starts in Kelso, California (where you'll find the park's visitor center) and runs generally south to its terminus at I-40. The peaks in this subsection are arranged south-to-north.

Kelso Dunes Highpoint (3,113)

What could be more sandy than a hike up a towering dune! There's excellent free (primitive) camping at its base, too.

Drive south from Kelso to a graded dirt road heading west directly toward the dunes.

-WGS84 Lat: 34.9035 deg N Lon: -115.7181 deg W

-II, Class 1 via Southwest Ridge ****

Descending the southwest ridge of Kelso Dunes Highpoint

Halloran Springs & Halloran Summit

The peaks in this section are located close to I-15. They are arranged here south-to-north.

Squaw Tit (3,950)

A good dirt road, approached as per Sawtooth, runs to within a mile of the southeast side of the mountain. I once found a large and well-preserved desert tortoise shell near the base of the peak.

-WGS84 Lat: 35.3626 deg N Lon: -115.8320 deg W

*-I, Class 1 from the Southeast Slopes **

Sawtooth (4,124)

A good dirt road (from Halloran Summit Road, off of I-15) leads to within 0.25 mile of the base of this tiny but striking peak. A large window in the summit block makes this peak stand out, as does its very steep, crumbly faces. The easiest route up the peak is via the northeast face. Although it's steep and exposed, the rock on that route tends to be decent. A scary knife-edge is crossed on the way to the summit. If this route was even *twice* as long as it actually is, the peak would be a desert classic. Sadly, it's super-short, and the thrill is over rather quickly.

-WGS84 Lat: 35.3711 deg N Lon: -115.8048 deg W

*-I, Class 3-4 via Northeast Face ****

Sawtooth from the northeast

Negro Head (4,185)

Negro Head is a short scramble from the dirt road between it and I-15 near Halloran Summit. It is a recognizable landmark along I-15, northeast of Baker.

-WGS84 Lat: 35.3979 deg N Lon: -115.8320 deg W

*-I, Class 3 via Northeast Ridge **

*-I, Class 3-4 via Southeast Face **

"Unnamed Benchmark" (4,750)

An old dirt road (gained via the Halloran Summit Road off of I-15) leads to within 0.2 mile of the summit on the northeast side. The peak is named for the unnamed benchmark that resides on its summit.

-WGS84 Lat: 35.4153 deg N Lon: -115.8178 deg W

*-I, Class 1 via Northeast Slope **

Solomons Knob (4,474)

This peak is near Turquoise Mountain. Approach initially by leaving I-15 at Halloran Springs Road (not to be confused with Halloran *Summit* Road, to the east) and head north. A dirt road will eventually leave the pavement and lead toward the peak.

-WGS84 Lat: 35.4256 deg N Lon: -115.8431 deg W

*-I, Class 2-3 via Northwest Face **

Turquoise Mountain (4,511)

The super-lazy (or mega-unmotivated) can drive a service road all the way to the top. Approach as if you're going to Solomons Knob, instead following the paved road all the way up.

-WGS84 Lat: 35.4358 deg N Lon: -115.9231 deg W

*-I, Class 1 from paved service road **

Cima Road

Cima Road runs southeast from I-15 (northeast of Baker) to its terminus at the ghostly ruins of Cima. Peaks in this subsection are arranged approximately south-to-north.

Wildcat Butte (5,179)

This little butte is due south of the summit of Cima Dome. It makes for a logical bonus peak after snagging the Dome.

-WGS84 Lat: 35.2434 deg N Lon: -115.5852 deg W

*-I, Class 2 from any direction **

Cima Dome (5,744)

This giant, low-angle mound is seen by countless people mindlessly blowing through I-15 on their way to and from Vegas. It's a surreal peak studded by Joshua trees and not much else. I found no cairn or register atop the indistinct highpoint.

Although Cima Dome can be approached from any direction, I found it pleasant enough to approach from the powerline road a few miles south of the summit. That approach leaves nearby Wildcat Butte as a logical bonus peak.

-WGS84 Lat: 35.2894 deg N Lon: -115.5853 deg W

*-II, Class 1 via South Slope ***

Teutonia Peak (5,725)

"Congratulations. You have reached obscurity." - Teutonia Peak summit register entry

Teutonia Peak is believed by some to be the last few granite crags poking out of an old, eroded and vanishing range, the last protuding fingers of rock not yet disappeared into the rounded and eroded Cima Dome.

Easy access to the mountain's route-laden three "summits" provides a good variety of scrambles and climbs on decent granite. From the summits, distant views of Telescope Peak and Charleston Peak, and closer, Clark Mountain, New York Mountain, and others, greet the random desert visitor.

The summit register is usually found on the central summit, which just barely scrapes by as the highest. Historically, the register entries are among some of the most bizarre I've ever come across. Weird drawings and odd poems seem to rendezvous here, with only the occasional legible, coherent and rational entry thrown into the mix.

To get there from Las Vegas, Nevada, take I-15 south into California. Passing Primm, NV, look for the Nipton Road exit (exit 286, just before Mountain Pass) and take it. Cross over the highway and take Nipton Road east for 3.5 miles until you reach the signed Ivanpah Road. Turn right and head south-ish on Ivanpah Road 1.5 miles to the signed Morning Star Mine Road. Turn right. After nearly ten miles, you will come to a stop sign, which also serves as a junction for Morning Star Mine Road, Kelso Cima Road, and Cima Road. Hang a direct right onto Cima Road. After first passing a few abandoned buildings, at 6.3 miles you will come to the signed dirt parking area (on the left) for Teutonia Peak. Teutonia Peak is the rather unimpressive cluster of crags to the left (southwest).

Alternatively, you can also continue south on I-15 past Mountain Pass and head for Baker, CA. Before reaching Baker, leave the highway at the signed Cima Road exit (exit 272, only a few miles past Mountain Pass). Once on Cima Road, head southeast for 11.3 miles to the signed trailhead on the west side of the road.

From the trailhead, follow the trail for less than a mile as it heads southwest across the desert, through the Joshua forest, and past a couple of mines to the base of Teutonia Peak. Although appearing from the trailhead as a small mountain, as you approach its flanks you will see that Teutonia Peak is more of a collection of crags on the northern slopes of Cima Dome. Not immediately apparent from the trail, once the "summit" is gained, one will notice that the mountain is comprised of three somewhat distinct "summits"—a north, a central, and a south. Again, the central is the highest.

Since the routes are various and worthy, I will describe a few usable routes to the three summits, including a subsidiary crag just north of the north summit that I felt to be the best of all.

The roundtrip is no more than 2.5 miles with 700 feet of elevation gain.

To get to the North Summit: Continue on the trail as it winds its way up onto the north ridge of the peak. After only a mile or so from the trailhead, the trail ends at a sort of saddle. There should be a cairn prominently displayed here. Immediately to the left is the aforementioned subsidiary crag, and immediately to the right is the north summit. Backtrack a few feet and look for a use trail that heads southwest along the north side of the north summit. Follow the use trail a short distance (less than 50 feet) until it leads you left to a kind of cave in the rocks. Sticking your head into the cave you will see that the route continues up a low class 5 chimney for maybe 15-20 feet. Climb the chimney. Once at the top, squeeze out and carefully make your way across class 2-3 terrain to the highpoint of the north summit, which is marked with a cairn.

To get to the Subsidiary Crag: From the saddle where the trail ends, the subsidiary crag is the precariously balanced boulder sitting atop the somewhat sheer protrusion above and to the immediate left. Backtrack a hundred feet or so on the trail and find yourself on the other side of the crag. From here, look for the path of least resistance. It involves a couple of class 3 moves up to a narrow ledge that you must lie down on and scooch a short distance (5 feet) across to a weird ramp-dihedral formation that you pull yourself up onto and then climb up. Go around a couple of quick bends and look up at the remaining 15 feet of impossible rock that leads up to the highpoint. Now work your way to the left and crawl up onto a short (10 feet) but narrow (3 inches) and fairly exposed (100 feet) fin of rock that juts out below the highest (summit) boulder above you. At the end of the fin, stand up on the 3 inches of exposed rock fin and you will see that your head should be just about eye level with the top of the summit boulder. Look for handholds and hoist yourself up to the top. The route is easier than it sounds, but not for those fearful of exposure.

To get to the Central Summit: From the aforementioned saddle between the north summit and the subsidiary crag, drop slightly east and head cross-country across, over and around boulders and then brushy terrain. Follow the crags to your right and look for a prominent notch between two obvious blocky crags ahead. There should be a cairn marking the bottom of a brushy, bouldery ramp leading up to the notch. Once the notch is gained, negotiate class 3 boulders and then a class 4 ramp section up and to the left until you see a class 2 ramp heading back to the right toward an obvious wide crack blocking further progress. Step or jump across the crack to a nearby boulder, then work your way upward over class 2-3 terrain to the summit.

To get to the South Summit: From the top of the aforementioned notch between the middle and south summits, follow class 3 terrain to the east/southeast and to the summit cairn.

-WGS84 Lat: 35.3001 deg N Lon: -115.5638 deg W
*-I, Class 3 to South Summit ****
*-I, Class 4 to Subsidiary Crag ****
*-I, Class 4 to Central Summit ****
*-I, YDS 5.2 to North Summit ****

Kessler Peak (6,163)

Kessler is the highpoint of the Ivanpah Mountains. It sits across the roadway from Teutonia Peak. Anticipating a roundtrip of 2 miles and just over a thousand feet of gain, Kessler's okay summit views are made-up for by the interesting granitic terrain encountered on its northwest face. Pick a line (class 2 to short class 5 can easily be found); just about any will do.

To get there, leave I-15 at exit 272 and follow the paved road south to a point along the roadway that seems about right. You can start hiking from there.

-WGS84 Lat: 35.3151 deg N Lon: -115.5294 deg W
*-I, Class 3 via Northwest Buttress ***

New York Mountains

The peaks in this subsection are arranged generally south-to-north. Although Hart Peak and a couple of others in and around the Castle Mountains are not part of the New York Mountains (as they sit to the east of the larger range), they are included in this subsection for convenience.

New York Mountains Highpoint (7,532)

This is a desert classic, and the 32nd most prominent peak in California. Climb it some wet spring when Carruthers Canyon is flowing! The final summit scramble is great fun too.

Get there by leaving I-15 at the Nipton Road exit. From Nipton Road, turn right onto Ivanpah Road, which is followed into the New York Mountains. From there, look for the New York Mountains Road. This will lead to Carruthers Canyon. The old mining road leading into Carruthers Canyon gets extremely rough. It is best hiked.

-WGS84 Lat: 35.2587 deg N Lon: -115.3112 deg W
-II, Class 3 via Carruthers Canyon ****

Barnwell Benchmark (5,150)

Barnwell Benchmark, just east of the townsite of Barnwell (where Hart Mine Road and Ivanpah Road intersect), is a short hike from Hart Mine Road.

-WGS84 Lat: 35.2943 deg N Lon: -115.2141 deg W
-I, Class 1 via South Slopes *

Linder Peak (5,580)

Linder Peak, the highpoint of the Castle Mountains, has 981' of prominence. It is an easy bonus peak after Castle Mountain (to the north), given the jeep road that goes to the northern base of the peak.

-WGS84 Lat: 35.3014 deg N Lon: -115.0919 deg W
-II, Class 2 via North Face **

"Castle Mountain" (5,492)

This well-guarded, aesthetic peak in the Castle Mountains sits between Linder Peak and Hart Peak. Decent jeep roads get one quite close to the peak on its northwest side.

-WGS84 Lat: 35.3122 deg N Lon: -115.0862 deg W
-II, Class 2 via Northwest Face **

Hart Peak (5,543)

In his classic desert peakbagging guidebook, *Desert Summits*, Andy Zdon has this to say about Hart Peak: "This sharp, volcanic peak is one of the more interesting in appearance within the region...Only sparse information is available on this peak."

With a short approach of about a mile, and perhaps a thousand feet of elevation gain, the only real work involved in getting to Hart Peak's summit is finding a break in the complex cliffs, ribs, fins, dry falls, caves, dead ends, arches, alcoves and other geologic obstacles taking residence on the upper mountain.

Zdon says that there is a reported class 2-3 weakness on the north slope of the peak, which is accessed from the obvious saddle to the north of the peak. The south side of the peak also has a reported class 2 weakness. Or you can try one of the sweet, direct lines I took on the northwest face—lines from class 2-5 can be found—one has only to look hard enough for the terrain one desires. Part of the fun of Hart's northwest face is the route-finding, never particularly hard but always entertaining.

There are two good options for getting to the peak. If coming from Las Vegas, Nevada, option #2 is faster. It's also better for passenger cars.

Option #1: Follow the directions given for Castle Peak to the junction of Ivanpah Road and Hart Mine Road. Hang a left and follow Hart Mine Road (high clearance suggested in good conditions; a good walking stick in bad) for 8.2 miles until you come to a stop sign and an intersection with a very well-graded dirt road. This is Walking Box Ranch Road. Hang a left and follow Walking Box Ranch Road for 4.2 miles to a small dirt road heading off to the right. You'll know you're in the area because Hart Peak will be the obvious eye-directing peak a mile or so to the east/northeast. Either park just off the road on this minor dirt road, or follow it for 0.5 mile and find a good place to park. Consider this the trailhead.

Option #2: From US-95 in Searchlight, Nevada (between Las Vegas and Henderson, NV and Needles, CA), turn onto SR-64 (Nipton Road) and follow it for 6.9 miles to a signed junction with Walking Box Ranch Road. From the junction, you'll be able to see Hart Peak as the distinctive peak to the south. Turn left onto Walking Box Ranch Road and follow it for 12.9 miles to a minor dirt road heading off to the left. This point will be immediately adjacent to the southwest side of Hart Peak, perhaps a mile away from the mountain. You can park here or head down the dirt road for 0.5 mile then park. A low-rider could make it to this junction in standard conditions.

To climb the peak, head cross-country for a mile or so to the base of the mountain. You'll be looking up at the northwest face. Although the upper portion of the mountain is essentially cliffy, you'll notice a steep weakness on the northwest face.

Working the weakness directly, you'll note that it's not as steep as it appeared from below, and that it forms into a sort of gully as you ascend. You can follow this weakness (class 2-3) to a shallow saddle between the summit (to the left) and something resembling a sub-peak (to the right). From there, follow your nose (class 2) to the summit.

Although impossible to describe in any real detail, you can alternatively head up along the more strenuous terrain to the right of the weakness, following any line that looks tempting. Taking this path, it's unlikely you'll find a way up easier than 3rd class, though I can confirm that it can be done at 4th class. As stated earlier, part of the fun of Hart Peak's northwest face is route-finding your way through the various obstacles along the way. Have fun and pick your own way.

-WGS84 Lat: 35.3430 deg N Lon: -115.0797 deg W

*-I, Class 2-3 via Northwest Face ***

As viewed to the north-northeast from Castle Peak (Dove Benchmark).
Note the GPS track on the map.

Castle Peak (5,834)

Castle Peak is one of the more technically challenging summits in the Mojave Desert region, due in no small part to steep faces and crumbly rock. Rising as a small mountain mass above the surrounding desert washes and hills of northern Mojave National Preserve, Castle Peak (also known as Castle Peaks) consists of a cluster of rather enticing and aesthetic volcanic spires. The summit of the highest spire in the primary Castle Peaks cluster, once marked by a now-missing "Dove" benchmark, requires a short bit of 5.2 climbing on poor rock.

Castle Peak lies at the northern end of the very picturesque and craggy New York Mountains. Not quite as picturesque or craggy as the central or southern portion of the range, excepting Castle Peak itself, the northern portion of the range primarily hosts your classic desert scene of washes and cacti and jackrabbits, not to mention miles of Joshua trees.

This fine little peak and its cluster of pinnacles is clearly visible as one drives between Los Angeles, California and Las Vegas, Nevada on I-15, right around Mountain Pass and the state line. Judging by the rough dirt roads on the approach, requiring a high clearance vehicle in the best of conditions, the mountain's lack of trails, the poor quality of the rock, and the technical difficulties required to reach the highpoint, Castle Peak is not commonly climbed.

The lesser spires of the Castle Peak cluster also hold climbing potential, though information on their routes is sparse-to-non-existent. They all have bad rock.

To get to the peak: From I-15 near Primm, Nevada and the California state line, get off at the Nipton Road exit (exit 286). Nipton Road is in California, just a few miles over the state line. Head east on Nipton Road 3.5 miles to the signed Ivanpah Road. Ivanpah Road takes you into Mojave National Preserve. Once on Ivanpah Road, follow it for 16.7 miles, ignoring the main turn-off (Morning Star Mine Road) for the Preserve and the fact that the road soon becomes graded dirt (generally in good shape; sometimes not), to the signed Hart Mine Road. Hang a left and follow Hart Mine Road (high clearance suggested in good conditions; a good walking stick in bad) for approx. 4.7 miles until you come to a dirt road branching off to the left. (Actually, in the 4.5 to 5.5 mile stretch, there are two dirt roads branching off to the left–either will work.) Get onto the left-branching dirt road and follow it nearly four miles to Castle Peak, the obvious collection of crags in the distance. Though some minor dirt roads branch off here and there, a little trial and error and basic route-finding skills, staying on the most traveled dirt road headed toward the peak, will land you at a wilderness boundary sign in a wash nestled amongst some hills. At the wilderness boundary, Castle Peak will be out of view behind one of the hills to the north/northeast. This is the trailhead.

From the wilderness boundary, follow the old and fading road for about 1.5 miles to a minor saddle next to a cluster of granite boulders on your left. From the saddle, Castle Peak comes clearly into view about 0.5 mile away to the northeast.

This is an ideal opportunity to identify which of the five visible spires is the highest. Though not apparent from the saddle, the highest (Dove Benchmark) is the second spire from the left. The left-most spire, incidentally, is North Castle Butte, about 0.75 mile north of Castle Peak.

Dropping from the saddle, continue along the dirt road to a point that feels about as close at it's going to get to the peak. Hike cross-country toward the highest spire. In case you forgot to identify the highest one from the saddle, it may also be recognized as the easiest-appearing high spire of the group. Its right (southeast) face/slope appears at a glance to be a walk-up, and practically is.

When you get to a likely looking spot, head up the desert slope to the saddle connecting the highpoint with the smaller crag to its south. From the saddle, head directly up the obvious class 2-3 crumbly slope/face to the left (northeast). Route-finding is not hard—just follow the path of least resistance. About 200-300 feet up, your upward progress will abruptly come to a halt. You've reached the summit block.

A quick review of the terrain on the summit block will reveal that it is near-vertical-to-overhanging on all sides, with only a couple of obvious weaknesses. The easiest appears to be an open book/crack on the east side of the block. Traverse to the right and around to the block's east side. An obvious weakness presents itself.

Being mindful of the poor quality of the rock, ascend the weakness through its 20 feet of difficulties. The bottom portion of the weakness (the crux; YDS 5.2) consists of an open book. After about 10 feet, a crack develops and the climbing becomes even easier (class 4). Above the major difficulties, a short bit of class 3-4 scrambling leads to easier scrambling and then the summit.

Roundtrip numbers are about 4 miles with 1,000 feet of gain.

-WGS84 Lat: 35.3695 deg N Lon: -115.1615 deg W

-II, YDS 5.2 to Dove Benchmark ****

"North Castle Butte" (5,894)

Those with extra energy after Dove Benchmark may want to wander a half mile to the northeast to tag the highpoint of the Castle Peaks. It can be bagged 4th class via a 15-foot crack on its south face. The rock is loose, and some might want a rope.

-WGS84 Lat: 35.3754 deg N Lon: -115.1572 deg W

-II, Class 4 via South Face ***

Crescent Peak (5,999)

Crescent Peak is a mostly forgettable mountain near Castle Peak and McCullough Mountain. Although a part of the New York Mountains, it is actually located in Nevada.

-WGS84 Lat: 35.4767 deg N Lon: -115.1293 deg W

*-I, Class 2 via Southwest Ridge **

Hole-in-the-Wall

The peaks in this subsection are clustered around the fantastically cool Hole-in-the-Wall area. Black Canyon Road is used to access this area. The road begins at Kelso Cima Road and runs initially east before turning south (and eventually becoming Essex Road) as it flows to I-40. The peaks are arranged here south-to-north.

Wild Horse Mesa (5,626)

The summit of this sprawling mesa affords excellent views of Mitchell Point and Edgar Peak in the nearby Providence Mountains. One of the opening scenes in Oliver Stone's 1991 film, *The Doors*, was shot from the top of this mountain.

-WGS84 Lat: 35.0467 deg N Lon: -115.4528 deg W

*-I, Class 3 via East Ridge ***

*-I, Class 3 via East Face ***

Views southwest to Mitchell Point (right) and Edgar Peak (left) from the top of Wild Horse Mesa.

Tortoise Shell Mountain (4,609)

This is a mostly forgettable peak. I suppose its isolation and loneliness make it a rewarding endeavor to those who dig that sort of thing, which, of course, I *do*.

-WGS84 Lat: 35.0392 deg N Lon: -115.3361 deg W

*-I, Class 2 via Southeast Slope **

"South Tower" (5,140)

Although maps show North Tower to be higher, South Tower sure appears to be a touch taller. Both this and North Tower are due west of Barber Benchmark.

-WGS84 Lat: 35.0478 deg N Lon: -115.4292 deg W

*-I, Class 2 via North Slope **

"North Tower" (5,108)

Andy Smatko named this small peak in 1970. It and South Tower can be combined in just a couple hours roundtrip from a car parked in Wild Horse Canyon.

-WGS84 Lat: 35.0511 deg N Lon: -115.4283 deg W

*-I, Class 3 via West Slope ***

North Tower from South Tower

Barber Benchmark (5,504)

While the peak's nothing spectacular, Hole-in-the-Wall is definitely worth visiting. To get you started on the Hole-in-the-Wall route, follow the Rings Trail (picked up near the Hole-in-the-Wall visitor center) in Banshee Canyon to a point immediately before the first set of rings. As you look down-canyon just before the rings, look for a class 4 groove in the wall to your right. Head up this for 30 feet or so then work right to some slabs that present a weakness leading to somewhat easier ground above. Above that, trend left for a couple hundred yards to gain the first plateau above the Hole-in-the-Wall cliffs.

-WGS84 Lat: 35.0554 deg N Lon: -115.4125 deg W
*-I, Class 2-3 via East Face **
*-II, Class 4 via Hole-in-the-Wall ****

Just above the point where one escapes Banshee Canyon in Hole-in-the-Wall

Woods Mountains Highpoint (5,590)
A good dirt road takes you right to the base of the northwest ridge. From there, pleasant scrambling leads to the unnamed highpoint of this range.

-WGS84 Lat: 35.0670 deg N Lon: -115.3647 deg W
-I, Class 2-3 via Northwest Ridge **

The Tawoo Peak summit register in January 2010

Twin Buttes – South (5,498)
Although not as fine a scramble as Twin Buttes - North, it is a very fun outing itself. Recommended! When I reached the summit alone one afternoon, I found the 41-year old register had only been signed once since the 'first recorded ascent' party left it in May 1969. The original party dubbed the butte Woota Peak.

-WGS84 Lat: 35.0908 deg N Lon: -115.3565 deg W
-II, Class 2-3 via North Slope ***

*-II, Class 3 via West Slope ****

Twin Buttes – North (5,649)

When Andy Smatko and his partners made the first ascent of this peak in May 1969, they dubbed it Tawoo Peak. My partner and I learned this when we made the second ascent of the peak 41 years later! It was terrific. The tiny summit is a fine perch from which to take in the high desert surroundings. And getting there is no walk in the park!

-WGS84 Lat: 35.0985 deg N Lon: -115.3613 deg W
*-II, Class 3-4 via North Face *****
*-II, Class 4-5 via Southeast Face ****

Table Top (6,177)

Good dirt roads lead you to the south side of the mountain. From there, a fine loop of Table Top and the Twin Buttes can be done in a few hours.

-WGS84 Lat: 35.1099 deg N Lon: -115.3677 deg W
*-I, Class 2 via South Face ***
*-I, Class 2-3 via Southeast Face ***

Matthew H. on the tiny summit of Twin Buttes–North. The view looks west.

Providence Mountains

The Providence Mountains, one of the most varied and striking ranges in the region, parallel the Kelso Cima Road and the southern portion of Kelbaker

Road, both of which run to the west of the range. The peaks are arranged here south-to-north.

Fountain Peak (6,988)

This is a terrific peak, one of the best in the region.

Drive there as if you were driving to Edgar Peak.

-WGS84 Lat: 34.9465 deg N Lon: -115.5375 deg W

-III, Class 3-4 via South Ridge from East Slope ****

-III, Class 3-4 via North Ridge from Edgar Peak ***

Edgar Peak (7,162)

While once descending this peak, my buddy Harlan took a big spill over a short rock band, somehow righting himself in mid-air just in time to save himself a broken neck. Pretty impressive, I think.

Leave I-40 at exit 100 and follow the paved road north to Providence Mountains State Recreation Area, which in recent years has not always been open to the public. The routes start from near the visitor center.

-WGS84 Lat: 34.9556 deg N Lon: -115.5363 deg W

-III, Class 2-3 via Southeast Slope **

-III, Class 3-4 via South Ridge from Fountain Peak ***

Columbia Mountain (5,672)

Taking good dirt roads to the base of this small peak, it's only about an hour's effort via the southeast face. My partner and I did it in 30 minutes car-to-car.

-WGS84 Lat: 35.0835 deg N Lon: -115.4728 deg W

-I, Class 1-2 via Southeast Face *

"Der Tooth" (5,800+)

Although the National Park Service recognizes this crag as 'Eagle Rocks', scrambler-types have been calling it Der Tooth since the late 60s. With some fine scrambling and climbing on its north face, if it was prominent enough to be a mountain (rather than just a crag), this would be a desert classic. Still, an ascent is a grand time, and the views are fabulous!

-WGS84 Lat: 35.1299 deg N Lon: -115.4473 deg W

-I, Class 4-5 via North Face ****

Mountain Pass

The peaks in this subsection are clustered around Mountain Pass, off of I-15 between Primm, Nevada and Baker, California. Here, they are arranged roughly south-to-north.

Striped Mountain (5,929)

Striped Mountain is near Kokoweef Peak and Kessler Peak. It is approached as if you were headed to Kokoweef Peak.

-WGS84 Lat: 35.3942 deg N Lon: -115.5311 deg W

*-I, Class 2 via East Ridge **

Der Tooth's class 4-5 north face route roughly follows the right skyline from about halfway up the crag.

Kokoweef Peak (6,088)

Supposedly there's a lost river of gold under this puppy. Google it.

Approach by leaving I-15 near Mountain Pass, taking the initially paved (then good dirt) Kokoweef Road generally south toward the peak. Be careful of private property as you near the peak.

-WGS84 Lat: 35.4200 deg N Lon: -115.4938 deg W

*-I, Class 2 via Northeast Slope **

*-I, Class 4 via East Headwall **

Mescal Range Highpoint (6,497)

I bagged this highpoint after work one afternoon while driving from Vegas to Los Angeles.

Initially approached as per Kokoweef Peak.

-WGS84 Lat: 35.4315 deg N Lon: -115.5460 deg W

*-I, Class 2 via East Ridge **

Mineral Hill (5,479)
For being a pretty lame summit, the views from the top are quite nice. A primitive dirt road picked up near Kokoweef Peak can actually be driven to the top, if one so chooses.

-WGS84 Lat: 35.4347 deg N Lon: -115.4769 deg W
*-I, Class 1 via West Slope **

"Climax Peak" (6,217)
This nice peak, named by Andy Smatko in 1978, is approached as per Mescal Range Highpoint (via a decent dirt road from the southeast). On my visit, I found no register sign-ins since 1987. Very good views from the top.

-WGS84 Lat: 35.4463 deg N Lon: -115.5339 deg W
*-I, Class 2 via South Ridge ***

Mohawk Hill (5,987)
One can easily walk the service road to the high summit with nice views of Clark Mountain and the Mescal Range highpoint. Mohawk Hill is north of I-15.

-WGS84 Lat: 35.4909 deg N Lon: -115.5580 deg W
*-I, Class 1 via Service Road **

Clark Mountain (7,929)
This is a fine mountain. I climbed it one spring during a fantastic wintry blizzard. It happens to be the 15th most prominent peak in California. There's a small plane crash on the mountain's flanks.

It is approached by leaving I-15 near Mountain Pass and following dirt roads to its base. The mountain is located north of I-15.

-WGS84 Lat: 35.5257 deg N Lon: -115.5888 deg W
*-II, Class 3 via East Ridge ****

"Coyote Peak" (5,278)
This mountain, northeast of Kokoweef Peak, has a dramatic appearance from I-15 near Nipton Road. From the vicinity of that junction, one can hike southwest through the desert (admiring some awesome displays of cactus blooms in spring) then pick one of several reasonable lines on the north face that lead to the top. The summit has excellent views.

-WGS84 Lat: 35.4392 deg N Lon: -115.4557 deg W
*-II, Class 2 via North Face ****

"Tess Mountain" (5,265)
This peak was named in 1983 by Andy Smatko and company. Upon my arrival to the summit in January 2011, I found the Smatko register, with no

sign-ins since their visit nearly 28 years before. A good dirt road leads from the rear parking lot of Whisky Pete's in Primm, Nevada to the toe of the peak's south ridge. Although the south ridge can also be climbed, my partner and I joyfully wandered the Zen garden-like southwest ridge to the top. From there, we hiked to the unnamed highpoint to the west, eventually dropping back down to the desert via a beautiful and sculpted wash between the two summits.

For purposes of general reference, this obscurity is near the California-Nevada border, a couple miles north of Clark Mountain.

-WGS84 Lat: 35.6123 deg N Lon: -115.5212 deg W
-II, Class 2 via Southwest Ridge ***

Outlying

The peaks in this subsection, though not technically a part of Mojave National Preserve, are noteworthy diversions while traveling near the western edge of the preserve on I-15 or along I-40 on the south side of the preserve. They are arranged here somewhat randomly.

Old Woman Statue (5,104)

This is the most technically challenging summit in the book. After a previous failed attempt, I recruited and returned with a brave and talented partner who gladly led what I lacked the nerve to lead and landed us safely on the summit.

After a pleasant, meandering hiking approach, a bit of class 3-4 scrambling near the base of this striking formation, which is visible from miles away, puts one at the base of a 70' open book/chimney feature (YDS 5.8). Once atop the pedestal at the top of that pitch, one is confronted with a short (30') but intimidating bolt ladder comprised of ancient, manky bolts that should not be trusted. A descent rappel is made from a bolt anchor on the summit.

-WGS84 Lat: 34.5198 deg N Lon: -115.1634 deg W
-III, YDS 5.8 C0 via the only feasible way ****

Elephant Mountain (2,674)

The summit of this eye-catching basalt mesa south of I-15, just west of Yermo, can easily be hiked (or driven to) via a 4WD service road.

-WGS84 Lat: 34.8860 deg N Lon: -116.8967 deg W
-I, Class 1 via Service Road *

Camp Rock (2,530)

Just off I-15 near Yermo, California, this short hike from Mule Canyon leads to an overlook of some fantastically colored rock.

In the classic Quentin Tarantino film Kill Bill Vol. 2, Uma Thurman's character, The Bride, stands on the summit of Camp Rock while looking down into Mule Canyon onto the trailer of her nemesis, Budd, as she plots his demise.

-WGS84 Lat: 34.9389 deg N Lon: -116.8395 deg W

*-I, Class 2 via West Saddle **

"Birthday of the Buddha Peak" (2,810)

This minor peak, immediately west of Camp Rock, makes for a very short, pleasant stroll on a cool summer morning.

-WGS84 Lat: 34.9394 deg N Lon: -116.8459 deg W

*-I, Class 1 via mining road from Mule Canyon- **

Cave Mountain (3,519)

Very impressive when traveling I-15 between Barstow and Las Vegas. Although it's tempting to approach it directly from I-15, it's more prudent to exit I-15 just northeast of the peak and take a couple miles of good dirt roads to the other side of the mountain.

-WGS84 Lat: 35.0709 deg N Lon: -116.3235 deg W

*-II, Class 2 via South Ridge ***

*-III, Class 3-4 via East Face ****

"Basin Peak" (1,441)

A minor peak easily accessed from the I-15/Basin Road exit near Cave Mountain. Park on the shoulder of the paved road and head up. The summit gives up nice views of the lonely desert spanning for countless miles around you.

-WGS84 Lat: 35.0992 deg N Lon: -116.2577 deg W

*-I, Class 2 via Northwest Slopes **

"Muppet Mountain" (3,323)

Muppet Mountain is closely southeast of Mount Walter. By going up and over a few bumps, the two can be easily combined in a short outing.

-WGS84 Lat: 34.8455 deg N Lon: -115.0258 deg W

*-II, Class 2 via Northwest Slopes **

"Mount Walter" (3,562)

Mount Walter is a nice peak with good views. It is most easily accessed from Mountain Springs Road, southeast of Goffs Butte. The peak has 823' of prominence.

-WGS84 Lat: 34.8504 deg N Lon: -115.0333 deg W

*-II, Class 2 via West Slopes ***

Goffs Butte (3,612)

This small mountain south of Goffs and north of I-40 (and southeast of Mojave National Preserve) is easily accessed by hiking a service road to the top. The mountain has 873' of prominence.

-WGS84 Lat: 34.8806 deg N Lon: -115.0683 deg W

*-II, Class 1 via service road ***

"El Tren Peak" (3,451)

El Tren Peak is east of Goffs Butte. From Mountain Springs Road, one can drive east on a gas pipeline road that leads over the saddle just north of the peak.

-WGS84 Lat: 34.8851 deg N Lon: -115.0340 deg W

*-I, Class 2 via North Slope **

"Whistle Peak" (3,159)

Whistle Peak is northeast of Goffs Butte. It is a short hike from the vicinity of Mountain Springs Road and the gas pipeline road.

-WGS84 Lat: 34.8977 deg N Lon: -115.0523 deg W

*-I, Class 2 via Southwest Slopes **

On the summit of Avawatz Mountains Highpoint

Avawatz Mountains Highpoint (6,154)

I put off doing this peak for many years because I thought it would be dull. As it turned out, it was a highly satisfying, lonely desert hike to a fine viewpoint. It also happens to be the 34th most prominent peak in California.

From Baker, California, follow SR-127 north for 19.1 miles to a dirt road on the left. Follow it as far as you're comfortable. 4WD will be needed after 5.5 miles or so, for a 100-yard stretch of gnarly stuff. After that, it's easier going all the way to a small parking area next to an antenna at 4,500 feet.

From the beginning of the 4WD spot, expect a roundtrip hike of 12 miles and 4,500 feet of elevation gain. Follow the road to the antenna. From there, follow the road another 0.5 mile (or slightly more) then cross left over a low ridge to a saddle and then scramble up the obvious white hill to catch the ridgeline to the summit (which is still two miles away).

-WGS84 Lat: 35.5126 deg N Lon: -116.3315 deg W
-III, Class 2 via Standard Route from the East ****

Shadow Mountain (4,197)
Out in the desert by Solomons Knob and Kingston Peak. Approached by leaving I-15 at exit 272 and heading north. Eventually, a dirt road branches off from the pavement and heads off toward the peak, which is clearly visible to the west.

-WGS84 Lat: 35.5693 deg N Lon: -115.7915 deg W
-I, Class 1 via Southwest Ridge *

Death Valley National Park

Another satisfying day high above Death Valley.

Panamint Range

The Panamint Range is the impossibly high-looking range towering to the west over the lowly depths of Death Valley. The Panamints are bordered by Death Valley to the east, Panamint Valley to the west, Towne Pass to the north, and miles upon miles of low mountains and obscure ranges to the south. The peaks are arranged here generally south-to-north.

Telescope Peak (11,049)

Telescope Peak is the highest point in Death Valley National Park. It is a classic summit whose views look east more than 11,000 vertical feet down to Badwater (-282 feet in elevation) and west to Mount Whitney (14,497 feet above sea level), the highest peak in the U.S. outside of Alaska. Telescope also ranks as the 7th most prominent peak in the entire state of California.

Drive or walk to Mahogany Flat (via Charcoal Kilns), which can be gotten to from either Panamint Valley or by leaving highway 190 east of Towne Pass and taking the Emigrant Pass road. From Mahogany Flat, follow the maintained trail to the top of the mountain. The views from the summit, and along the entire route, are breathtaking.

-WGS84 Lat: 36.1700 deg N Lon: -117.0892 deg W
-III, Class 1 via maintained trail ****

Bennett Peak (9,980)

Rogers Peak's southern neighbor, this peak is *barely* worth doing on its own; rather, it makes for a semi-worthy bonus peak while traveling to or from Telescope Peak.

-WGS84 Lat: 36.2065 deg N Lon: -117.0930 deg W
-II, Class 1-2 via North Slope *

Rogers Peak (9,994)

This is a semi-popular winter snow climb in Death Valley National Park. Approached as per Telescope Peak.

-WGS84 Lat: 36.2181 deg N Lon: -117.0858 deg W
-II, Class 1 via South Slope *

Wildrose Peak (9,064)

Wildrose Peak lies several miles north of Rogers Peak. With a maintained trail leading from the trailhead to the peak, and excellent summit views, it is another summit worth visiting. It has been many years since I was last there, but I think it's time I paid it another visit!

Wildrose Peak has over 1300' of prominence.

-WGS84 Lat: 36.2755 deg N Lon: -117.0789 deg W

*-II, Class 1 via Trail ****

"South Fork Peak" (6,444)

Named for South Fork Canyon, to the peak's south, this easy peak is a worthwhile endeavor while hiking the other easy highpoints in the vicinity.

-WGS84 Lat: 36.3490 deg N Lon: -117.0576 deg W

*-I, Class 1 via Northeast Slope **

Aguer Benchmark (6,428)

This is an easy, 10-minute diversion from the saddle between it and Aguereberry Point to the immediate east.

-WGS84 Lat: 36.3570 deg N Lon: -117.0526 deg W

*-I, Class 1 via East Slope **

Aguereberry Point (6,433)

I drove up here once to escape a nasty storm that was spawning flash floods down low that would eventually close CA-190 for a few days, and catch some sleep after a busy summer weekend in the Sierra. I was blown away by the majesty of the views. This is a wonderful spot, despite what it lacks as a mountaineering objective.

-WGS84 Lat: 36.3580 deg N Lon: -117.0481 deg W

*-I, Class 1 via Road *****

"Petes Peak" (6,075)

A striking peak in a striking position, this is a short, easy scramble from Aguereberry Point. Despite the looseness and unpleasantness of some of the rock, Petes Peak stands out for its appearance and its commanding presence over Death Valley, some 6,000 feet below the summit.

-WGS84 Lat: 36.3599 deg N Lon: -117.0379 deg W

*-I, Class 2 via West Face ****

Death Valley Junction

Death Valley Junction is a reformed ghost town at the CA-190/CA-127 crossroads north of Shoshone, California, located a few miles east of the park boundary along CA-190 near the Nevada border. With a neat old Opera House, a funky motel, and a restaurant I will not recommend, the place puts out enough weird vibes that you can't help but be drawn to it (or repelled from it).

The peaks in this subsection are arranged here roughly south-to-north.

Brown Peak (4,947)

We climbed this mountain one afternoon after waiting out a morning rainstorm inside the depths of nearby Plumbers Cave. You should have seen all the black widow spiders in the cave!

The peak is readily approached by driving a decent dirt road generally southwest from CA-127, west of Eagle Mountain. At a point that seems about right, park in a safe spot and head across the desert to the peak.

-WGS84 Lat: 36.1151 deg N Lon: -116.3855 deg W
-III, Class 2-3 via (the convoluted) Northwest Face **

Eagle Mountain (3,806)

Although not actually in Death Valley National Park, this awesome desert peak is close enough to the park (and Death Valley Junction) for me to situate it here in the book and still maintain a clear conscience.

It is approached via a short bit of decent dirt road heading north from CA-127 to a point just west of the summit. Although there are lots of cairns, a use trail and other signs of use along the route, take care with your route-finding.

-WGS84 Lat: 36.2113 deg N Lon: -116.3564 deg W
-II, Class 3 via West Face ****

"Slabby Acres Peak" (3,700)

This peak has nice views, despite its minor stature. It is a short but pleasant hike from Slabby Acres, along CA-190 west of Death Valley Junction.

-WGS84 Lat: 36.3163 deg N Lon: -116.5967 deg W
-I, Class 1 via North Slopes *

Devair Benchmark (4,423)

While a network of dirt roads heading south from CA-190 west of Death Valley Junction can take one close to the summit, it's a bit more adventurous to cross-country it from the informal campground known as Slabby Acres, northeast of the summit. Regardless, this is a neat area, if not particularly dramatic.

-WGS84 Lat: 36.3089 deg N Lon: -116.6466 deg W
-II, Class 1 via jeep roads **
-II, Class 2 from the northeast ***

Bat Mountain – South Summit (4,950)

Most people scrambling up Bat Mountain stop on the south summit, perhaps because some sources describe this as the highpoint. The north summit appears to be higher by some four feet, and both summits host registers. The south summit is the easier to reach, most enjoyably via the long southwest ridge directly from CA-190.

-WGS84 Lat: 36.3446 deg N Lon: -116.5039 deg W
*-II, Class 3 via Southwest Ridge ***
*-II, Class 3 via North Ridge from Main Summit ****

Bat Mountain (4,954)
Bat Mountain's big west face is impressive when viewed from CA-190. A scramble to the main summit via the south ridge and south summit is an enjoyable half-day out, though one must leave the crest at a point between the two summits and drop down a bit to the east in order to work around a troublesome tower. A nice loop can be completed by dropping into the bowl southeast of the main summit, working down to the desert, and then hiking out while paralleling the southwest ridge of the south summit on its east side.

Start hiking directly from highway 190, west of Death Valley Junction. The peak will be to the northeast. Neither Bat Mountain nor its prominent south summit lie within the boundaries of Death Valley National Park – but they're close!

-WGS84 Lat: 36.3542 deg N Lon: -116.5012 deg W
*-II, Class 3 via South Ridge from South Summit ****
*-II, Class 3-4 via Southeast Face ***

Funeral Mountains Wilderness Highpoint (5,340)
This interesting, rugged, steep and dangerous peak sits just northeast across CA-190 from Slabby Acres. With 1360' of prominence, it is a dominating peak with interesting route-finding required to climb it safely. We chose to descend the talus-heavy southeast face, figuring it to be safer than descending our ascent line up the southwest face.

-WGS84 Lat: 36.3749 deg N Lon: -116.5705 deg W
*-II, Class 2-3 via Southwest Face ****
*-II, Class 2-3 via Southeast Face ***

Pyramid Peak (6,703)
A big, colorful and imposing peak near Death Valley Junction, home of the Amargosa Opera House. It is the 24th most prominent peak in California. You approach it directly from CA-190, crossing open desert on foot to get to the base of the uphill stuff.

-WGS84 Lat: 36.3918 deg N Lon: -116.6123 deg W
*-III, Class 2 via Southeast Ridge ****

Daylight Pass

Daylight Pass is located northeast of Stovepipe Wells, along NV-374/Daylight Pass Road, near the Nevada border outside of Beatty, Nevada. The peaks in this subsection are arranged here roughly south-to-north.

Chloride Cliff (5,279)

The nearby (technical) Keane Canyon has some awesome mining relics in it from the Keane Wonder Mine, for those so inclined. (I'm told that Keane Canyon is now closed to visitation. This should not affect access to Chloride Cliff.)

The peak is initially approached by leaving NV-374 (Daylight Pass Road) near the California-Nevada border and following a dirt road initially south (and later southwest) toward the peak.

-WGS84 Lat: 36.6950 deg N Lon: -116.8802 deg W

*-I, Class 2 via Northeast Slope **

Death Valley Buttes (3,017)

The east ridge is a fun route up this rugged little mountain. Good views too. The summit has been marked with a benchmark stamped 'Red Top'.

I recommend you start hiking from the self-pay fee station parking lot at the junction of Daylight Pass Road and Daylight Pass Road Cut-off.

-WGS84 Lat: 36.7116 deg N Lon: -117.0045 deg W

*-II, Class 3 via East Ridge ****

Corkscrew Peak (5,804)

I climbed this in a heavy snowstorm one New Year's Day. Afterward, I drove down to Jubilee Mountain and hiked it under beautiful sunshine!

Drive west from Daylight Pass until you see the sign pointing out Corkscrew Peak to the northwest. Park near there, and start hiking.

-WGS84 Lat: 36.7706 deg N Lon: -117.0041 deg W

*-II, Class 2 via Southeast Slope ***

"Daylight Peak" (5,510)

This excellent viewpoint just west of Daylight Pass harbors 770' of prominence.

-WGS84 Lat: 36.7856 deg N Lon: -116.9453 deg W

*-II, Class 1-2 via East Slope ***

"The Loner" (4,663)

Located just inside of Nevada, this small peak lies closely off the highway, northeast of Daylight Pass.

-WGS84 Lat: 36.7968 deg N Lon: -116.9146 deg W

*-I, Class 1 via North Slope **

"Prospect Peak" (5,055)

Prospect Peak lies along NV-374 near the California-Nevada border, just north of Daylight Pass. The terrain on the southeast face is remarkably steep dirt and gravel, so it's a bit more pleasant to approach the summit via the east ridge.

-WGS84 Lat: 36.8110 deg N Lon: -116.9290 deg W

*-I, Class 2 via Southeast Face **

*-I, Class 2 via East Ridge ***

Bullfrog Mountain (4,757)

Bullfrog lies *just* within Death Valley National Park. After my beloved grandfather's death in February 2009, I hiked up the mountain and wrote a short tribute note to him in the summit register.

Bullfrog Mountain is initially approached as per Sawtooth Mountain and the other peaks above Rhyolite (and near Beatty, Nevada).

-WGS84 Lat: 36.9086 deg N Lon: -116.8821 deg W

*-I, Class 2 via Northeast Ridge ***

Titus Canyon Road

The peaks in this subsection, arranged here east-to-west, lie close to Titus Canyon Road, a scenic and interesting 27-mile-long one-way road between NV-374 (two miles east of the park boundary, and west of Beatty, Nevada) and northern Death Valley. The road must be driven east-to-west.

"Pot Peak" (5,252)

Pot Peak is south of Titus Canyon Road, just inside Nevada, very close to the California border.

-WGS84 Lat: 36.8223 deg N Lon: -116.9613 deg W

*-II, Class 1 via Northwest Aspect **

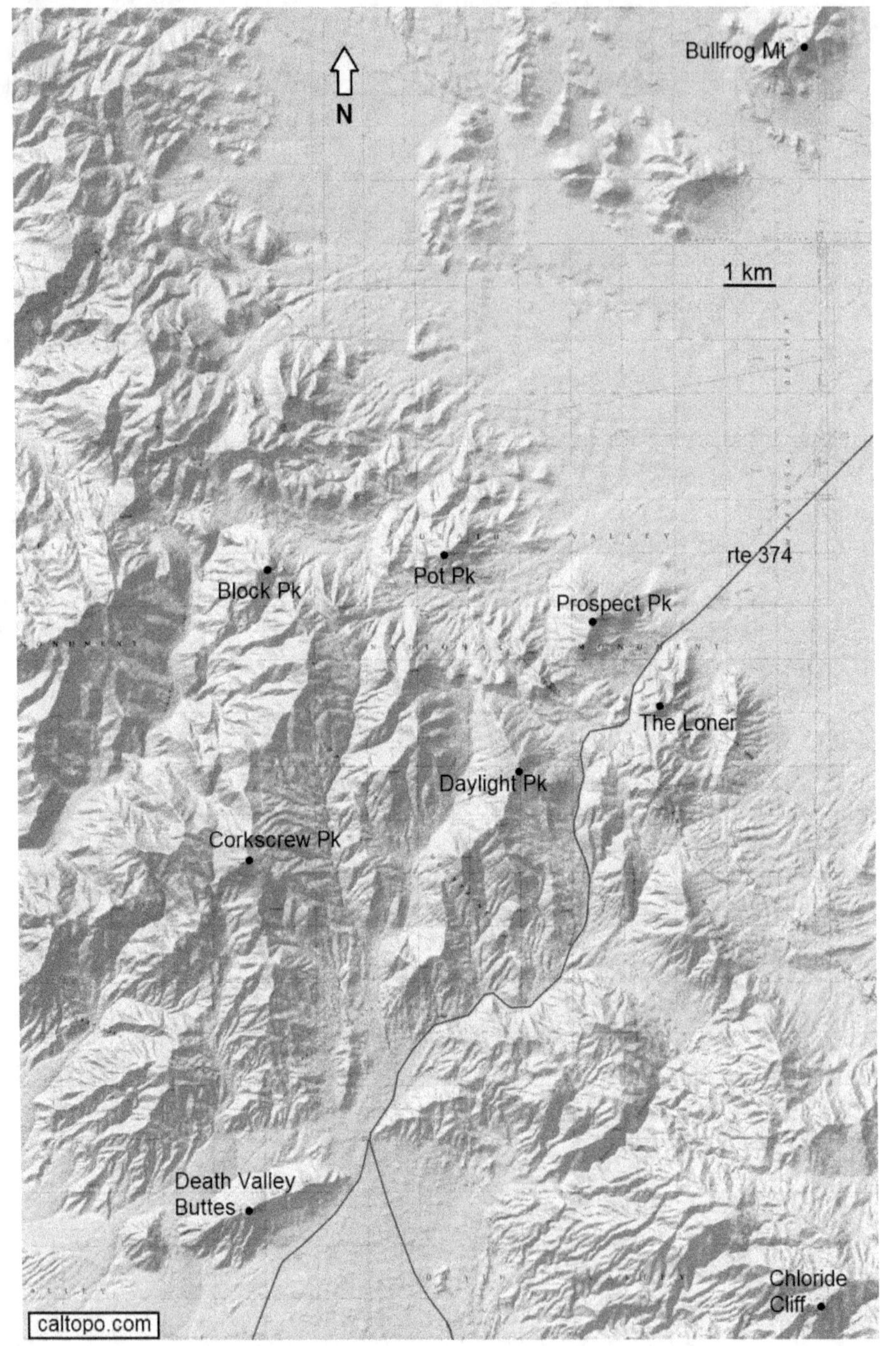
N
Bullfrog Mt
1 km
rte 374
Block Pk
Pot Pk
Prospect Pk
The Loner
Daylight Pk
Corkscrew Pk
Death Valley
Buttes
Chloride
Cliff
caltopo.com

"Block Peak" (5,921)

Block Peak is south of Titus Canyon Road, due west of Pot Peak. A crumbly, steep block marks the highest point, from which excellent views can be had.

-WGS84 Lat: 36.8198 deg N Lon: -116.9999 deg W

*-I, Class 2-3 via North Face ***

"Titanothere Point" (5,380)

Titanothere Point, sitting just northwest of Block Peak and south of Titus Canyon Road, is near the head of Titanothere Canyon. It makes for a short hike with some fun meandering as the top is approached. There are good views of the higher peaks surrounding it on all sides.

-WGS84 Lat: 36.8258 deg N Lon: -117.0131 deg W

*-I, Class 2 via Northwest Ridge **

"Red Pass Peak" (5,860)

Red Pass Peak, immediately northeast of Red Pass, is an impressively steep and crumbly peak. Interesting route-finding is required to find (and follow) a relatively safe route to the summit, where big drop offs down the front side greet visitors.

-WGS84 Lat: 36.8313 deg N Lon: -117.0290 deg W

*-II, Class 2-3 via Southwest Face ***

"Thimbles Shadow" (6,140)

This peak is south of Titus Canyon Road at Red Pass. It makes for a logical bonus peak while traveling to or from the much sweeter Thimble Peak, just to the southwest.

-WGS84 Lat: 36.8167 deg N Lon: -117.0334 deg W

*-II, Class 1 via North Ridge ***

Thimble Peak (6,381)

This is the nice-looking, sharp peak one sees east of northern Death Valley and to the northwest of Corkscew Peak. Start your hike by heading south from Red Pass along Titus Canyon Road (one-way, running east-to-west). Pick up Titus Canyon Road off of NV-374 near the park boundary. It is a signed dirt road on the north side of the highway.

-WGS84 Lat: 36.8120 deg N Lon: -117.0404 deg W

*-II, Class 2-3 via North Ridge from Red Pass ***

"Titus Peak" (4,620)

This little peak showcases an intimidatingly steep southern aspect as one passes through the Titus Canyon narrows northwest of the ghost town of Leadfield. Fortunately, one can park in the narrows east of the summit, where a gap comes in from the north. The gap allows easy access around to the backside and to the northwest slope, which is an easy scramble to the top.

-WGS84 Lat: 36.8540 deg N Lon: -117.0714 deg W

-II, Class 2 via Northwest Slope **

Northern Grapevine Mountains

The peaks in this subsection are best accessed via Phinney Canyon, on the east side of the range. The dirt Phinney Canyon Road heads west off US-95, north of Beatty, Nevada.

Grapevine Peak (8,738)

Grapevine Peak, the highpoint of the Grapevine Mountains, which run along the eastern edge of Death Valley in the northern portion of the national park, is an enjoyable hike. The mountain, with 4,558 feet of prominence, ranks as the 17th most prominent peak in the state of Nevada. From Beatty, Nevada, drive north on US-95 to a dirt road on the left 0.6 mile north of mile marker 71. Follow this mostly-good dirt road 20.8 miles (going right at a major fork a bit over 12 miles in) to a nice primitive camp spot on the right in the upper reaches of Phinney Canyon. From there, one simply hikes the worsening road to its end at a saddle, then hangs a right and follows the southeast ridge of the mountain to the summit. Expect a roundtrip of 6.5 miles and 3,100 feet of elevation gain.

-WGS84 Lat: 36.9652 deg N Lon: -117.1497 deg W

-II, Class 2 via Southeast Ridge **

Wahguyhe Peak (8,628)

Though its relatively modest 1,128 feet of prominence hardly compares to the massive prominence of the nearby range highpoint, Grapevine Peak, this much less visited mountain (the register averages about one sign-in per year) is more aesthetic and its summit views are absolutely outstanding. *This* is the peak to do! Follow the directions given for Grapevine Peak to the Phinney Canyon camp spot at 20.8 miles. From there, hike 100 yards east on the road and then follow a major draw southwest toward a saddle northwest of Wahguyhe Peak's summit. You can either continue to the saddle and then head southeast of very steep talus to the summit, or leave the draw at any reasonable point and wander up the comparable (though less talus-prone) north slope of the mountain. As you near the summit, the trees part and the views expand. From here, everything from Charleston Peak to Telescope Peak to Mount Whitney to Boundary Peak can be seen. Awesome! Keep your eyes peeled for wild horses too!

-WGS84 Lat: 36.9396 deg N Lon: -117.1052 deg W

-II, Class 2 via North Slope or Northwest Slope ***

Nearing the summit of Grapevine Peak.
Wahguyhe Peak, to the southeast, is the prominent mountain in the upper-right corner.

Jubilee Pass & Salsberry Pass

Jubilee Pass and Salsberry Pass are located along CA-178 in southern Death Valley. This lonely stretch of road offers a number of obscure peaks that are worth visiting. This is one of my favorite parts of Death Valley National Park.

The peaks in this subsection are widely scattered but arranged roughly west-to-east.

Cinder Hill (-75)

At one time, this was the lowest peak (in terms of elevation in relation to sea level) I'd ever climbed. If approaching the summit from the northeast you gain about 130 feet of elevation to reach the *below sea level*-summit! Could this be the lowest named summit in the Western Hemisphere? It's not—but it's close!

You get to it off the Badwater Road, many miles south of Badwater. Alternatively, you can get there by taking highway 178 west from Jubilee Pass.

-WGS84 Lat: 35.9400 deg N Lon: -116.7355 deg W

-I, Class 1 from any direction ***

Smith Mountain (5,913)

High and remote. Best approached from Gold Valley (infrequently maintained dirt road access) via the decent dirt Greenwater Valley Road.

-WGS84 Lat: 36.0181 deg N Lon: -116.6890 deg W
*-II, Class 1-2 via Northeast Slope ***

"Gold Valley Peak" (5,172)
A winding and meandering ridge with lots of ups and downs leads to this prominent summit and its nice views.

-WGS84 Lat: 36.0028 deg N Lon: -116.6278 deg W
*-II, Class 2-3 via Northeast Ridge ***

On the summit of Wahguyhe Peak, looking southwest.
Mount Palmer can be seen in the right foreground and Telescope Peak is at distant left.

"Virgin Spring Peak" (807)
A very short scramble south directly from highway 178 west of Jubilee Pass. Nice views of southern Death Valley.

-WGS84 Lat: 35.9039 deg N Lon: -116.6320 deg W
*-I, Class 2 via North Face ***

Jubilee Mountain (2,527)
This little mountain gives up really nice views of the southern portion of Death Valley. The views are so nice, I've been up there twice.

Approach directly from highway 178 by hiking south from Jubilee Pass.

-WGS84 Lat: 35.8976 deg N Lon: -116.5830 deg W

*-I, Class 2 via North Ridge ***

Epaulet Peak (4,765)

From Greenwater Valley Road, a surprisingly enjoyable hike leads to this outstanding viewpoint of the region. The peak has 986' of prominence.

-WGS84 Lat: 35.9727 deg N Lon: -116.5243 deg W

*-II, Class 2 via North Face ***

Rhodes Hill (2,860)

The tranquil summit of Rhodes Hill has pleasant views of Salsberry Peak, Sheephead Mountain, Ibex Peak, Epaulet Mountain, as well as a number of unnamed peaks in the area. The uphill hiking starts five minutes from the shoulder of highway 178, south of the peak.

-WGS84 Lat: 35.9232 deg N Lon: -116.4999 deg W

*-I, Class 2 via South Ridge ***

Salsberry Peak (4,254)

The peak is notable for its spectacular coloration. Start hiking north directly from highway 178.

-WGS84 Lat: 35.9465 deg N Lon: -116.4553 deg W

*-II, Class 2 via South Slopes ***

Ibex Peak (4,752)

A good dirt road (leaving the pavement of highway 178 just west of Salsberry Pass) can be followed generally south for a bit less than 1.5 miles to the wilderness boundary. From there, walk the road to the saddle west of the peak, then hang a left and follow the meandering ridge to the summit.

-WGS84 Lat: 35.8787 deg N Lon: -116.4167 deg W

*-II, Class 2 via West Ridge from the Dirt Road ****

Sheephead Mountain (4,274)

There's a distinct notch between the summit and the north sub-summit. The notch can be seen from miles away. Park just off highway 178 at Salsberry Pass and start cruising southeast to the top!

-WGS84 Lat: 35.9200 deg N Lon: -116.4101 deg W

*-II, Class 2 via Northwest Slopes **

Dante's View

Dante's View is the finest tourist viewpoint in all of Death Valley. It is a spot not to be missed. Get there by taking Dante's View Road south from CA-190, southeast of Furnace Creek.

The peaks in this subsection are arranged south-to-north.

Nearing the top of Ibex Peak,
as the high peaks of the Panamints rise in the distance to the northwest.

Funeral Peak (6,384)

The highpoint of the Black Mountains. The east ridge is a somewhat pleasant slog. The views from the top are surprisingly mediocre, considering that we're talking about the 33rd most prominent peak in all of California.

Take Greenwater Valley Road from either direction (from the north, off Dantes View Road via CA-190; or from the south, off highway 178) to a point east of the peak. Park as best you can along the side of the road (not much of a shoulder through here), and start hiking across the open desert to the base of the peak.

-WGS84 Lat: 36.1031 deg N Lon: -116.6240 deg W
-II, Class 1-2 via East Ridge **
-II, Class 2 via Southeast Face *

"False Coffin Peak" (5,500)

A bump one passes over on the way to Coffin Peak. Approach as per Coffin Peak.

-WGS84 Lat: 36.2176 deg N Lon: -116.7105 deg W
-I, Class 1 via Northwest Slopes *

Coffin Peak (5,490)

The named point is actually a touch lower than the 5,500-foot peak 100 yards west of it. Park below Dante's View for this short hike.

-WGS84 Lat: 36.2143 deg N Lon: -116.7058 deg W
-I, Class 1 via West Slope **

On the summit of Funeral Peak, looking west to the high peaks of the Panamint Range.

Dante Benchmark (5,704)
The views are perhaps a touch more classic than the mega-classic views given up by Dante's View, a mere 0.5 mile to the south.
-WGS84 Lat: 36.2262 deg N Lon: -116.7256 deg W
-I, Class 1-2 via South Ridge ***

Mount Perry (5,716)
On the glorious ridge north of Dante Benchmark. From Dante's View, hike along the ridge up and over Dante Benchmark, then keep hiking. You'll see it, way over there.
-WGS84 Lat: 36.2736 deg N Lon: -116.7244 deg W
-III, Class 2 via South Ridge *

Towne Pass & Panamint Valley

Towne Pass sits along CA-190 between Death Valley and Panamint Valley. I acknowledge that this subsection is anemic in its scope—it's an area of the park I've not yet spent much time exploring.

Lake Hill (2,008)
An isolated hill out in northern Panamint Valley, I climbed this puppy in *August* one year—yikes! I think it was about 125 degrees out. Reward yourself with a tasty and very pricey smoothie and a veggie burger in Panamint Springs afterward!

From CA-190 east of Panamint Springs, a good dirt road heads north toward (and beyond) the peak. Park on the shoulder as the road eases along the east side of the peak.

-WGS84 Lat: 36.3846 deg N Lon: -117.4044 deg W
-I, Class 2 via (the short and pleasant) East Gully *

Towne Benchmark (7,287)
There's a significant plane crash not far below the summit. Start your hike from Towne Pass along CA-190. The peak is on the north side of the road.

-WGS84 Lat: 36.4198 deg N Lon: -117.3182 deg W
-II, Class 1 via East Slope **

Furnace Creek

Furnace Creek is the epicenter of the Death Valley tourist experience. It's where you'll find the visitor center, a golf course, RV and tent camping, a pool, showers, and a couple of restaurants. It is located on CA-190, a couple miles north of the Badwater Road junction, in Death Valley.

The peaks in this subsection are arranged south-to-north.

"20-Mule Team Peak" (2,191)
This peak shares the same approach as Artist Palette Peak, starting along the dirt 20-Mule Team Road off of CA-190 east of Zabriskie Point. As you near the summit, the scene is reminiscent of a cross between the lunar surface and the high slopes of Aconcagua.

-WGS84 Lat: 36.3791 deg N Lon: -116.7755 deg W
-I, Class 1-2 via West Slope ***

"Artist Palette Peak" (2,230)
This is a fine hike with excellent history and outstanding, funky scenery the whole way. The colors seen from the summit are mind-blowing! An awesome approach (class 4) is up the canyon that divides Artist Palette Peak and 20-Mule Team Peak. Route-finding is required.

Start your hike along the dirt 20-Mule Team Road off of CA-190 east of Zabriskie Point.

-WGS84 Lat: 36.3782 deg N Lon: -116.7938 deg W
-II, Class 2 via East Ridge ****

An interesting inscription from the year 1911 found on the way to 20-Mule Team Peak

Mars Hill (-170)

This officially named peak, so named in 1991 by the U.S. Geological Survey after a proposal from the International Association of Astronomical Artists, is the lowest named peak I've ever summited. As the name suggests, the summit area of the peak recalls scenes of the surface of Mars.

The "peak," with a *massive* prominence of probably ten feet above the miles of open desert and salt flats around it, lies immediately west of the junction of Badwater Road and the northern exit to Artist Drive.

-WGS84 Lat: 36.3818 deg N Lon: -116.8524 deg W

-I, Class 1 from the Badwater Road **

"Cerro Blanco" (1,300+)

I first heard about this small and obscure summit above 20-Mule Team Canyon through a buddy who picked it up in an excellent local guidebook whose name I never learned.

The initial driving approach is as per Artist Palette Peak.

-WGS84 Lat: 36.3962 deg N Lon: -116.7808 deg W

-I, Class 1 via Southeast Ridge **

-I, Class 2 via Northeast Face *

Expansive and outrageously colorful scenes from the top of Artist Palette Peak. This view looks northwest toward Tucki Mountain.

"Furnace Peak" (1,820)

A small peak near Zabriskie Point and Hole-in-the-Wall. To get to it, leave CA-190 at the Hole-in-the-Wall turn-off (east of Zabriskie Point). Follow the dirt Hole-in-the-Wall road to the northern base of the peak. Be very careful hiking amongst all the loose rubble on this peak.

-WGS84 Lat: 36.4029 deg N Lon: -116.7592 deg W

-I, Class 2-3 via North Face **

Manly Beacon (820)

This is a classic summit. As you near the top, soft dirt and noticeable exposure require care. Get here via Golden Canyon, approached from either Zabriskie Point (along CA-190) or the Golden Canyon trailhead (off Badwater Road) in Death Valley.

-WGS84 Lat: 36.4235 deg N Lon: -116.8261 deg W

-I, Class 2 via Northeast Ridge from Golden Canyon ****

"Red Cathedral" (980)

By leaving the crowds of Zabriskie Point behind to hike up this small mountain, you get equally rewarding views of Golden Canyon, Manly Beacon and Death Valley.

Red Cathedral sits just northeast of Manly Beacon.

-WGS84 Lat: 36.4271 deg N Lon: -116.8240 deg W

-I, Class 2 via East Ridge **

Surreal views southeast toward Zabriskie Point (barely visible at left) from the summit of Manly Beacon.

Stovepipe Wells

Stovepipe Wells is mostly famous for being absurdly hot in summer. It's situated along CA-190 in Death Valley, northeast of Towne Pass and northwest of Furnace Creek. There's a small ranger station, a gas station, a not-so-great restaurant, camping, and a motel here. The main reason to spend time around Stovepipe Wells is the awesome sand dunes nearby!

"High Dune" (200)

A hike to the highpoint of the ever-shifting sand dunes above Stovepipe Wells is a life-changing and surreal experience that is sure to mystify. Or, at least that's what I got from it!

Start your hike from the nice parking lot on the north side of CA-190, east of Stovepipe Wells.

-WGS84 Lat: 36.620 deg N Lon: -117.1102 deg W

-II, Class 1 via South Slopes ****

Kit Fox Hills Highpoint (883)

This neat hike to a funky viewpoint in Death Valley has a register on the highest point. Don't be fooled into thinking that scrambling up one of the steeper aspects guarding the approach to the summit is a breeze—it can be but it can also lead to steep, exposed dirt scrambling that is not recommended. A safer alternatively is to hike up one of the open canyons from the road then route-find across mellow terrain leading to the gentle slopes ascending to the highpoint.

-WGS84 Lat: 36.6673 deg N Lon: -117.0450 deg W

-I, Class 1 from the northwest **

Middle-of-Nowhere

Hundreds of Death Valley peaks could aptly be placed in this subsection. For now, pay a visit to ultra-classic, middle-of-nowhere Ubehebe Peak.

Ubehebe Peak (5,678)

Ubehebe Peak, with an extended visit to the surreal and trippy Racetrack (and a climb of the YDS 5.2 north face of The Grandstand), is a classic desert experience. Best done in the nude.

Get here by taking the highway north into northern Death Valley, aiming for Ubehebe Crater (a must-see!). After your visit to the crater, follow the main dirt road to the Racetrack. Drive slowly, for many folks have gotten flat tires along this long stretch (about 26 miles) of lonely road.

-WGS84 Lat: 36.6908 deg N Lon: -117.5860 deg W

-II, Class 2 via trail from the Racetrack ****

West of Panamint Valley

Peaks in this subsection are scattered along the western outskirts of Death Valley between Panamint Valley and Owens Valley. They are arranged here roughly south-to-north.

Ophir Mountain (6,019)

Just north of the townsite of Darwin, Ophir Mountain is a short hike to a decent viewpoint of the area. Afterward, be sure to visit the excellent mining ruins and miner's cabin nearby.

Ophir Mountain has 845' of prominence.

-WGS84 Lat: 36.2901 deg N Lon: -117.5991 deg W

-II, Class 2 via South Ridge **

Darwin Benchmark (5,979)

This is an easy hike to a nice, simple peak sitting north of Ophir Mountain. There are interesting mining ruins nearby.

-WGS84 Lat: 36.3180 deg N Lon: -117.5990 deg W

-II, Class 2 via Southwest Slopes **

"508 Peak" (5,850)

This is a short hike from the mining ruins just off the Darwin road.

-WGS84 Lat: 36.3158 deg N Lon: -117.6428 deg W
*-I, Class 2 via Southwest Slope ***

"Talc Hill" (5,580)
This small peak just south of Talc City is easily accessed via a short dirt road running north from CA-190.

-WGS84 Lat: 36.3256 deg N Lon: -117.6769 deg W
*-I, Class 1 via Southeast Slopes **

Talc City Hills (5,706)
This short, semi-interesting hike is accessed by just a short drive down a good dirt road from CA-190 to the south. Parking at the base, an easy scramble leads to the top.

-WGS84 Lat: 36.3356 deg N Lon: -117.6765 deg W
*-I, Class 2 via Southeast Face ***

Eagle Point (5,171)
A very short hike to a little peak just northwest of Talc City Hills. A network of decent dirt roads leads one closely to the west base of the peak, about a mile from CA-190.

-WGS84 Lat: 36.3407 deg N Lon: -117.6933 deg W
*-I, Class 2 via West Face **

"Skunk Stripe Peak" (5,300)
This short, easy peak, just north of Eagle Point and northwest of Talc City, has good views of the area.

-WGS84 Lat: 36.3477 deg N Lon: -117.6872 deg W
*-I, Class 1-2 via West Slope **

"Panamint Gate – South" (2,822)
This minor but excellent overlook sits closely northwest of Panamint Springs. Several funky cairns dot the flattish summit area.

There's a small pull-out along CA-190 at the base of the west ridge.
-WGS84 Lat: 36.3462 deg N Lon: -117.4832 deg W
*-I, Class 1-2 via West Ridge ***

Shoshone Area

Shoshone

The peaks in this subsection are part of the Dublin Hills complex, more or less west of Shoshone. Shoshone's a funky town, with interesting history (the Manson Family used to live here) and okay-for-obscurity food. Although not further discussed herein, me and some friends once re-discovered a nearby, long-forgotten technical cave with pioneer relics at its terminus. Cool stuff.

Dublin Hills Highpoint (3,046)

This range highpoint, due west of Shoshone and shown as 'Beck' on some maps, is easily accessed from Dublin Gulch and the mud houses of Shoshone.

Dublin Hills Highpoint has 865' of prominence.

-WGS84 Lat: 35.9746 deg N Lon: -116.3198 deg W

-II, Class 2 from the east **

"Shoshone Point – South" (2,302)

This is the forgettable southwest summit of Shoshone Point.

-WGS84 Lat: 35.9758 deg N Lon: -116.2917 deg W

-I, Class 2 via Southwest Face *

-I, Class 2 via Northeast Slope *

"Shoshone Point" (2,365)

This small peak is just northwest of Shoshone.

-WGS84 Lat: 35.9836 deg N Lon: -116.2826 deg W

-II, Class 2 via Southwest Ridge **

-II, Class 2 via Southeast Face *

Resting Spring Range

The Resting Spring Range runs east of CA-127, Shoshone and Death Valley Junction, and more or less west of CA-178 as it bends its way from Shoshone toward Pahrump, Nevada, where it becomes NV-372.

The peaks in this subsection are arranged south-to-north.

Ring Benchmark (3,267)

On the divide between Shoshone and Chicago Valley. Approach directly from CA-178, east of Shoshone. The peak is just south of the highway.

-WGS84 Lat: 35.9813 deg N Lon: -116.2143 deg W

-I, Class 2-3 via (crumbly) Northeast Face *

-I, Class 3 via North Ridge **

"Stewart Point" (5,265)

Some folks regard Stewart Point as a classic desert summit. I don't understand why.

Approach the mountain from CA-178, southeast of the peak, at the north end of the Nopah Range.

-WGS84 Lat: 36.1661 deg N Lon: -116.2080 deg W

-II, Class 2 via Upper South Ridge from Southeast **

-II, Class 2 via Upper East Ridge from Southeast **

Shadow Mountain (5,069)

This is a prominent, rounded mountain between Pahrump and Death Valley Junction. Approach from the paved Ash Meadows Road, which starts at the north end of Pahrump as Bell Vista Avenue and dead-ends at CA-127 at Death Valley Junction.

-WGS84 Lat: 36.2632 deg N Lon: -116.2582 deg W

-II, Class 2 via North Ridge *

Hunch Benchmark (2,829)

This small peak is at the northern end of the range. A short hike from Ash Meadows Road (paved), from east of Death Valley Junction, leads to an okay viewpoint from the summit.

Be sure to visit Devil's Hole while you're in the area. It's really neat.

-WGS84 Lat: 36.3248 deg N Lon: -116.2864 deg W

-I, Class 1 via East Ridge *

Nopah Range

The Nopah Range lies west of Pahrump, Nevada, and east of CA-178 and CA-127, south of Shoshone. It is a dramatic range with plenty of excellent scrambling to be found.

The two peaks in this subsection are arranged south-to-north

Nopah Range Highpoint (6,394)

This is the 27th most prominent peak in the state of California. A number of variations are possible on the western approach (accessed via dirt roads off of CA-178). Look carefully to avoid harder climbing that lurks nearby on the lower mountain.

-WGS84 Lat: 36.0063 deg N Lon: -116.0806 deg W

-III, Class 3 via West Slopes ***

Pahrump Benchmark (5,740)

This is a classic desert peak. Get to it by looking for a short spur road (rough dirt) that heads northeast from CA-178 directly toward a prominent canyon at the western base of the peak. From there, follow occasional cairns, signs of use, and your good judgment to reach the top. If lacking all of the above, retreat, head home, and flip on the television. (It's safer there, anyway.)

-WGS84 Lat: 36.0991 deg N Lon: -116.1398 deg W

-III, Class 2-3 via West Slopes ****

Kingston Range

The Kingston Range is an outstandingly interesting range located southeast of Tecopa, California. Most of the peaks in the range are most easily reached via Excelsior Mine Road off of I-15, northeast of Baker, California.

The peaks in this subsection are arranged south-to-north.

Kingston Peak (7,323)

This is one of the most impressive and rugged peaks in the region. It is also the 23rd most prominent peak in California.

Initially approach as per Excelsior Mine Peak. Rather than leave Excelsior Mine Road at the network of dirt roads southeast of *that* peak, find yourself a couple miles west of there (and roughly 28 miles from I-15). You'll eventually leave the car and begin hiking cross-country generally southwest through a brushy valley of sorts to a saddle. Head west from the saddle and work to gain the interesting north ridge of the peak. The north ridge is followed to the top.

Best of luck to you! I'd hold your hand, but that's just not my style—and I know it's not yours either.

-WGS84 Lat: 35.7267 deg N Lon: -115.9156 deg W

-III, Class 3 via North Ridge ***

"Excelsior Mine Peak" (4,886)

Gordon MacLeod and Barbara Lilley named the peak and placed a register on top in 1984. In 2009, I was the next person to sign in.

To get there, gain the Excelsior Mine Road (alternatively rough paved and mostly good dirt) from either the southeast side of Tecopa (stopping for some dates at China Ranch Date Farm while you're nearby) or by leaving I-15 at exit 272 and heading north. This is the Excelsior Mine Road. A network of dirt roads leaving Excelsior Mine Road southwest of the peak will lead you to a point closely northwest of your objective.

-WGS84 Lat: 35.7849 deg N Lon: -115.8390 deg W
*-I, Class 2 via Northeast Face **
*-I, Class 2 via North Ridge **

"Jupiter Mine Peak" (5,177)

This small peak is the northern neighbor of Excelsior Mine Peak, and sits northeast of the highly aesthetic Kingston Peak. Gordon MacLeod and Barbara Lilley named this peak and placed a register on the summit in 1984. There had been only one sign-in after theirs—9 years before mine.

Approach as per Excelsior Mine Peak.

-WGS84 Lat: 35.7911 deg N Lon: -115.8351 deg W
*- I, Class 2 via Southwest Slope **
*-I, Class 2-3 via West Face ***

Tecopa

Tecopa, California is located just off of CA-127, south of Shoshone. It is a weird place with some developed hot springs (and some *un*developed ones), and not much else. Oh yeah, there's also China Ranch Date Farm, which is sort of cool.

Tecopa Peak (2,692)

Start hiking from the vicinity of CA-127 and the Old Spanish Trail Highway, just west of Tecopa. When you get to the top, you'll see that someone's placed a plaque on the summit rocks. Once you're done here, head to China Ranch Date Farm for some fresh dates!

Although you'll probably need a bath after hiking and passing through town, I'd recommend avoiding the primitive hot springs they have out there in the open desert outside of town – I once emerged barefoot from the springs and nearly stepped on an exposed hypodermic needle in the sand! Yikes.

-WGS84 Lat: 35.8342 deg N Lon: -116.2758 deg W
*-II, Class 2 via Northeast Ridge ***
*-II, Class 2 via North Ridge ***

"Athel Hill" (882)

This little peak is situated right off CA-127, south of Tecopa and next to Salt Creek. The area is rich in history and fascinating remnants of past cultures can be found nearby.

-WGS84 Lat: 35.6299 deg N Lon: -116.2803 deg W
*-I, Class 2 via South Slope **

Salt Benchmark (1,376)
This nice, rugged peak is east of Amargosa Spring (and the neat mining ruins there) and southeast of Little Dumont Dunes, near Tecopa, California.

-WGS84 Lat: 35.6361 deg N Lon: -116.2644 deg W
*-II, Class 2 via Northwest Slopes ***

"Old Spanish Mountain" (3,914)
This is a nice hike to an outstanding viewpoint. The peak is easily accessed from the paved Old Spanish Trail Highway, east of Tecopa, California, parking near Emigrant Pass.

-WGS84 Lat: 35.8979 deg N Lon: -116.0676 deg W
*-II, Class 1-2 via Southeast Slopes ****

Scattered

Sprawling California has a diversity of mountain landscapes that's hard to contain. Thus, a selection of peaks scattered across the desert in deep southern California is included here.

Needles Area

The peaks in this subsection are located along highway 95, south of I-40 and Needles, California. They are arranged here south-to-north.

"Umpah Point" (3,553)
Umpah Point and its northern sister, Mopah Point, are two of the most sought-after peaks in the desert southwest. Umpah, with 1080' of prominence, is the higher of the two. The two peaks are accessed from highway 95, south of Needles.

-WGS84 Lat: 34.2973 deg N Lon: -114.7648 deg W
*-II, Class 2-3 via Northeast Face ****

"Mopah Point" (3,530)
Mopah Point, with 955' of prominence, is a striking and exciting peak that every peakbagger should endeavor to climb. Although I've heard arguments that Umpah is the better peak, I think Mopah is. Regardless, they're both outstanding and worthwhile objectives.

-WGS84 Lat: 34.3104 deg N Lon: -114.7651 deg W
*-II, Class 3 via Eastern Aspect *****

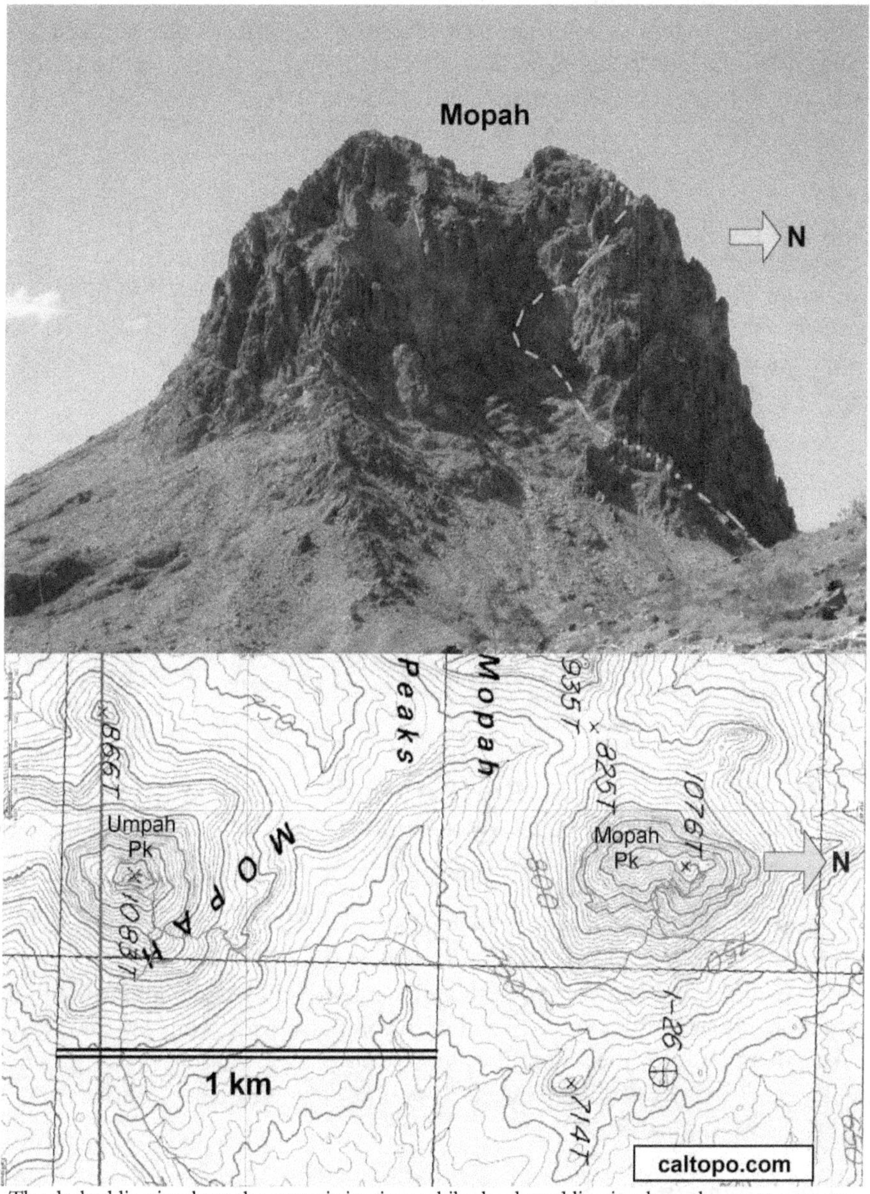

The dashed line is where the route is in view, while the dotted line is where the route goes out of view behind rocks. Note the GPS track on the map.

Sawtooth Range Highpoint (2,340)
This minor range highpoint is east of highway 95, a few miles southeast of Snaggletooth. Dirt roads make this hike very short and easy, though loose, gravelly slopes will be encountered near the summit.

-WGS84 Lat: 34.5564 deg N Lon: -114.6013 deg W
*-I, Class 2 via West Slope **

Snaggletooth (2,110)
Snaggletooth is an easily overlooked but aesthetic small peak just west of highway 95, south of Needles. The very enjoyable class 4-5 south arête/face is the easiest route to the summit. The nearby western summit is also supremely enjoyable.

-WGS84 Lat: 34.5904 deg N Lon: -114.6372 deg W
*-I, Class 4-5 via South Face ****

Sharp Benchmark (2,070)
Though unofficially named, this peak has a California DOT "Sharp" benchmark on the summit. The peak is just west of highway 95 north of Lobecks Pass and south of Needles.

Delightfully, the upper mountain features about 200 feet of really nice scrambling.

-WGS84 Lat: 34.6776 deg N Lon: -114.6268 deg W
*-II, Class 2-3 via East Face ****

Blythe Area

Blythe is a place perhaps best forgotten. Other than the intaglios and the odd aesthetic peak, there's not much to draw the scrutinizing peakbagger.

Thumb Peak (1,375)
Thumb Peak, a part of the Palo Verde Mountains, is a very intimidating, steep butte that has a remarkably easy (though exposed and frightening) route to its summit. I'll leave it up to you to sniff around and see if you can find it. It's likely that the only other summit routes are class 5.

-WGS84 Lat: 33.4064 deg N Lon: -114.8665 deg W
*-II, Class 2 via ? ****

Black Mountain (2,165)
Black Mountain, south of Blythe, California, has a paved service road leading to its summit from CA-78 to the northwest.

-WGS84 Lat: 33.0548 deg N Lon: -114.8279 deg W
*-I, Class 1 via Service Road ***

Quartz Peak (2,178)
Quartz Peak is north of Black Mountain. With 1078' of prominence, it is the highpoint of a feature also known as Peter Kane Mountain. Peter Kane Peak (2,051), a nearby subsidiary summit reachable by traveling across some interesting terrain, is a convenient bonus.

Quartz Peak has 1078' of prominence.

-WGS84 Lat: 33.0891 deg N Lon: -114.8229 deg W

*-II, Class 2 from the west ***

Yuma Area

Picacho Peak is the big draw in the Yuma, Arizona area. A system of good dirt roads allows access deep into this remote area, where obscure, chossy peaks beckon.

Although Muggins Peak is just over the border in Arizona, I've included it in this subsection due to its proximity to Yuma.

Pebble Mountain (1,007)
Pebble Mountain is super-lame but makes for a shamelessly easy bonus peak for those coming from or going to a real mountain like Picacho Peak.

-WGS84 Lat: 32.9269 deg N Lon: -114.6383 deg W

*-I, Class 1 via West Slope **

"Mine Peak" (1,365)
Mine Peak is east of Picacho Road, southeast of Picacho Peak, and northeast of Pebble Mountain. It is a pleasant hike to a good viewpoint. The summit is marked with a large cairn.

-WGS84 Lat: 32.9493 deg N Lon: -114.6130 deg W

*-II, Class 2 from the west ***

Picacho Peak (1,930)
Picacho Peak is a jaw-dropping butte located near Yuma, Arizona. The easiest route, a desert classic by any definition, requires some interesting route-finding, enjoyable scrambling, a leap across a spooky chasm, climbing a ladder, and re-ascending a rope on the return. A 30m rope is adequate for the route. Start the climb from the end of the 4WD A278 road.

Picacho Peak has 1107' of prominence.

By the way, this peak is commonly referred to as Little Picacho. This is confusing because there is an officially named Little Picacho just to its north. The "Little Picacho" nickname was given by DPS scramblers to differentiate it from another DPS peak called El Picacho del Diablo (or "Big Picacho").

-WGS84 Lat: 32.9714 deg N Lon: -114.6643 deg W

*-II, Class 4 A0 via West Aspect *****

Muggins Peak (1,424)

This splendid mountain offers a righteous amount of bang for the buck. With some of the finest scrambling in the region, speedy types can reach the summit in under an hour from the 2WD trailhead.

Leave I-8 at exit 21 (east of Yuma), proceed east through the small community then turn north, following signs to Muggins Mountains Trailhead, 1.5 miles southwest of the peak. From there, follow the now-4WD road to the base of the peak then scramble up the southwest face below the saddle. An exposed class 3 arete splits the two steep gullies leading to the saddle. Turn left at the saddle then traverse left until you can climb back up to the right to gain the peak's southeast arête (class 3). Scramble the arête to the false summit then scramble 50' north to the summit.

-WGS84 Lat: 32.7455 deg N Lon: -114.2518 deg W

*-II, Class 3 from the southwest *****

Petroglyphs in sandstone

Appendix

CP's 25 Favorite Scrambles

Given the outrageous amount of great scrambles to be had in places like Red Rock, Valley of Fire, Sedona and Grand Canyon, compiling a list of just 25 of the highest-quality scrambles within the scope of this book proved to be an exercise in frustration. But I think you'll enjoy my favorites, which are listed here.

I've tried to arrange the list in descending order, from my very favorite to my least favorite *favorite.* It was no easy task. Status was based upon a combination of mountain appearance, position and setting, quality of the route, and the improbability of the route.

☐ **Coronado Butte** (7,162) – P1132 / Class 3-4 via South Ridge & East Face
☐ **Weavers Needle** (4,553) – P1013 / YDS 5.0 via East Gully
☐ **Baboquivari Peak** (7,780) – P4204 / YDS 5.3 via Forbes Route
☐ **O'Neill Butte** (6,071) – P331 / YDS 5.4 via North Face
☐ **Picacho Peak (Yuma)** (1,930) – P1107 / Class 4 A0 via West Aspect
☐ **Mount Wilson** (7,070) – P690 / Class 4-5 via Cleaver Crack
☐ **Haystack Peak** (2,783) – P923 / Class 3 via full West Ridge
☐ **High Peak** (2,716) – P1006 / Class 4 via Upper West Face (with SE Ridge descent)
☐ **Playground Peak** (5,266) – P591 / YDS 5.2 via Southwest Face
☐ **Picacho Peak (Tucson)** (3,370) – P1573 / Class 3 via Hunter Trail
☐ **Muggins Peak** (1,424) – P674/ Class 3 from the southwest
☐ **Fountain Peak** (6,988) – P394 / Class 3-4 via South Ridge from East Slope
☐ **Valley of Fire Summit** (2,972) – P626 / Class 4-5 via South Ridge from the East
☐ **Jumbo Peak** (5,761) – P3317 / YDS 5.3 via West-Northwest Chimney
☐ **Goodman Peak** (6,600) – P150 / Class 3-4 via Northeast Gully
☐ **Bridge Mountain** (6,990) – P722 / Class 3 via standard route
☐ **Mopah Point** (3,530) – P955 / Class 3 via Eastern Aspect
☐ **Castle Dome Peak** (3,788) – P2098 / Class 3 via Northwest Wash
☐ **Moapa Peak** (6471) - P1691 / Class 3 via Southwest Slope
☐ **Morning Glory Spire** (5,260) – P360 / Class 4 via Northwest Ridge
☐ **Rainbow Mountain** (6,810) – P240 / Class 4 via West Ridge
☐ **Escalante Butte** (6,536) – P876 / Class 4 via South Slope or East Slope
☐ **Crimson Staircase** (2,454) – P436 / Class 4 via Southwest Aspect
☐ **The 5-Arch** (2,313) – P427 / Class 4 via North Gully
☐ **Cheops Pyramid** (5,401) – P800 / Class 3-4 via Northwest Ridge

The Fifteen 10,000+ foot, P300 Peaks of the Spring Mountains

There are fifteen summits in the Spring Mountains that are at least 10,000 feet above sea level with a prominence of 300 feet or more. Prominence? A summit's prominence is the number of feet it rises from the saddle between it and the closest higher neighbor. These 10,000+ foot, P300 peaks are listed below:

- ☐ **Charleston Peak** (11,915) – *P8257*
- ☐ **Mummy Mountain** (11,527) – *P816*
- ☐ **Griffith Peak** (11,059) – *P446*
- ☐ **Mummys Nose** (10,751) – *P400*
- ☐ **McFarland Peak** (10,744) – *P1181*
- ☐ **Bonanza Peak** (10,396) – *P833*
- ☐ **Fletcher Peak** (10,252) – *P459*
- ☐ **Mount Reagan** (10,187) – *P460*
- ☐ **The Sisters** (10,177) – *P811*
- ☐ **Clinton Peak** (10,160) – *P662*
- ☐ **Amargosa Overlook** (10,154) – *P460*
- ☐ **Divide Peak** (10,068) – *P341*
- ☐ **North Sister** (10,042) – *P348*
- ☐ **Macks Peak** (10,036) – *P1129*
- ☐ **Harris Mountain** (10,014) – *P943*

The Clark County P2000 List

Clark County, Nevada is fortunate to have a lot of mountains. Of those many hundreds of summits, ten of them have at least 2,000 feet of prominence. Here they are:

- ☐ **Charleston Peak** (11,915) – *P8257*
- ☐ **Hayford Peak** (9,912) – *P5412*
- ☐ **Jumbo Peak** (5,761) – *P3317*
- ☐ **Virgin Peak** (8,087) – *P3215*
- ☐ **Potosi Mountain** (8,514) – *P3012*
- ☐ **Muddy Mountains Highpoint** (5,431) – *P2931*
- ☐ **Spirit Mountain** (5,639) – *P2899*
- ☐ **Arrow Canyon Range Highpoint** (5,226) – *P2446*
- ☐ **McCullough Mountain** (7,026) – *P2220*
- ☐ **Gass Peak** (6,943) – *P2043*

The Nine P1000 Peaks of Lake Mead National Recreation Area

☐ **Spirit Mountain** (5,639) – P2899
☐ **Gold Cross Peak** (3,422) – P1470
☐ **River Mountain Benchmark** (3,789) – P1409
☐ **Redstone Peak** (3,510) – P1312
☐ **Northshore Peak** (3,330) – P1132
☐ **Salt Spring Mountain** (3,973) – P1113
☐ **Arch Mountain Highpoint** (3,763) – P1024
☐ **Willow Beach Peak** (2,321) – P1021
☐ **Salt and Pepper Mountain** (2,700) – P1011

The Fourteen P300 Peaks of Valley of Fire State Park

☐ **North Fire Peak** (3,743) - P807
☐ **Thin Peak** (3,694) - P626
☐ **Peak 3,077** (3,077) - P502
☐ **Duane Peak** (3,002) - P689
☐ **Gregg Peak** (2,999) - P358
☐ **Valley of Fire Summit** (2,972) – P626
☐ **Weekapaug Mountain** (2,674) - P328
☐ **Cairn Peak** (2,497) - P381
☐ **Crimson Staircase** (2,454) - P436
☐ **Peak 2,431** (2,431) - P315
☐ **Baseline Mesa** (2,378) - P361
☐ **The 5-Arch** (2,313) - P427
☐ **The Orphan** (2,280) - P328
☐ **Sitting Monkey** (2,260) - P324

General Ticklist

Red Rock Canyon NCA Sandstone

- ☐ Beer and Ice Peak
- ☐ Big Bird Peak
- ☐ Black Velvet Peak
- ☐ Boot Boulder
- ☐ Bridge Mountain
- ☐ Bridge Point
- ☐ Bridge Vista Peak
- ☐ Burlap Buttress
- ☐ Cactus Flower Tower
- ☐ Calico Hills-South
- ☐ Calico Peak
- ☐ Dead Horse Point
- ☐ Deception Peak
- ☐ Decision Peak
- ☐ Divided Sky, The
- ☐ East Monument Peak
- ☐ Evas Tower
- ☐ First Creek Peak
- ☐ Fork Peak
- ☐ Global Peak
- ☐ Goodman Peak
- ☐ Gunsight Notch Peak
- ☐ Hidden Peak
- ☐ Holiday Peak
- ☐ Hollow Rock Peak
- ☐ Ice Box Peak
- ☐ Indecision Peak
- ☐ Juniper Peak
- ☐ Kraft Mountain
- ☐ Lost Creek Peak
- ☐ Magic Mountain
- ☐ Mescalito
- ☐ Mikes Tower
- ☐ Monument, The
- ☐ Mount Wilson
- ☐ North Peak
- ☐ Oak Peak
- ☐ Pine Creek Peak
- ☐ Rainbow Mountain
- ☐ Rainbow Wall
- ☐ Ramp Peak
- ☐ Red Book Point
- ☐ Red Cap
- ☐ Rose Tower
- ☐ Sandstone Peak
- ☐ South Peak
- ☐ South Wilson
- ☐ Tank Peak
- ☐ Terrace Canyon Peak
- ☐ Tinaja Peak
- ☐ Tunnel Vision Peak
- ☐ Whisky Peak
- ☐ White Rock Peak
- ☐ White Rock Pinnacle
- ☐ White Rock Spring Peak
- ☐ Willow Springs Overlook
- ☐ Wilsons Pimple
- ☐ Windy Peak
- ☐ Yoga Peak

Greater Red Rock Area

- ☐ Barricade Peak
- ☐ Blue Diamond Hill
- ☐ Burnt Peak
- ☐ Crest Peak
- ☐ Damsel Peak
- ☐ East La Madre Peak
- ☐ El Bastardo
- ☐ El Padre
- ☐ First Creek Overlook
- ☐ Gateway Peak
- ☐ Goat Bed Peak
- ☐ Greycap
- ☐ La Madre Mountain
- ☐ Lonely Pinon Mountain
- ☐ Mount Golden Eagle
- ☐ Mount Gottlieb
- ☐ Mount Woody
- ☐ Mountain Spring Benchmark
- ☐ New Peak
- ☐ Nony Peak
- ☐ Oak Creek Overlook
- ☐ Pondview Peak
- ☐ Rainy
- ☐ Red Benchmark
- ☐ Summerlin Peak
- ☐ Turtlehead Mountain
- ☐ Ugly Brown Lump
- ☐ Willow Benchmark
- ☐ Wilson Ridge
- ☐ Windy

Spring Mountains NRA

- ☐ Amargosa Overlook
- ☐ Bee Canyon Peak
- ☐ Black Rock Sister
- ☐ Bluebird Peak
- ☐ Bonanza Hill
- ☐ Bonanza Peak
- ☐ Bootleg Spring Peak
- ☐ Burro Peak
- ☐ Cactus Flower Point
- ☐ Cathedral Rock
- ☐ Charleston Peak
- ☐ Chase Mountain
- ☐ Claret Peak
- ☐ Clinton Peak
- ☐ Cockscomb Peak
- ☐ Dead Badger Peak
- ☐ Dead Horse Mountain
- ☐ Devil Peak
- ☐ Divide Peak
- ☐ Dull Mountain
- ☐ Edge Benchmark
- ☐ Fletcher Peak
- ☐ Freddie Peak
- ☐ Gap Peak
- ☐ Graduation Peak
- ☐ Grapevine Spring Point
- ☐ Green Monster Benchmark
- ☐ Griffith Peak
- ☐ Harris Mountain
- ☐ Horse Benchmark
- ☐ Indian Benchmark
- ☐ Indian Springs Peak
- ☐ Indian Ridge
- ☐ Indian Ridge-North
- ☐ Ison Peak
- ☐ Jagged Peak
- ☐ Jaybird Benchmark
- ☐ Kyle Benchmark
- ☐ La Madre Mountain Wilderness Highpoint
- ☐ Lead Mountain
- ☐ Lee Peak
- ☐ Little Devil Peak
- ☐ Lucky Strike Mine Peak
- ☐ Lucky Strike Peak
- ☐ Macks Peak
- ☐ McFarland Peak
- ☐ Mesa Benchmark
- ☐ Mine Peak
- ☐ Misty Mountain
- ☐ Mount Alexander
- ☐ Mount Bulworth
- ☐ Mount Everest
- ☐ Mount Hualapai
- ☐ Mount Pumpkin
- ☐ Mount Reagan
- ☐ Mount Stirling
- ☐ Mud Hole Mountain
- ☐ Mummy Mountain
- ☐ Mummys Chin
- ☐ Mummys Forehead
- ☐ Mummys Nose
- ☐ Mummys Toe
- ☐ North Macks Peak
- ☐ North Potosi Peak
- ☐ North Sister
- ☐ Pas Rump
- ☐ Peak 4,773
- ☐ Peak 4,839
- ☐ Peak 4,930
- ☐ Peak 4,945
- ☐ Peak 5,035
- ☐ Peak 5,475
- ☐ Peak 6,742
- ☐ Peak 6,830
- ☐ Peak Four
- ☐ Pepper Peak
- ☐ Pioneer Rock
- ☐ Point of Rocks Peak
- ☐ Potosi Mountain
- ☐ Potosi Mountain-South
- ☐ Profile Point
- ☐ Ragged Peak
- ☐ Rainbow Point
- ☐ Ridge View Peak
- ☐ Ridge View Peak-East
- ☐ Roasting Pit, The
- ☐ Seldom Seen Peak
- ☐ Sexton Ridge
- ☐ Shaft Peak

☐ Shenandoah Peak
☐ Sisters, The
☐ Smith Benchmark
☐ Snow King
☐ Spring Peak
☐ Table Mountain
☐ Tio Grande
☐ Traction Benchmark
☐ Whale Peak
☐ Wheeler Benchmark
☐ Wild Horse, The
☐ Willow Peak

Gold Butte

☐ Black Butte
☐ Bonelli Peak
☐ Condor Peak
☐ Gold Butte
☐ Gold Cross Peak
☐ Iceberg Peak
☐ Jumbo Peak
☐ Mica Peak
☐ Packard Peak
☐ Peak 3,068
☐ Peak 3,123
☐ Peak 5,003
☐ Playground Peak
☐ Rattlesnake Peak
☐ Scanlon Hill
☐ South Tramp Point
☐ Tramp Ridge

Greater Lake Mead NRA Area

☐ After-Work Peak
☐ Anniversary Narrows Peak
☐ Arch Mountain
☐ Arch Mountain Highpoint
☐ Basalt Peak
☐ Bearing Peak
☐ Bighorn Peak
☐ Bill Gays Butte
☐ Bitter 3
☐ Bitter Ridge Highpoint
☐ Black Mesa
☐ Black Mountain (Boulder City)
☐ Black Mountain (Cottonwood)
☐ Blowing Peak
☐ Blue Point
☐ Booth Pinnacle
☐ Boulder Peak
☐ Bowl View Peak
☐ Boxcar Rock
☐ Capuchin Peak
☐ Cathedral Peak
☐ Christmas Tree Peak
☐ Copper Mountain
☐ Copper Mountain-West
☐ Cove Peak
☐ Coyote Skull Peak
☐ Dam View Point
☐ Devils Thumb
☐ Division Peak
☐ Double, The
☐ East Bitter Peak
☐ East Longwell Ridge
☐ East Longwell Ridge-South
☐ East Redstone Peak
☐ Echo Hills
☐ Endless Peak
☐ Falls Peak
☐ Fire Benchmark
☐ Fortification Hill
☐ Glyph Point
☐ Golden Mine Peak
☐ Guardian Peak
☐ Knife Peak
☐ Knob Peak
☐ Hamblin Butte
☐ Hamblin Mountain
☐ Hamblin Mountain-West
☐ Hanging Valley Peak
☐ Harlan Peak
☐ Iguana Peak
☐ Indigo Peak
☐ Knife-Edge Peak
☐ Land's End Peak
☐ Lava Butte
☐ Little Peak
☐ Little Pyramid
☐ Long View Peak
☐ Manganese Peak
☐ Middle Bitter Peak
☐ Midway Peak
☐ Mine View Peak
☐ Minefield, The
☐ Mount Graybeard
☐ Mount Mangreed
☐ Mount Newberry
☐ Mount Wilson
☐ Mud Crag
☐ Mud Hill
☐ Mud Tower
☐ Murphys Peak

☐ Mystery Cairn Peak
☐ North Crag
☐ North Fire Peak
☐ North Fire Peak-East Summit
☐ North Peak
☐ Northshore Peak
☐ Northshore Peak-West
☐ Paint Pots
☐ Peak 1,804
☐ Peak 1,876
☐ Peak 2,159
☐ Peak 2,421
☐ Peak 2,474
☐ Peak 2,500
☐ Peak 2,674
☐ Peak 2,740
☐ Peak 2,890
☐ Peak 3,153
☐ Peak 3,537
☐ Pellet Peak
☐ Pilot Mesa
☐ Pinnacle
☐ Pinto Ridge
☐ Pipeline Hill
☐ Pluto
☐ Polytick Peak
☐ Promontory Point
☐ Pyramid Peak
☐ Ram Skull Peak
☐ Raven, The
☐ Razorback Ridge
☐ Red Fox Peak
☐ Red Mountain
☐ Red Needle
☐ Redstone Peak
☐ River Mountain Benchmark
☐ River Mountain Peak
☐ Rough Benchmark
☐ Saddle Mountain
☐ Salt and Pepper Mountain
☐ Salt Spring Mountain
☐ Sentinel Peak
☐ Slabs Peak
☐ South Crag
☐ Spirit Mountain
☐ Stock Ridge
☐ Tall Cairn Peak
☐ Talus Mound
☐ Triple, The
☐ Unity Peak
☐ Uranus
☐ Vista Peak
☐ Walts Ridge
☐ West Bitter Peak
☐ West Longwell Ridge
☐ White Eagle Peak
☐ Yucca Camp Mountain

Arrow Canyon Range

☐ Arrow Canyon Peak
☐ Arrow Canyon Range Highpoint
☐ Arrow Peak
☐ Bedrock Peak
☐ Birthday Peak
☐ Broken Arrow Peak
☐ Cave Butte
☐ Cliff Benchmark
☐ Dead Man Hill
☐ Dry Benchmark
☐ Dry Lake Peak
☐ False Arrow Peak
☐ Fossil Peak
☐ Gunshot Peak
☐ Hidden Benchmark
☐ Hidden Wash Peak
☐ Landfill Peak
☐ Lytle Benchmark
☐ Marble Mountain
☐ Mount of Caves
☐ Painted Prow
☐ Pasture Mountain
☐ Question Mark Peak
☐ Reale Peak
☐ Red Barrel Peak
☐ South Arrow Cone
☐ South Arrow Peak
☐ Spider Peak
☐ Table Mountain
☐ Tortoise Peak
☐ Trench Peak

Desert NWR

☐ Bald Knob
☐ Banded Ridge-North
☐ Banded Ridge-South
☐ Big John
☐ Castle Rock
☐ Cow Camp Peak
☐ Dike Benchmark

☐ Dike Benchmark-East Summit
☐ Dike Benchmark-Middle Summit
☐ First Peak
☐ Fossil Benchmark
☐ Fossil Ridge
☐ Gass Peak
☐ Gumbo Peak
☐ Gumby Peak
☐ Hayford Peak
☐ Iko Iko Peak
☐ Johns Peak
☐ Little Sawmill Peak
☐ Little Smokey
☐ Lost Yucca Peak
☐ Marble 2 Benchmark
☐ Mount Freedom
☐ Naked Peak
☐ Peak 4,300
☐ Peak 4,608
☐ Peak 6,252
☐ Peak 6,610
☐ Peak 7,265
☐ Quartzite Mountain
☐ Sheep Peak
☐ Tri-Lambs-Dudley, The
☐ Tri-Lambs-Gilbert, The
☐ Tri-Lambs-Louis, The
☐ Twin Buttes
☐ Yucca Benchmark

Bare Mountains

☐ Bare Mountain
☐ Bare Mountain Peak
☐ Barely Peak
☐ Meiklejohn Peak
☐ Razorback Ridge
☐ Wildcat Peak

Greater Beatty Area

☐ Beatty Mountain
☐ Black Peak
☐ Black Cone
☐ Black Marble
☐ Bonanza Mountain
☐ Burton Mountain
☐ Busch Peak
☐ Coba Mountain
☐ Elizabeth Peak
☐ Foundation Peak
☐ Ladd Mountain
☐ Little Cones
☐ Montgomery Mountain
☐ Paradise Mountain
☐ Pioneer Mine Peak
☐ Rainbow Mountain
☐ Red Cone
☐ Sawtooth Mountain
☐ Sharp Benchmark
☐ Skeleton Hills-West
☐ Springdale Mountain
☐ Springdale Mountain-Northeast
☐ Sutherland Mountain
☐ Velvet Peak
☐ West Sawtooth Peak

Valley of Fire SP

☐ 5-Arch, The
☐ Baseline Mesa
☐ Boneyard Peak
☐ Cairn Peak
☐ Crimson Staircase
☐ Duane Peak
☐ Gibraltar Rock
☐ Gregg Peak
☐ Orphan, The
☐ Peak 2,431
☐ Peak 3,077
☐ Prospects Peak
☐ Silica Dome
☐ Sitting Monkey
☐ Thin Peak
☐ Valley of Fire Summit
☐ Weekapaug Mountain
☐ West White Dome
☐ White Dome

South of Las Vegas (General)

☐ Bad Hill
☐ Bird Peak
☐ Bird Spring Range Highpoint
☐ Canine Crag
☐ Christmas Gift
☐ Cottonwood Peak

☐ Cottonwood Peak-North
☐ Dog Skull Mountain
☐ Ecru Peak
☐ Escarpment Peak
☐ Feline Fang
☐ Flowered Peak
☐ Hole-in-the-Top
☐ Jingle Bells, The
☐ Joshua Peak (4,231)
☐ Joshua Peak (4,300)
☐ Joshua Tree
☐ Mount Roses Are Free
☐ North Twin
☐ Peacock Mountain
☐ Peak 3,970
☐ Pleasant Peak
☐ Sheep Mountain
☐ Sloan Peak
☐ South Twin
☐ Sutor Benchmark
☐ Tortoise Foot Hill
☐ Trident

McCullough Range & Railroad Peaks Area

☐ Black Hill
☐ Black Mountain
☐ Fishhead Peak
☐ Fortress, The
☐ Fracture Ridge Peak
☐ Henderson Benchmark
☐ Indian Point
☐ Jack, The
☐ King, The
☐ Maid of Rubble
☐ McCullough Mountain
☐ McCullough Point
☐ North McCullough Peak
☐ Peak 3,954
☐ Peak 4,089
☐ Queen, The
☐ Railroad Hill
☐ Railroad Peak
☐ Rattlesnake Mountain
☐ Tortoise Shell Peak
☐ Wee Thump Joshua Tree Wilderness Highpoint
☐ White Gold #7

Highland Spring Range

☐ Castle Peak
☐ Highland Juniper Peak
☐ Highland Peak
☐ Highland Spring Range Highpoint
☐ Mount Alex
☐ Mount Tappen
☐ North Castle Peak
☐ Peak 4,540
☐ Possible Mesa
☐ Sleeping Indian Peak

Laughlin

☐ Center Benchmark
☐ Conical Peak
☐ Hiko Peak

Searchlight

☐ Doherty Mountain
☐ Light Benchmark
☐ Morning Glory Mountain

Nelson & Boulder City Area

☐ Arch Back
☐ Aztec Mountain
☐ Bard Peak
☐ Bootleg Mountain
☐ Eagle Peak
☐ Easter Island Peak
☐ Gold Strike Mountain
☐ Goldstrike Pass Peak
☐ Hoover Peak
☐ Ignorant Fool, The
☐ Ireteba Benchmark
☐ Knob Hill
☐ Keyhole Peak
☐ Knoll, The
☐ Leaning Arch Peak
☐ Little Hands Peak
☐ Lonesome Peak
☐ Mount Duncan
☐ Mount Stocker

☐ Nelson Benchmark
☐ Neslon Peak
☐ Pass Benchmark
☐ Peeper Benchmark
☐ Pigs in Zen Peak
☐ Pilot Cone
☐ Point of Redemption
☐ Techatticup Peak
☐ Windbreak Peak

Urban Las Vegas

☐ Cheyenne Mountain
☐ Frenchman Mountain
☐ Lone Mountain
☐ Mesa Mesa
☐ Mount Turtle Island
☐ NE Frenchman Peak
☐ NW Frenchman Peak
☐ Peak 2,980
☐ Pipe Benchmark
☐ Sunrise Mountain

Apex Area

☐ Bark Benchmark
☐ Blissful Peak
☐ Divided Peak
☐ Friendship Peak
☐ Game Benchmark
☐ Hidden Arch Mountain
☐ Mount Formidable
☐ Peak 3,235
☐ Sneaky Peak
☐ Tony Benchmark
☐ Tracked Peak

Muddy Mountains

☐ Buffington Peak
☐ Colorock Summit
☐ Midridge Peak
☐ Muddy Mountains Highpoint
☐ Muddy Peak
☐ Piute Point
☐ Piute Point Highpoint
☐ Surprise Peak
☐ White Basin Overlook
☐ White Benchmark

Ute

☐ Peak 2,963
☐ Peak 3,001
☐ Peak 3,284
☐ Ute Benchmark

Virgin Mountains

☐ Billy Goat Peak
☐ Juanita Benchmark
☐ Little Virgin Peak
☐ Quail Point
☐ Virgin Benchmark
☐ Virgin Peak
☐ Whitney Pocket Point

Coyote Springs & Alamo

☐ Center Benchmark
☐ Dinosaur Fins
☐ Elbow Butte
☐ Elbow Range Highpoint
☐ Fleur de Lis Peak
☐ Hand Peak
☐ Juniper Benchmark
☐ Meadow Valley Mountains Highpoint
☐ Mount Irish
☐ Oak Spring Peak
☐ Pahroc Summit Peak
☐ Perkins Peak
☐ Pincher, The
☐ Sanderson Mountain
☐ Secret Point
☐ South Pahroc Range Highpoint
☐ Tikaboo Benchmark
☐ Toy Train Peak

North of Las Vegas (Other)

☐ Beacon Peak
☐ California Ridge
☐ Candy Benchmark
☐ Davidson Peak
☐ Glen Benchmark
☐ Glendale Point
☐ Huntsman Hill
☐ Little Davidson Peak
☐ Moapa Peak
☐ Mormon Mesa
☐ Mormon Peak
☐ Peak 2,050
☐ Peak 2,335
☐ Sharks Tooth

☐ Sheep Canyon Peak
☐ Tabeau Peak

Pahrump & Crystal

☐ Black Butte
☐ Crystal Mountain
☐ High Peak
☐ Mount Montgomery
☐ Mount Schader
☐ North Chance Peak
☐ Skull Peak

Great Basin NP

☐ Baker Peak
☐ Bald Mountain
☐ Buck Mountain
☐ False Pyramid Peak
☐ Jeff Davis Peak
☐ Mount Moriah
☐ Pyramid Peak
☐ Wheeler Peak

Quinn Canyon Range

☐ Quinn Canyon Range Highpoint
☐ Sage Mountain
☐ Sage Mountain-North
☐ Steep Mountain

Pioche Area

☐ Comet Peak
☐ Connor Peak
☐ Highland Peak

Lida Summit Area

☐ Blue Dick Benchmark
☐ Magruder Mountain
☐ Palmetto Mountain

Schell Creek Range

☐ Middle Schell Peak
☐ North Schell Peak
☐ Ptarmigan Peak
☐ Uinta Peak

Ruby Mountains Area

☐ Favre Benchmark
☐ Greys Peak
☐ Lake Peak
☐ Liberty Peak
☐ Peak 10,500
☐ Peak 10,545
☐ Tri-Lake Peak
☐ Wines Peak

White Pine Range Area

☐ Currant Mountain
☐ Duckwater Peak
☐ Eagle Feather Peak
☐ Troy Peak

Hualapai Mountains

☐ Aspen Peak
☐ Dean Peak
☐ Hualapai Peak
☐ Peak 7,680
☐ Peak 7,745

Bullhead City & Oatman

☐ Battleship Mountain
☐ Boundary Cone
☐ Negrohead
☐ Sugarloaf Mountain
☐ Sugarloaf Peak

Dolan Springs Area

☐ Housholder Peak
☐ Mount Perkins
☐ Mount Tipton

Colorado River (Arizona)

☐ Fire Mountain
☐ Fortress Peak
☐ Gold Bug Peak
☐ Kenny Peak
☐ Liberty Bell Arch Peak
☐ Malpais Flattop Mesa
☐ Mohave Mine Peak
☐ Peak 1,712
☐ Peak 2,060
☐ Peanut Peak
☐ Sheep Tank Peak
☐ Sarada Devi
☐ Sugarloaf Mountain
☐ Willow Beach Peak

Williams Area

☐ Bill Williams Mountain
☐ Boxcar Hill
☐ Moore Benchmark
☐ Squaw Peak
☐ Summit Mountain

Greater Flagstaff Area

☐ Doyle Peak
☐ Elden Mountain

☐ Humphreys Peak
☐ Kendrick Peak
☐ Mars Hill
☐ Red Butte
☐ Slate Mountain
☐ Woody Mountain

Sunset Crater National Monument

☐ Crater 7,480
☐ Crater 7,682
☐ Darton Dome
☐ O'Leary Peak
☐ O'Leary Peak-West
☐ Robinson Mountain

Sedona Area

☐ Battlement Mesa
☐ Brins Butte
☐ Capitol Butte
☐ Cockscomb, The
☐ Coconino Point
☐ Bear Mountain
☐ Doe Mountain
☐ Fin, The
☐ Grassy Knolls
☐ Little Sugarloaf
☐ Loy Butte
☐ Mescal Mountain
☐ Morning Glory Spire
☐ Scheurman Mountain
☐ Sugarloaf Mountain
☐ Table Top Mountain
☐ Three Sisters
☐ West Twin Butte
☐ Wilson Mountain
☐ Windmill Mountain
☐ Woodchute Mountain

Grand Canyon NP

☐ Battleship, The
☐ Cardenas Butte
☐ Cedar Mountain
☐ Cheops Pyramid
☐ Coronado Butte
☐ Desert View Point
☐ Escalante Butte
☐ Grandview Benchmark
☐ O'Neill Butte
☐ Sinking Ship
☐ Unnamed Butte
☐ Whites Butte

Grand Canyon-Parashant NM

☐ Black Knolls
☐ Cinder Knoll
☐ Diamond Butte
☐ Hudson Point
☐ Last Chance Knoll
☐ Little Black Mountain
☐ Mount Dellenbaugh
☐ Mount Logan
☐ Mount Trumbull
☐ Point of Rock
☐ Seegmiller Mountain

Lake Havasu City Area

☐ Goat Hill
☐ Little Haystack
☐ Shangri La Butte

Kofa NWR Area

☐ Castle Dome Peak
☐ Haystack Peak
☐ High Peak
☐ Ibex Peak
☐ Kofa Butte
☐ La Cholla Peak
☐ Little Cholla Peak
☐ Old Smokey Mountain
☐ Peak 2,550
☐ Polaris Mountain
☐ Signal Peak
☐ Spaghetti Peak
☐ Yellowfin

Superstition Mountains

☐ Fremont Peak
☐ Superstition Peak
☐ Weavers Needle

Tucson Area

☐ Baboquivari Peak
☐ Kitt Peak
☐ Peak 2,540
☐ Picacho Peak
☐ Ragged Top
☐ Razorback Ridge

Greater Mojave National Preserve Area

☐ Avawatz Mountains Highpoint
☐ Basin Peak
☐ Birthday of the Buddha Peak

☐ Cairned Ridge Peak
☐ Camp Rock
☐ Cave Mountain
☐ Cima Dome
☐ Clark Mountain
☐ Climax Peak
☐ Coyote Peak
☐ Crater 3,152
☐ Crater 3,221
☐ Cowhole Mountain
☐ El Tren Peak
☐ Elephant Mountain
☐ Goffs Butte
☐ Hanks Mountain
☐ Kelso Dunes Highpoint
☐ Kelso Peak
☐ Kessler Peak
☐ Kokoweef Peak
☐ Little Cowhole Mountain
☐ Mescal Range Highpoint
☐ Mineral Hill
☐ Mohawk Hill
☐ Mount Walter
☐ Muppet Mountain
☐ Negro Head
☐ Nickel Mountain
☐ Old Dad Mountain
☐ Old Woman Statue
☐ Otto Mountain
☐ Sawtooth
☐ Shadow Mountain
☐ Solomons Knob
☐ Squat Hill
☐ Squaw Tit
☐ Striped Mountain
☐ Tess Mountain
☐ Teutonia Peak
☐ Turquoise Mountain
☐ Unnamed Benchmark
☐ Whistle Peak
☐ Wildcat Butte

New York Mountains

☐ Barnwell Benchmark
☐ Castle Mountain
☐ Castle Peak
☐ Crescent Peak
☐ Hart Peak
☐ Linder Peak
☐ New York Mountains Highpoint
☐ North Castle Butte

Hole-in-the-Wall

☐ Barber Benchmark
☐ North Tower
☐ South Tower
☐ Table Top
☐ Tortoise Shell Mountain
☐ Twin Buttes-North
☐ Twin Buttes-South
☐ Wild Horse Mesa
☐ Woods Mountain Highpoint

Providence Mountains

☐ Columbia Mountain
☐ Der Tooth
☐ Edgar Peak
☐ Fountain Peak

Panamint Range

☐ Aguer Benchmark
☐ Aguereberry Point
☐ Bennett Peak
☐ Petes Peak
☐ Rogers Peak
☐ South Fork Peak
☐ Telescope Peak
☐ Wildrose Peak

Titus Canyon Area

☐ Block Peak
☐ Pot Peak
☐ Red Pass Peak
☐ Thimble Peak
☐ Thimbles Shadow
☐ Titanothere Point
☐ Titus Peak

Dante's View Area

☐ Coffin Peak
☐ Dante Benchmark
☐ False Coffin Peak
☐ Funeral Peak
☐ Mount Perry

Furnace Creek Area

☐ 20-Mule Team Peak
☐ Artist Palette Peak
☐ Cerro Blanco
☐ Furnace Peak
☐ Manly Beacon
☐ Mars Hill
☐ Red Cathedral

Greater Death Valley NP Area

☐ 508 Peak
☐ Bat Mountain
☐ Bat Mountain-South Summit
☐ Brown Peak
☐ Bullfrog Mountain
☐ Chloride Cliff
☐ Cinder Hill
☐ Corkscrew Peak
☐ Darwin Benchmark
☐ Daylight Peak
☐ Death Valley Buttes
☐ Devair Benchmark
☐ Eagle Mountain
☐ Eagle Point
☐ Epaulet Peak
☐ Funeral Mountains Wilderness Highpoint
☐ Gold Valley Peak
☐ Grapevine Peak
☐ High Dome
☐ Ibex Peak
☐ Jubilee Mountain
☐ Kit Fox Hills Highpoint
☐ Lake Hill
☐ Loner, The
☐ Ophir Mountain
☐ Panamint Gate-South
☐ Prospect Peak
☐ Pyramid Peak
☐ Rhodes Hill
☐ Salsberry Peak
☐ Sheephead Mountain
☐ Skunk Stripe Peak
☐ Slabby Acres Peak
☐ Smith Mountain
☐ Talc City Hills
☐ Talc Hill
☐ Towne Benchmark
☐ Ubehebe Peak
☐ Virgin Spring Peak
☐ Wahguyhe Peak

Shoshone Area

☐ Athel Hill
☐ Dublin Hills Highpoint
☐ Excelsior Mine Peak
☐ Hunch Benchmark
☐ Jupiter Mine Peak
☐ Kingston Peak
☐ Nopah Range Highpoint
☐ Old Spanish Mountain
☐ Pahrump Benchmark
☐ Ring Benchmark
☐ Salt Benchmark
☐ Shadow Mountain
☐ Shoshone Point
☐ Shoshone Point-South
☐ Stewart Point
☐ Tecopa Peak

Needles Area

☐ Mopah Point
☐ Sawtooth Range Highpoint
☐ Sharp Benchmark
☐ Snaggletooth
☐ Umpah Point

Blythe Area

☐ Black Mountain
☐ Thumb Peak
☐ Quartz Peak

Yuma Area

☐ Mine Peak
☐ Muggins Peak
☐ Pebble Mountain
☐ Picacho Peak

Index

5-Arch, The 195
20-Mule Team Peak 364
508 Peak 368
After-Work Peak 129
Aguer Benchmark 351
Aguereberry Point 351
Amargosa Overlook 93
Anniversary Narrows Peak 130
Apex Peak (see Game Benchmark) 234
Arch Back 223
Arch Mountain 154
Arch Mountain Highpoint 154
Arrow Canyon Peak 172
Arrow Canyon Range Highpoint 165
Arrow Peak 166
Artist Palette Peak 364
Aspen Peak 272
Athel Hill 373
Avawatz Mountains Highpoint 348
Aztec Mountain 221
Baboquivari Peak 318
Bad Hill 206
Baker Peak 256
Bald Knob 181
Bald Mountain 259
Banded Ridge North 182
Banded Ridge South 182
Barber Benchmark 340
Bard Peak 330
Bare Mountain 186
Bare Mountain Peak 188
Barely Peak 187
Bark Benchmark 234
Barnwell Benchmark 333
Barricade Peak 76
Basalt Peak 134
Baseline Mesa 195
Basin Peak 347
Bat Mountain 353
Bat Mountain – South Summit 352
Battlement Mesa 290
Battleship, The 299
Battleship Mountain 275
Beacon Peak 243
Bear Mountain 292
Bearing Peak 135
Beatty Mountain 190
Bedrock Peak 161
Bee Canyon Peak 92
Beer and Ice Peak 56
Bennett Peak 350
Big Arrow Peak (see Arrow Canyon Range Highpoint) 165
Big Bird Peak 69
Big John 185
Bighorn Peak 144
Bill Gays Butte 157
Bill Williams Mountain 284
Billy Goat Peak 240
Bird Peak 204
Bird Spring Range Highpoint 204
Birthday of the Buddha Peak 347
Birthday Peak 171
Bitter 3 138
Bitter Ridge Highpoint 138
Black Butte (Gold Butte) 128
Black Butte (Sandy Valley) 251
Black Cone 190
Black Hill 213
Black Knolls 308
Black Marble 189
Black Mesa 129
Black Mountain (Blythe) 376
Black Mountain (Cottonwood Cove) 157
Black Mountain (Henderson) 211
Black Mountain (River Mountains) 145
Black Peak 190
Black Rock Sister 97
Black Velvet Peak 27
Blissful Peak 235
Block Peak 357
Blowing Peak 129
Blue Diamond Hill 67
Blue Dick Benchmark 262
Blue Point 144

Bluebird Peak 113
Bonanza Hill 115
Bonanza Mountain 190
Bonanza Peak 101
Bonelli Peak 120
Boneyard Peak 195
Boot Boulder 64
Booth Pinnacle 141
Bootleg Mountain 227
Bootleg Spring Peak 111
Boulder Peak 135
Boundary Cone 273
Bowl View Peak 132
Boxcar Hill 285
Boxcar Rock 128
Bridge Mountain 58
Bridge Point 55
Bridge Vista Peak 54
Brins Butte 294
Broken Arrow Peak 169
Brown Peak 352
Buck Mountain 260
Buffington Peak 237
Bullfrog Mountain 355
Burlap Buttress 29
Burnt Peak 76
Burro Peak 93
Burton Mountain 190
Busch Peak 191
Cactus Flower Point 112
Cactus Flower Tower 41
Cairn Peak 196
Cairned Ridge Peak 324
Calico Hills-South 72
Calico Peak 73
California Ridge 241
Camp Rock 346
Candy Benchmark 242
Canine Crag 208
Capitol Butte 291
Capuchin Peak 130
Cardenas Butte 305
Castle Dome Peak 310
Castle Mountain 333
Castle Peak (Mojave National Preserve) 336
Castle Peak (Highland Range) 217
Castle Rock 176
Cathedral Peak (see Meadow Valley Mountains Highpoint) 248
Cathedral Peak (Lake Mead) 142
Cathedral Rock 89
Cave Butte 164
Cave Mountain 347
Cedar Mountain 306
Center Benchmark (Elbow Range) 247
Center Benchmark (Laughlin) 219
Cerro Blanco 365
Charleston Peak 89
Chase Mountain 108
Cheops Pyramid 299
Cheyenne Mountain 227
Chloride Cliff 354
Christmas Gift 205
Christmas Tree Peak 156
Cima Dome 330
Cinder Hill 359
Cinder Knoll 308
Claret Peak 114
Clark Mountain 345
Cliff Benchmark 171
Climax Peak 345
Clinton Peak 108
Coba Mountain 191
Cockscomb, The 290
Cockscomb Peak 89
Coconino Point 297
Coffin Peak 362
Colorock Summit 236
Columbia Mountain 343
Comet Peak 262
Condor Peak 128
Conical Peak 219
Connor Peak 261
Copper Mountain 158
Copper Mountain – West 157
Corkscrew Peak 354
Coronado Butte 304
Cottonwood Peak 202
Cottonwood Peak – North 202
Cove Peak 152
Cow Camp Peak 177
Cowhole Mountain 325
Coyote Peak 345
Coyote Skull Peak 150

Crabby Appleton Peak (see Ramp Peak) 47
Crater 3,152 (Mojave) 325
Crater 3,221 (Mojave) 326
Crater 7,480 (Flagstaff) 285
Crater 7,682 (Flagstaff) 285
Crescent Peak 338
Crest Peak 75
Crimson Staircase 196
Crystal Mountain 252
Currant Mountain 268
Dam View Point 152
Damsel Peak 76
Dante Benchmark 363
Darton Dome 286
Darwin Benchmark 368
Davidson Peak 243
Daylight Peak 355
Dead Badger Peak 111
Dead Horse Mountain 106
Dead Horse Point 37
Dead Man Hill 171
Dean Peak 273
Death Valley Buttes 354
Deception Peak 63
Decision Peak 35
Dellenbaugh, Mount 307
Der Tooth 343
Desert View Point 305
Devair Benchmark 352
Devil Peak 117
Devils Thumb 156
Diamond Butte 308
Dike Benchmark 173
Dike Benchmark – East Summit 173
Dike Benchmark – Middle Summit 173
Dinosaur Fins 247
Divide Peak 98
Divided Peak 235
Divided Sky, The 65
Division Peak 149
Doe Mountain 291
Dog Skull Mountain 207
Doherty Mountain 219
Double, The 150
Dove Benchmark (see Castle Peak – Mojave National Preserve) 336
Doyle Peak 287
Dry Benchmark 161
Dry Lake Peak160
Duane Peak 197
Dublin Hills Highpoint 370
Duckwater Peak 268
Dull Mountain 83
Eagle Feather Peak 267
Eagle Mountain 352
Eagle Peak 221
Eagle Point 369
Eagle Rocks (see Der Tooth) 343
East Bitter Peak 130
East La Madre Peak 77
East Longwell Ridge 143
East Longwell Ridge-South 143
East Monument Peak 31
East Peak (see East Monument Peak) 31
East Redstone Peak 140
Easter Island Peak 226
Echo Hills 141
Ecru Peak 208
Edgar Peak 343
Edge Benchmark 92
El Bastardo 77
El Hijo (see New Peak) 69
El Padre 77
El Tren Peak 348
Elbow Butte 247
Elbow Range Highpoint 246
Elden Mountain 287
Elephant Mountain 346
Elizabeth Peak 191
Endless Peak 131
Epaulet Peak 361
Escalante Butte 305
Escarpment Peak 203
Evas Tower 56
Excelsior Mine Peak 372
Exploration Peak (see Pipe Benchmark) 233
Falls Peak 146
False Arrow Peak 167
False Coffin Peak 362

False Pyramid Peak 256
Favre Benchmark 266
Feline Fang 208
Fin, The 293
Fire Benchmark 144
Fire Mountain 280
First Creek Overlook 75
First Creek Peak 35
First Peak 177
Fishhead Peak 210
Fletcher Peak 89
Fleur de Lis Peak 246
Flowered Peak 204
Fork Peak 32
Fortification Hill 153
Fortress, The 213
Fortress Peak 283
Fossil Benchmark 182
Fossil Peak 171
Fossil Ridge 177
Foundation Peak 189
Fountain Peak 343
Fracture Ridge Peak 211
Freddie Peak 108
Frenchman Mountain 233
Friendship Peak 235
Funeral Mountains Wilderness Highpoint 353
Funeral Peak 362
Furnace Peak 366
Game Benchmark 234
Gap Peak 114
Gass Peak 176
Gateway Peak 78
Gibraltar Rock 197
Glen Benchmark 242
Glendale Point 242
Global Peak 26
Glyph Point 136
Goat Bed Peak 74
Goat Hill 309
Goffs Butte 348
Gold Bug Peak 280
Gold Butte 126
Gold Cross Peak 120
Gold Strike Mountain 224
Gold Valley Peak 360
Golden Mine Peak 155
Goldstrike Pass Peak 225
Goodman Peak 62
Graduation Peak 92
Grandstand, The 268
Grandview Benchmark 304
Grapevine Peak 358
Grapevine Spring Point 91
Grassy Knolls 292
Green Monster Benchmark 116
Gregg Peak 198
Greycap 73
Greys Peak 266
Griffith Peak 87
Guardian Peak 137
Gumbo Peak 183
Gumby Peak 182
Gunshot Peak 161
Gunsight Notch Peak 146
Hamblin Butte 134
Hamblin Mountain 133
Hamblin Mountain – West 133
Hand Peak 245
Hanging Valley Peak 149
Hanks Mountain 325
Harlan Peak 135
Harris Mountain 87
Hart Peak 333
Hayford Peak 181
Haystack Peak 315
Henderson Benchmark 215
Hidden Arch Mountain 234
Hidden Benchmark 168
Hidden Peak (Arrow Canyon Range – see Hidden Benchmark) 168
Hidden Peak (Red Rock) 29
Hidden Wash Peak 171
High Dune 367
High Peak (Kofa) 312
High Peak (Pahrump) 252
Highland Juniper Peak 216
Highland Peak 215 (Highland Spring Range)
Highland Peak (Pioche) 262
Highland Spring Range Highpoint 216
Hiko Point 219
Hole-in-the-Top 203
Holiday Peak 57

Hollow Rock Peak 21
Hoover Peak 225
Horse Benchmark 109
Housholder Peak 280
Hualapai Peak 271
Hudson Point 307
Humphreys Peak 288
Hunch Benchmark 371
Huntsman Hill 242
Hyko Benchmark (see South Pahroc Range Highpoint) 249
Ibex Peak (Death Valley) 361
Ibex Peak (Quartzsite) 315
Ice Box Peak 61
Iceberg Peak 127
Ignorant Fool, The 224
Iguana Peak 156
Iko Iko Peak 184
Indecision Peak 34
Indian Benchmark 104
Indian Point 210
Indian Ridge 104
Indian Ridge – North 104
Indian Springs Peak 105
Indigo Peak 157
Ireteba Benchmark 220
Ison Peak 103
Jack, The 213
Jagged Peak 116
Jaybird Benchmark 107
Jeff Davis Peak 258
Jingle Bells, The 205
Johns Peak 183
Joshua Peak (Bird Spring Range – North) 205
Joshua Peak (Bird Spring Range – South) 202
Joshua Tree 204
Juanita Benchmark 241
Jubilee Mountain 360
Jumbo Peak 123
Juniper Benchmark 245
Juniper Peak 45
Jupiter Mine Peak 373
Kelso Dunes Highpoint 327
Kelso Peak 326
Kendrick Peak 288
Kenny Peak 281
Kessler Peak 332
Keyhole Peak 220
King, The 215
Kingston Peak 372
Kit Fox Hills Highpoint 367
Kitt Peak 318
Knife Peak 130
Knife-Edge Peak 149
Knob Hill 220
Knob Peak 130
Knoll, The 224
Kofa Butte 311
Kokoweef Peak 344
Kraft Mountain 68
Kyle Benchmark 92
La Cholla Peak 312
La Hija (see Kraft Mountain) 68
La Madre Mountain 78
La Madre Mountain Wilderness Highpoint 85
Ladd Mountain 191
Lake Hill 364
Lake Peak 265
Landfill Peak 164
Land's End Peak 138
Last Chance Knoll 307
Lava Butte 148
Lead Mountain 117
Leaning Arch Peak 226
Lee Peak 90
Liberty Bell Arch Peak 283
Liberty Peak 266
Light Benchmark 220
Linder Peak 333
Little Black Mountain 309
Little Cholla Peak 313
Little Cones 189
Little Cowhole Mountain 325
Little Davidson Peak 243
Little Devil Peak 118
Little Hands Peak 221
Little Haystack 309
Little Peak 156
Little Picacho (see Picacho Peak – Yuma) 377
Little Pyramid 138

Little Sawmill Peak 184
Little Smokey 175
Little Sugarloaf 290
Little Virgin Peak 241
Lone Mountain 229
Lonely Pinon Mountain 78
Loner, The 355
Lonesome Peak 223
Long View Peak 146
Lost Creek Peak 64
Lost Thing Mountain (see Hanks Mountain) 325
Lost Yucca Peak 177
Loy Butte 293
Lucky Strike Mine Peak 92
Lucky Strike Peak 93
Lytle Benchmark 172
Macks Peak 98
Magic Mountain 49
Magruder Mountain 262
Maid of Rubble 211
Malpais Flattop Mesa 281
Manganese Peak 141
Manly Beacon 366
Marble 2 Benchmark 173
Marble Mountain 164
Mars Hill (Death Valley) 365
Mars Hill (Flagstaff) 287
McCullough Mountain 210
McCullough Point 210
McFarland Peak 98
Meadow Valley Mountains Highpoint 248
Meiklejohn Peak 189
Mesa Benchmark 110
Mesa Mesa 233
Mescal Mountain 292
Mescal Range Highpoint 344
Mescalito 50
Mica Peak 125
Middle Bitter Peak 139
Middle Schell Peak 263
Midridge Peak 237
Midway Peak 159
Mikes Tower 56
Mine Peak (Spring Mountains) 102
Mine Peak (Yuma) 377
Mine View Peak 132
Minefield, The 150
Mineral Hill 345
Misty Mountain 115
Moapa Peak 243
Mohave Mine Peak 281
Mohawk Hill 345
Montgomery Mountain 191
Monument, The 30
Moore Benchmark 285
Mopah Point 374
Mormon Mesa 242
Mormon Peak 244
Morning Glory Mountain 220
Morning Glory Spire 293
Mount Alex 218
Mount Alexander 111
Mount Bulworth 106
Mount Duncan 221
Mount Everest 101
Mount Formidable 234
Mount Freedom 173
Mount Golden Eagle 79
Mount Gottlieb 79
Mount Graybeard 136
Mount Hualapai 11
Mount Irish 250
Mount Logan 308
Mount Mangreed 147
Mount Montgomery 252
Mount Moriah 260
Mount Newberry 157
Mount of Caves 161
Mount Perkins 279
Mount Perry 363
Mount Pumpkin 93
Mount Reagan 108
Mount Roses Are Free 204
Mount Schader 252
Mount Stirling 107
Mount Stocker 222
Mount Tappen 215
Mount Tipton 278
Mount Trumbull 307
Mount Turtle Island 233
Mount Walter 347
Mount Wilson (Hoover Dam) 150
Mount Wilson (Red Rock) 38
Mount Woody 80

Mountain Spring Benchmark 74
Mud Crag 129
Mud Hill 129
Mud Hole Mountain 98
Mud Tower 129
Muddy Mountains Highpoint 236
Muddy Peak 236
Muggins Peak 378
Mummy Mountain 90
Mummys Chin 94
Mummys Forehead 94
Mummys Nose 95
Mummys Toe 90
Muppet Mountain 347
Murphys Peak 133
Mystery Cairn Peak 140
Naked Peak 177
NE Frenchman Peak 233
Negrohead 275
Negro Head 329
Nelson Benchmark 222
Neslon Peak 221
New Peak 69
New York Mountains Highpoint 332
Nickel Mountain 324
Nony Peak 81
Nopah Range Highpoint 371
North Castle Butte 337
North Castle Peak 219
North Chance Peak 252
North Crag 138
North Fire Peak 144
North Fire Peak – East Summit 144
North Macks Peak 100
North McCullough Peak 211
North Peak (Christmas Tree Pass) 156
North Peak (Red Rock) 63
North Potosi Peak 113
North Schell Peak 263
North Sister 97
North Tower 339
North Twin 207
Northshore Peak 135
Northshore Peak-West 135
NW Frenchman Peak 232
Oak Creek Overlook 75
Oak Peak 42
Oak Spring Peak 250
Old Dad Mountain 325
Old Smokey Mountain 310
Old Spanish Mountain 374
Old Woman Statue 346
O'Leary Peak 286
O'Leary Peak – West 286
O'Neill Butte 301
Ophir Mountain 368
Orphan, The 198
Otto Mountain 324
Packard Peak 121
Pahrock Summit Peak 249
Pahrump Benchmark 371
Paint Pots 154
Painted Prow 161
Palmetto Mountain 262
Panamint Gate-South 369
Paradise Mountain 191
Pas Rump 114
Pass Benchmark 225
Pasture Mountain 164
Peacock Mountain 205
Peak 1,712 (Colorado River) 281
Peak 1,804 (Callville) 130
Peak 1,876 (Hoover Dam) 152
Peak 2,050 (Glendale) 242
Peak 2,060 (Colorado River) 282
Peak 2,159 (Callville) 130
Peak 2,335 (Glendale) 242
Peak 2,421 (Bowl of Fire) 132
Peak 2,431 (Valley of Fire) 195
Peak 2,474 (Bowl of Fire) 133
Peak 2,500 (River Mountains) 146
Peak 2,540 (Tucson) 319
Peak 2,550 (Kofa) 311
Peak 2,674 (Cathedral) 142
Peak 2,740 (River Mountains) 146
Peak 2,890 (Longwell) 143
Peak 2,963 (Ute) 239
Peak 2,980 (Sunrise Mountain) 231
Peak 3,001 (Ute) 239
Peak 3,068 (Gold Butte) 128
Peak 3,077 (Valley of Fire) 195
Peak 3,123 (Gold Butte) 128
Peak 3,153 (Christmas Tree Pass) 157

Peak 3,235 (Apex) 235
Peak 3,284 (Ute) 240
Peak 3,537 (Bowl of Fire) 133
Peak 3,954 (Railroad Peaks) 213
Peak 3,970 (Sloan) 209
Peak 4,089 (Railroad Peaks) 213
Peak 4,300 (DNWR) 175
Peak 4,540 (Highland Spring Range) 215
Peak 4,608 (DNWR) 175
Peak 4,773 (Lost Cabin Springs) 110
Peak 4,839 (Indian Springs) 105
Peak 4,930 (Indian Springs) 105
Peak 4,945 (Indian Springs) 105
Peak 5,003 (Gold Butte) 126
Peak 5,035 (Indian Springs) 104
Peak 5,475 (Indian Springs) 104
Peak 6,252 (DNWR) 180
Peak 6,610 (DNWR) 180
Peak 6,742 (Trout Canyon) 110
Peak 6,830 (Trout Canyon) 111
Peak 7,265 (DNWR) 181
Peak 7,680 (Hualapai Mountains) 273
Peak 7,745 (Hualapai Mountains) 273
Peak 10,500 (Ruby Mountains) 265
Peak 10,545 (Ruby Mountains) 266
Peak Four 112
Peanut Peak 282
Pebble Mountain 377
Peeper Benchmark 223
Pellet Peak 142
Pepper Peak 112
Perkins Peak 247
Peter Kane Peak (see Quartz Peak) 377
Petes Peak 351
Picacho Peak (Tucson) 319
Picacho Peak (Yuma) 377
Pigs in Zen Peak 222
Pilot Cone 224
Pilot Mesa 160
Pincher, The 246
Pine Creek Peak 50
Pinnacle 147
Pinto Ridge 136
Pioneer Mine Peak 192
Pioneer Rock 93
Pipe Benchmark 233
Pipeline Hill 146
Piute Point 239
Piute Point Highpoint 238
Playground Peak 125
Pleasant Peak 209
Pluto 152
Point of Redemption 224
Point of Rock 308
Point of Rocks Peak 108
Polaris Mountain 311
Polytick Peak 132
Pondview Peak 81
Possible Mesa 216
Pot Peak 355
Potosi Mountain 113
Potosi Mountain – South 117
Profile Point 112
Promontory Point 152
Prospect Peak 355
Prospects Peak 198
Ptarmigan Peak 263
Pyramid Peak (Death Valley) 353
Pyramid Peak (Great Basin) 256
Pyramid Peak (Lake Mead) 141
Quail Point 241
Quartz Peak 377
Quartzite Mountain 182
Queen, The 214
Question Mark Peak 167
Quinn Canyon Range Highpoint 261
Quo Vadis Peak 213
Ragged Peak 116
Ragged Top 318
Railroad Hill 214
Railroad Peak 211
Rainbow Mountain (Beatty) 192
Rainbow Mountain (Red Rock) 44
Rainbow Point 112
Rainbow Wall 44
Rainy 81
Ram Skull Peak 136
Ramp Peak 47
Rattlesnake Mountain 214
Rattlesnake Peak 121
Raven, The 143
Razorback Ridge (Bare Mountains) 187
Razorback Ridge (Lake Mead) 136

Razorback Ridge (Tucson) 319
Reale Peak 171
Red Barrel Peak 170
Red Benchmark 70
Red Book Point 72
Red Butte 289
Red Cap 70
Red Cathedral 366
Red Cone 190
Red Fox Peak 147
Red Mountain 144
Red Needle 147
Red Pass Peak 357
Red Top Benchmark (see Death Valley Buttes) 354
Redstone Peak 140
Rhodes Hill 361
Ridge View Peak 117
Ridge View Peak – East 117
Ring Benchmark 370
River Mountain Benchmark 145
River Mountain Peak 145
Roasting Pit, The 112
Robinson Mountain 286
Rogers Peak 350
Rose Tower 48
Rough Benchmark 151
Saddle Mountain 141
Sage Mountain 261
Sage Mountain-North 261
Salsberry Peak 361
Salt and Pepper Mountain 159
Salt Benchmark 374
Salt Spring Mountain 155
Sanderson Mountain 250
Sandstone Peak 32
Sarada Devi 282
Sawtooth 328
Sawtooth Mountain 192
Sawtooth Range Highpoint 376
Scanlon Hill 120
Scheurman Mountain 297
Secret Point 247
Seegmiller Mountain 308
Seldom Seen Peak 100
Sentinel Peak 137
Sexton Ridge 85
Shadow Mountain (Baker) 349
Shadow Mountain (Pahrump) 371
Shaft Peak 112
Shangri La Butte 309
Sharks Tooth 244
Sharp Benchmark (Beatty) 192
Sharp Benchmark (Needles) 376
Sheep Canyon Peak 243
Sheep Mountain 205
Sheep Peak 181
Sheep Tank Peak 281
Sheephead Mountain 361
Shenandoah Peak 116
Shoshone Point 370
Shoshone Point-South 370
Signal Peak 313
Silica Dome 199
Sinking Ship 302
Sisters, The 95
Sitting Monkey 200
Skeleton Hills-West 189
Skull Peak 252
Skunk Stripe Peak 369
Slabby Acres Peak 352
Slabs Peak 130
Slate Mountain 289
Sleeping Indian Peak 216
Sloan Peak 209
Smith Benchmark 105
Smith Mountain 359
Snaggletooth 376
Sneaky Peak 235
Snow King 91
Solomons Knob 329
South Arrow Cone 160
South Arrow Peak 164
South Crag 137
South Fork Peak 351
South Pahroc Range Highpoint 249
South Peak 20
South Tower 339
South Tramp Point 127
South Twin 207
South Wilson 38
Spaghetti Peak 310
Spider Peak 170
Spirit Mountain 156

Spring Peak 109
Springdale Mountain 192
Springdale Mountain-Northeast 192
Squat Hill 324
Squaw Peak 285
Squaw Tit 328
Steep Mountain 261
Stewart Point 370
Stock Ridge 141
Striped Mountain 344
Sugarloaf Mountain (Black Mountains) 277
Sugarloaf Mountain (Colorado River) 283
Sugarloaf Mountain (Sedona) 290
Sugarloaf Peak 277
Summerlin Peak 81
Summit Mountain 284
Sunrise Mountain 231
Surprise Peak 237
Sutherland Mountain 193
Sutor Benchmark 207
Tabeau Peak 244
Table Mountain (Arrow Canyon) 172
Table Mountain (Goodsprings) 116
Table Top 342
Table Top Mountain 297
Talc City Hills 369
Talc Hill 369
Tall Cairn Peak 140
Talus Mound 159
Tank Peak 72
Tawoo Peak (see Twin Buttes – North) 342
Techatticup Peak 223
Tecopa Peak 373
Telescope Peak 350
Terrace Canyon Peak 47
Tess Mountain 345
Teutonia Peak 330
Thimble Peak 357
Thimbles Shadow 357
Thin Peak 200
Three Sisters 292
Thumb Peak 376
Tikaboo Benchmark 248
Tikaboo Peak (see Tikaboo Benchmark) 248
Tinaja Peak 72
Tio Grande 113
Titanothere Point 357
Titus Peak 357
Tony Benchmark 236
Tortoise Foot Hill 207
Tortoise Peak 170
Tortoise Shell Mountain 339
Tortoise Shell Peak 215
Towne Benchmark 364
Toy Train Peak 246
Tracked Peak 234
Traction Benchmark 103
Tramp Ridge 127
Trench Peak 161
Trident 203
Triple, The 150
Tri-Lake Peak 265
Tri-Lambs (Dudley), The 174
Tri-Lambs (Gilbert), The 175
Tri-Lambs (Louis), The 174
Troy Peak 267
Tunnel Vision Peak 66
Turquoise Mountain 329
Turtlehead Junior (see Red Cap) 70
Turtlehead Mountain 72
Twin Buttes (DNWR) 181
Twin Buttes – North (Mojave National Preserve) 342
Twin Buttes – South (Mojave National Preserve) 341
Ubehebe Peak 368
Ugly Brown Lump 82
Uinta Peak 263
Umpah Point 374
Unity Peak 150
Unnamed Benchmark 329
Unnamed Butte 302
Uranus 151
Ute Benchmark 240
Valley of Fire Summit 201
Velvet Peak 193
Virgin Benchmark 241
Virgin Peak 241
Virgin Spring Peak 360
Vista Peak 139
Wahguyhe Peak 358
Walts Ridge 149

Wee Thump Joshua Tree Wilderness Highpoint 210
Weekapaug Mountain 210
West Bitter Peak 138
West Longwell Ridge 143
West Sawtooth Peak 193
West Twin Butte 290
West White Dome 202
Whale Peak 116
Wheeler Benchmark 102
Wheeler Peak (Great Basin National Park) 257
Wheeler Peak (Spring Mountains - see Wheeler Benchmark) 102
Whisky Peak 29
Whistle Peak 348
White Basin Overlook 236
White Benchmark 238
White Dome 202
White Eagle Peak 147
White Gold #7 214
White Pinnacle Peak (see White Rock Pinnacle) 36
White Rock Hills Peak (see White Rock Peak) 66
White Rock Peak 66
White Rock Pinnacle 36
White Rock Spring Peak 66
Whites Butte 299
Whitney Pocket Point 240
Wildcat Butte 329
Wildcat Peak 186
Wildrose Peak 350
Wild Horse, The 116
Wild Horse Mesa 338
Willow Beach Peak 282
Willow Benchmark 82
Willow Peak 101
Willow Springs Overlook 62
Wilson Mountain 294
Wilson Ridge 82
Wilsons Pimple 42
Windbreak Peak 224
Windmill Mountain 297
Windy 83
Windy Peak 24
Wines Peak 264
Woodchute Mountain 295
Woods Mountains Highpoint 341
Woody Mountain 287
Woota Peak (see Twin Buttes – South) 341
Yellowfin 31
Yoga Peak 52
Yucca Benchmark 179
Yucca Camp Mountain 160

www.ingramcontent.com/pod-product-compliance
Lightning Source LLC
LaVergne TN
LVHW051448080426
835509LV00017B/1697

* 9 7 8 0 6 9 2 3 8 1 3 1 1 *